MARIO CUOMO

Also by Robert S. McElvaine

Down and Out in the Great Depression:
Letters from the "Forgotten Man"

The Great Depression: America, 1929–1941

The End of the Conservative Era:
Liberalism after Reagan

MARIO CUOMO

A BIOGRAPHY

Robert S. McElvaine

Charles Scribner's Sons

NEW YORK

Grateful acknowledgment is made to the following: Random House, Inc., for excerpts from *Forest Hills Diary: The Crisis of Low Income Housing*, by Mario M. Cuomo, © 1974 by Mario M. Cuomo, and *Diaries of Mario M. Cuomo: The Campaign for Governor*, by Mario M. Cuomo, © 1984 by Mario M. Cuomo; Paul Simon Music, for excerpts from "Mrs. Robinson," by Paul Simon, copyright © 1968 Paul Simon, used by permission; SBK Entertainment World, for excerpts from "Leader of the Band," by Dan Fogelberg, © 1981 April Music Inc. and Hickory Grove Music, all rights controlled and administered by April Music Inc., all rights reserved, international copyright secured, used by permission; TRO, Hollis Music, Inc., for excerpts from "Some Children See Him," lyrics by Wihla Hutson, music by Alfred Burt, © copyright 1954 (renewed 1982) and 1957 (renewed 1985), used by permission.

Charles Scribner's Sons
Macmillan Publishing Company
866 Third Avenue, New York, NY 10022
Collier Macmillan Canada, Inc.

Library of Congress Cataloging-in-Piblication Data
McElvaine, Robert S., 1947–
    Mario Cuomo: a biography / Robert S. McElvaine.
        p.   cm.
    Bibliography: p.
    Includes index.
    ISBN 0-684-18970-4
    1. Cuomo, Mario Matthew.   2. New York (State)—Governors—
Biography.   I. Title.
F125.3.C86M34   1988
974.7′043′0924—dc 19
[B]   88-2041
                                                                        CIP

Macmillan books are available at special discounts for bulk purchases for sales promotions, premiums, fund-raising, or educational use. For details, contact:

Special Sales Director
Macmillan Publishing Company
866 Third Avenue
New York, NY 10022

10 9 8 7 6 5 4 3 2 1

Designed by Jack Meserole

PRINTED IN THE UNITED STATES OF AMERICA

For

and a Player to Be Named Later

Contents

Preface

It may strike some readers as an odd undertaking—especially for a historian—to write a biography of a man who may just be beginning the most important phase of his life. The record, like the life, is far from complete. But in the view of vast numbers of Americans, Mario Cuomo is the most intriguing figure in American public life today. It is widely believed that he has a good chance of becoming president of the United States at some point in the not too distant future. It seems to me, especially in view of the long series of less than wholly satisfactory presidents during the past two decades, that it is desirable to know as much as possible about potential national leaders *before* we elect them. Of course we will know more about Mario Cuomo in the future, but I decided that was no reason to refrain from trying to find out as much as I could about him now, and relaying those findings to the public.

Regardless of whether Mario Cuomo ever seeks the presidency, he is a fascinating person who has had a major impact on American politics. I believe a biography of him at this point in his life is entirely justified, quite apart from his presidential aspirations.

I must say a few words about the genesis of this book. I have been interested in Mario Cuomo since early 1983, when his first gubernatorial inaugural address came to my attention. I quickly concluded that he was a person almost certain to become a major force in American politics. I remained interested in Governor Cuomo through the next few years. At the beginning of 1986, I interviewed him for a book on which I was then working (*The End of the Conservative Era*). As a result of that meeting, my interest in Cuomo grew. Unlike the other major national politicians I was interviewing for the project, Cuomo did not use canned excerpts from speeches to answer my questions. It was clear that he was actually *thinking* while he was talking. I found this remarkable in a politician.

Later that year, as I completed the manuscript I had been working on when I first interviewed Cuomo, it occurred to me that he would make a fascinating subject for a biography. I got in touch with the governor and was surprised to learn that no one had yet undertaken such a project. He was hesitant at first to cooperate in my endeavor. His concern was that his cooperation would be interpreted as a sign that he planned to seek the presidency. Late in 1986 he agreed to participate in the project under the conditions that I had outlined when I proposed it. The most important of those understandings were that he would grant me several extensive interviews; would tell family members, staff, associates, and friends that he had no objection to their talking with me about him; and that he would have no control over the outcome.

This is *not* an authorized biography in the usual sense of that term. I was free to interview anyone and to publish anything I found. I have done just that, and while my overall assessment of Governor Cuomo is favorable, there are in the pages that follow many revelations that I am sure he would rather not see published and several assessments of his actions at various points in his life with which he will not be pleased.

This book is mine, not Mario Cuomo's. It has, however, benefited greatly from his openness and accessibility during its creation. I had several long in-person interviews with the governor, spent full days with him, and was able to talk with him via telephone whenever I so desired. He has told me many things that one might normally expect to find only in a genuine or an "as-told-to" autobiography. It is my hope that the result combines the objectivity of a critical biography with the intimate insights of an autobiography. I have sought to make it more than a simple narrative of Cuomo's life. I have tried also to interpret and explain that life.

I believe that this is an objective book. It will be plain to readers that I like Mario Cuomo and think highly of him. I have striven, though, not to let these feelings for my subject distort my vision. Governor Cuomo is, like all of us, a long way from perfection. I have detailed all the imperfections that I was able to uncover. Nothing has been held back; no punches have been pulled. This does not mean, however, that I attempted to create an artifically "balanced" view of the man to give the book the false appearance of objectivity. I believe that a biography in which the author does not hesitate to state straightforwardly his conclusions is decidedly preferable to one in which he attempts to balance each positive statement with an equivalent negative one. The sum of the latter sort of exercise must, after all, be zero.

The result of this biography is not zero. When the various positive and negative numbers are added, the outcome is on the positive side of the number line. Some critics, I anticipate, will find fault with this result. There has built up among us—especially among political writers—over the past two decades of growing cynicism a tendency to believe that the only good investigative writing must be negative. "If you can't say anything bad about a public figure, then don't say anything at all about him," seems to be the slogan of many of those who write on public life in America today.

That is not the way I see it. Objectivity requires that one tell the good along with the bad. I *have* found some "bad things" to say about Mario Cuomo, and I have said them. But what I found most notable about him was that, unlike so many other modern politicians, his positive side appears to be considerably larger than his negative.

The negativism of most writing about public figures is understandable. It reflects the sorry state into which American public life has fallen in recent years. Most of us find it hard to believe in anyone. But cynicism is an utterly unsatisfying attitude. People *want*—desperately so, in many cases—to find someone worthy of their trust and belief. The extraordinary popularity of biographies in the 1980s is, I suspect, a reflection of this yearning. People are searching for a hero. The public today amounts to a sort of collective Diogenes. They are seeking one good man or woman, and biographies serve as their lanterns.

If it is a hero they seek, readers will be disappointed in these pages—as I think they will be wherever they look. Heroes can be dangerous. They rarely, if ever, prove to be as perfect as they at first appear.

But if the modern-day Diogenes will settle for a good but imperfect person, he may find this biography more to his liking. Part of our trouble, I believe, lies in thinking that we are going to find on this earth someone without fault—or, as Mario Cuomo would be more likely to put it, without sin. That is a hopeless quest.

Three of the historical figures Cuomo most admires are Thomas More, Abraham Lincoln, and Franklin Roosevelt. The reason, he told me, is that all three had serious human failings, but managed to do great things anyway. "It's nice to be able to admire them as heroes, even as you accept them as humans," Cuomo said to me. "It would be a helluva world if all the saints were perfect—I mean, what would you aspire to?"

Clearly Cuomo associates himself with these men. It gives him some comfort to know that one need not be perfect to be worthy. In his 1950 assessment of FDR, *Roosevelt in Retrospect,* John Gunther listed some of that President's shortcomings: "dilatoriness, two-sidedness (some would say plain dishonesty), pettiness in some personal relationships, a cardinal lack of frankness . . . , inability to say No, love of improvisation, garrulousness, amateurism, and what has been called 'cheerful vindictiveness.' " Yet none of these flaws prevented Roosevelt from ranking with Lincoln (of whom a similar lengthy list of failings could easily be assembled) as one of our two greatest presidents. Mario Cuomo's faults are not, for the most part, those from which FDR suffered, but they are as numerous. As in the cases of Lincoln and Roosevelt, though, it appears that Cuomo's flaws are outweighed by his virtues and abilities.[1]

In doing the research for this biography, it was necessary to rely heavily on interviews. The reader should be aware that many of the statements quoted from Cuomo's past are based upon the recollections of people who were present. I have enclosed such passages in quotation marks, even though in most cases the words cannot be assumed to be exactly those spoken at the time.

A biography of someone in mid-career would be impossible without the willingness of a large number of people who have known him through the years to grant interviews. I greatly appreciate the kindness of the following people in giving of their time and their memories: Philip Astuto, Joe Austin, Bernard Babb, Governor Bruce Babbitt, Herman Badillo, Carol Bellamy, Senator Joseph Biden, Jenny Brand, Senator Dale Bumpers, Patrick Caddell, Eugene Callender, Lou Carnesecca, William Carrick, Governor Bill Clinton, Representative Tony Coelho, Donna Cuomo, Frank Cuomo, Immaculata Cuomo, Joan Cuomo, Maria Cuomo,

Governor Mario Cuomo, Matilda Cuomo, Rosario Cuomo, Sal Curiale, Arlene D'Arienzo, Nicholas D'Arienzo, Michael Del Giudice, Peter DeNunzio, Patricia Derian, Senator Christopher Dodd, Governor Michael Dukakis, Janie Eisenberg, Arthur Foster, Gary Fryer, Representative Richard Gephardt, John Gerity, Roy Goodman, Richard Goodwin, Senator Gary Hart, John Iaccio, Rev. Jesse Jackson, Peter Johnson, Senator Edward Kennedy, Mayor Edward Koch, Mary Anne Krupsak, Alexander Levine, Mayor John Lindsay, Joseph Mattone, William Modell, Jack Newfield, Fabian Palomino, Peter Quinn, Joseph Rauh, Governor Charles Robb, Felix Rohatyn, Timothy Russert, Nicholas Sallese, Anthony Sarno, Arthur Schlesinger, Jr., Stephen Schlesinger, Representative Patricia Schroeder, Senator Paul Simon, Beth Smith, Judge James Starkey, Richard Starkey, Martin Steadman, William Stern, Robert Sullivan, Margaret Swezey, Mary Tragale, Jacques Tuchler, Representative Morris Udall, Marie Cuomo Vecchio, Ted Vecchio, Judge Sol Wachtler, Richard Wade, Speaker Jim Wright, and Drew Zambelli.

Special thanks are owed to Governor Cuomo himself, who cooperated so fully in an undertaking over which he had no control; to Rose and Bob Lee of Mahopac, and Paul and Sue Murray of Albany, who provided accommodations, conversation, and cheer on my many trips to New York; to Ross Moore and his amazing one-man clipping service; to my editor, Edward T. Chase, and my agent, Mel Berger; and, for a variety of assistance, to Carol and Charlie Boyle, Kathy and Hugh Boyle, Karen Carlley, Nancy and Jim Condangelo, Susan Garcia, Julie and John Heyman, Bishop William Houck, Anna and John Lee, Joan and Ron Marks, Joan and Charlie Meehan, Karen and Chuck Meehan, Susan and Brian Meehan, Judy Page, Linda and Michael Raff, Stephen Schlesinger, Doreen and Joey Shelton, Rev. Elvin Sunds, and Mary Tragale.

I never would have been in a position to write a book such as this had it not been for the guidance and inspiration provided over many years by my parents, Ruth and Edward McElvaine. That they are not here to share my excitement in completing the book is one of my greatest sorrows.

The book is dedicated to four of my loves: my daughters Kerri, Lauren, and Allison, and a yet-to-be-named person who was conceived while the book was being written and who is expected to see the light of the world at about the same time it does.

My greatest love, Anne, shared more in the gestation of this life story than I am able to share in that of the new life that has been simultaneously developing within her.

ROBERT MCELVAINE
Clinton, Mississippi
December 1987

MARIO CUOMO

Introduction

ENIGMA

AFTER a narrow victory in his first race for the state's highest office during the height of the Republican ascendancy in Washington, New York's Democratic governor won an overwhelming reelection victory. The next day the state Democratic party chairman said he did not see how the governor could "escape becoming the next presidential nominee of his party, even if no one should lift a finger to bring it about."

The year was 1930 and the governor was Franklin D. Roosevelt, but a similar situation seemed to exist for the man who took FDR's position in Albany in 1982. Four previous New York governors—Martin Van Buren, Grover Cleveland, Theodore Roosevelt, and FDR—had moved on to the White House. And in this century alone, five others—Charles Evans Hughes, Al Smith, Thomas Dewey, Averell Harriman, and Nelson Rockefeller—had made strong efforts to do so. Mario M. Cuomo was reelected in 1986 by a larger margin than any of these illustrious predecessors had ever won in a New York gubernatorial contest.

Then in February 1987 Governor Cuomo startled the political world by announcing that he would not seek his party's highest honor in 1988. Since he would not rule out the possibility of being drafted, some suggested that Cuomo was "running by not running." Although many fingers had in fact been lifted to make Roosevelt the party's standard-bearer in 1932, perhaps Cuomo wanted to see if *he* could win the nomination *without* a finger being lifted. If that was his intent, it seemed a dubious strategy. Other politicians have found that it is easy to grow old waiting for a nomination to seek you. Nominations are notoriously poor pathfinders. Yet if anyone was ever likely to be sought by a major

3

party's presidential nomination, Mario Cuomo seemed like a good bet.

In any case, a man who was already among the most intriguing public figures in America became even more interesting when he appeared to turn away from the very prize that most successful politicians seek with all their strength.

New York's governor will never be a matinee idol. On television he appears to be of moderate stature and stocky build, but he is actually six feet tall and muscular. The large, sagging pouches under his eyes testify to his habit of sleeping no more than five hours each night. He says his face has the appearance of "a tired frog." The eye bags combine with a gap-tooth smile to make him a cartoonist's delight. His dancing dark brown eyes mark him as a man who enjoys a good time, but on occasion those eyes suddenly turn brooding. He is often told by surprised people meeting him for the first time, "You know, Cuomo, you're not as ugly in person as you are on television." He is not ugly, but neither is he likely to compete for the role of national sex symbol. Yet he has about him a magnetism that has led many women who have been around him to become infatuated with him. Many females of all ages who come into his presence cling to his arm.[1]

He looks like a man who would be at home in a neighborhood tavern in his native Queens—and who could acquit himself well in a barroom brawl, should the need arise. The casual observer might easily conclude that he is a middle-aged man who used to be a good athlete and has not lost the build that made him a standout in high school sports—one whose "glory days," like those of the hero of Bruce Springsteen's song, have passed him by. His gnarled hands and powerful, stubby fingers label him as a manual laborer. Or he might be the sort of parish priest who knows how to have a good time and enjoys those pleasures of life from which he has not taken vows to abstain.

With the exception of a laborer, Mario Cuomo is all of these things. Except for his work in his father's grocery store while he was growing up, he has not been gainfully employed in anything like manual labor. But legend has it that on at least one occasion when he found himself in a barroom altercation, he proved to have a quite respectable right hook. He was not only a high school athlete of considerable renown, but a talented semiprofessional basketball player and a minor-league outfielder in the Pittsburgh Pirates organization. And—until he met Matilda Raffa—he gave some consideration to entering the priesthood.

When he opens his mouth, though, the impression is dramatically altered. Suddenly the image of Mario Cuomo ceases to be that of a fun-loving, simple man of the lower middle classes. He becomes instead a scholar, a man with an intellect of the first rank. A one-sentence question put to him is likely to trigger a fifteen-minute discourse. He speaks as readily about the philosophy of Thomas More as about the hitting technique of Joe DiMaggio. His intellect is a match for his passion. His zest for life is reflected in his hunger for ideas and his love of debate.

Superior intelligence is not necessarily an asset for one who seeks high political office, as Ronald Reagan proved by negative example. Arthur Schlesinger reminds us of a positive example of the same point when he says that he sees Cuomo as "another Adlai Stevenson." (It may be worth pointing out to some readers that Schlesinger means this as a compliment.) It is a partially apt analogy. Like Stevenson, Cuomo is more intellectual than most politicians. He has an ability to inspire people to get involved in politics and believe that government can accomplish good. But, inspiring as Stevenson was, Mario Cuomo is an even better public speaker than the 1952 and 1956 Democratic presidential candidate was. This is to say nothing negative about Stevenson. Cuomo is the best speaker American politics has produced in at least the last half century. He is to political orators what Vladimir Horowitz is to pianists or Wayne Gretzky is to hockey forwards: the standard against which all others are measured, the ideal toward which all others strive.

It was a string of magnificent speeches that brought Cuomo to the nation's attention: his address to the New York Democratic convention in 1982, his inaugural address as governor in 1983, his speech at the 1984 Democratic National Convention, his statement on religion and public service at Notre Dame University later in 1984, and commencement addresses at Harvard and Stanford in 1985. Such political speeches, many said, had not been heard since the days of Franklin Roosevelt—if then. "Mario Cuomo is probably the most eloquent, articulate person in public office today," his two-time political rival Ed Koch said to me. "Some read speeches as well as he does—none better. [Ted] Kennedy reads speeches extremely well, but there's no question in my mind that if you put Kennedy and Cuomo on the same platform, without a piece of paper to read from, Cuomo would wipe the floor with him," New York's mayor said. "I can't think of anyone who's gone so far on the basis of a couple of speeches," Beth Smith, who served as Gary Hart's communications director, told me in 1986 with more than a touch of envy in her voice.

But Cuomo's speaking ability would not have carried him so far if that were his only attraction. "Cuomo touched everybody," former Assistant Secretary of State Patricia Derian said of the keynote address at the 1984 convention, "not because he had at that point demonstrated a long record of great leadership, but because he was able to *articulate* an idea of the country." In short, Cuomo's speeches inspire people not just because of the way he delivers them, but even more because of what he says.[2]

Cuomo's philosophy and politics begin with the optimism of the Jesuit scientist-theologian Pierre Teilhard de Chardin, who maintained that God did not create the world to be an obstacle course of dangers and evils to be avoided, but as a context in which people were expected to work out their divine mission. Therefore, the faithful should not seek to escape the world but to embrace it and try to make it better. Cuomo feels that he's been given more than he deserves and more than most others, and that he owes a debt to society. This perspective leads the New York governor to believe that "the political power one wins is good for the good it can do. . . . The joy of winning is the joy of having the opportunity to do the good." Politics ought genuinely to be an opportunity for service. Cuomo insists that he is in politics "in order to serve because it's good to serve." Coming from many a politician, such statements would be greeted with cynicism—and rightly so. Coming from Governor Cuomo, they are often greeted with tears and enthusiastic applause.

People *believe* Mario Cuomo because he offers them something worthwhile and uplifting to believe in. This is desperately needed in late twentieth-century America. A series of political scandals has nearly destroyed the faith of most Americans in their leaders and institutions. It was ironic that, prior to the Iran-contra scandal of late 1986, Ronald Reagan had succeeded in restoring some confidence in the very "gub-mint" he had run against. But, as Seymour Martin Lipset and William Schneider have shown, even at the peak of his popularity Reagan had not restored faith in governmental leaders and institutions among the private sector. The "crisis of confidence" Jimmy Carter warned of in 1979 has not yet passed, and as President Reagan sank ever more deeply in 1987 into scarcely credible defenses of his actions, the problem worsened once more. The temporary (one hopes) infatuation in the summer of 1987 of a significant portion of the American public with Oliver North indicated just how desperate people were to find someone in Washington they could trust. North's degree of truthfulness was limited to a willingness to admit, under a grant of immunity, that he had repeatedly lied to the elected representatives of the people (in order to advance the cause of democracy)—and was proud of it. When any sizable number of Americans could take such a man as a hero, it was clear that the country was in a dangerous state. The yearning for a leader with integrity had become so great that many were prepared to accept someone who was at least truthful about the fact that he was a liar. Under the circumstances, the public was anxiously seeking a leader in the White House who could and would shoot straight.

Washington Post book reviewer Jonathan Yardley probably articulated the feelings of a majority of Americans when he wrote in the spring of 1987: "Where once I believed that politics is an honorable, if not noble, calling, I now see it as a refuge of opportunists and self-aggrandizers, if not scoundrels." "With the rarest of exceptions," Yardley went on to say, "serious people no longer run for office, because television is inherently inhospitable to seriousness. Those blow-dried egotists now lining up for the presidency radiate all the intellectual and moral acuity of Max Headroom, who probably would make a better president than any of them." Whatever one may think of Cuomo, who was not a candidate at the time Yardley delivered his opinion, the New York governor plainly does not belong in the category of mindless, valueless, blow-dried or computer-generated politicians.

There is a large and growing group of Americans who hunger for something good to believe in. Cuomo understands this. "Before everything else," he wrote in 1982, "they want to believe in something uplifting, pure, good. The vacuum I've sensed for years is more obvious to me now than ever." "Most of all," the new governor wrote after the extremely favorable response to his 1983 inaugural address, "I think people want to feel good about themselves and the world. We are often a cynical people, but we don't want to be. We'd prefer to believe, to love, to hope."

There can be little question that there is a widespread desire among the American people for some*thing* worthwhile in which to believe. But it is equally clear that after a long series of failed presidencies and politicians beset with scandals, many Americans are also searching for some*one* in whom they can believe, someone who will restore a sense of trust in the American political system and who will present a vision of America, based upon the nation's best values, around which people can rally.

Cuomo provides people with an alternative to the cynicism that has gripped the nation since the days of Vietnam and Watergate. He gives them something that can fill the cavity in the heart of the "Me generation." "Believing is better than not believing," he says simply. "My whole case is an affirmative one that is aggressively confident of our ability to help ourselves. Most people like that more than they like surrender." After hearing a Cuomo campaign speech in 1982, an elegant, elderly Republican woman told the candidate, "It's nice to be able to vote for somebody who believes in something—even if you don't agree with all of it."[3]

That was a large part of the secret of Ronald Reagan's appeal. He appeared to believe in something, so many people were willing to go along with him, even if they did not much like his direction. But Cuomo claims to offer more: not simplistic answers to all problems, not pandering to popular prejudices, but innovative leadership that dares to go against prevailing opinion when Cuomo believes prevailing opinion to be wrong.

Can someone who disagrees with "the people" on several important issues be a "leader"? Cuomo thinks so. He believes that a campaign should be used to educate and enlighten citizens and that if one merely goes along with popular opinion, "you are not a shepherd but simply part of the flock." Cuomo expresses disdain for politicians who allow opinion polls to lead them. "If leaders will not lead," he inquires rhetorically, "who will?"

Unlike some Democrats of the 1980s, Cuomo never made any effort to move closer to Republican positions. He thought they were wrong. He understood, moreover, that "me-tooism" is defeatist politics and, in any event, the conservative tide was ebbing. Democrats, Cuomo argued throughout the Reagan years, must demonstrate their sharp philosophical differences with Republicans.[4]

* * *

Many of Mario Cuomo's personal qualities are of the sort that enhance his appeal. He says what he thinks. In his unsuccessful attempt to become mayor of New York City in 1977, Cuomo was asked why he thought he would make a good mayor. He quickly answered that he *didn't* think he would make a good mayor and proceeded to explain why he thought *no one* could be a good mayor, because it is a job that is impossible to do well. This sort of direct approach in a politician is unusual and refreshing.

He prides himself on maintaining complete honesty and keeping his commitments. "Credibility means everything to me," he says. "You can't govern without it." He says it is necessary to be open with the press, even if this results in some negative stories; but he has often engaged in feuds with members of the media. Cuomo looks on politics with a healthy degree of skepticism, but he is not cynical. He insists that he refuses to alter his positions to gain popularity. "I don't waffle," he proudly states. If true, this would make him a remarkable politician indeed. It is one of the many claims that Cuomo makes about himself that will be carefully examined in the pages that follow.

There seems to be little chance that Cuomo would ever be directly involved in a scandal. He is, by all accounts, "squeaky clean." He has remarkably little interest in wealth or material comforts. "I think if he had his druthers, living as a monk would not have hurt him at all," his wife told me. His family has never lived in a high style, and he gave up an opportunity to bring in a greater income after his political career began by ending his law practice, even though he was not required to do so and all previous New York secretaries of state had practiced law on the side. The only income he has comes from his salary, the books he has written and some of his speeches. His children have, for the most part, been educated in state universities. Cuomo's lack of greed is directly connected to his deeply rooted philosophy. His major objective is to avoid being motivated by a desire for self-advancement. He strongly believes that it is our obligation to exist to serve others.[5]

Cuomo holds himself to the highest personal standard of morality—sufficiently so that some might describe him as a prude. Yet unlike most people who bear that label, he is tolerant, within broad limits, of the behavior of others. He is very far from being a bluenose. He does not believe that we have the right to judge the souls of others. That is God's task and, as Cuomo often reminds anyone who will listen, "I am not God."

"I don't ever want to be in a position of saying, 'I'm a good and moral person,' " Cuomo told me. "I don't want to hold myself out as a moral leader—a hard worker, yes, but I'm not so good. I'm religious because religion is for sinners, not saints."

While all the evidence indicates that Cuomo is absolutely committed to faithful monogamy on a personal level—"When I was growing up," he says, "we had a clear standard of morality: 'If it was fun, it was a sin; if it was a lot of fun, it was a mortal sin.' "—he has no objection to (indeed, seems to enjoy) listening to tales of the sexual adventures of others. Presumably he, like Jimmy Carter and virtually all other men, lusts in his heart; but if so, unlike Carter, he does not feel the urge to tell others about it. Several of our presidents and presidential aspirants went further and lusted with other parts of their anatomy, but Cuomo confines any lusting he may engage in to his heart.

If reports were to circulate that he had sailed off to Bimini with an actress, Cuomo said after Gary Hart's first political demise in the spring of 1987, his wife, Matilda, "would split her sides laughing." It appears that he has always adhered to a remarkably high personal standard of conduct in such matters. A teammate on the Brunswick, Georgia, minor-league baseball club for which Cuomo played in 1953 says that he would go out at night and pick up girls, sometimes bringing back an "extra" for Matt (as Cuomo was called while playing baseball in a part of the country where, as South Carolina Democratic National Committeeman Don Fowler would note early in 1986, "there aren't many Marios"). "Jesus, when you play in those little towns in Georgia, you got all these women," he said. "I'd bring women home for him [Cuomo], and he'd chase me out of the room. I said he didn't even have to pick them up, I'd bring them, but he'd chase me out of the room."

Longtime friend and associate Fabian Palomino underscores Cuomo's personal morality by saying: "Mario is the only Italian male I've ever known who was a virgin when he got married. The *only* one. I won't go any further on how I know, but [it's a fact]."[6]

                    Mario Cuomo sometimes seems too good to be true. "Will Mario Cuomo throw his halo into the ring in 1988?" mused Democratic activist and soon-to-be candidate for the United States Senate Mark Green early in 1986. Those of us who have been burned in the past by believing in leaders who turned out to be vastly different from what they had once seemed are especially reluctant to accept another apparent savior. It is among the major purposes of this book to find out whether Cuomo is "just another politician" who has skillfully created an attractive image for himself or someone who might genuinely be capable of restoring belief in our political system, compassion for others, and idealism in the American people.

It must be made clear from the outset that Mario Cuomo does not possess a halo. Although he seems almost saintly in some respects, he is wholly human in others. His faults are real and far from insignificant.

On the question of whether Cuomo is for real or just another carefully crafted image, on at least one occasion in 1984 he appeared to condemn himself. "Perception is the key," the governor told a reporter. "Reality often doesn't matter in politics. I believe in symbolism, and I want to convey a certain message in everything I say and do." Cuomo went on to declare that he wanted the audience for his Notre Dame speech on religion and public service to take his presentation as a serious intellectual statement, so he would put on his eyeglasses about thirty seconds after beginning his speech.

To say that reality often doesn't matter in politics is only to accept the obvious truth. To believe in the importance of symbolism is to recognize what is necessary to motivate people. The crucial question is whether the symbols coincide with reality. If they do, Cuomo qualifies as a refreshing, cleansing breeze in American politics; if they do not, he can be categorized as another misleader of the people, albeit one who is more skillful than most.

New York's governor is a most introspective man. In keeping a diary, he tries to come to grips with his own motivations, sort out his thoughts, and constantly remind himself of his principles and his reasons for being in politics. "How should I try to spend the rest of my time so that I hurt as few people as possible and help as many as possible?" he wrote in a typical diary entry at the beginning of 1982. "Always, the nagging truth is that I should be something else—a person who gives only to give, who works only to provide, who speaks only to soothe or persuade for the good, who strives only for others." Cuomo holds himself up against an impossible standard and, inevitably, finds himself wanting. "In the end, I am a man who knows what to do but knows even more sharply that he has failed by his own standards to do it as well as it can be done."

Like a surprisingly large number of successful politicians, Mario Cuomo says he prefers privacy to the public life that he leads. "Loneliness has never been the threat to me that the world has been," he says. "The more deeply I have become involved in opening myself, revealing myself, discussing myself, the more vulnerable I have felt." At the time of major events in his life, Cuomo says, "I want to close my eyes and think and feel . . . alone." Cuomo seems to have a sort of emotional "balance wheel that drives me back toward the center." "Whether in tragedy or triumph, my psyche seems incapable of going all the way."[7]

A good sense of humor is essential for a politician who hopes to persuade people to follow him. Cuomo is, despite the seriousness of most of the subjects he addresses, quite capable of making people laugh. Yet his sharp wit can be the proverbial double-edged sword. His appearance before the House Ways and Means Committee in the summer of 1985, to testify against President Reagan's proposal to eliminate the deductibility of state and local taxes, demonstrated both his sense of humor and the danger of wounding himself with his wit. In his prepared testimony, the governor said that one of the main reasons the administration offered for ending deductibility was, "We need the money." "It reminds me," Cuomo deadpanned, "of what Willie Sutton said when he was apprehended after his last bank robbery. He was asked, 'Why did you do it, Willie?' And he answered exactly the same thing: 'I need the money.' "

Then Cuomo was questioned by Congressman Judd Gregg (R., N.H.), who asked why the people of his state should subsidize the high taxes in New York. After making an excellent statement on the cooperative nature of sharing benefits and burdens in our federal Union, in which he pointed out that if we gave back to every state exactly what it contributed, we wouldn't need a union, Cuomo said: "That's federalism. That's how the Union works. If the people of New Hampshire want a different union that says we want *only* what we raise ourselves within our borders, that's terrific—then New Hampshire can secede from the Union!" The pointed remark brought the house down with laughter, but it was not a wise statement for one who might someday participate in a primary election in the Granite State.

During the same appearance before the House Ways and Means Committee, Governor Cuomo was questioned by Representative John J. Duncan (R., Tenn.), who said in a rather nasty tone, "I never heard of anyone in Tennessee who wanted to retire to New York." "Maybe they don't admit that they're from Tennessee after they've retired," Cuomo shot back. On another occasion he said that Senator Hollings's comment that "people in Alabama think the nuclear freeze is a dessert" was one of the funniest statements he had ever heard. Perhaps it was, but saying so was not very diplomatic.

Cuomo's greatest liability is his well-deserved reputation for being overly sensitive to criticism and having a volatile temper that sometimes escapes his control. "He's got a short fuse, let's put it that way," says his brother Frank.

It is clear that Cuomo is especially sensitive to ethnic slurs. There is nothing wrong with that, but there is a danger of carrying his legitimate concern too far. In December 1985 he spent forty-five minutes talking to reporters about why they should not use the word "Mafia" and other ethnic stereotypes. Although his main point was the unarguable one that the public should not be led to the outrageous conclusion that most people of Italian ancestry are criminals, he did say at one point that the notion that the Mafia is an organization is "a lot of baloney." He minimized the damage by backing off that statement quickly.

Senator Christopher Dodd (D., Conn.), in a generally favorable 1986 assessment of Cuomo, said to me that he worries that the governor "has a very thin skin. You've gotta be able to take your lumps in this business. In fact, you've got to be able to take your lumps and turn them around in a positive way," Dodd said. "If your counterpunch is a negative one, with a tone of nastiness in it, you won't last long." Dodd said this "may only be a temporary problem with him; I like other things about him tremendously."

One of the most damning criticisms of Cuomo ever to reach print came in 1985 from a liberal Democratic congressman who, understandably, wished to remain anonymous: "Mario is an Old Testament Christian rather than a New Testament Christian. He's vindictive. He has an enemies list. I sort of view him as a liberal Nixon."

Surely the last charge is excessive, but the problem is there, and both Cuomo and his close friends know it. At several points in his *Diaries,* he wrote of how hard it is for him to control his anger and avoid unnecessary arguments. "Tired, I find the instinct to hit back hard difficult to resist," he said during the general election campaign of 1982. Even within his family, the problem sometimes arises. In his diary entry for Thanksgiving Day 1980, Cuomo wrote: "I argued too much as usual: even *I* found it unpleasant." A certain degree of combativeness can be a political asset, but Mario Cuomo will have to be very careful to avoid turning his argumentative style into a serious liability.[8]

One close friend says that the governor is "unpredictable, both as to positions he will take on particular issues and on how he will treat you when he knows you well." Friends and associates describe him as "moody," and on occasion cutting and nasty. He is noted for trying to find out who among his staff was a "source who did not wish to be identified" and said something to the press that Cuomo did not appreciate.

These lapses notwithstanding, Mario Cuomo is generally loyal to his friends and they to him. One who noted his capacity for slashing remarks still insisted that one of his great attractions is his personal warmth and his ability to make you feel good. Even loyalty, however, can be seen in a negative light. Cuomo has left himself open to the charge of "cronyism" in filling administrative posts in the state government.

Another potential problem for the New York governor is his penchant for being a "micromanager." "Cuomo's a one-man band," Bill Carrick, then Ted Kennedy's political director and later Dick Gephardt's campaign manager, told me in 1986. "He has a weak staff and does everything himself." "I think Cuomo has a great deal going for him," former JFK speechwriter Dick Goodwin said, "and that he could make it [to the presidency] if he would get around him some people with experience in a national campaign. Without that, he'll be in trouble. But I'm very impressed with him. He's certainly the most intelligent of the prospective candidates," Goodwin concluded in mid-1985.

Like his quick temper, Cuomo's tendency to try to do too much himself is a problem of which he is aware. He knows he is a workaholic. "The one great sin," he has declared, is "wasting existence. "I have always felt" Cuomo wrote in his diary, "—despite the shibboleths—that I should be aggressively involved in my own campaigns." After his election as governor, Cuomo said: "I must resist the temptation to deal with so much of the detail, but it's not easy. I've spent a lifetime doing things for myself, and that habit has grown quite strong after half a hundred years."[9]

Being aware of one's potential problems is an important plus, but the danger remains.

Another of Cuomo's problems is that he seems the consummate New Yorker. There is, to begin with, the question of his accent. New York City speech is not popular in the rest of the nation. Many people in the nation's heartland cringed when they heard Al Smith speak over what he called the "raddio" during his 1928 presidential campaign. But Cuomo's accent is closer to that of a New York intellectual than to Smith's Fulton Fish Market inflection. (Cuomo's use of the Rooseveltian pronunciation "a-gain" for "again" sometimes seems out of place.) New York intellectuals are not all that popular in the hinterlands, either, but there is at least one example in our recent history of an accent peculiar to a limited region of the country enhancing a politician's image. Although Jimmy Carter's southern accent condemned him from the start with many "liberals," John F. Kennedy's Boston cadence was a net plus. People laughed at it, but it added to his luster, his aura of quality.

But the New York problem is more than a superficial question of accent. Cuomo, like many New Yorkers, has not often traveled far from the city. Aside from his few months as a professional baseball player in Georgia and his time in Albany since entering politics, he has lived his entire life in Queens and only occasionally exposed himself to other parts of the nation, much less the world. "Roots" are important to a national leader, but Cuomo's vines have not spread far enough to give him a wide variety of experience.[10]

There is also the charge that Cuomo is an "old-style New Dealer" and therefore is out of step with the American electorate. To head Cuomo off, both Democratic rivals and Republicans have tried to tar him with being the representative of "the failed policies of the past," that is, "liberalism." "I think Mario Cuomo automatically inherits the mantle of Ted Kennedy and Walter Mondale," former Virginia Governor Chuck Robb told me. "He doesn't want to be dubbed the heir apparent to the Kennedy-Mondale-Tip O'Neill wing of the party." Doubtless. But it is a title that political opponents will continue to try to attach to Cuomo. "I know the thing that hurts me most is that I am not perceived as 'new,' " he wrote in 1982. "The irony is that I have many more new ideas than the public has heard in along time."

Realizing that the label "liberal" has fallen into disrepute, Cuomo has sought other terms to describe his political philosophy: "not a way to fool people into 'buying' the same old politics disguised as something new, but a way to make them listen to what I was saying without concluding that it was somehow out of date." He has used such terms as "progressive pragmatism" and "family" to describe his vision of what is essentially a new form of liberalism.

The new progressivism for which Mario Cuomo speaks retains the traditional liberal values. It seeks a greater degree of cooperation among various segments of American society. A concert of interests among business, government, labor, and the public, Cuomo believes, can promote economic growth and make America more competitive in the world economy. An understanding of the interconnectedness of our society will make it easier to persuade those who have "made it" of the necessity to help those who have not. Unlike some liberals of the past, Governor Cuomo is not hostile to legitimate business interests; but unlike many who style themselves conservatives, he does not advocate letting business and the rich do whatever they please, regardless of the social consequences. He seeks instead to replace confrontation with cooperation.

Cuomo summarized this view well when he said to me: "I give tax cuts, not so the people with pinky rings can buy another pinky ring, or a Mercedes, but to encourage them to do business in this state, because I need the wealth they help to create to take care of the people in wheelchairs." "And," the governor continued, "we're constantly talking about the relationship between economic growth and the other mission that we see for government, which is taking care of people who are not going to be [directly] benefited by that growth." The guidelines for the new progressive pragmatism are to employ common sense and reasonableness in seeking new and more effective ways to reach the unchanging liberal goals and to strive, as Cuomo puts it, "to do more with less"—fiscal responsibility combined with social responsibility. In New York, Cuomo says, "we don't apologize for government; we use it intelligently, reasonably, proudly." "I don't accept that the price of progress for the majority of us is that the government must forget the rest of us," Cuomo told an audience at Yale early in 1985.[11]

It is clear that Mario Cuomo is the Democrat Republicans fear most as an opponent in a presidential election. As early as 1981, before Cuomo had ever won an elective office on his own, Reagan operatives in the White House were reported to be concerned about him winning the Democratic nomination for governor. During his 1982 primary against Mayor Edward Koch, Cuomo said the question of his campaign was "Can you beat electricity with light?" Cuomo saw Koch as a charismatic figure—"a kind of male 'Evita' "—and himself as one who was making rational arguments on the issues. Although Cuomo won, he had reason to doubt that his arguments carried the day. At a big rally in Utica after his primary victory, Cuomo told me, a man rushed up to him, threw his arms around him, kissed him on the cheek, and said to him: "You showed that bastard. You're right. We gotta burn 'em all!" "I thought," Cuomo said, " 'You've got to be kidding.' Twenty percent of the campaign was spent arguing the death penalty, and he thought I was *for* it!"

So much for light. What really worries Republicans is that Mario Cuomo can combine electricity with light. That would be a difficult combination to beat.

It sounds, in fact, a lot like the qualities possessed by such previous leaders as Franklin Roosevelt and John Kennedy. And in some respects Mario Cuomo is similar to those earlier Democrats. Like them, his appeal goes beyond traditional Democratic voters. His approval ratings in the normally Republican suburban counties around New York City have been almost as high as his ratings in the Democratic city. In June 1986, for example, Cuomo was approved by 71.6 percent of the people in Westchester, Rockland, Nassau, and Suffolk counties, and by 72.3 percent in the five boroughs of New York City. And like FDR and JFK, MMC (as he refers to himself in his diaries) is that curious American hybrid, a pragmatic idealist. Like Kennedy, Cuomo asks more of people than he promises to give them. He is, furthermore, an inspirational leader and orator in much the way those two Democratic presidents were.[12]

Cuomo is the first American politician since the assassination of Robert F. Kennedy who seems capable of bringing together a coalition similar to that of the New Deal—one comprised of middle-class whites (including ethnics), blacks, Hispanics, organized labor, and liberal intellectuals. The reason for this potential in Cuomo, ironically, is that he is in fact so *different* from the Roosevelts and the Kennedys, and indeed from most people who call themselves liberals today.

It is not going too far to say that no one like Mario Cuomo has ever before approached the pinnacle of American politics. Like the Roosevelts and the Kennedys, he is a champion of "the people." Unlike them, he began life as *one of* the people. He is not, of course, the first progressive politician in our history who could justly make that claim. But he differs from other liberals in several fundamental ways. A comparison with President Kennedy is instructive in this regard.

John F. Kennedy was said to be the first representative of urban, immigrant, Catholic America to reach the White House. But the Kennedys were far from immigrants when JFK was born. His great-grandfather arrived in the United States around 1850 (following the Irish Potato Famine), nearly seventy years before the future president was born. JFK's was the family's third generation born in this country. By contrast, Mario Cuomo's older brother was born in Italy and his mother arrived in New York less than five years before the future governor's birth. His mother still pronounces her remarkable gems of wisdom through a thick Italian accent.

Although the America into which John Kennedy was born in 1917 was not without some lingering prejudice against people of Irish ancestry, any ethnic hostility he faced was minimal in comparison to that which still confronted Italian-Americans when Mario Cuomo was growing up. Cuomo's experience was very close to that of the immigrant masses of southern and eastern Europe; Kennedy's was only slightly removed from that of the old-stock "native" American Yankees with whom his father sought full equality and acceptance.

Kennedy's Catholicism was more perfunctory and cultural than it was committed or theological. At the age of twenty, JFK had an audience with the pope. At a similar age, Cuomo's contacts in the hierarchy did not go above his parish priests and his Vincentian professors at St. John's. No one familiar with the habits and practices of the two men could fail to conclude that Cuomo is far more religious than Kennedy ever was.

Both of JFK's grandfathers were politically powerful figures—one was the mayor of Boston. His father was a multimil-
lionaire who held positions of great influence in the Roosevelt
administration. Cuomo's parents were so little interested in politics that when he became New York's secretary of state in 1975,
his father was concerned that Mario was giving up his position as
a lawyer to become a secretary. John Kennedy grew up completely
immersed in a political milieu; Mario Cuomo grew up in an atmosphere in which politicians were at best ignored and at worst
considered the corrupt enemy.

The difference between Kennedy and Cuomo is the difference
between Hyannis Port and South Jamaica; between gifts of ponies
and sailboats and never having a bicycle; between Choate and P.S.
50; between the "gentleman's C" at Harvard and the scholarship
student's A at St. John's; between having a "gentleman's gentleman" to look after your needs as a college student and your wife
doing most of the household chores for thirty years; between writing a popular book at the age of twenty-two and being rejected by
the leading Manhattan law firms despite finishing at the top of
your class; between winning a seat in the United States Congress
at the age of twenty-nine and winning no elective office on your
own until age fifty; between a reputation for never losing an election and one for being a loser.[13]

Mario Cuomo reached liberalism via a remarkably different
route from that followed by FDR, JFK, and most modern liberals.
He became a liberal because of his deep religious commitment, his
understanding of Teilhard de Chardin and Pope John XXIII, and
his own experience. It is because of this unusual course that
Cuomo is in a nearly unique position to bridge the vast gulf that
opened in the late 1960s between liberal intellectuals and the
"common people" they professed to champion. In the simplest
terms, Cuomo can heal that breach because he is *both* a "common
person" and a liberal intellectual.

                         Because Mario Cuomo seems so
different from most other politicians, and because he appears to
embody as well as to articulate a vision of America at its best, he
has become a truly remarkable political phenomenon. When Edward M. Kennedy announced late in 1985 that he would not be a
candidate for the presidency in 1988, his decision was readily ac-

cepted. Three months after Governor Cuomo made a similar statement in February 1987, national opinion polls showed him far
ahead of all active candidates as the choice for the Democratic
nomination. He became the only noncandidate whose every move
and statement were intently scrutinized by the media. A public
jaded by the experience of a long line of presidential aspirants who
coveted power too avidly to be trusted with it was all the more
attracted to a man who said he preferred to remain at his duties
as governor.

Some said that Cuomo did not have the necessary "fire in the
belly" to be president. His response was to the point: Do we want
"a guy with fire in the belly sitting down with Gorbachev? Sitting
down next to the phone with the red button—with fire in his belly?
Show me a man with fire in his belly and I'll put seltzer in his
mouth." Many Americans seemed to think that they had seen
enough presidents with fire in their bellies. One suspects that if a
poll were taken on which post–World War II presidents were the
most trustworthy—not the most popular or most approved—the
names that would most often be mentioned are Truman, Eisenhower, and Ford, the only three who did not spend years seeking
the office.

One of the reasons Cuomo decided he could not run for president while serving as governor was that political strategists told
him people in Iowa expect to see a candidate in their living rooms,
and that he would have to spend at least fifty days in the state to
have a chance of winning the caucuses there. But a *Des Moines
Register* poll in May 1987 found that 32 percent of Iowa Democrats
said they would support the New York governor at a time when
he had never set foot in the state. This figure placed him far ahead
of all of the active candidates, many of whom had adopted Iowa
as their second home. It appeared that Cuomo now fit the lines of
one of his favorite songs: "Where have you gone, Joe DiMaggio? /
A nation turns its lonely eyes to you / . . . 'Joltin' Joe' has left and
gone away."

Conservative columnist George F. Will had noted in 1984 the
degree to which Cuomo already stood out in the political field
when he said that if Democrats are not able to spot him as their
obvious leader of the future, "they cannot spot a rose among the
rutabaga."

Here, obviously, is an intriguing man. Many observers have
labeled him an enigma. "He's a funny guy," Massachusetts Gover-

nor Michael Dukakis said to me of his New York counterpart in a 1986 interview. His reference was not to Cuomo's sense of humor. Mario Cuomo is indeed, as *Newsweek* said in 1986, "the one man nearly everybody wants to know more about."[14]

Can he be for real? A cynical public that wishes someone would give it a reason to believe appears to hope so. As the pages that follow will show, there is a considerable basis for that hope.

1

HERITAGE

Southern Italy in the late
nineteenth and early twentieth centuries stood in something of the
same relationship to the rest of that nation as did the American
South to the United States of the same era. During the period in
which this country was confirming its unity through a civil war,
Italy was belatedly establishing its unity. The results were similarly disadvantageous for the feudal-agrarian southern regions of
the two nations. While in the 1870s and subsequent decades northern regions in both countries experienced rapid industrialization,
land remained the only significant resource in the southern regions, and land ownership became even more concentrated there
than it had been in earlier years. In southern Italy, as in the
American South, much land was acquired by wealthy absentee
owners from the north.

In the southern regions of both countries, there were memories—personal or historical—of better, grander times. The inhabitants of southern Italy and Sicily called the region the
Mezzogiorno—the center of the earth, and at times in the distant
past so it had seemed. But now the population of southern Italy
was divided into a small number of wealthy landowners and numerous illiterate peasants living in abject poverty. Among the
southern aristocracy and most residents of northern and central
Italy, the southern peasants were categorized as an undifferentiated, vastly inferior, scarcely civilized mass. This view was not
unlike the attitude of Americans outside the South and the southern aristocracy toward both poor whites and blacks in the southern United States. And, just as many landless Americans of both
races in the South were obliged to enter into exploitative sha-

23

cropping arrangements, southern Italian peasants took up similar sharecropping contracts, called *mezzadrie*.

The world of the *contadino*, the south Italian peasant, was a small one, usually not extending far beyond the borders of his village. These peasants were clannish, placing a heavy emphasis upon their families—to the point of calling all those who were not members of the family *forestieri*—"strangers." Those who came from outside the village were viewed with suspicion. The governments of Italy were at best unhelpful to these poor people, and often the government was considered an enemy. Certainly it was not to be trusted. Most southern Italian peasants considered government officials to be "thieves" and laws to be the rules those thieves used to help them steal.

The village itself, though, was a community in which one felt completely "at home," a member who *belonged*. People in the village worked together for the common good. They prized their individuality, but did not subscribe to a doctrine of individual*ism*. Survival necessitated cooperation. Peasants had to be willing to share, to make contributions to their joint interests; but there were distinct limits to their cooperativeness. It did not go beyond the family and the village: strangers were neither to be trusted nor helped. "It is impossible," wrote Leonard Covello in *The Social Background of the Italo-American School Child* (1944), "to imagine the *contadino* in South Italy contributing to the Red Cross."

This attitude is readily explained. The peasants of the Mezzogiorno were in no position to try to cure the ills of outsiders or to help the poor of the world. They themselves *were* the poor and had all they could do to try to deal with the immediate problems facing their families and villages. There sharing made sense, but they had nothing to share with anyone beyond the horizon.

The last two-and-a-half decades of the nineteenth century witnessed a severe international agricultural depression. Its causes included a prolonged deflation that had disastrous effects on long-term debtors (a category into which most farmers fell) and caused the prices of farm products to collapse; vastly improved modes of transporting agricultural products, creating a truly worldwide, highly competitive market; the opening of large amounts of new land to farming in many parts of the world, the introduction of efficient new machinery into the fields in the United States and elsewhere; and the rapid transformation of the economy of the Western world from an agricultural to industrial one.

The effects of the agricultural transformation and collapse of the late nineteenth century were disruptive everywhere and absolutely devastating in many regions. The disruption in the American South led to the Populist movement; the devastation in southern Italy led to mass emigration. There production of olive oil and wine fell far behind the growth in population and the price for citrus fruits fell by two-thirds. But other woes also befell the *contadino*. Deforestation increased the swamplands of southern Italy and after 1860 malaria reached near-plague levels. Then in the 1890s phylloxera, a plant parasite, destroyed most of the region's grapevines. French wines rapidly replaced Italian wines in the world market. On top of these problems, the new government of united Italy placed heavy new taxes on the people of the South. The local and provincial governments did the same.

The Italian government, suffering a series of crises, realized that it had many more people in the South than it could find any productive use for. Population density in Italy, with its limited land area and large peasant families, was greater than that in India and China. The government therefore strongly encouraged the emigration of unemployed peasants. Although the United States' economy in these years was unstable, swinging erratically between boom and bust, during the years of prosperity the demand for labor in this country seemed insatiable. This made the United States an attractive destination for the Italian emigrants, but many made their way to South America, other parts of Europe, and North Africa. Nearly 3 million Italians entered Argentina between 1857 and 1926, roughly three-fifths of the number migrating to the United States.

The Italian peasant, like his counterpart in other countries, was by nature conservative. Change was a mortal threat to those living on the edge of existence. Innovation *might* make things better, but there was always the risk that it would make things worse. That was a chance that a family with no surplus—no margin for error—could not afford to take. The result of the failure of a new method was likely to be starvation. The old ways had not provided much, but they were dependable. The peasant's very existence testified to the efficacy of the old methods: had they not worked well enough to provide survival, his ancestors who employed those same methods would have perished and he would never have been born.

Change came to such a peasant only when there was no alternative. To leave his village for an unknown land thousands of miles away was to abandon his entire world. But by the late nineteenth century, there was no choice. Life of any sort was no longer possible for millions of residents of the Mezzogiorno. Their departure was in most cases effected only with great reluctance, but reality had finally to be confronted.

Understandably, though, most of the emigrants left with the intention of making enough money in the new lands of opportunity (a category that included such nations as Argentina, Brazil, and Uruguay as well as the United States) that they would be able to return to their homeland and survive. This was generally true of the southern and eastern European groups that made up the "New Immigration" to the United States after 1880. Except for those—particularly the Jews of eastern Europe—who were driven out more by persecution than by economic deprivation, most of the migrants hoped to return to their old countries. The Italian migration of the late nineteenth century consisted primarily of men who left their families behind and for the most part intended to return to them rather than bring them to America. Between 1899 and 1910, only 21 percent of the Italian immigrants to the United States were women. A startling number of the men who planned to go back home did just that. In the nine years between 1908 and 1916, for instance, more than 1.2 million Italians left the United States, most of them to return to their native land. Ironically, though, those who did so often encouraged others to follow their path to America. The new homes and relative prosperity of many of those who had made the trek to the golden land enticed others to try their luck across the Atlantic.

By the 1920s, conditions in Italy had in some respects become less hospitable, and the nature of emigration from the nation was transformed into a permanent one in which men brought their families with them or planned to do so as soon as possible. Policies on both ends of the route combined in that decade to slow Italian migration dramatically. Benito Mussolini's Fascist regime in Italy, with its militaristic dreams of establishing a new Roman Empire, saw a large population as a national asset and so prohibited most emigration after 1922. The Immigration Acts of 1921 and 1924 in the United States established national quotas for immigration into this country. These quotas discriminated against such non–Anglo-Saxon groups as the Italians.

Yet by the 1920s, Italian-Americans had become a significant

portion of the population of the United States. The vast majority
of the 4.6 million people of Italian birth or parentage living in this
country when the 1930 census was taken entered the country
through New York. More than 1 million of these first- and second-
generation Italian-Americans, along with about 300,000 members
of the third generation, remained in the New York metropolitan
area in 1930. They constituted approximately one-sixth of the
city's population, ranking Italian-Americans second only to those
of Jewish ancestry among New York ethnic groups.[1]

Almost all of the immigrants to
the United States from southern Italy were illiterate and unskilled
in tasks for which there was a demand in America. They were,
moreover, a completely rural people who had suddenly to cope
with an urban environment in a strange land where they understood neither the language nor the customs. All they had to offer
was their physical strength. The bulk of these immigrants started
life in the Western Hemisphere in the most menial and backbreak-
ing forms of unskilled labor: railroad and subway construction,
sewer-digging and -cleaning, general construction work, textile
factories. Beginning in 1900, subway construction in New York
City, previously the preserve of Irish- and Polish-American labor-
ers, became almost exclusively the work of newly arrived workers
from Italy. The small stature of most Italian men of that era combined with their willingness to engage in hard physical work for
pitiful wages made them a most attractive source of labor for the
cramped subway tunnels. The peasant immigrants were accustomed to such a low standard of living that, despite the very low
rate of pay, many of them were able to save a portion of their
meager income, whether for the purpose of returning home,
bringing the family to America, or establishing a small business in
the new country.

Like most other sizable immigrant groups, the Italians clus-
tered in neighborhoods populated by their countrymen, often by
migrants from their province or even their own village. These
ethnic enclaves served as "decompression chambers" in which
immigrants re-created as much as they could of their old ways and
adapted at their own pace to the practices of their new country.
The Italians who populated "colonies" in American cities
amounted to what sociologist Herbert Gans aptly termed "urban

villagers." Their conservative village traits for the most part survived in a new and sharply different environment. The goal of remaining "free from strangers" carried over from Italian village to American neighborhood. Advancing the family was the primary objective, and there were no obligations to outsiders. One could depend upon others in his family, but all strangers were to be dealt with warily, if at all.

One unfortunate consequence of the practices of the urban villagers was that the new arrivals depended completely upon neighborhood leaders, who found them work and looked after their wages and savings. The *padrone* was not a "stranger," so he was trusted. This was almost invariably a mistake. Most of the *padroni* were unscrupulous characters who took advantage of their illiterate countrymen by skimming a large percentage off their wages.

Although the well-being of the family was the foremost concern of most southern Italian immigrants, their conservatism placed strict limitations on their ambitions in their early years in America. Most showed little interest in education, which took children away from what they saw as productive employment. The goal of owning a small business—a store, restaurant, or trucking firm—was as far as the family ambitions usually went. Through tireless labor and remarkably long hours, many succeeded in these enterprises and attained a comfortable middle-class standard of living. When they did, the usual practice was to stay in the neighborhood village and make improvements in the old home, not move on to more affluent areas. Thus it was often whole neighborhoods, rather than individuals, that experienced upward mobility.

The family-village loyalty that the *contadino* brought with him from the old country was not the only reason for group rather than individual mobility. Italian-Americans were confronted with greater hostility than were most other immigrant groups. They were often excluded from "white" (that is, fair-skinned and Protestant) communities and activities. In the 1930s and 1940s, people of Italian heritage were near the bottom of the totem pole of American ethnic prejudice, by some accounts ranking only somewhat ahead of blacks.

Oddly, being victimized by prejudice does not always inoculate one against it. Not only did many Italians join in the American pastime of stigmatizing other ethnic, racial, and religious groups, but some were not above prejudice against their own countrymen who came from other regions of Italy. Among the first generation, there was a considerable amount of mutual distrust and prejudice between mainland southern Italians and Sicilians.

Other large ethnic groups suffering from persecution have moved rapidly to seize political power on the local level and to begin to redress some of their grievances. The Irish were especially notable for their quick achievements in the realm of politics in localities where they were numerous. Italian-Americans moved into the political arena with considerably less celerity. Their general distrust of government and its agents, carried over from their experience in the old country, was a large part of the reason. In addition, they had had little previous experience with democracy of any sort; had no notion that government under democratic institutions might be made their servant and ally rather than their oppressor, were reluctant to change their ways or trust others with whom they might have to cooperate in building political coalitions, and were accustomed to accepting hierarchical arrangements in both church and government. To most Italian-Americans of the first generation, politics was hardly a suitable profession for themselves or their offspring.

Fiorello La Guardia, who was elected to Congress for six terms beginning in 1917 and who served as mayor of New York City from 1934 to 1945, enjoyed singular gifts and a personality that enabled him to achieve political success in New York years before other Italians did so. But La Guardia was the exception that proves the rule. He was not a product of the New Immigration, was not descended from southern Italians, and was a Protestant. He was a reformer closely aligned with the city's WASP and Jewish reformers. In some of his elections, La Guardia actually won a substantially higher percentage of the votes of non-Italians than he did of Italian-Americans. As mayor, the Little Flower was nevertheless a source of pride to many New Yorkers of Italian extraction.

With the exception of La Guardia and a very few others such as the ultraliberal Manhattan congressman Vito Marcantonio, New York Italians did not begin to achieve positions of political power in the city until the mid-to-late 1940s, and when they did, it was not usually as progressive reformers. Italian-Americans were less enthusiastic about the New Deal than were most other ethnic groups. Their village conservatism persisted, and their usual status as small homeowners and middle-class merchants and businessmen reinforced that conservative outlook. The first real power among the New York Italians who came from the South was Carmine DeSapio, who took command of Tammany Hall in 1949 and could hardly be labeled a "reformer" or a "liberal." DeSapio's prominence among Democratic regulars did not, however, deter many Italians from drifting into the more conservative ranks of the Republican party.[2]

The comparatively slow rise of Italian-Americans in New York politics is underlined by the fact that, their large numbers in the state electorate notwithstanding, the first person of Italian ancestry ever to be elected governor of New York did not achieve that distinction until 1982. His name was Mario M. Cuomo.

The village of Nocera Superiore, located in the mountains northwest of Salerno, did not differ significantly in the late nineteenth century from most southern Italian villages. Families were large and poor, work was hard to find, and two families owned almost everything. The children of the poor stole fruit from the lands of the rich. Most of the peasants subsisted on a diet of pasta, bread, beans, and potatoes. If times were good, they might have meat once a week. A peasant family was considered to be doing well if it could kill one pig a year. Families of ten or more lived in two-room cottages without bathrooms or running water. Women carried water from streams or wells in large barrels that they rested on their heads. Chickens, dogs, cats, mice, and other creatures freely entered the cottages through openings in the walls. Those with access to land had vineyards and grew wheat, corn, figs, oranges, and chestnuts. The village economy was based more upon barter than cash exchanges.

In 1870 Donato Cuomo was born to one of the landless families of Nocera Superiore. As a teenager, he took up the trade of woodcutting. Woodcutters went into the mountains and sought chestnut wood, which was nonabsorbent and therefore could be used for barrels to hold wine and olive oil. In 1896 Donato Cuomo joined the human tidal wave sweeping from the Mezzogiorno to America. Like so many of his countrymen, he came only to earn enough money to return home and live the sort of life that had been denied the poor peasants. While in Brooklyn, in 1901, Donato Cuomo and his wife, Maria, became the parents of a son, Andrea. Three years later the new family returned to Italy.

Back in Nocera Superiore, the Cuomos were able to build a new home of a somewhat higher quality than the cottages occupied by those who had not ventured to the land across the sea. The new home even contained a wine cellar. Donato ran a cantina, where he and his family sold wine, sandwiches, and coffee. The old folks would play cards there, and lunch was served to others. Donato also returned to working during the week as a woodcutter. The money was good by the standards of the peasants of the province of Salerno. The Cuomos had a decent home, could regularly put food on the table and buy a modest but adequate amount of clothing. Although quite poor by any modern American standard, they certainly were not considered to be poor by their neighbors. Poverty is, after all, much more a relative than an absolute standard. In the context of early twentieth-century southern Italy, to be poor meant to be a beggar, and the Cuomos were well removed from that status.

When they were teenagers, Andrea and his cousin Rosario Cuomo joined other boys in swiping fruit and vegtables from the fields and orchards of the two families that owned most of the land in the area. After Italy entered World War I, Rosario was taken into the army. Andrea was still too young for military service. Rosario was taken prisoner by the Germans and spent a year in a loose form of captivity on a farm in Czechoslovakia. When the war was over, he decided to emigrate to the United States. He arrived in this country in 1921 and was soon sending favorable reports back to cousin Andrea. Andrea left Nocera during the mid-twenties and found work in the village of Tramonti, on the farm of the Giordano family. The Giordanos were considerably better off than the Cuomos, their estate comprising hundreds of acres of orchards, vineyards, croplands, and pastures. They raised dairy cattle and sheep as well as fruit and vegetables. In the mid-twenties, the Giordano farm included ten sheep and seventy-five goats, along with seven dogs and a few head of cattle. They hired many workers.

While the Giordano family was much better off than those of the peasants, it was just as large: six daughters and four sons. Among the daughters was Immaculata, with whom young Andrea Cuomo fell in love. They were married in 1925. Having been born in the United States, Andrea was an American citizen and was unaffected by both Mussolini's restrictions and the new American immigration laws. The new couple thought long and hard about whether to migrate to America. Finally Andrea decided to take the chance of joining his cousin Rosario and trying his luck in the promised land. But when he was ready to leave in 1926, his wife was pregnant and it was decided that it would be unwise for her to travel across the Atlantic and face uncertain facilities in the United States. She told me that when her family learned that she was to have a baby, they asked, "You got a house there?"

"No," she answered.

"You got relatives there?"

"No."

"Then you can't go yet."

So when Andrea sailed from Naples, Immaculata Cuomo remained in Italy until after the birth of her first son, Frank. She and the baby joined Andrea in New Jersey in the fall of 1927.[3]

Andrea Cuomo's first adult experiences in the promised land were not promising. He walked with a limp as a result of a hip injury that had been left untreated, stood five feet six inches tall, and weighed 155 pounds. Andrea went to work in Jersey City for his mother's brother, who was a moderately well-to-do construction contractor. The uncle worked Andrea—and the rest of his employees—like a dog. Family connections meant nothing to him. Andrea was put to work as a common laborer, building and cleaning storm sewers. On the weekends, he made extra money as a guard-watchman looking after his uncle's supplies of bricks and lumber. Working day and night, seven days a week, Andrea earned twenty dollars a week.

This experience was hard on the prideful Andrea. He was more than willing to work hard, but he hated to think that he had brought Immaculata from her life of relative comfort in Italy to an existence of poverty and drudgery in America. His hopes for a better life for his children seemed unlikely to materialize if he continued to work for the meager wages paid by his cruel uncle. During his first years back in the United States, young Andrea Cuomo often cried in the presence of his wife, saying he wanted to return to Italy.

Although she says that *she* did not cry, Immaculata Cuomo also wondered whether they had made a mistake in coming to America. "When I came," she told me, "I no like. [During the first few years] I was very unhappy in this country. We came to this country with no money, no house. Stuck in a room." It was not at all like an

Italian village. There were no trees; quarters were extremely cramped in an apartment.

The birth in 1928 of a daughter, Marie, and in 1930 of a son, Mario (who died of what apparently was pneumonia before reaching the age of two), combined with the continuing bleak outlook in the employ of his uncle to lead Andrea Cuomo to the decision to leave Jersey City and start his own business. His wife was particularly distressed at the loss of her infant son, and new surroundings might help her to recover. Andrea used the small savings that he had managed to accumulate to start a grocery store in South Jamaica, Queens, in 1931.

Andrea got up at 2:30 A.M. and his work day usually started about a half hour later when he would go to the market to obtain the day's produce off trucks. One frigid morning he slipped and fell down the stairs at the produce market while carrying a large sack of potatoes and avoided freezing to death only because he was found and revived by a couple of other men. On a typical day Andrea was back by six o'clock to open the store for construction workers who came in for coffee and for sandwiches to take to their work sites. During the day the store served as a neighborhood grocery. In those days city dwellers shopped in the neighborhood grocery store every day, often more than once a day, buying a few items at a time. Cuomo's remained open until at least 11 P.M., when late meals were available for the workers in the sweater factory across the street. On weekends hardworking recent immigrants who were still saving to bring their families to America would buy beer by the case. The store was filled with such delights as Genoa salami, provolone, prosciutto, and seasonal fresh fruits. It was often open twenty-four hours a day. Even on holidays Cuomo's was open for at least a part of the day. The family would have a holiday meal together, but about four in the afternoon Andrea would open the store.

It was a family enterprise. The Cuomos lived in a large room behind the store and three bedrooms upstairs. Immaculata worked in the store and raised the family at the same time, leaving much of the "mothering" of the two boys (another son, also named Mario, was born the year after they moved to Jamaica) to her daughter, Marie. As soon as Frank was old enough, he began making deliveries to his father's customers. In the winter he used a sled, and the rest of the year he carried the groceries on a three-wheeled cart. Later Frank's young brother Mario made deliveries, too.

It was a hard life that left little time for anything but work. Although Andrea Cuomo did everything for his family, he had little time to be with them. There was never a vacation. It was always work, work, and more work, even after this was no longer financially necessary. Andrea finally worked himself into ill health. "When I got older," Frank Cuomo said to me, "I'd tell Pop, 'You can't work around the clock. Close the store on Sunday so you can eat with the family.' But he wouldn't listen. Mario used to get mad; I used to get mad; my sister used to get mad."

When the long hours are considered, the money was not very good, but it was far better than digging and cleaning sewers. And during the Great Depression, having a steady income of any kind had to be considered a substantial blessing. Most Italian-Americans in those days would not use anything that came in a can except olive oil and tomato paste. This custom kept business in fresh produce steady.

A few years after buying the grocery, Andrea feared that someone would open a supermarket in a larger vacant building on the corner down the street from his store, so he bought the building and moved his store there. The whole family, along with many of the teenagers in the neighborhood, worked through the night to pack all the groceries in boxes and move everything to the new location. By daybreak Frank had even constructed a new display of tomato-paste cans in the window.

When he started in the grocery business, Andrea Cuomo could speak scarcely any English and was illiterate. A woman in the neighborhood used labels on items in the store to teach him how to read and spell a bit. The rest, he taught himself. He eventually came to value education and to realize the doors it could open for his children. "My father was a big believer in education because he realized his own shortcomings," Frank Cuomo maintains.

Immaculata Cuomo never did learn to read very well in English. It was unnecessary for first-generation immigrant women in New York's ethnic neighborhoods to learn much English. They could get along very well in their native tongues. In fact, Immaculata Cuomo did not even bother officially to become a citizen until a few years before her husband's death. When she went before a judge to obtain her citizenship, he asked her several questions that she could not answer. One was "How many stars and stripes are there in the American flag?" When he had finished, Mrs. Cuomo said, "Judge, can I ask you something? I spent all my life in the food business. Do *you* know how many hands of bananas there are on a stalk?" When he admitted that he didn't, she proudly said, "Well, *I* do." Her citizenship was promptly approved.

The neighborhood in South Jamaica was inhabited by a diverse ethnic population. It was almost entirely working-class. Some of its residents were determined to make good via whatever means they found available, inside or outside the law. Andrea Cuomo was different; he lived by a strict code of values. Right and wrong were clearly distinguishable, and he insisted that his family would always be on the side of right. He demanded absolute honesty. No breaking of rules was ever tolerated. He summarized his philosophy of life in lectures to his sons: "Don't fool around with women—only your wife. Don't ever hurt anybody. And don't steal. Just do your work."

He was a compassionate man, one who was constantly concerned about the needs of his neighbors. Cuomo sold to many of his customers on trust. He kept a black marbled composition book with a record of what people owed him. By the time he sold the business in 1954, some people owed him in excess of a thousand dollars each. He simply forgave most of these debts when he retired.

Andrea Cuomo's attitude toward government and politicians was essentially the same as that of most of his contemporaries among Italian immigrants. In Italy, at the family's cantina, he had experienced government in the form of the *carabinieri*. According to Mario Cuomo, in the view of his father and most southern Italian peasants, the typical *carabiniere* was "the bum who would sleep with your sister if he got the chance; who would take money from you as bribes; who never arrested anyone unless it was an act of public violence. He wasn't good."

Andrea Cuomo's notion of government improved only slightly in this country. When he opened his store, he knew nothing of licenses and regulations. So government to him in New York became city regulations—like the health department coming and telling him he was doing something wrong. Then, with American entry into World War II, government became more palpable. It rationed products and set prices. And ultimately it made his oldest son go to war. Andrea went along with all this, because of his sense of right and wrong, and because he wanted to show his love for the United States and the opportunities it had provided for his family. Although there were many merchants in his area who evaded the wartime rationing laws, Cuomo refused all offers for black-market sales. He had no reason, though, to look kindly upon government or the politicians who ran it.

Like most ethnic men of his day, Andrea Cuomo was the unquestioned ruler of his household. It was unthinkable for one of the children to talk back to him or argue with him. The children had great respect for their father and his authority. When he made a decision, it was usually his alone and the rest of the family had to go along. The best example of this came in 1949, when he decided to move the family out of South Jamaica. Immaculata was in Europe visiting her sister, and Andrea made the decision on his own. He found a new house in Holliswood, Queens, bought it, and moved there while his wife was away. When she returned to the old home, he simply took her to the new one. "That's the way it was in those days," Frank told me. "She didn't have any say."

To leave the old neighborhood was to break with the Italian-American tradition of staying put and improving the old home. Some of the Cuomos' relatives and neighbors were upset with them. One was Mrs. Cuomo's cousin, who had been with her on the trip to Italy. Her family owned a fish store on Jamaica Avenue, and they could easily have afforded to move to Holliswood themselves, but believed this was not proper. She said the Cuomos had "outgrown their roots," thought they were "above" everybody else, and had moved to "the rich section." Who were the Cuomos, she asked, to move while her family stayed put? She considered it a disgrace to leave the neighborhood. "Use your money to improve things *here*; keep the family *here*"—that was the accepted practice. For years afterward she refused to talk to her cousin Immaculata.

If the Cuomos' move was not popular among some of their Italian neighbors in Jamaica, it was even less so among some of their new neighbors in Holliswood. This was basically a white Anglo-Saxon Protestant area. When Immaculata Cuomo first returned from her trip to Italy and took up residence in her new home, she was outside sweeping the sidewalk when three proper-looking but *"fredde"* (cold) ladies came up to her. "You must be the Italian woman," they said. "Well, we want you to know you are welcome here, but please remember to keep the tops on your garbage pails."[4]

It is out of such arrogance, prejudice, and insensitivity that lasting ethnic consciousness and pride arise. It was an experience common to many upwardly mobile members of the New Immigration as they sought to enter fully into the promise of American life. That promise is one that for them has been largely, but not yet completely, fulfilled.

The New Immigration from southern and eastern Europe constituted an important part of the development of modern America. Its members have made contributions to the nation ranging from the physical labor of building our cities and transportation systems and working in the factories of our expanding industries, through popular culture, to the highest achievements in the arts, sciences, and professions. Yet no one representing this vast segment of American society has ever approached the nation's highest office.

The same can accurately be said of the urban America where most of those immigrants made their home. Even as the United States became an increasingly urban society in the twentieth century, its mythology has remained steadfastly agrarian and small-town. The closest that someone who truly represented the modern American city has ever come to the presidency was the 1928 campaign of New York Governor Alfred E. Smith—and Smith was crushed by Herbert Hoover. Smith's campaigns in 1924 and 1928 ignited the interest of many urban ethnics in the political process for the first time. Franklin Roosevelt's New Deal kept them involved and attracted millions of others who had not previously participated. But Roosevelt was a protector of the urban masses, not their product. John Kennedy spent a portion of his youth in metropolitan Boston, but he too was far removed from the experience of the typical American city dweller.

This failure of the American political system fully to embrace the people of the New Immigration is surprising. When the electorate expanded to include the so-called "common man" in the second quarter of the nineteenth century, a representative of this new force in American politics won the presidency almost immediately. Yet more than a century after the processes of urbanization and immigration began, urban, immigrant America still awaits its Andrew Jackson. This fact is an uncomfortable reminder that our nation has never completely lived up to its promise and values where non-WASPs and urbanites are concerned.

A leading liberal Democrat from Texas told Geraldine Ferraro in 1984 that a national ticket including a candidate whose name ended in a vowel could never hope to carry the Lone Star State. We had learned eight years earlier that in some places, such as southwestern Georgia, even the most prominent citizens do not know how to pronounce "Italian." But more is involved here than names and complexions. In the twenties Middle America showed that it would not vote for a Catholic even if his name was Smith and his pigmentation as fair as theirs. "The society which miraculously opened to [Al Smith] his greatest opportunity," as historian Oscar Handlin has put it, "spitefully tripped him up when he attempted to seize it."

Ethnics and urbanites have been expected to know their place in America. That place has greatly expanded, but it still has never included the highest place the nation has to offer. And though John Kennedy seemingly showed once and for all that a Catholic could be elected president, it is worth remembering that Kennedy was not only the first Catholic to win the White House, he also remains the *last*, nearly three decades after his narrow victory.

After Jackson's "Revolution of 1828," it became almost obligatory for an aspirant to national office to place a log cabin in his background, even if none had actually been there. American voters repeatedly demonstrated their preference for candidates who posed as frontiersmen. As the old frontier began to wane in the late nineteenth century, a new one was opening in the cities of the nation. Those who migrated from the countrysides of Europe to the cities of America were as much daring pioneers as were those who traveled from the cities of America to the nation's countryside. The Wickersham Commission's report on crime in the United States argued in 1931 that assertions of an unusual level of criminal activity among Italian-Americans "should be compared with the kind of lawlessness that has been prevalent in certain frontier conditions in America. Here, representatives of the oldest American stock were often responsible for rude justice summarily administered."

But the urban, largely eastern, frontier was not as glamorous as its rural western predecessor. Nor did it seem as "American." The notion that what made America unique was its open, rural–small-town society and what made Europe wicked were its teeming cities was deeply ingrained in the American psyche by the late nineteenth century. The new urban frontier did not match the self-image to which most Americans clung. If the urban frontier was a reflection of the western frontier, this was one mirror into which vain Americans preferred not to gaze. Many of these Americans were attracted to the city and its amenities, but they continued to praise the rural life and to insist that it represented the "real America."

Mario Cuomo has tried to make the link between the two American frontiers by associating the efforts of his immigrant forebears with the image of a covered wagon moving toward a new frontier.[5] The election of Cuomo or another truly urban, ethnic "frontiersman" to the presidency of the United States would mark an important point in American history. It would mean that we were maturing as a nation in the sense that we were finally prepared to bring our self-image more closely into line with our practice and our reality.

2

YOUTH

MARIO MATTHEW CUOMO
was born on June 15, 1932, in the urban equivalent of a log cabin:
a room above the family grocery store in South Jamaica, Queens.
His father was an urban frontiersman, as much of a self-made man
as the heroic figures of the nineteenth-century American West.

Cuomo's sister, Marie, who was four at the time, remembers his
birth. She was standing on the staircase and a doctor with a little
case passed her. A little while later she heard a cry from the
bedroom upstairs, the new baby's greeting to the world. Marie told
me that Mario was the only one of her mother's four children
whose birth was attended by a physician.

There are said to be more different ethnic groups in Queens
than anywhere else in the world. Certainly South Jamaica in the
thirties and forties was as polyglot a neighborhood as was to be
found anywhere. Italians rubbed shoulders with Greeks, Jews,
Poles, Irishmen, blacks, Czechs, Portuguese, and a half dozen other
ethnic groups. It was the sort of neighborhood that helped to
define what it means to be an "American" in the twentieth century. Speaking more than four decades later and contrasting South
Jamaica in those years with what the area is today, an old-timer
from the neighborhood said in 1987: "It used to be Polish, Italian,
and Irish. Now it's Indians, blacks, Spanish—everything. There
are very few Americans around here anymore. They all moved
away."

It has never been entirely clear what makes one an American,
but it seems that most of the groups that lived in South Jamaica
when Mario Cuomo was a boy have now been accepted as "Americans." Some of their successors, though, are as excluded today as
the Italians and others were two generations ago.

South Jamaica was in some respects a typical outer-borough New York neighborhood in the 1930s; in other ways, though, it was unusual. Its ethnic mix was what most set it apart. Mario Cuomo tells stories of Kelly, the Irish scrap dealer, Lanzone the Italian baker, Kaye the Jewish tailor, and Rubin the Jewish roofer, as well as of Poles and many others. Here people of different backgrounds lived in a wary but generally peaceful coexistence. The various immigrants learned from each other. Cuomo recalls that Mrs. Kessler, the wife of the man who owned the building that housed the Cuomo grocery, taught his mother to count and Immaculata taught Mrs. Kessler to make tomato sauce alla marinara.

It was the sort of New York ethnic neighborhood in which on Sundays in the summer residents sat on the front stoop (for those uninitiated in the parlance of New York, this term refers to brick or cement steps). Children played the games of the city: ring-a-levio, Johnny-on-the-pony, kick-the-can, tag, stickball, stoopball, and, in the winter when snow was plowed into high mounds, king-of-the-mountain.

Although the first-generation immigrants were almost invariably law-abiding avoiders of trouble, their children were sometimes overly eager to achieve a standard of living on a par with that of "native" children with whom they attended school. When they found that many of the doors of legitimate opportunity were not open to New Immigrants and their offspring, some among the second generation struck back at society. The 103rd Precinct in South Jamaica, like other ethnic neighborhoods, had its share of kids who got into trouble with the law. It was an area in which getting into trouble was not difficult. Gang wars and more ad hoc acts of violence, while not nearly as prevalent as they are in many urban neighborhoods today, were a fact of life. "Everybody fought," Cuomo says. "You occasionally had gang wars and someone might even stick you with a knife." His brother Frank remembers that several of the boys that they knew when they were growing up—although none of their close friends—wound up in serious trouble with the law.[1]

"I had no youth," Mario Cuomo asserts. "It was just school and the store—always the store. It never changed—only the displays in the windows changed. But I never did what most kids did. My time was always occupied, but

I never had a youth like most kids. It was very uninteresting; it would only bore people."

This recollection is partly correct. Cuomo's youth *was* unusual, though hardly extraordinarily so. Uninteresting and boring, however, it was not.

When I asked Cuomo what his earliest memory is, he paused a moment and said, "Macaroni boxes."

He spent a great deal of his time as a child alone in the back room of the store, because his mother was working in the store and afraid to let him out where he might get hurt. He entertained himself when he was three or four by taking twenty-pound boxes of spaghetti and macaroni and moving them around to build houses and forts. Sometimes he would manage to get a box open and take out a long, hollow piece of dry pasta. If he could also open a carton of very small dried peas, he had both weapon and ammunition.

"You could use them as peashooters until the end of the macaroni got soggy from the moisture of your mouth, and then you had to break off a piece," Cuomo explained to me. "So your peashooter was constantly getting shorter and shorter, until you ran out of peashooter. It should only happen to the Pentagon!"

Immaculata and Andrea Cuomo were tolerant of the antics of their "baby," but a boy who worked in the store, Tony, was not at all happy with Mario's games. Tony had to put the boxes back where they belonged, and that proved to be a never-ending task.

There was in most Italian immigrant families a strong tie between mother and son. Italian mothers are noted for being overprotective of their children. Up to a point, Immaculata Cuomo fit this stereotype. She was, moreover, a mother who had already lost one son. She was quite close to her sons, Frank and Mario, and on several occasions her concern for their safety led her to deny them forms of recreation that most boys enjoyed. This was especially the case with Mario, who was not only the baby of the family, but was in some sense a "replacement" for his deceased sibling of the same name.

Immaculata Cuomo is a wise woman. Although lacking in formal education, she has long been able to make penetrating insights into people and their motivations. It is plain that her folk wisdom had a lasting impact on her younger son. Much less palatable were the doses of cod-liver oil that she poured down her children's throats against their wills. It was pure torture, Frank insists. "She had tablespoons that weren't tablespoons—they were *shovels.*" Both boys would run out of the room and hide when they saw their mother take out the bottle. Mrs. Cuomo believed the syrupy fish oil to be the antidote for any illness or physical malady. "You could be bleeding, have a broken arm—she'd give you cod-liver oil," Frank says. "This is *good* for you, Mario," she'd say as she forced it down his gagging throat. But this practice, according to Mrs. Cuomo herself, was not part of folk belief. "The doctor told me," she explains.

But Immaculata could not spend as much time with her children as she wanted to. There was always something to be done in the store. When Mario was an infant, a boy who lived across the street, Peter DeNunzio, often watched his baby carriage and pushed him around in it on the sidewalk in front of the store. Mrs. Cuomo gave the boy treats from the store in exchange.

A bit later Immaculata appointed her daughter, Marie, to be the "little mother" for her brothers. She ordered them around and threatened them with reports to their parents. "You scrub the stairs the right way! Otherwise I'll tell Momma." "It was always: 'I'll tell Momma and Poppa,'" Frank remembers. These arrangements did not invariably work out for the best. On one occasion when Mario was about four or five, his mother had to work in the store and left Marie in charge of the toddler: "You take care of Mario. Walk him. Hold him by the hand." But as they passed the Golden Cup bakery down the block, a delivery truck roared up an inclined alley at them. In her fright Marie let go of her little brother's hand, and he fell. The truck went right over him. Thinking her brother had been killed, Marie ran away screaming. She went into hiding at Rufus King Mansion Park. When Marie finally came back, she went in tears to a neighbor across the street whom they called Tia (Aunt) Paulina, although she was not related. She told the woman her sad tale and asked her to go and break the news to her parents.

In fact, the truck wheels had completely missed Mario and Tia Paulina found him sitting at home having cookies and milk and "being treated like a king." He didn't have a scratch on him. "Typical Mario luck," the governor said to me.

And lucky he was. Another incident in which he might easily have been killed took place when he was five or six. A milk truck was making a delivery at the family store. The driver went inside and left the engine running. Milk trucks at that time had open cabs, with no doors, and a stool on which the driver sat. Little Mario got into the truck while no one was looking, engaged the gears, and started driving down the street. He had gone a half block before the milkman caught up with him, hopped in, and averted disaster.

The Cuomos' first apartment in South Jamaica had no bathtub. The governor remembers his mother washing him with brown Octagon soap in a black metal tub about the size of a sink. When the family moved down the block to the apartment above the corner store, they had more spacious accommodations. The apartment consisted of three bedrooms, a dining room, a living room, and a kitchen. All the rooms were large by apartment standards. But the neighborhood could hardly be described as attractive. It was an industrial area in which grass was a rare sight. To see nice houses with lawns, one had to cross to "the right side of the tracks," north of the Long Island Railroad, in Jamaica Estates.

Although the Cuomos were better off than many of their unemployed neighbors during the Depression, money was very tight during Mario's early years. Mrs. Cuomo had to take the children out to buy them clothes; Marie was still too young to be put in charge of this duty. The mother could not be away from the store for long, though, so she had no time to waste on shopping expeditions.

One of the first commercial items that Mario desperately wanted was a two-gun cowboy holster set, with a belt studded with artificial diamonds. "Of all the stupid luxuries," Cuomo says today in disbelief of his childish desires. "First of all, she didn't like guns," he said of his mother. "Secondly, they didn't waste money."

When Mario saw the holster set in a store on Jamaica Avenue, he said, "Ma, I gotta have this."

"No, Mario," Immaculata replied, "I gotta buy you a suit."

"I *want* it," the boy insisted.

"Whattaya gonna do with a pistol?" his mother asked. "You don't even have kids to play with in the backa the store. So whattaya gonna do, knock over a sack of rice and pretend that it's a horse?"

This is just what Mario intended to do. "Oh, I raised hell," he told me. "I said, 'If you don't give me this, I'm going to go on the railroad'—the elevated railroad tracks."

"Okay, we're going to take that," Immaculata told the salesman. This quieted Mario down, but his mother also said to the man in a whisper, "I'm coming back. I'm bringing this back."

Immaculata quieted Mario all the way home. Once they got inside, he recalls, "She pushed me—bang. 'Shut up. When I tell you you can't have it, that's it!' She went all the way back to the store and got her money back."

The holster set cost seven dollars, as Immaculata Cuomo remembers it, and she was in no position to engage in that sort of extravagance. As she told me in 1987, "We no hadda the money."

The cowboy holster disappointment was due to a shortage of money, but even after the family's financial position improved, the Cuomo youngsters suffered other disappointments that resulted from their mother's caution and protectiveness. Frank wanted a bike, but his mother said that the street was too small and busy: "You'll go out in the middle with the cars."

"No, no, I'll go on the sidewalk," he assured his mother. She then asked if he would give little Mario rides. Frank agreed, and Mrs. Cuomo laid out thirty-five dollars for a new bicycle. No sooner did he get it, though, than, in his mother's words, "he go right in the street—cars go zing, zing, zing." She warned him, but he would not listen, and when he went back into the street, she took the bike away from him. "Mario cried and Marie cried," Frank says, "because I pulled this stupid stunt and they would never get to ride a bike." And that's just what happened. When Frank returned from the navy years later, he found the bike still hanging in the garage, rusting. The Cuomo children got second chances, but not third chances.

Mario never got a bicycle. Nor did he have roller skates or ice skates. When he got older, his mother went out one Christmas and bought a sled for him. "My mother, uncharacteristically, thought she would surprise me," he told me. "I guess the two of them felt bad. My mother and father felt I was deprived, but I wasn't deprived. I never felt deprived. I ate well; I had a good life. But I guess they felt sorry for me. . . . So she went off and bought me a sled."

When Immaculata brought the sled home, she said to Mario, "I have a surprise for you!"

"I don't want a sled," the boy responded. He did this, Cuomo told me sadly, "because I was perverse. So my mother took the sled back, heartbroken. She never admits to anybody that she's heartbroken, but as I look back now, she must have been."[2]

As a boy, the future governor of New York was both a prodigious and an undiscerning eater. He loved his mother's pasta and other Italian dishes, but would eat almost anything, especially if there was a lot of it. "Put a plate in front of him," Frank remembers, "and he'd devour it." There is nothing unusual about this in a boy. The only oddity was that young Mario did not go in much for sweets. The glorious pastries and cookies that his mother prepared for the holidays were not among his favorites.

In every group of kids, there is usually a home of one that is identified as the best place to go for snacks. It is hardly surprising that among young Mario Cuomo's friends his home was considered the eatery of choice. It was, after all, located behind a grocery store. His mother remembers that Mario often brought his friends home for lunch. He would also sneak off with a few pounds of potatoes from the store so that the kids could make "Mickeys"— whole potatoes that were baked by placing them directly into a fire or on hot coals until they were blackened on the outside—in the lot where they played ball. Although Frank had gotten into trouble for similar escapades a few years earlier, the Cuomos were in a better position to afford such provisioning of neighborhood youngsters when Mario did it, so the parents tolerated it.

Mario liked to sing, and did so loudly. Unfortunately he was not at all good at it. "He do nothing wrong," his mother says, "he just sing loud and not know what he sing." His general loudness got him quite literally into hot water once when a woman who lived upstairs and liked to sleep during the day tried to shut him up by throwing a bucket of hot water out the window onto the boy. This was not the sort of action that Immaculata Cuomo found it easy to forgive, as she let the somnolent lady know in no uncertain terms.

Recreation was not plentiful in the work-centered Cuomo household, but even in the early years Mario found pleasure in occasional family outings. He has fond memories of Sunday mornings, after early mass, spent at the beach or at Cunningham Park. He especially loved it when his father would take the family on hot summer weekend nights in the station wagon to Rockaway Beach. Andrea had bought a spoke-wheeled, wooden Ford station wagon of which he was very proud. He would throw a blanket in the back and take everyone to the beach. They pulled the car right up on the sand and slept in the station wagon, with the tailgate down, enjoying the cool ocean breezes until dawn, when they had to return to open the store. These expeditions to Rockaway Beach were classified as "adventures" by the three Cuomo kids. Life couldn't get any better.

Another favored family activity, the governor's sister informed me, was going to the movies on Sunday afternoons. Since the prices went up after the early afternoon, they would have their Sunday dinner in the late morning or around noon, "then [Pop] and my brothers would walk to the movies and get the tickets before the price changed," Marie Vecchio said, "and would wait for my mother and me, who had to clean up the dinner dishes."

Yet young Mario did not always need the family or friends in order to enjoy himself. He was already able to find great pleasure in the world of his own imagination. His older brother and sister excluded him from their crowds—he was too young, and they wanted to keep him out of trouble. From those first years, when his protective mother would not let him out in the street and he had no friends his own age, Mario remembers "being behind the store, alone, with the boxes of pasta piled high and the sacks of rice and coffee. I remember pushing over the sacks and tying a cord to the two gatherings at the top of the sack that stuck up like ears and riding the sack like a horse." It was a wonderful place all his own. "I remember a thousand days being alone in my own quiet world while all the neighborhood's activity was going on steps away on the other side of the door. . . . Alone, but not really lonely."

An often solitary boy could also derive pleasure from the radio. Cuomo recalls that his favorite shows included "Fibber McGee and Molly," "Just Plain Bill," "Lorenzo Jones" (the theme of which he sang for me), "Mandrake the Magician," and, of course, "The Shadow." He also distinctly remembers hearing, at the age of nine, the radio announcement of the bombing of Pearl Harbor.

It is not entirely surprising that a boy who cherished his solitude, had a strong imagination, and liked to engage in speculative thinking would become religious. Frank Cuomo remembers that when his mother sent him (Frank) to church, he would check the missal to see what color the priests were wearing that day. Then he could go off and play and later tell his mother what the priest wore so she would think he had been to mass. "But Mario actually went!" Frank reports with some degree of amazement. "He even became an altar boy. . . . He was just a good kid."*

---

*Catholicism is one of the central influences in the life of Mario Cuomo, and that influence will be explored in detail in the next chapter.

The polyglot neighborhood of South Jamaica also provided young Cuomo with exposure to other religions. When he was about thirteen years old, he served on Friday nights in the Orthodox synagogue down the block as a Shabbos goy—a good Gentile who did the chores, such as snuffing out the candles and turning off the lights, that Orthodox Jews were not permitted to do on the Sabbath.

The Catholic altar boy was struck by the similarities between the services in the synagogue and those in his church. "So much of it was the same to my young mind," he said nearly four decades later. "The Gregorian chant from the priest was very much like the chanting I heard at the synagogue, and the incense and candles at St. Monica's Catholic Church on Sunday gave the altar and the whole chamber an aroma, an aura—mysterious, strangely but benevolently powerful—that I felt also in the synagogue on Friday nights . . . a Latin I didn't understand and a Hebrew I didn't understand. . . ."[3]

"Do not make your child better than you are," says a southern Italian proverb. Such an attitude did not seem strange in a static peasant society. There change was feared. It often implied not progress but regression. But the idea that one's children should not be allowed—indeed, encouraged—to reach for something better is so completely antithetical to the "American" creed of progress that it seems incomprehensible to most people in this country. It was inevitable that most Italian immigrants would eventually abandon the notion of keeping their children in their station and join other Americans in the quest for betterment. But the pace at which Italian-Americans changed their outlook varied greatly.

Many first-generation Italian-Americans saw no point in educating their children. They were getting along with little or no formal education themselves. They were working and in some cases beginning to prosper without the benefits of much schooling. Why should it be any different for their children? What good was school? It prepared you for positions to which people from Italian peasant stock thought they could not aspire. School took time away from productive labor. Why waste your time with books and useless information when you could be helping out in the family business? The school system was, moreover, the domain of women,

and self-respecting "real" men wanted no part of a female-domi-
nated institution.

"Most of the Italian boys took out working papers when they
were fourteen," one of Cuomo's professors at St. John's said to me.
"In my community, for a guy to go to high school and college—I
had to hide my books—you'd be thought of as a sissy."

Given these widespread attitudes, it was to be expected that
truancy and dropout rates would be especially high among Italian-
American children, and so they were. In their study of ethnic
groups in New York City, *Beyond the Melting Pot*, Nathan Glazer
and Daniel Patrick Moynihan assert that among first-generation
Italian-Americans "it was the 'bad' son who wanted to go to school
instead of work."

Fortunately for Mario Cuomo, his parents soon moved beyond the negative views of education prevalent among their
countrymen. "Since he was the oldest of the children," Mario
Cuomo says, "the burden of the family's hard early days fell
mostly on Frank." The five-year span between his brother's age
and his own meant that by the time Mario reached school age the
family was in a somewhat better economic position and had had
more exposure to the American idea of advancement by means of
education. Frank's presence also meant that there was less demand for the labor of the younger boy in the store. "He was the
first in the house," Mario said of Frank, "which means he had to
do all the heavy lifting in the store. My father couldn't afford
anybody in the beginning."

"I didn't have the advantages that he had," Frank says. "I was
the first. I had to go to school, but I also had to work like a dog after
school—day and night, work in the store. But they [his parents] got
smarter and they realized what education could do, so they said,
'Mario's going to go to college.' " Immaculata Cuomo insists that
she tried to get Frank to take school seriously, too, but that he was
not interested.

The elder Cuomos understood little about education. "My
mother never went to school," the governor said to me. "She
claims now she went a little. She hates saying she never went at
all." "All they knew [about education] is that you had to get all you
can." Andrea insisted that Mario get all A's. "He'd look at the card,
and if I didn't get an A, he'd be all upset, and he'd tell you—and
he was very persuasive—and he would say, 'You know this is a
chance that I never had. How can you not make the most of it?

How can you be so stupid? I'm working here so you don't have to
work here.'

"You felt great guilt," Cuomo says. "You felt guilty because
this guy was killing himself." The burden of being the outstanding
son of an ambitious immigrant family fell squarely on Mario. He
was expected to make good. Neither time nor opportunities could
be wasted.

It would be difficult to imagine someone of Mario Cuomo's
intelligence not finding his way to an education, regardless of his
parents' attitude. Once when Frank, in my presence, asked his
mother how Mario got so smart, she replied, "How I know? He'sa
born like that." But even his parents' newfound appreciation for
schooling left young Mario facing serious obstacles when he entered P.S. 50 in Jamaica. One was going to a school where the
language was different from the Italian spoken in his home, to a
school where, as Cuomo put it in a 1986 speech in San Antonio,
noting the similarity between his situation and that of Representative Henry Gonzalez, "the words sounded hard-edged and tight
compared to the rolling, rounded rhythms of his mother and father's tongue."

It is remarkable, in view of the fact that he became such a great
master of the English language, that Mario Cuomo spoke scarcely
any English at the time he entered school. His parents always
spoke Italian at home, and communicated as best they could in
very broken English with non-Italian customers in the store. Having little contact with people outside the home and store, Mario
remained at the age of five largely ignorant of English. As a result,
he was not happy in his first few years of school. "I didn't like it,"
he told me, and he remembers almost nothing of it. He was surprised in 1987 when a woman who had been in school with him
sent him a photograph of them in a kindergarten play, "with me
as Happy, of all things, in the Seven Dwarfs."

Cuomo's school records from P.S. 50 show a large number of
absences in the first two years. He missed forty-five days of first
grade. He was not at all a sickly child, so the governor believes that
his poor attendance record in those years was a result of his difficulty with the language. His sister remembers him practicing his
English at home, speaking by himself or with Frank and Marie.

Cuomo has a great facility for foreign languages to complement
his obvious gift for spoken English, and at about the age of eight
he cleared the language hurdle, although he claims, "I wasn't too

good at it [English] even in high school." Another handicap was that his parents were unable to help him with his schoolwork. Andrea Cuomo never sat down and said, "Mario, I'll help you with this." He couldn't. What Mario learned, he had to learn in school and on his own. His habits of self-reliance and particularly of thinking for himself started early.

Mario Cuomo's intellectual abilities were apparent from quite early in his days in the Jamaica public schools. When he was in the fifth grade, his teacher sent a note home, asking his mother or father to come in to talk about him. Since her mother did not speak English, Marie was the family spokesperson. When she went to talk to Mario's teacher, the woman told her that Mario was very inquisitive. He would question everything, and always had his hand up to answer questions. "I always thought of that as odd," Marie told me. "Why talk to the parent if the child was doing a good thing?"

On another occasion, Mario's teacher came to the store. She was wearing lipstick and makeup and didn't look like a regular customer. Andrea asked Marie, in Italian, who it was.

"That's Mario's teacher," Marie replied.

Andrea called Mario out and promptly slapped him across the face. It turned out that the teacher had come because Mario was doing so well that she wanted to talk about his skipping a grade.

Mario differed markedly from the typical boys in the neighborhood, in that he loved to read. His sister, Marie, recalls him studying or reading all the time. School was his main occupation. "Mario—school, school, school," his mother says simply. But even at home, he loved to sit "alone in the summer's heat lost in a book." He liked to cut himself off from the outside world and become completely engrossed in reading. It is a habit that he has not fully abandoned even in the governorship, much to the consternation of his assistants and other political leaders. "I read a lot and wrote a lot," Cuomo told me, "but I was no good at speaking. I love to read everything—I loved *A Swiss Family Robinson* before any teacher assigned it to me." He was fond of Dickens and Poe and anything difficult. "I read a lot. [It was] my salvation," he maintains.

When he was eleven, in 1943, Mario Cuomo moved briefly from the public schools to junior high at St. Monica's School. He stayed there for all of one day, during which a teacher hit him with a ruler. This was a common practice in parochial schools; however, to Andrea Cuomo's way of thinking discipline was fine, but a father was the only person who had any right to hit his children. Mario was promptly transferred to Shimer Junior High, a public school in Jamaica, and his Catholic school experience was deferred for two more years.

The primacy of education for Mario is evident in his mother's response to an inquiry from her son Frank. "What was Mario's job around the house?" he asked. "Marie had to clean the rooms and I had to work in the store. What did Mario have to do? What did Mario have to do?" Eighty-five-year-old Immaculata Cuomo smiled and said in a low voice, "He had to go to school."[4]

Mario Cuomo's childhood may not have been a "regular" one, but he was, for the most part, able to do the things he most wanted to do. Like many boys with older brothers, he always wanted to do everything his brother did. "He was a tough little kid," Frank remembers. "He always wanted to play with the big guys. Wherever we went, he wanted to go." Frank always discouraged this, not only because he didn't want his kid brother hanging around all the time, but because he wanted to shield Mario from the potential for trouble. "Frank didn't want me to have anything to do with them," Mario says, "because, instinctively, he was brother enough—and father enough—to know that a lot of the things they were doing I shouldn't be doing—smoking cigarettes, who knows what they were doing with girls—and he was very protective of me." Frank and his friends deliberately kept Mario out of their society. "It was more than a membrane," the younger Cuomo told me, "—it was a Berlin Wall."

When Frank and his friends were fifteen or sixteen and Mario was ten or eleven, the older boys played a type of "chicken" in the tunnels of the Long Island Railroad. They would try to see how close they could come to the trains without being hit. They also used the railroad tunnels as hiding places in games of hide-and-seek. If the person who was "it" had enough nerve, he would go into the tunnel looking for those who might be hiding there, worrying constantly that he would in the process be hit by a train. One day Mario begged Frank to take him along to play with the big guys, who were going into the tunnel. Frank told him, "No, you gotta go home. You're too small to play the games we play. I don't want you going on the railroad. No, no, no." But Mario persisted, becoming a "real pain in the neck." The two of them got into a big argument and Frank, who at the time was much bigger than Mario, beat the stuffing out of his little brother. "He knocked my head against the lumberyard wall," Mario relates.

Mario went home and told his father his version of what had happened. "Now, you don't tell your father something like that— my father being the type of man that he was," Frank says. When Frank came home and they sat down to eat, his father didn't say a word before slugging him so hard that he knocked him out of his chair. "You almost killed your brother!" Andrea screamed. "You banged his head against the wall." Frank's attempts to convince his father that he *wasn't* trying to kill Mario, but to protect him, to *keep* him from being killed in the railroad tunnel, were to no avail. Neither Andrea nor Mario accepted that explanation then, and Mario still does not. "That's not true; you just beat the daylights out of me for no reason," he tells Frank. But Frank maintains that his version is the truth, and that the beating was for Mario's "own good."

Most of the time Mario was left to hang around with the younger kids. His brother's group was beginning to go out with girls, while Mario and his friends were too young to consider such a course. And Mario's group tended to stay out of trouble to a greater extent than did the older gang. Frank admits that he used to swipe quarters from his parents and get caught, but says that Mario never took anything—except the potatoes for the kids at the ball field. The older kids got into trouble for minor acts of vandalism, but Mario was never in this sort of difficulty. Frank and his friends "were more of a gang—we'd go looking for trouble. But [Mario and] his friends weren't really a gang. They didn't go looking for trouble; they went to play ball."

Mario's two best friends in his grade school years were Willie Golowski and Artie Foster. "It's interesting," Foster told me, "— one Italian kid, one Jewish kid, and one Polish kid. We were always horsing around, playing ball, doing something." "We were regional," Foster said, "—not that there were gangs or anything, but you really didn't go too far from your neighborhood." They played stickball all the time. The only requirements were, of course, a stick and a ball. "We'd go out and try to find an old broom," Foster told me. "Sometimes we'd take an old broom from his father's store and whack off the bristles. [But] we always had trouble finding balls."

The space to play stickball in the street was never large enough.

Balls frequently landed on nearby roofs, and to retrieve them the kids would have to shinny up the poles on which women hung clothes. Sometimes they climbed on the roof just for the fun of it. Places to play were limited, and they made the best of fire escapes and alleys.

Cuomo's youth seems as if it came out of an ethnic, urban Norman Rockwell painting. Dictograph had a factory in the neighborhood. During World War II, it was engaged in defense work, had a night watchman, and was surrounded by a barbed-wire fence. The boys hung around there on summer evenings and listened to the watchman tell stories. On occasion, some of them would go back later at night and try to get inside the fence. "Boy, if you could find your way under the barbed wire," Cuomo said to me, "—'I was on the Dictograph roof last night! Shhh!' Thrilling business."

Frank Cuomo says he doesn't fear saying anything about Mario's past that might hurt him, because he never did anything bad. "I have never heard my brother use foul language . . . never heard him tell an off-color joke, never heard him make an ethnic slur—not even joking—it wasn't him."

"He never hurt anybody," Frank says of his brother with conviction. "He was never even picked up because he broke windows."[5]

If Mario Cuomo's boyhood seems too good to have been true, it was. He was not quite the perfect child that sticks in the memory of relatives and friends. He was, to be sure, an extraordinarily "good kid," but he did have a few minor brushes with imperfection.

To cite a trivial example of the sort of trouble all children get into at one time or another: once when Mario's mother bought him a new suit for Christmas, he went out and climbed a fence in it, ripping the coat. Afraid to take it to his mother, he went instead to a woman across the street, who sewed it so that he would not have to tell his mother what happened. Two days later Immaculata Cuomo decided to send the suit to the cleaners. Seeing the repair job, she exclaimed, "My God, he give me a bad coat!" She was about to return it to the merchant when little Mario stopped her by owning up to what had happened—not because he could not tell a lie, but because he had been caught in a small one.

Nor, it seems, did young Mario work quite as much in the store as he often remembers. Arthur Foster remembers helping him "stock the shelves with cartons of sugar, corn flakes, stuff like that," but the youngest Cuomo child did not work in the store nearly as much as his brother. Mario began making deliveries only at the age of twelve, when Frank went into the navy late in World War II. Mario only made deliveries on Saturdays. Frank had started working in the store at a much younger age and worked every day after school, in addition to Saturdays.

The small businesses started by Italian immigrants were often financially successful, but they held little attraction for their better-educated sons. It was clear to the Cuomos that Mario's destiny was not to be found in the grocery business. He worked at it while his brother was gone, because his father needed help, and "you didn't go out and hire help when you had sons." So for several years when his friends went to the movies on Saturdays, Mario worked for his father, making the weekly deliveries to regular customers. He also took other jobs, working in the summer as a stock boy at Gertz department store and making deliveries for a local dental lab. This was a somewhat unusual line of work. He delivered completed false teeth to the patients of local dentists.

But Mario soon had a convenience that his older brother had not enjoyed when he was making deliveries: Poppa's brand-new Ford station wagon. It was this new mode of delivery that got Mario into his only significant trouble as a teenager. He started driving the station wagon to make deliveries when he was about fifteen and not old enough to drive legally. The police picked him up for driving without a license. The officers at the 103rd Precinct in Jamaica knew Andrea Cuomo and they took his young son home. They said they were supposed to report the incident, but it was around Easter and maybe if they were given "a little something" they could forget about it. "It wasn't bribery or anything," Frank says. It was just an exchange of favors. But any cash payment to the cops would have constituted a breach of Andrea Cuomo's strict ethical code. "You know," he said to his sons, "I think they want something like eggs." The boys thought their father was kidding. "No, Poppa," Mario said, "it's not eggs that they want." But Andrea proceeded to get out a basket and fill it with two dozen eggs. He gave the basket to the officers and said, "Thank you for bringing my son home. I'll take care of the problem with my son." The policemen looked in the basket and didn't see what they wanted, but they couldn't come right out and ask for a five-dollar bill, so they had no choice but to leave. Andrea turned to his sons, who were mortified by his seeming ignorance, and offered a one-word explanation: "Easter."

Somewhat later there was more trouble involving the wooden station wagon. While Mario was making a delivery on Liberty Avenue, he left the door on the driver's side open. A truck came by and knocked the door completely off the station wagon. Mario was afraid to tell his father what had happened, but the police had to make an accident report. They informed the Cuomos that it was illegal to get out of a car into the street from the driver's side, even though everyone did so. The report, however, placed blame for the accident on the driver of the truck, who was speeding.[6]

When he was not in school, reading, or working in the store, the preteen and teenage Mario Cuomo divided his time between baseball fields, basketball courts, and the street corner in front of Tiedemann's ice cream parlor on Jamaica Avenue. Baseball became for him a passion that was at least the equal of his love of learning. In order to have a place to play, the kids in the neighborhood worked to clean up a large lot filled with all sorts of rubble up to the size of bedsprings. They dug a hole so large that they had to use ropes and buckets to get the dirt out. Then they dumped all the trash into it, covered it with dirt, and leveled it off to make a baseball diamond.

When he reached his teens, Mario moved from pickup games to an organized team. The Austin Celtics derived their name from coach Joe Austin and his ethnic background. He had started coaching sandlot teams in South Jamaica in 1932, and always took a keen interest in the welfare and development of youngsters in the area. Several of his players attracted the interest of major-league scouts.

Cuomo's hero was Yankee star Joe DiMaggio and his dream and goal was the same as that of thousands of other boys of that era—to become another DiMaggio. That, of course, was not to be, but Cuomo was an outstanding outfielder and a fierce competitor. Austin helped greatly in developing his natural skills to the point where he was offered a contract in 1951 to play in the Pittsburgh Pirates organization. He continued to play with Austin's teams up until that time. Austin remembers Cuomo as "a very amiable guy who always kept everybody loose. He was comical, always engaged in chatter."* [7]

At Tiedemann's ice cream parlor, Cuomo and his friends established a "Cornerville" society outwardly similar to that described in William F. Whyte's classic 1943 study of Boston's North End, *Street Corner Society*. The emphasis in Italian culture on male camaraderie and exhibitionism led to the establishment of peer groups of teenage boys who engaged in frequent verbal sparring, not unlike black ghetto youths who played "the dozens" on street corners. It was quite possible for a bright youngster such as Cuomo to hone his verbal skills to a fine precision in these street-corner debates.

While Mario Cuomo was a part of the Tiedemann group, he remained something of an exception to the typical picture of a member of such a society. He hung out with the others, but had more outside interests than most of the rest did, and he maintained a certain distance from them. "I didn't really fit in," he told me. "The only reason they accepted me was because of my playing ball. They were into racing cars—it didn't interest me."

Cuomo was *in* the street-corner society, but in important respects he was not *of* it. Nor did he go along with the general emphasis in such peer groups on demonstrating sexual prowess. The lessons he learned from his father and his church seem to have outweighed the peer pressures to "score" with girls. Immaculata Cuomo only recalls her younger son taking one girl to a show while he was in high school. As the governor himself put it: "Dating? Sure, a little, but it wasn't a big thing with me."

It was also part of the custom of Italian male street-corner groups that members should not "desert." Only a few made the break to go to college and seek personal advancement. This break, which Cuomo made, was as sharp a departure from the Italian-American norm of the time as was his father's decision to move from South Jamaica to Holliswood. Significantly Mario took the first step toward his break with tradition and the neighborhood four years before his father did. "He didn't want to go to Jamaica High School," Frank says of his brother. "That's where we all had

*Cuomo's athletic skills and competitiveness were such an important part of his developing character that they will be dealt with in a separate chapter (see Chapter 4).

to go. In our neighborhood, when you graduated from public school, you had to go to Jamaica High school. When a friend went in 1945 to take the entrance exams for St. John's Preparatory School in Brooklyn, Mario Cuomo went with him and decided to take the test himself. As a result, he became a student at a Vincentian prep school far from the old neighborhood. (See next chapter.) Despite some misgivings, Andrea and Immaculata Cuomo agreed to their studious son's daily trek to Brooklyn. He continued to live at home and to hang out at times with the old gang, but a decisive break had been made when Cuomo was only thirteen years old.[8]

While there can be no question that Mario Cuomo's Italian heritage shaped him in critical ways, it is equally important to take note of the ways in which he deviated—even in his youth—from the attitudes and practices usually associated with his culture.

Cuomo's hunger for knowledge and formal education set him apart from many of his contemporaries in the Italian-American communities of New York. In this, however, he was merely somewhat unusual. The second-generation Italian-Americans who craved knowledge and sought to enter the professions were breaking with expectations, but their numbers were sufficiently large to make them an important minority within the community.

In other respects, though, Mario Cuomo's differences with the usual practices of second-generation males of his ethnic background were striking and extremely significant. The usual desire for material goods was almost completely absent in Cuomo. Except for a brief period as a young lawyer when he sought to make money just to see if he could do it, he never had any interest in money or the material possessions and comforts it could buy. Nor did Cuomo ever share the sensuality and emphasis on conquest of females that was so common among young Italian-American men. He is, in fact, a sort of Catholic Puritan, if one does not push the latter term too far. He combines, as one of his longtime friends points out, the vitality of a Catholic ethnic with the academic curiosity and love of knowledge of the traditional Protestant New Englander.

Another crucial difference between Mario Cuomo and most of his peers while they were growing up was his strong religious interest. Southern Italian males had not been noted for their

church attendance or interest in religion. That did not change
noticeably when the culture was transplanted to urban America.
Nor was it altered significantly by the second generation. It was
not unusual for young Italian-American boys to be faithful
churchgoers while they were still close to their mothers, but as
they got older, most saw the Church as an insufficiently masculine
institution and so rejected it. Young Cuomo's identification with
the Church—a Church that in New York was almost entirely
Irish, even in Italian areas—was one more characteristic that set
him apart from most males of his age and background.

Among most immigrant groups there developed a conflict between the Americanized second generation and the immigrant
parents. In addition to the usual generational conflict between
parents and children, there was for most immigrants a "culture
gap" in which the children turned against the old-country ways of
their parents. There was a bit less of a split between the first and
second generation among Italians than there was among many
other ethnic groups, but it clearly existed.

Mario Cuomo was not immune to this phenomenon. As a teenager, he was embarrassed by his parents' broken English and
immigrant practices. He made excuses to keep his parents from
attending school events at St. John's Prep. But unlike most second-
generation ethnics who sought to lose their heritage in the process
of "Americanization," Cuomo never rejected the basic values he
had learned at home. Instead, he kept them as a base and expanded
upon them and transformed them. He took the southern Italian
and Italian-American urban villager's emphasis on family and
community and transformed it from an *exclusive* principle of working together for the good of a narrow group into an *inclusive* notion
of the larger "family" of New York, of America, and even of all
humankind. This led him to stand the *contadino*'s fear of government on its head. He saw that, under American democratic conditions, it was possible to use the government to advance the larger
sense of family and community he had developed out of his traditional Italian values.

Cuomo summed up his debt to his Italian heritage in a speech
in 1982: "My traditional—conservative, if you will—values have
guided me in my personal and public life. Because I love a merciful
God, I believe that government must never lose the quality of
compassion. Because I love my country, I believe America is ill-
served by setting class against class and young against old. Because

I love my family, and because I believe in the value of family, I believe we must fulfill our contract with our elders. Because I love my children, I believe we must not defeat the aspirations of the next generation, which is willing to work to fulfill its potential. And because I believe in the fundamental value of dignity through labor, I believe jobs should not be sacrificed on the altar of economic sleight of hand."

"All of these," Cuomo noted, "are Italian values. You don't have to be Italian to believe them—but it helps." He was only partially correct. The *basis* of these values is indeed Italian, but as he outlined them, they are a greatly expanded version of Italian-American values, created by Mario M. Cuomo.

Mario Cuomo was, as his brother Frank put it, "just an American boy growing up with immigrant parents." The example set by those immigrant parents and the experiences of his American youth combined with the basic religious principles he arrived at to provide Cuomo with the foundation he needed to develop his hybrid value system.[9]

3

CATHOLIC

THE ROLE of religion in politics
has become a hotly debated topic in recent years in this country.
Ninety percent of Americans profess a belief in God, and more
than half of the nation's people attend religious services on a more
or less regular basis. Mainline churches became active in the civil
rights movement of the 1950s and 1960s, and by the late 1970s
right-wing, fundamentalist Christians were making their presence
felt in the Republican party. Various churches have taken vocal
stands on political issues ranging from abortion and homosexuality to nuclear war and the American economy. The distinction
between Caesar's realm and that of God has become ever more
blurred.

Jimmy Carter went beyond the usual politician's lip service to
religion by openly proclaiming himself to be a "born-again Christian." The support he received in 1976 from white evangelicals and
black churchgoers of all denominations was essential to Carter's
winning of both the Democratic nomination and the general election. In 1980 Carter lost a majority of the white "born-again" vote
to Ronald Reagan, a man who said all the things the right-wing
Christians wanted to hear. They apparently thought these words
were of more importance than whether he went to church or
practiced many of the virtues that he preached.

In 1984 an ordained minister, the Reverend Jesse Jackson, made
a sustained bid for the Democratic presidential nomination. Reverend Jackson again pursued his party's nomination in 1988 and was
joined in the race on the Republican side by television evangelist
Marion G. "Pat" Robertson.

Within this context an examination of any major politician's
religious beliefs would seem to be in order. But where Mario

Cuomo is concerned, the reason for delving deeply into his faith goes far beyond current political fashion. For while Ronald Reagan *acts* religious, Mario Cuomo *is* religious. His religion is central to everything he believes and does.

The recent politicizing of religion (and vice versa) led Cuomo to address the subject directly. He feared that "the whole question of religion in politics is in danger of being co-opted by a single kind of religious group [right-wing fundamentalists]." By "brandishing religious values," Reagan was "moving into a vacuum." Cuomo's response was to reclaim religious values for liberal Democrats by emphasizing the Christianity of the Sermon on the Mount.

But Cuomo's raising of the standard of liberal religious values was no simple political reaction to the fundamentalists. Indeed, the New York governor had undertaken a campaign for these values long before Reagan "wrapped himself in religiosity." During his unsuccessful campaign in the 1977 New York mayoralty race, for example, Cuomo addressed the congregation at the Church of the Master, in Harlem. "One of our moral obligations, as Catholics, as Christians," the candidate told his audience of black Protestants, ". . . is to be involved." "The sense of all religions is love," Cuomo continued. "Love means doing good things for those who are less fortunate, for the poor, the hungry, the abused, the sick, the prisoners. That kind of love is the basis of government and politics as well. The predicate of your involvement in politics and mine is the same—the obligation to love."

When Cuomo began using liberal religious themes in his political speeches, there seemed to be no political gain to be had in such a course. In fact, when he entered politics in the early seventies, religious belief was something that practically disqualified a politician seeking "liberal" support. It had, as *New York Daily News* columnist Pete Hamill noted in 1977, "become fashionable in many political circles to sneer at people who still believe in God." How could anyone who still believed in God understand "the Issues," sophisticated liberals asked each other. Oh, they realized that it might be politically necessary for a candidate to pose for photographers in front of a church on Sunday mornings. That was acceptable, so long as it was understood that the action was hypocritical. But in Cuomo's early political career, Hamill pointed out, liberals looked upon him with suspicious eyes, "because he is a Catholic who believes in the basic strictures of his faith, who has studied them in detail, and feels them passionately."

There is, in fact, no more important key to comprehending Mario Cuomo than his faith. As he himself has put it: "My Catholic faith and the understanding it gives me of stewardship aren't a part of my politics. Rather, my politics is, as far as I can make it happen, an extension of this faith and the understanding." "I am a governor, I am a Democrat," he said on another occasion, "but I am a Catholic first—my soul is more important to me than my body." "I will remain true to my belief and a member of the Church," Cuomo has declared, "which is more important to me than remaining a member of the Democratic Party." Some other politicians might make statements like these before certain audiences they thought would like to hear them, but by all indications Cuomo was sincere.

A couple of incidents illustrate the centrality of religion to Cuomo's thinking. When one of his aides, Richard Starkey, informed him during the 1986 gubernatorial campaign that there was speculation in the press that because William Ellinghaus, the former president of New York Telephone Company and current chairman of the board of Channel 13, had accepted the position of chief fund-raiser for Cuomo's Republican opponent, Andrew P. O'Rourke, the governor might "get even" by reducing the funding for public television, Cuomo's private response was startling. "I could never do that," he said. "That would be a sin." Coming from most politicians, such a statement would be either a joke or sheer hypocrisy intended to win votes. But when one gets to know Mario Cuomo, it becomes clear that his comment was utterly serious and truthful. "I thought to myself," Starkey told me, " 'Nobody would believe me; nobody in this country would believe that there's a man that's being considered for president of the United States who would, without being facetious, say "I couldn't do that; it would be a sin." ' I couldn't use that phrase," Starkey said, "but I knew that he was being sincere."

On another occasion, this one early in 1987 when Cuomo was having difficulty getting the state legislature to agree to an anticorruption commission to be headed by Joseph Califano, Starkey called the governor on a Saturday morning to give him his daily press briefing. He was surprised to learn that his 8 A.M. call had awakened the normally early-rising Cuomo. Surprise gave way to astonishment when the governor told him why he had overslept. "I got up at three o'clock—I bolted out of bed at three o'clock," the governor explained, "—an inspiration from the Holy Spirit—an idea about the Califano Commission." "Again," Starkey told me, "your first tendency is to say he's pulling your leg, he's being facetious—but he's *not*. I'm constantly amazed." (It should be noted that in this case Cuomo was not suggesting that he had actually been visited by the Holy Spirit. Starkey's point was only that Cuomo is comfortable speaking in such terms.)

Stories such as these are indicative not of a religious fanatic, which Mario Cuomo plainly is not, but of a man whose religious commitment is deep and powerfully motivating. Cuomo tries to avoid being photographed entering or leaving church. As president, Dwight Eisenhower went to church because he thought it was his duty to set a good example for those who needed it. Mario Cuomo goes to church because he *wants* to, to fulfill his own needs, not to create an image or set an example for others. He frequently attends daily mass at a small church in Albany. Although he does not often talk directly about his religion, it has always formed the core of his beliefs.

The Catholic Church in which Cuomo was raised had a lasting impact upon him, but it was only a transformed understanding of the Catholic view of the proper human place in the world and of God's intention for people while they are in this world that led Cuomo to conclude that public service is a vocation second only to the priesthood in importance. He came, indeed, to see politics as a sort of secular ministry. "Politics is the highest vocation after the religious vocation," he contends, "because the business of politics and government is to distribute the goods of the world in such a way as to improve the condition of people's lives." "I see a priest as being selfless," Cuomo told me. "A politician is not. At its worst, politics is a way to get rich. But at its best, politics can be a way to serve and help." That is a far cry both from the light in which his parents and most other Italian immigrants saw politics and from the attitude most Americans today have toward politics and politicians.[1]

In most respects the fact that Cuomo's values stem from Catholicism, rather than from another religious framework, holds no particular import. The values he espouses are universally appealing. But in one sense it *is* significant that Cuomo's values are rooted in Catholicism. The important distinction is that Catholics do not believe that people are "saved" at some moment in their lives. The Catholic view is that salvation is an ongoing, lifelong process. One must work day-by-day at being as good as one can be.

That can never be good enough to merit salvation, so God's grace is also necessary. Thus there are never, in the Catholic way of thinking, two groups, the saved and the damned. Rather, the Catholic sees everyone living on earth as existing in a state of imperfection, but capable of achieving salvation if they work at it.

This worldview contains direct implications for social policy, and Mario Cuomo has drawn those implications and worked them into a philosophy that guides his public career.

The relationship between Cuomo and his religion is a complex one. This chapter will trace and explore that relationship from his days as an altar boy at St. Monica's Church in South Jamaica, through his Vincentian education at St. John's, his exposure to the new Catholic philosophy taught by the French Jesuit scientist Pierre Teilhard de Chardin and the reforms of Pope John XXIII, to the role that his faith plays in his contemporary political career and how his religious beliefs might affect a bid for national office.

Catholicism was not notably strong among southern Italian immigrants to the United States prior to about the 1940s. Churchmen and scholars alike spoke of "The 'Italian Problem' in the Catholic Church of the United States." Although most Italian-Americans were nominally Catholic, relatively few observed the sacraments with any degree of regularity. Part of the problem was the domination of the Church by an Irish-American clergy. Even in Italian parishes, the priests were often Irish. There were few Italian priests, and a good many of that number were not very effective. The paucity of Italian priests was the result both of a general disinterest in the Church on the part of southern Italian males and of the requirement of priestly celibacy. "A man is supposed to be a man," Glazer and Moynihan wrote in *Beyond the Melting Pot*, "and celibacy has always been something of a problem for the South Italian culture, which tends to see sexual needs as imperative and almost incapable of suppression or moderation."

What Italian religious life there was in New York was vibrant. The Catholicism that the immigrants carried with them was essentially a folk religion, with a heavy emphasis on ceremony and emotional expression. The immigrant church was one of simple and unquestioned theological beliefs. The traditional ceremonies at once demonstrated the power of the Church and provided the assurance of salvation for those who would follow the prescribed course.

It was in this simple, static, awe-inspiring, and ceremonially impressive Church that Mario Cuomo was introduced to his faith. "Ours was a Catholicism closer to the peasant roots of its practitioners than to the high intellectual traditions of Catholic theology and philosophy," he has said. "We perceived the world then as a sort of cosmic basic-training course, filled by God with obstacles and traps to weed out the recruits unfit for eventual service in the Heavenly Host."

Those obstacles were a source of worry to a young boy who took his religion seriously. Cuomo describes the basis of the faith that was taught to him and his contemporaries as "the ultimate 'carrot and stick' approach to religious philosophy, with the stick being a lot more ominous than the carrot was appealing." Most—perhaps all—of the material world and its temptations were to be avoided. We were not on this earth to achieve success or happiness here, but to be tested for our worthiness to spend eternity with God. This was indeed a "vale of tears," and it was to be endured, not enjoyed; rejected, not embraced, "until by some combination of luck and grace and good works, we escaped final damnation." Anyone imbued with this concept would find it difficult to accept material success in the earthly realm, and this has certainly been true of Cuomo.

The Catholic Church in which Mario Cuomo was brought up was preoccupied with the presence of evil in the world. Heavy doses of guilt were administered to the faithful in Sunday morning masses, and the communicants in turn were expected to cleanse themselves of that guilt in the confessional. Cuomo's lifelong habits of questioning the motives behind all of his actions and of holding himself up against an almost saintly standard can be traced back to his youthful days in the confessional opposite Father Eugene Erny, when he "prayed that the old German pastor wouldn't recognize the voice from the darkened cubicle on the other side of the screen."

The Church's ritual commanded respect, even if it was difficult to follow in Latin. A young altar boy at St. Monica's learned to make his way through such prayers as the *Confiteor* and the *Suscipe* without entirely deciphering their meaning.

But there was more to the Catholic Church in those days than a pervasive sense of guilt and an impressive ritual in an unfamiliar tongue. St. Monica's Church and School were also populated by a group of Sisters of Charity. As their name implies, their mission was to encourage the finding of inner peace through giving and helping others. Cuomo liked the nuns. "As I think about it now," he said to me, "what I liked about the nuns was their passion—they were *totally* committed. I like that about people." Because they were not always so charitable in dealing with students in their charge ("I tell the nuns now whenever I see them—I say, 'You're not Sisters of Charity—you're Sisters of *Justice!*'—and they like that"), Mario Cuomo was not directly educated by the nuns, but their emphasis on helping those in need was to become a central feature of his version of Catholicism.[2]

The guilt-centered Church of Mario Cuomo's youth inevitably induced anguish and torment among many of its frail, sinful communicants. Mario Cuomo was one of this number. Not only did he have worries about the destiny of his immortal soul when he was young, Cuomo told me, he still does. "We all do, all of us who went through that period. You never escape it—that guilt. Forget about Jewish guilt. Jewish guilt is nothing [in comparison]. Old-fashioned Catholic guilt is the absolute best. It ruins everything. After a while, you conclude: if you enjoy it, it's wrong."

But young Mario Cuomo found great comfort in Sunday school. "I don't know who asked me to go to Sunday school, or who *made* me go to Sunday school," he said. "I guess you had to if you wanted to be confirmed. But it was a very good experience for me. I *liked* Sunday school; I liked the books. I liked—that's interesting—I *liked* the catechism. I have never thought of this before," he told me in mid-1987. The Baltimore Catechism in use when Cuomo was preparing for confirmation answered the question "Why did God make me?" with "God made me to know Him and to love Him and to serve Him in this world and to be happy with Him in the next."

The catechism struck an inquisitive young mind ("I was always looking and wondering—curious") as "a neat, complete, plausible, comfortable statement of profound truths." "Somehow it appealed to my sense of logic," Cuomo told me. "You know, it was so nice. It was *all* the answers, wrapped up, the whole game." "Here," he went on, "all of life was described for me: there's a God, the

Ultimate Being, and here's how you relate to *Him* ('Him' because he had a beard), and it was wonderful. I liked the neatness of it; I liked the sureness of it."

As he grew older, Cuomo would find more to question in his faith, but the basic belief that there is a reason for us to exist has continued to guide his inquisitive mind throughout his life. He summarized his basic belief by recounting to me what his brother Frank had said after the death of his young son. "Frank said: 'Look, I'm not smart enough to understand God. Either there is something that makes sense which I don't understand, or there isn't. If there isn't, I can't make it. I don't want to go through with it with my other kids. I can't handle it if the rest of my life just doesn't make sense. I don't want to live that way. So I think that there must be something that makes sense that I can't perfectly figure out.' " Mario's response to his brother's statement was: "From all I know, that's a perfect description of Christianity. . . . You can't understand it, but it makes sense—a much better way to live."[3]

That young Mario Cuomo was much more religious than most of his peers is another indication of the strong maternal influence on the boy. Of course he loved such male pursuits as playing ball, but he also engaged in activities that many boys of his time and place considered "feminine"—such as reading and taking church seriously. And, as he has throughout his life, Mario Cuomo in his youth—his tough and highly competitive male nature notwithstanding—drew the line at activities that he considered to be sinful. Frank Cuomo not only says that he can never remember hearing his brother curse (he picked up the practice in later years, but uses only the mildest of oaths), but also states that Mario always asked himself on every decision that he faced: "What's moral? What's immoral?" "He always wanna do the righta thing," adds Immaculata Cuomo.

He was always a tough competitor, longtime friend Bernard Babb says of Cuomo, "but not in a manner that might be destructive. He was not a destructive person at all. He was always a very warm and giving person." "You can be tough and competitive on the outside, but soft on the inside," said Professor Anthony Sarno, who directed the intramural athletic program when Cuomo was at St. John's College. "That's Mario." "He was a hard, ungiving player," Cuomo's friend Nicholas D'Arienzo says of him, "but off the [basketball] court, he'd probably do anything" for you. It was Cuomo's makeup, another friend, Joe Mattone, told me, "to seek a peaceful way out of things. He wasn't a tough guy in that sense. He was the kind of guy who knew he could handle himself and didn't feel a need to prove it. Maybe that's a sense of security."

It seems that Mario Cuomo was able to blend the best of what our culture often classifies as "female values" into his solidly masculine exterior. "I can talk about values," he told me, "because of the way I look, my hands, my build, my face. No one is going to call me 'effete' or a 'wimp' when I talk about values and compassion."

Although his bookish and religious interests were out of the ordinary for boys from his background, Cuomo's most significant departure from the expectations for young Italian males was his refusal to "make it" with girls. The contention of his best friend, Fabian Palomino, referred to earlier, that Cuomo is the only Italian male he has ever known who was still a virgin on his wedding day, is illustrative of the man's religious commitment. He remained celibate until marriage not, it seems, because he was lacking in either desire or opportunity, but because, as his mother said, he always wanted to do the right thing. Lust is among the seven cardinal sins, and this religious young man made it a point to avoid all of them. (Indeed, as I shall show throughout the book, much of Cuomo's character can be understood in terms of his quest to avoid what his Church teaches are the seven deadly sins and to practice what his religion classifies as the four cardinal virtues.)

"He was always a prude when it came to women," Palomino said, "*always* a prude. He was never a womanizer, a woman's guy. . . . [But] one thing that was nice about him, he was not judgmental of other people. Whatever standards they had when it came to sex, that was their business."*

Utterly prudish in his personal standards, Cuomo was nonetheless eager to hear stories of the sexual adventures of friends. "He liked to hear of the exploits of other guys who were scoring all the time," Palomino told me, "because I think he wondered about it: 'How in the hell can they be up to that? What's so great about it?'—or whatever. He was just not driven that way, I guess." Former law associate Sal Curiale has a slightly different explanation.

*It is worth noting that these assessments of Cuomo's attitudes toward sex were collected *before* the exposure of Gary Hart's proclivities in this area raised its political importance.

"The man is a passionate individual—strong feelings, very attractive—but also a tremendously *moral* man," Curiale says of Cuomo. "I always felt like there was this volcano ready to explode, but he just kept the lid on it because he was so strong," he told me. "But I really think he was preoccupied by the exploits he never permitted himself to have." Cuomo himself offers yet another motive for his readiness to listen to the tales of other men's conquests: "I knew some of them had a need to tell these stories, so I listened."

An Italian-American boy who was deeply religious and willing to restrain his sexual appetite was an attractive prize for the Church. "The priests come to me and say, 'Tell your son to be a priest,' " Immaculata Cuomo recalls. "I say, 'I no tell him to be a priest. I tell him to go to school and he can be anything he wants.' " But, for a time, young Mario *did* want to be a priest. "He *liked* the idea," his mother told me, "because really the priests was educated people. He *liked* them; he had good friends."

Nick D'Arienzo says "there was always the feeling of his spiritual background. He could have very easily become a priest." If he had gone that route, D'Arienzo adds only half-jokingly, Cuomo "probably would have been at least a cardinal—or the pope."

Mario Cuomo's thoughts of becoming a priest went the way of the same intentions on the part of many another young Catholic man. Immaculata Cuomo put it succinctly: "Then he met Matilda—and no more priest!"

"Father Caufield really had his eye on Mario," Matilda Cuomo told me. One day he wanted to meet her and had Father Murray introduce him. "This is Matilda Raffa," Father Murray said. Father Caufield just stared at her. "I felt like I had done something wrong," she said to me. Father Murray later told her what Father Caufield had said after she left: "So *she*'s the person who put the kink in [our plans]."

She did not then know quite what that meant, but Mario later explained that he had had some sessions with the priests. "They did recruit," she affirmed.

After he met Matilda Raffa, Cuomo no longer felt that he had the calling to be a priest. He did not think that he could give up marriage and children, so he decided not to enter the seminary but to go on to other things, such as baseball and the law. In any case, he now says, "I soon realized that I didn't have sufficient goodness and selflessness to be a priest. And I've had that confirmed many times since." As with other committed Catholic men who decided to marry, though, Cuomo did not completely abandon the idea of devoting his life to God. If he could not be good and selfless enough to be a priest, he could at least strive to be as good and selfless as he possibly could. It would, however, take several years and the introduction of new ideas into Catholicism before he would find a suitable outlet for his desire to live a properly religious life in this world.[4]

By the time he made the decision to exchange vows with Matilda Raffa rather than with Mother Church, Mario Cuomo had already spent several years in an environment of strict, religiously centered education at St. John's Prep and St. John's College.

Cuomo came to be a student at the Vincentian preparatory school only because he accompanied his friend who went there to take the entrance examination. "For kicks," he says, "I took the test, too." As a public school product, Cuomo had been educated in a different manner from the parochial school students who constituted the bulk of the St. John's Prep applicants. Consequently he was not well prepared for the sort of questions that were asked and he failed the test. Mario Cuomo has never been one to calmly accept defeat or rejection, and his failure led him to decide that he really wanted to get into the prep school. "I think I wanted to go to the school because I failed the test, to be honest with you," Cuomo told me. He went to see the headmaster, Father John P. Cotter, and pleaded his case. The audacity of a thirteen-year-old from a relatively poor family who came in on his own—without even telling his parents—and argued that the test had not accurately reflected his ability impressed Father Cotter. "He decided on the spot," Cuomo believes, " 'Well, I'm going to help this kid.' "

The approval of the headmaster, however, was only half the battle. Young Mario still had to convince his father that he should attend a school that was in distant Brooklyn and that cost money. Andrea Cuomo saw no reason why anyone should pay to go to school when there were free schools available. His son acted as his own attorney once more, arguing that St. John's was a good school and that he would work hard there. Always interested in the betterment of his children, Andrea Cuomo agreed to shell out fifteen dollars a month for tuition, plus daily carfare, so that his youngest and brightest child could obtain a quality education.

St. John's Prep was a school that maintained strict discipline. "You had to be sitting in your seat at nine—no talking in the hallways. That kind of stuff was strictly enforced," recalls one of Cuomo's contemporaries. Although he enjoyed a good time, Cuomo had no problem with discipline. By his second year at the school, Mario had earned a full scholarship. But after two years he wanted to quit. He felt that it was not his kind of place. The school was not populated by his "kind of people." He did not know many of his fellow students very well. "They were all one generation ahead of us," he told me. "They spoke the language; they had a more sophisticated cultural background than I did—all of them. They had done things and been places that I knew *nothing* of. I was just out of it. I could compete with them—better—at everything they were doing in the classroom, or on the ball field. But the cultural difference—I just didn't understand it."

Close friend Joe Mattone says that "there were a lot of better-dressed guys [at the Prep] than he and I. The Irish were kind of middle-class—by *our* standards—and we weren't." Mattone remembers conversations while they were at the Prep in which Cuomo said, "I don't see myself fitting in here." But, Mattone told me, "if he had some self-doubts, he wasn't one to share them. I think he was a kind of shy guy at the time. He got along with the fellows; he was a guy who was known—it wasn't that he was a loner."

During these years Cuomo came to feel ashamed of his ethnic and class background. "Most of the kids were of the Irish 'elite,'" he has said. "You see, in those years, to be a Catholic was to be an *Irish* Catholic. Italians were something else, something not as good." He would not invite his mother and father to functions such as parents' days at St. John's Prep. "They wouldn't have understood the language," he explains. "I would have embarrassed them and embarrassed myself." "I didn't like those kids," he says, "but I didn't want them to know that my parents didn't speak English well." "I came to regret that in later years—the self-hate syndrome." "I could cry now, thinking of how I didn't want them to come," Cuomo says.

In the end, Father Cotter persuaded Cuomo to go out for the varsity basketball and baseball teams, and there he found his niche.

"I think what he did," Mattone said, "was get himself on a career track, become goal-oriented."

Cuomo was one of only twelve members of his class selected for the Moore Honor Society, "the school's most coveted recognition." Membership was based upon "character, school spirit, and achievement." He showed no interest in politics, was not involved in student government, and did not join the debate club. He was, however, during his senior year a member of the Forum Club, the stated purpose of which was "to prepare the young men of today to be the civic leaders of tomorrow; that by discussing and dissecting the world problems they might be able to grasp the torch . . . to weld the Catholic world of the future."[5]

Cuomo was offered an athletic scholarship to Hofstra, but the coaches there wanted him to run track. He intended to play basketball and baseball, and decided that he was better off accepting the academic scholarship proffered by St. John's College. That way he wouldn't "have to worry about what ball I want to play." So he continued his education across the street from his prep school. In the days when he was an undergraduate at St. John's College (1949–53), the school was a small, highly disciplined community. It was an all-male institution, still housed in a single building on Lewis Avenue in the Bedford-Stuyvesant section of Brooklyn. Rules were strictly enforced. All students were required to wear jackets and ties. "You couldn't have free rein in a clerical school," as Joe Mattone put it. In this atmosphere, Cuomo's already highly developed self-discipline grew stronger. Yet his brilliance and ability to concentrate allowed him to get by—indeed, to excel—without spending a large amount of time at his studies. Nicholas D'Arienzo tells a revealing story of the night before their biology final. They decided to study together and D'Arienzo went to Cuomo's home for the evening. They had dinner and then went for a long walk. When they got back to the house, Cuomo said, "It's too early to study." So they took another walk. This time upon their return, Cuomo said it was too *late* to study. The only thing to do, he said, was to try to figure out what the questions would be and work out answers to them. "We went through about a dozen questions," D'Arienzo told me. "I think about nine or ten of them were on the exam. We both got A's, but it was a terrifying experience."

"He had great retentive power," Mattone remembers. "He could really hear something once and it was his for good." "I have never seen *anyone* make use of time the way he did, scholastically," Bernard Babb says of Cuomo. "He'd say, 'I have an assignment in philosophy,' or in English or in Spanish, or whatever, and he would find a nook in the cafeteria and he'd sit down and in forty-five minutes or an hour or an hour and a half, he'd complete an essay. He was able to shut out everything and get it done." And, according to one of his major professors, Nicholas Sallese, "anything he turned in was always of superior quality." "He was exceptionally good in the way he spoke and handled himself, and in the things that he wrote, which were grammatically correct and well-organized," Spanish professor Philip Astuto said of his former pupil. "He had his head together well, and he came out as a good student—more than just good—an *excellent* student."

The only reason that Cuomo was not selected for Phi Beta Kappa was the very good one that there was no chapter of the organization at St. John's. He was, however, tapped into the highly exclusive Skull and Circle Honor Fraternity, the St. John's equivalent of Phi Beta Kappa. Membership in the Skull and Circle was based upon "a general excellence in the scholastic, social, and athletic fields, with the emphasis on a diversity of activities." The skull symbolized intellectual achievement and the circle all-around activity. A maximum of fifteen members of the junior class were chosen by the senior members of the organization each May. Cuomo was the fifth student chosen and one of only twelve members of his class picked in 1952.

Cuomo "was awarded every honor the college had to offer," as Anthony Sarno remembers it. He was one of only nine members of his class named to Who's Who Among Students in American Universities and Colleges. His intellectual abilities were so great that he was able to excel in his studies and still have plenty of time for other activities. "Mario outside the classroom was always one of the boys who stood out," said Sarno. All seniors at St. John's wore academic gowns, and members of the honor fraternity displayed a skull-and-circle insignia on theirs. This was one of the many indications that Mario Cuomo was a classic example of the Big Man on Campus. But his actions did not endear him to all of his classmates. "He *seemed* very, very self-assured," one of them told me. "For those of us who liked to make ourselves invisible, he seemed a little ostentatiously visible, a little *brazenly* self-confident.

He wasn't a sympathetic figure to some of us. My image of the governor as a student," he went on, "is being in the back of the student cafeteria, surrounded by other noisy friends." They would *"dominate* the scene in the cafeteria. So his was a larger-than-life image."

In addition to repeating such words as "gregarious," "brilliant," "fun-loving," and "intense," other students and professors I asked have described Mario Cuomo as an undergraduate as "cocky," a "cutup," "brash," an "arrogant SOB," and a "pain in the ass." All of these comments were made by people who came to admire Cuomo greatly in later years, which makes their descriptions of his attitude as a seventeen-to-twenty-one-year-old all the more telling. "Most anyone will tell you the same thing," Judge James Starkey said. "Mario would probably admit to it himself. Later he was somewhat embarrassed by the way he had acted in college."

An example of Cuomo's use—or misuse—of his intellect at St. John's came when the dean of men saw him standing in a second-floor hallway with a lighted cigarette in his hand. This was a clear violation of the college's rule against smoking above the first floor. The dean told Cuomo to report to his office.

"Why?" the student inquired.

"Because smoking here is against the rules."

"Did you see me smoking?" Cuomo responded. "Is there a rule against carrying a lighted cigarette?"

"Do you mean to tell me that you were not smoking?" the dean asked.

"No, Father, I'm not going to say that I wasn't, but I'm not going to say that I was, either. I have shoes on, but I'm not walking," said the smart-assed student.

The dean was less than amused by Cuomo's argument, and at the next student assembly he criticized students who have "cheating, technical minds."

"He could change anything and everything," D'Arienzo says of his college friend. "He really had a quick mind." When Cuomo handed in a paper late on one occasion, Dr. Sallese gave him a B+ on what was clearly an A paper. "I want you to look at this again," Cuomo said to his professor. "I think it was worth an A. You know I'm going to medical school." The veracity of Cuomo's claim can be judged by the comment of Nick D'Arienzo, now a pediatrician, who told me that medicine "is about the only thing he's not great at." The professor knew exactly how to characterize his student's assertion.

"Bullshit!" Sallese said. "You're not going to medical school. You're on the varsity team and you're going into big-league ball."

"Mario was brilliant. He could have majored in anything," one of his professors told me. As it happened, he became a triple major, concentrating in English, Spanish, and inter-American affairs. He still showed no interest in politics. He was not a member of the Political Affairs Organization, which existed for "students interested in current events and political theory and practice." During the 1952–53 academic year, club members discussed such topics as the Eisenhower-Stevenson presidential race, McCarthyism, the Soviet Union, Western European federation, and the South African racial problem. Apparently these subjects were of less interest to the future governor than were the American League standings and playing basketball at St. Monica's gym.

"[I had] zero interest in politics, all through college," Cuomo told me. He said he was aware of Roosevelt, the war, Eisenhower, "all of that, but no real interest. . . . I had no strong opinions and no heroes."

But there were some signs in his undergraduate career of where Mario Cuomo might wind up. He wrote a paper on Domingo Faustino Sarmiento, the "teacher president" of Argentina, for a Latin American history course. In it Cuomo wrote that Sarmiento believed man has three passions: "the passion to study, the passion to teach, and the passion to govern." Although he was writing about a long-gone Argentine politician, Cuomo may actually have been subconsciously looking in a mirror when he put this statement in his paper.

There were, in any case, ways at St. John's in which social concern could be shown other than participation in political discussions. The college had both an ethnic and a class mix, but perhaps 75 percent of its student body came from working-class families. A substantial number were older men attending college on the GI Bill. Unlike students from higher social strata who took college for granted, these first-generation collegians were on the rise and knew how important getting an education was. They knew they were there for a purpose and they were generally serious about it.

St. John's was not without its share of the ethnic prejudice of the day. "In those days," one of Cuomo's professors recalls, "boy, those Irish gave the Italians a hard time." "It wasn't fashionable to walk around with a handle like 'Mario.' " When Cuomo's first name was read from attendance rolls, other students sometimes laughed.

Italian-Americans—particularly those from recent immigrant, working-class backgrounds, had not been readily accepted into the St. John's fraternities. An Italian-American fraternity, AID, had existed on the campus, but the dean abolished it around 1940 because he believed that fraternities should not be based on ethnic lines. In its place an organization dedicated to promoting cultural ties with Latin America was formed in the early forties. After World War II the Pan-American Society became a fraternity, Pi Alpha Sigma. It provided a social organization open to Italian-American students, who constituted more than half of the membership. While many of the group's Italian-American members were Big Men on Campus, PAS had become a fraternity that took in students who were not always welcome in other organizations. By the time Mario Cuomo joined in 1949, PAS was also serving as a haven for others who would not be accepted into many campus social organizations. In Cuomo's senior year PAS membership included approximately twenty students with Italian surnames, fewer than ten of Irish ancestry, and a sprinkling of Germans and Poles. More significant is the fact that the only two blacks in the senior class and two black underclassmen were also Pi Alpha Sigma members. This number amounted to nearly the entire black population at St. John's in 1953. The fraternity also included John Gerity, a blind student who was—and is—a close friend of Mario Cuomo.

Joe Mattone, a fraternity brother of Cuomo's, says: "I guess we were kinda the catch basin for the kids nobody else wanted—in Pi Alpha Sigma. I think we had the best cross-section of personalities. We were more democratic than the other fraternities."

There is no question that Cuomo approved of the inclusive, open-door policy of his fraternity. He spent many hours as an undergraduate and in law school studying and listening to tapes with John Gerity. On at least one occasion when a group of students went into a restaurant that refused to serve the very light-skinned black Bernard Babb, Cuomo led a struggle that, as he puts it, "*got* our constitutional rights—we were served."

Although the St. John's fraternities were less formalized organizations than their counterparts at residential colleges, they engaged in many of the activities common to such organizations during the fifties. Hazing was taken seriously, and after suffering the application of numerous sticks to his posterior during his own induction, Cuomo became cochairman of the PAS "vigilance committee," which oversaw the installation of new members. "He was *rough*," says Nick Sallese, the group's faculty adviser. "He swung a mean paddle."[6]

Despite the existence of a bit of ethnic friction, St. John's in its days on Lewis Avenue in Brooklyn was a small, generally caring community. "It was a warm, small, family type of school," says Anthony Sarno. "St. John's catered to poor Catholics," Nick Sallese declares. "If they had money, they went elsewhere." "The attitude was to help the little, nice kid from Brooklyn whose parents couldn't afford to send him to college," according to Sarno. "We all got to know each other very well; it was tiny," Phil Astuto says wistfully. Professors would meet informally and talk about students. "And Cuomo's name would come up a lot, either as a cutup or as a good student—one way or the other."

"You can get a lot closer to people when you have a student body of maybe six hundred or seven hundred," Joe Mattone noted. "It was a different atmosphere, a different conviviality. We knew the whole gamut. There's a little more intimacy—including the faculty. If you had a problem, you could see the prof and address it."

The experience of community—albeit incomplete—at St. John's presumably added to young Cuomo's growing concept of a larger, more inclusive social "family."

Although St. John's was a clerical school, it was not a seminary. The college encouraged free and open discussion. The prelaw or liberal arts student was definitely encouraged to engage in debate. Mario Cuomo was one to take advantage of this openness. Fellow students recall that he was never reticent and was already a good speaker, but not in the same league with the best student speaker on the campus, whom Cuomo greatly admired. "He would take an unpopular position on an issue, just for the sake of stirring the waters," Mattone remembers of Cuomo. "He was, in that sense, a provocateur—for the purpose of generating a discussion. He wasn't shy on that." "He feasted on the idea of ideas—that was his feast."

Mario Cuomo the college student often displayed a good sense of humor, but behind his wit there was always the serious purpose to be the best that he could be. He joined with a small group of friends to form an organization they called the AMC—the "Academy of Mutual Criticism." This was an informal gathering of about five students who convened on Friday afternoons at three-thirty to criticize each other from an attitude of "how do we make ourselves better?"

Cuomo's participation in this mutual criticism/self-improvement group is suggestive of his approach to life during his college years. "That's all I recall," Babb told me, "—just this constant drive to make himself better."

Yet *self*-improvement could never be allowed to become the primary motive. The notion of our obligation to each other, engrained in Mario Cuomo as a boy, was heightened in his years under the tutelage of the Order of St. Vincent de Paul. The Vincentians are a missionary order, many of whose members had been working in China before being driven out by the Communist advances in the late forties. Some of these missionary priests wound up teaching at such Vincentian schools as St. John's. They sought to transmit their missionary spirit to the students.

More important, though, than the missionary spirit of the priests was the St. John's requirement that all students take a full complement of religion and philosophy courses. "All of us wound up with a minor in philosophy, not by choice, but by fiat," a former student says. They studied logic, epistemology, ontology, the history of philosophy, and ethics, including social ethics. Cuomo was especially fond of his ethics professor, Father Moynihan, an earthy but serious priest who taught ethics in a way that was readily understood by undergraduates. These courses instilled moral values in Cuomo more deeply than had his previous experiences. Students "were constantly exposed to the idea of what you owe to your fellowman," Mattone told me. Cuomo seems to have absorbed this concept to a greater extent than did many of his classmates. He emerged from St. John's with a large and growing social consciousness.

It was also at St. John's (the prep school as well as the college) that Cuomo was exposed to a structured study of the full theology behind his religion. Having attended public elementary school, he had not had an overflow of religious dogma poured into him at a very young age. By the time he was more fully exposed to Catholic theology, he was a bright and reflective young man who was able to raise questions, interact with the faith, and begin to work his own views into a way of life. "He always questioned, always asked. He would never just accept in a sheepish manner what the clergy said," Cuomo's brother-in-law Ted Vecchio recalls. "He was always very inquisitive in religion." It would be several years, however, before changes in the Church would make its doctrine fully compatible with the worldview that Cuomo was developing.[7]

It is significant that the Church hero with whom Mario Cuomo most identified was Thomas More, the English humanist of the late fifteenth- and early sixteenth-centuries who had been canonized in 1935. When he graduated from college, Cuomo won the Thomas More Scholarship to St. John's Law School. What especially impressed Cuomo was More's dedication and steadfastness, his refusal to deviate, even for the king or to keep his own head.

But Cuomo's fascination with More did not rest solely upon the English saint's willingness to face martyrdom rather than abandon his beliefs. There were several aspects of More with which Cuomo could readily identify. More was a brilliant scholar noted alike for his sense of humor and his piety. "From childhood he had such a love for witty jests that he seemed to have been sent into the world for the sole purpose of coining them," the Dutch humanist Desiderius Erasmus wrote of his friend More. "He never descends to buffoonery, but gravity and dignity were never made for him." While most of the English clergy during More's youth had adopted lives of comfort, More was attracted to those, such as the Carthusian monks, who practiced austere lives of fasting and prayer. He engaged in many of their practices and almost decided to enter the priesthood himself. "But," Erasmus relates, "as he found he could not overcome his desire for a wife, he decided to be a faithful husband rather than an unfaithful priest." "Nothing would have pleased him more," a recent biographer has written, "than to have been able to be a married priest." After his marriage, and despite the wealth available to him through most of his life, More continued to follow monastic austerities, including the wearing of a hair shirt beneath his outer clothing.

Cuomo could find many foreshadowings of his own life and beliefs in the career of Thomas More. The English saint was, for example, noted for his ability to mediate disputes and reconcile them in a manner that satisfied both sides. He knew, too, that the Church taught that all human endeavor was doomed and that good Christians should reject this world and concentrate instead on eternity. But he could not bring himself to follow this counsel. In his role as undersheriff of London, More saw extreme poverty and suffering and wanted to remedy it. His "charity was without bounds," a friend wrote, "as is proved by the frequent and abundant alms he poured without distinction among all unfortunate persons."

Thomas More is of course best known for his 1516 book *Utopia*. In it he portrayed an ideal society that merged Christian virtues with the social and political objectives of the Renaissance humanists. Although the inhabitants of More's imaginary island had never heard of Jesus, they practiced His teachings far more faithfully than did most of the Christians of Europe. The society of Utopia was based upon the family unit, and it operated in a cooperative fashion that made the entire community resemble a family.

King Henry VIII sought out More to serve him at the court. While More was well aware that the corruption and worldliness of the English monarchy were probably beyond cure, he accepted the position offered so as not to "forsake the commonwealth." Rather than reject the corrupted world, as a medieval monk would have, More saw it as his duty to do his best to improve the world to whatever extent proved possible. That which he could not turn to the good, More believed he was obliged to "so order that it be not very bad." Here was the kernel of Mario Cuomo's emerging view of what his religion required of him in this world.

In 1529 Henry appointed More as his chancellor, making him the first layman to hold that office. As a public official, More acted, Erasmus said, as one who "had been appointed public guardian of those in need." But More soon ran afoul of Henry VIII's growing conflict with the pope over the king's desire to have his marriage annulled. As a result of his refusal to take an oath required of English subjects by the Act of Succession, More was arrested in 1534 and beheaded a year later.

Mario Cuomo did not find the Catholic Church of his day to be in the corrupt state in which the Church of the Renaissance wallowed. But More's experience was instructive to him because he was wrestling with many of the same questions about the role of a Christian in this world that had confronted the English martyr. What most impressed Cuomo about More, he told me, was "his humanity, not his saintliness. We have plenty of saints—so many that we can afford to drop a few, like St. Christopher. But More was *human.*" More was "a man of great principle, and yet he didn't go rushing to meet death. He tried to keep his life *and* his principles. And that is evidence of humanity," Cuomo has said. "He got caught up in the ways of his world; sometimes he got compromised by it. In the end, he did the right thing, most of the time, in most people's estimate."

Here, to be sure, was "an appropriate symbol" for Mario Cuomo, whose goal is also to "do the right thing, most of the time," which he knows is the best an imperfect human can hope for.[8]

Thomas More's life provided the basis for the solution to Mario Cuomo's problem of acting within the world, but it took a modern Catholic thinker to convince the young New Yorker that God really wanted people to work to improve life on earth.

Cuomo first read Pierre Teilhard de Chardin's *The Divine Milieu* in 1960 or 1961. It was a revelation to him, if only in the sense that it provided striking confirmation for the direction in which his own thoughts had been moving for several years.

Teilhard was a French Jesuit geologist-paleontologist who attempted to reconcile his faith with the findings of modern science. By 1924 Teilhard's new vision of the universe got him into trouble with his religious superiors, who criticized him for "errors of theological interpretation" and barred him from teaching. He continued to work as a geologist in China. In 1951 he went to live in New York, where he persisted in writing about his views on the relationship between God and the physical universe. The Church continued to reject Teilhard's views, and his superiors placed new restrictions upon him in 1954. He died the following year, but his impact on Catholic thought was only in its early stages.

Teilhard began by not merely accepting the fact of evolution but by glorifying it and identifying it as God's plan. The whole universe, he insisted, is an evolution—a "genesis" rooted in the interconnectedness of the parts that compose the universe. There is, Teilhard argued, a necessary "mutual or reciprocal dependence" among the elements of the world. There is not, therefore, a separation between matter and spirit. Rather, they are "two distinct aspects of one single cosmic stuff."

Although his lifetime coincided with some of the worst horrors of the twentieth century, Teilhard was an incorrigible optimist. The evolution that he found in the world was one of progress toward the ideal perfection of God. Despite the existence of evil, he insisted, the world was moving in a positive direction. If the real world cannot be made ideal, Teilhard believed, it can be made more to *resemble* the ideal.

Teilhard's belief in the unity of God and the world led directly to his belief in the unity of humankind. He believed that the power that pulls the world on its upward path is the force of love. By love Teilhard meant sympathy with others and diminution of the self. When confronted with apparent evil, Teilhard looked for the saving, not the damning, element in others. The one sin that he would not tolerate was cynicism and disgust with life.

It was his notion that our work in the world was part of God's ongoing creation that allowed Teilhard de Chardin to reconcile science and religion. The vastness and marvels of the world discovered by scientists seemed to some people to make individual humans insignificant. Some observers preferred to reject the world and preserve their religious beliefs. Others came to worship the world to the neglect of God. Teilhard insisted that there is no contradiction between loving God and loving the world. Since we exist for God and the world exists for us, he contended, it follows that the world, through us, exists for God. It is therefore not only possible, but necessary, to combine a love of God with a love of the world.

After a reading of Teilhard de Chardin, the world suddenly looks very different from what it appeared to be in the Catholicism under which Mario Cuomo was raised. It is no longer simply a "fallen" place, a place of evil and temptations that must be avoided in order to achieve eternal salvation. Rather, it is something to be embraced and improved. It is worth remembering that Christians pray, "Thy will be done, on earth as it is in Heaven." It is *God's* world, not Satan's. God is to be served by working *in* His world, not by withdrawing from it or renouncing it. It made no sense, Teilhard pointed out, for followers of God to reject the work of the world and leave it to be done by the irreligious. Why should the work of the world not be done by those who would consciously do it with the intent of serving God?

"The will to succeed, a certain passionate delight in the work to be done," Teilhard wrote, "form an integral part of our creaturely fidelity." Cuomo must have loved this concept, with which he could readily and fully identify. It permitted him—indeed, encouraged him—to seek worldly success (so long as its purpose was to help others) while simultaneously serving his God. After exposure to Teilhard's analysis, Cuomo came to see public service, and eventually political leadership, as a Christian duty.

Cuomo has called Teilhard's message "a wonderful consolation to those of us who didn't want to think of the world as God's cruel challenge." The Jesuit showed, Cuomo said, that "God did not intend this world only as a test of our purity but, rather, as an expression of his love. That we are meant to live actively, intensely, totally in this world and, in so doing, to make it better for all whom we can touch, no matter how remotely."[9]

What Teilhard was doing was blending the traditional Catholic emphasis on good works with something of the Puritan ideal of serving God through one's calling and the Protestant social-gospel ideal of serving God by serving one's fellow human beings.

But Teilhard's concepts were not without precedent in Catholic thinking. They were actually a rebirth and modernization of the approach of St. Francis of Assisi in the early thirteenth century. Francis had come to understand that most of the dedicated religious people of his day were following the wrong path. Entering a monastery and renouncing the world is not the best way to serve God. This act of apparent self-denial is, in fact, a *selfish* act. Who is helped by the monk's withdrawal from the world? He takes his vows in order to save *himself*. This may be somewhat difficult for us to see, because of the value most of us place on physical comforts. But to a medieval monk, the only commodity of value to be obtained in this world was salvation, and in essence what he was saying was: "It's every man for himself. To hell with everyone else; I'm going to save myself."

St. Francis rejected what amounted to a pre-Darwin Darwinian approach to salvation. He and his Franciscan friars dedicated their religious lives to helping others. Like monks, the friars wanted to save their own souls, but they sought to do so by immersing themselves in the problems of the world, not by separating themselves from that world. To the friars, the world provides the context in which one works out his salvation.

Although Pierre Teilhard de Chardin urged the religious to accept a Darwinian view of the biological and physical world, he completely rejected a survival-of-the-fittest approach to either society or salvation. Instead, Teilhard prescribed something of a Franciscan approach to human relations for all of us. Mario Cuomo found this prescription to be most congenial. "Ours is not a faith," he declared in his 1984 speech at Notre Dame, "that encourages its believers to stand apart from the world, seeking their salvation alone, separate from the salvation of those around them."[10] Cuomo seems to have set for himself the goal of becoming a sort of secular St. Francis—a political friar.

Mario Cuomo was not alone in being affected by the ideas of Teilhard de Chardin. Angelo Giuseppe Roncalli, like Cuomo a Catholic of Italian parentage, had begun to see the relationship of the Church to the world in a way quite similar to Teilhard's conception. This exact contemporary (both were born in 1881) of the Jesuit paleontologist became Pope John XXIII three years after Teilhard's death. John XXIII's short reign as pope (1958–63), the most important in the modern history of the Church, combined with the ideas of Teilhard to give Cuomo his new outlook on how God wants us to fit into the world and what is expected of us.

Beginning as far back as the Council of Trent in the mid-sixteenth century, the Catholic Church had tied itself to the past by adopting a medieval worldview. The Church was seen in the way of a medieval castle that protected the faithful against the chaotic world outside the walls. The Church retreated further into its fortress mentality in the second half of the nineteenth century, when Pope Pius IX issued the *Syllabus of Errors* (1864). In this document the pope denounced science and rationalism and insisted that he as leader of the Church should not "reconcile and align himself with progress, liberalism, and modern civilization." In 1870 Pius IX convened the first ecumenical council of the Church since Trent, more than three centuries earlier. Rather than move toward any accommodation with modernity, though, the Vatican Council proclaimed the doctrine of papal infallibility.

In the decades following the death of Pius IX, the Catholic

Church did take some steps in the direction of recognizing the modern world and its social problems. In his 1891 encyclical *Rerum Novarum* (Of Modern Things), Pope Leo XIII expressly endorsed the right to private property, but indicated that unrestrained capitalism created vast social problems and that Christian employers must respect the dignity of their workers and not treat them as "chattels to make money by." The social ideas of *Rerum Novarum* were reaffirmed by Pius XI in his 1931 encyclical, *Quadragesimo Anno.*

Still, in the mid-twentieth century the Catholic Church was drastically out of touch with the modern world. There was little reason to expect that the seventy-seven-year-old John XXIII would alter that state of affairs, but he did.

John's intention was, he said in 1959, "to let fresh air into the Church." He did just that by boldly moving his Church into direct contact with the world and its social and international problems. John XXIII and the ecumenical council he convened in 1962, the Second Vatican Council (popularly known as Vatican II), said in essence that salvation was not to be found within the walls of the castle church, but outside among the poor banished children of Eve. They moved the Church out of its fortress and directed its concerns outward instead of inward. The narrow notion of a City of God separate from a contaminated City of Man was abandoned in favor of a mission for the Church to improve this world. The Church would no longer be an exclusive club. Instead, it "must bring Christ into the world." It "must follow man into the mud as well as the sky." Pope John believed that Christian values were relevant to the vast problems of the modern world.

The way for these changes was paved by Teilhard and other modern theologians whose ideas had not previously been welcomed by the Church. But John XXIII sensed the new spirit crying out for change and realized that the time was ripe for reform. The "progressive" churchmen who supported the pontiff at Vatican II tried to make the Church more catholic by making it less Roman. That is, they sought to make Christian values meaningful to people the world over. In order to accomplish this goal, the Church had to try to develop "diversity within unity" (a concept which, perhaps coincidentally, parallels Mario Cuomo's vision of American society as a "mosaic.")

Among the most fundamental shifts marked by Vatican II was the effort to turn the Church away from coercion and toward persuasion. While by no means complete, this alteration in course started the Church back toward what it had been in its first three centuries, when it won converts by the force of its message, not the power of the state. From the time of the conversion of Constantine up until modern times, however, the Church had generally depended upon governments and laws to enforce its doctrines. Vatican II recognized both that this was no longer possible in most secularized nations and that it had never been desirable. The values of Christianity must be adopted voluntarily if they are to be meaningful. Placing the sanction of the state behind religion perverts the religion. Colonial American dissenter Roger Williams put it best: "Forced religion stinks in God's nostrils."

Vatican II also liberalized and modernized the Church by making it less authoritarian. John XXIII called upon those in attendance to speak freely and practice "holy liberty." By the time the council ended in 1965, it had partially accommodated the Church to the modern concept of democracy by tempering its hierarchical authority and recasting the concept of the Church from a hierarchy of bishops into a community of clergy and lay people. Mario Cuomo was among those Catholics who took the expanded role for the laity seriously and welcomed it. "We are the Church, all of us together," he said in a 1986 interview.

In addition to calling the Second Vatican Council, Pope John XXIII revolutionized his Church's relationship with the world through two landmark encyclicals. In 1961 his *Mater et Magistra* (literally "Mother and Teacher," but known in English as "Christianity and Social Progress") continued down the road started upon by Leo XIII by stating that socialization for the common good was acceptable and calling upon the wealthier nations to share their resources with poor regions. More important was John's last encyclical, issued shortly before his death in 1963. *Pacem in Terris* (Peace on Earth) was the first papal encyclical in the Church's history to be addressed not just to Catholics but to "all men of good will." In this encyclical John called for a peaceful world based upon justice, liberty, democracy, and the protection of human rights.

The revolution John XXIII launched in the Catholic Church and in the influence of religious values on the world remained in its infancy when the pontiff died. "The Holy Father is only planting the seed, you know," said his secretary, Louis Capovilla, shortly before John's death. "He knows that somebody else will reap the harvest."

One of those who may reap the harvest was a thirty-year-old attorney in Brooklyn at the time of John's death. The dramatic changes in the Church that resulted from the efforts of John XXIII and Vatican II had a profound impact on Mario Cuomo. First, the direction in which Teilhard had pointed him was confirmed. A Catholic was now encouraged to involve him- or herself, as Cuomo has put it, in "the concerns of this world, rather than feeling that you had failed because you had not gone into a monastery to weave baskets to fill the uncomfortable interval between birth and eternity."

Cuomo saw Pope John XXIII, he told me, as a "round, jolly, living version of the ideas of Teilhard de Chardin." He was one of those, Cuomo said, "who makes me wonder why we don't pronounce the word 'Christ-ian.' He went back to the three years of Christ's work on earth and tried to restore the Church to those values. Prior to John, the Church was Jimmy Breslin's Church—girls not wearing patent leather shoes, constant worries about sex, prohibitions. John XXIII restored the Christianity of the Good Samaritan, of helping the prostitute and the leper."

More specifically John XXIII's *Pacem in Terris* contained two statements that seemed to speak directly to Cuomo and his developing philosophy. One declared the interdependence and unity of "the human family." The notion of a worldwide, inclusive "family" was in sharp contrast to the previous exclusive, fortress concept of the Catholic Church. It provided young Cuomo with an image for the way in which he, like Pope John, believed the world should operate. John also said that "the moral order" needs "public authority in order to promote the common good," and that such authority must be effective in attaining the common good. Here was an open invitation for Catholics to become socially concerned and to enter public service in order to work for the benefit of all people. It was an invitation that Mario Cuomo could not long decline.[11]

Over the years since Vatican II, Mario Cuomo's understanding of the proper relationship among religion, the secular world, and politics has continued to evolve. His deep religious commitment is the major basis of his progressive social philosophy. This makes him markedly different from most "liberals." Many of his policies and goals coincide with theirs, but he reached them along a very different route. "I think Mario slept through the sixties," his friend Jack Newfield told me. None of the events and upheavals of that decade that shaped the political beliefs of so many Americans seems to have had much of an impact on Cuomo. But his basic moral and religious values, crystalized by Teilhard and John XXIII, produced in him a social consciousness more profound than that of many liberals who trod the more usual path to their beliefs.

Cuomo's very different route to social consciousness enables him to make a much broader appeal than have secular liberals of the last two decades. While those sophisticates were looking down their noses at people who believed in God and worked for a living, the people they were rejecting were abandoning their traditional allegiance to the Democratic party and liberal social policy and being welcomed into a "holy" but unnatural alliance with conservative Republicans. The last progressive politician who was successful in appealing both to liberal intellectuals and religious, working-class ethnics was gunned down in the kitchen of a Los Angeles hotel in 1968. The religious basis of Mario Cuomo's liberal values makes him the first politician since Robert Kennedy who has a realistic chance of restoring the Democratic coalition.

The centrality of religion to Cuomo's value system should not be misinterpreted. He is by no means a religious fanatic. "Religion was not something that took over his life," Marie Cuomo Vecchio says of her brother. "It was *part* of his life." His religious views leave him tolerant of those who disagree with him, whether they be of another religious persuasion or without belief in the supernatural. "He has his standards, but he won't impose them on other people," Cuomo's friend Fabian Palomino says. Cuomo believes that it is the obligation of good people to become better and set an example that will help others to become better, too. Setting an example, not condemning others, is the way to improve the world. That is why he always holds himself to such a high standard. Cuomo firmly believes that only God has the infinite wisdom needed to judge people.

Here again he follows the lead of Pope John XXIII, who was always eager to communicate with "anyone who does not call himself a Christian but who really is so because he does good." Cuomo's is not the easy toleration of one who is indifferent to religious belief. It is the more difficult tolerance of one with firm beliefs who nevertheless is "respectful of all opinion on every subject of thought."

If Mario Cuomo is deeply religious without being a zealot, he is also a confirmed humanist without being "secular" in the sense that is so feared by fundamentalists. As did the intellectuals of the Northern Renaissance, such as Erasmus and More, Cuomo blends religion and humanism. For him religious belief directs his human concern.

He is spiritual without being other-worldly. Cuomo's conception of hell, he says, is "a place where there is nothing for you to believe in." "I mean, can you imagine," he asked me, "if you didn't feel like writing books; if you didn't feel like teaching; if you didn't give a damn about politics or *anything* else—there was *nothing* you really cared about?" Cuomo fears that many people in our society are already in a sort of hell-on-earth, and he does not mean just those who lack material comforts. "There's *nothing* they really care deeply about."

Cuomo's is a religion of persuasion, not coercion; of compassion, not condemnation; of seeking the good in people, not damning the evil in them; of love, not hate; of inclusion, not exclusion; of optimism, not pessimism. He echoes Teilhard and John when he says that we "are obliged by the commitment we share to help one another, everywhere, in all we do, and in the process, to help the whole human family. We see our mission to be 'the completion of the work of creation.' "

The New Catholicism of the post-Vatican II era is one that, as Cuomo sees it, has replaced guilt with an emphasis on responsibility and has "made negativism a sin." Cuomo's religion differs not only from the old Catholicism in which he was brought up, but even more sharply from that of the right-wing self-proclaimed Christians of today. "What some [fundamentalists] want is Christianity without the Sermon on the Mount," Cuomo contends. "They want Christianity without the prostitute that was forgiven. . . . They're forgetting that Christ never made a speech on abortion or birth control, but he made all kinds of speeches about taking care of the sinner, the penitent and the poor person, about sharing our goods with the rest of the world. Theirs is the most comfortable kind of Christianity—condemnatory Christianity."[12]

*　*　*

The New Catholicism is considerably less monolithic, absolutist, and coercive than the old, but there are still some dilemmas to be faced by Catholics who seek public office in pluralistic, secular states. No other Catholic politician has confronted these problems as directly as Mario Cuomo has. The basic question, he says, is "where private morality ends and public policy begins—how I involve myself in the political life of a world broad enough to include people who don't believe all the things I believe about God and conduct."

During the early stages of his political career, Cuomo was more willing to try to legislate private morality than he has been since the late seventies. During his 1974 campaign for the Democratic nomination for lieutenant governor, for example, Cuomo stated that "had he been a member of the Legislature he would have voted against the 1970 law that relaxed abortion curbs in the state." Such liberal friends as Janie Eisenberg argued with Cuomo for years before convincing him that abortion and homosexuality, while clearly moral issues, were matters of *private* morality that ought not to be dictated by the government. Eventually Cuomo concluded that this was the case and that the Church and its adherents should "teach by example rather than through legislation."

While this approach won Cuomo admirers among much of the non-Catholic public and the Catholic laity, it brought him into conflict with the leadership of his own Church. Cuomo's positions on such controversial subjects as abortion and homosexual rights are by no means unique among Catholic politicians. When he spoke at the Reverend Jerry Falwell's Liberty Baptist College in 1983, Senator Edward Kennedy took almost exactly the same stand as Cuomo on the proper relationship between religion and government action. Religious values should guide us in "questions which are inherently public in nature," Kennedy maintained. "The real transgression," the Massachusetts Democrat said, "occurs when religion wants government to tell citizens how to live uniquely personal parts of their lives." But the distinction may have been easier for Kennedy to make, since it would be generally conceded that he is less concerned with theological questions than is Cuomo. Cuomo takes Catholic moral teachings very seriously. Senator Daniel Patrick Moynihan also holds views similar to Cuomo's on matters of private morality. But "as a practical [as opposed to "practicing"] Catholic," Moynihan said with a grin in 1986, "I have made it my business not to know so much about Catholic doctrine that I know when I am in error."

It is not so easy for Mario Cuomo. He is more a practicing Catholic than a practical one. He *does* know a great deal about Catholic doctrine. There are in the political realm many nominal Catholics who have taken stands similar to Cuomo's as a matter of political convenience. The evidence strongly suggests that this is not the case with the governor of New York. He rarely if ever lets the popularity of a particular position determine his stand on an issue. He altered his positions on abortion and homosexual rights only after much soul-searching and careful theological reasoning.

Cuomo was absolutely serious when he said in 1984 that he cares more about his soul than his body. He has no desire for rebuke from the Catholic hierarchy. He could not have been pleased when John J. O'Connor, the new archbishop of the New York Archdiocese, arrived in 1984 and, after his first mass at St. Patrick's Cathedral, stepped up to Cuomo in a receiving line and said, "Mayor, I've always wanted to meet you."

"He's the mayor," Cuomo had to say, pointing to Ed Koch. "I'm the governor." There is no way to determine whether the archbishop's "error" was intentional.

In any case, it was not long before relations between New York's leading prelate and the state's governor deteriorated. Cuomo was upset when the Catholic bishops criticized the position that he and many other Catholic politicians had taken on abortion: that they are personally opposed to it but do not support legal prohibitions against it. Cuomo was more than upset in June 1984 when he sat with his wife and his son Christopher, who was fourteen at the time, watching Archbishop O'Connor being interviewed on television. "I do not see," the archbishop said, "how a Catholic in good conscience could vote for a candidate who explicitly supported abortion." This was disturbing, but expected. Then the interviewer asked O'Connor, "Don't you think we should excommunicate the governor?" The archbishop let the question linger for a moment and never flatly rejected the idea. Christopher Cuomo jumped up and started to cry, his mother told me. "What are you saying—excommunicate my father?" the boy exclaimed. "And Mario got so white, so pale, and he stands up and leaves the room," Matilda Cuomo recounts. "They hit us like a hammer in the head."[13]

When Mario Cuomo is hit in the head, he responds. As his wife said to herself right after the O'Connor interview, "Boy, did he pick on the wrong person." She seemed to mean that the governor is such a good Catholic that the Church should not single him out for criticism, but her statement applied in another sense as well. Cuomo was, in any case, upset by President Reagan and the right-wingers having seized the banner of religion for themselves. He wanted to make a general statement on the proper role of religion in public affairs, and he wanted to attack those religious leaders on the political right who were intruding directly in politics. Archbishop O'Connor's statements provided him with an opportunity to address all these issues and to do so most effectively by focusing his remarks on the hierarchy of his *own* Church, rather than on the Protestant fundamentalists. The latter would, of course, also receive criticism, but they would not be the featured target.

Whether entirely conscious and intentional or not, it was an ingenious strategy. By launching what a *New York Times* reporter called "an unusual challenge to the Catholic church by a Catholic politician," Cuomo was able to demonstrate to non-Catholics that while he was a faithful believer, his political positions were completely independent of the Church. At the same time, he made a forceful statement of his own views on the place of religious values in public life, scored several hits on Reagan and the fundamentalists, and went a long way toward reclaiming religious values for liberalism by placing his brand of positive, compassionate, inclusive religion in opposition to the right's negative, proscriptive, and exclusive type.

Cuomo began his offensive with an interview in the *Times* in August 1984. He could have ignored the archbishop's statement, as most other prochoice Catholic politicians were doing. Instead, the governor took a bold but calculated political risk by precipitating a debate with the hierarchy. "Cuomo is the first Catholic politician to pick a fight with a prelate," wrote columnist Mary McGrory. Not so long ago," she noted, "such an initiative on the part of a Catholic politician would have been nothing less than suicidal."

While Cuomo did "pick a fight with a prelate," it is important to note that he never made a personal attack on Archbishop, later Cardinal, O'Connor. The governor was hurt personally by O'Connor's attack. "When he's really doing what he thinks is the right thing and has to argue with the Church, I think it's a big drain on him," Frank Cuomo said of his brother. But those close to the governor all agree with his friend Peter Johnson, who said, "I have never heard him say an ill word about the cardinal."

In his interview with the *Times*, Cuomo charged that his church had become more "aggressively involved" in politics than ever before. The accuracy of this contention is open to question, but it is likely that Cuomo was actually warning of a general trend toward excessive intrusion of religious leaders into politics. His own church was not only the example with which he was most familiar, but the one that was safest for him to confront. He defended his position of personally opposing abortion but not demanding that others follow his position. "For me to preserve my right to be a Catholic means preserving your right to be a Jew," he said.

There was an immediate response from Archbishop O'Connor. He said that he had been misunderstood and was not telling anyone for whom they should or should not vote. The governor said he was "delighted to have the clarification."

But now that the subject had been broached, Cuomo wanted to make a full statement on religious belief and public morality. This he did in his widely praised address at Notre Dame in September 1984. "I accept the Church's teaching on abortion," Cuomo declared in that speech. "Must I insist you do?" His brilliantly argued answer was "No." Moral positions, he maintained, should only be enacted into law when there was "a consensus view of right and wrong . . . shared by the pluralistic community at large. Such a consensus for outlawing abortion plainly does not exist. In the face of vast public opposition, such laws even if enacted would not have the desired effect. "It would be 'Prohibition' revisited, legislating what couldn't be enforced and in the process creating a disrespect for law in general."

In any case, Cuomo pointed out, "the hard truth is that abortion isn't a failure of the government. No agency or department of government forces women to have abortions." The answer, he said, is to persuade people that it is wrong to abort their fetuses and to provide means that make it easier for them to carry their pregnancies to term. "Are we asking government to make criminal what we believe to be sinful because we ourselves can't stop committing the sin?" he asked.

At Notre Dame Cuomo contended that the decision on whether to try to enact into law "certain articles of our belief as part of public morality is not a matter of doctrine: it is a matter of prudential political judgement." He is a practical man. "The

Church's approach," Cuomo's friend John Gerity suggests, "is 'what *should* be,' and I think his approach is 'what *can* be.' . . . You can *aspire* to the ultimate, but you have to live what is accomplishable." Cuomo believes that society and individuals can be improved, but that you basically have to deal with people as they are, with their shortcomings.

The argument for a "practical idealism" or "progressive pragmatism" is attractive, but one of the examples Cuomo chose to illustrate his point was dubious. He cited the degree of public opposition to abolitionism as a justification for the failure of Catholic bishops to take a public stand against slavery before the Civil War. The bishops' silence on the issue of slavery was, he contended, "a measured attempt to balance moral truths against political realities."

Well. This comes perilously close to saying that if there is too much opposition to one's position on a moral issue, he or she has no obligation to take a public stand or attempt to right the wrong. That is not *progressive* pragmatism; it is crass pragmatism.

Mario Cuomo's case for the proper relationship between religious values and public policy is, for the most part, extremely persuasive. But the abortion question remains the chief sticking point. The issue can readily be linked with that of capital punishment, which Cuomo, along with his Church, opposes, but which a substantial majority of the people of his state and the nation as a whole supports. Cuomo himself never places his opposition to the death penalty on moral or religious grounds. Instead, he stresses practical reasons for opposing it. But the possible connection to the abortion question remains, and it is a dangerous linkage. "We must keep in mind always that we are a nation of laws," Cuomo told his Notre Dame audience, "—when we like those laws, and when we don't." But where would this leave the governor if the New York legislature ever passed a capital punishment law over his veto? Would he then be obligated to carry out death sentences in accordance with the law, even though he personally opposed the law? If he did not, could he justly be accused of protecting the lives of the guilty but not the lives of the innocent?

There is the key point in the whole abortion controversy: the *lives* of the innocent. The entire issue revolves around one question: is a fetus a living human being? If it is not, then there is no problem justifying abortion. If, however, it is once accepted that an unborn child *is* a human life, all the pragmatic arguments go out the window. Then abortion is murder, and the obligation of the government to try to prevent that crime is clear. "It is absurd to say," Bishop James W. Malone, then president of the National Conference of Catholic Bishops, pointed out in 1984, "I am personally against murder, but I will not impose my views on anyone else."

Governor Cuomo tries to avoid the fundamental question of the humanity of a fetus. When reporter Ken Auletta pressed him hard for an answer late in 1984, Cuomo finally said, "I have to conclude that the fetus is life or so close to life that it ought not to be disposed of casually." That leaves him on thin ice. He much prefers to say that a determination of when a new human being begins is a religious question that can never be satisfactorily answered. This position of doubt makes the "I believe it's wrong, but I won't impose my views on you" approach tenable; indeed, it makes it the only sensible stance. The commonsense solution toward which Cuomo—and much of the American public—seems to be drifting is that since it is clear on the one hand that a newly fertilized egg is only a *potential* human and, on the other, that an unborn child in the later months of pregnancy is wholly human, early abortions should be left a matter of private morality, but later ones rightly fall within the scope of public policy.[14]

                           The conflict between Governor Cuomo and the Archdiocese of New York continued to simmer after 1984. In September 1986 the vicar general, Bishop Joseph T. O'Keefe, issued a directive to pastors in the archdiocese warning them to avoid inviting to their parishes speakers whose "public position is contrary to and in opposition to the clear and unambiguous teaching of the Church." Cuomo saw this as a retreat from the "holy liberty" of Vatican II—as well as a possible attempt to silence him—and publicly protested the "restraint of intellectual activity." "We lay people have a right to be heard," the governor said. Cardinal O'Connor supported his vicar general. "People get confused," he said, "when someone who's well known for disagreeing with the Church in a substantive matter, not an insignificant matter, is given a platform."

Although both the vicar general and the cardinal said that the ban had not been aimed at Cuomo, both responded angrily to his comments on the directive. Some of the governor's friends have suggested that the reason O'Connor has been so vehement in his opposition to Cuomo is that he "has the wrong name." "Why are the searchlights on Governor Cuomo, who happens to be Italian," asks Notre Dame theologian Reverend Richard P. McBrien, "and were never put on Governor Carey, who not only had the same agenda but married outside the Church?"

The possibility of ethnic bias (which in the hierarchy's bitter denunciations of 1984 Democratic vice presidential candidate Geraldine Ferraro may have combined with gender bias) on the part of Irish prelates should not be dismissed, but there is a larger reason for the singling out of Cuomo for attack: his intellectual brilliance and theological knowledge. A weak and unworthy foe is more easily tolerated than a formidable one. Cuomo is "so smart he would confuse young people," Bishop O'Keefe said, declaring that he would never invite the governor to address a graduation. Cuomo's nuanced views would, the vicar general said, be likely to confuse the faithful.

For his part, Cuomo continues to assert his loyalty to the teachings of the Church but to defend the right of dissent. "How, after all," he asked rhetorically in an October 1986 speech at the Cathedral of St. James in Brooklyn (which is not part of the Archdiocese of New York), "has the Church changed and developed through the centuries except through discussion and argument?"[15]

It is impossible even to begin to understand Mario Cuomo without a careful examination of his religious beliefs. From an early age his inquisitive mind sought explanations—the world had to "make sense." For a time the Baltimore Catechism provided sufficient answers, but as Cuomo grew older, he needed the changes brought to his religion by Teilhard de Chardin, John XXIII, and Vatican II to reconcile his own inner drive and desire to participate in the affairs of the world with his need to serve his God.

It is trite, but nonetheless true, that Mario Cuomo is an exceedingly complex person. On one level he is much like other success-oriented people. He wants to advance himself and his career. But his idea of success has little to do with money or material rewards. And because of his deep religious convictions, the goal of personal success in any form is unacceptable as a motive. He is never able to feel ectasy in a moment of victory. "When the news is best, the applause the loudest," he noted in his diary in 1982, "—my throttle slows things down. . . . I seem incapable of enjoying it [victory] the way people expect me to. In the moments that seem right for exultation, my head turns to analysis."

" 'Selfish.' That's the word," Cuomo wrote in a 1980 diary entry. "As long as you think about what *you* need, *you* want, *you* feel—as long as you are selfish—you are doomed to frustration. 'Me' is a bottomless pit which cannot be filled no matter how much in achievement, glory, acclaim, you try shoveling into it." "For God's sake," he lectured himself, "you know the truth! The truth is that the only way to make anything of your life is to be what you know you're supposed to be."

Cuomo does not, his friend Joe Mattone says, "wear a big cross on his chest and say, 'I'm here to save the world.' " But he always has to believe that he is doing good in order to justify his doing well.

In this religiously based desire to dedicate his life to helping others rather than advancing himself is to be found the most important, although probably unconscious, reason why Cuomo decided in 1987 not actively to seek the presidency. To those who do not understand Cuomo, his seeming position that he would not seek the presidency, but would let it seek him, appears to be the height of vanity. In fact, it is just the opposite. Cuomo is always troubled by the possibility that he might be doing something for selfish reasons. If he *sought* the presidency, how could he ever be sure that he was doing it for the right reasons, that it was not an ego trip? "The worst sin," he told Anthony Lewis in a 1986 interview, "would be going [for the presidency] because I need it: 'Look, Mama!' "[16]

Note that Cuomo, typically, used the term "sin." Seeking the presidency to gratify personal ambition might constitute the cardinal sin of pride. But if the nation came to him and said it *needed* him, then it would be clear to him that he was pursuing the public good, not the advancement of his own ego.

As he said, "old-fashioned Catholic guilt is the absolute best. It ruins everything."

4

COMPETITOR

IF his deep religious values are the primary component of the complex personality that is Mario Cuomo, the second most obvious feature is his fierce competitive spirit. Like his religiosity, Cuomo's competitiveness has been a part of him from an early age. Ever since his childhood Cuomo has had a love for contest and for winning. "Mario Cuomo is the kind of guy that has to win; he can't lose," Nicholas Sallese says of his former student. "He always hated to lose and had a great desire for competition and winning," agrees Judge James Starkey, a Cuomo friend since college.

A passionate desire to win can easily come into conflict with the obligation to serve one's fellow human beings. Realizing this, at least intuitively, Cuomo has never been able to savor triumphs as fully as might be expected of one who so much desired to win. Victory was always sweeter in the anticipation than it was in the actuality. Winning solely for the self was unacceptable for someone also motivated by the religious duty to exist for the benefit of others. Hence the achievement of victory, so passionately desired, brought with it feelings of guilt. *Washington Post* writer Paul Taylor was not far from the mark when he suggested that Cuomo is composed "of equal parts hubris and guilt."[1]

Much of the first four decades of Mario Cuomo's life can be seen as an attempt to reconcile his values with his love of winning.

A feature of Cuomo's love of competition is his enjoyment of being in the role of underdog. A contest must be tough for him to enjoy it. There is no delight to be found in defeating an unworthy opponent. The greater the odds to be overcome, the better. This trait was visible when Cuomo was a boy. His aforementioned desire to play with his older brother and his friends amounted, at least in part, to a quest for stiffer competition.

Competition was a means to self-improvement. Although an opponent was needed, Cuomo's basic competition has always been with himself. From an early age he has been a compulsive achiever. Meeting difficult challenges was a way to perfect himself. Games and sports provided the major arena for Cuomo's youthful competition, but his quest for personal betterment through overcoming challenges took many forms. A book could become an opponent to be conquered. As in any other type of contest, the greater the competition, the better. "I loved thick books with little, dark print," he told me. "You think you're going to discourage me?"

It was never easy—if at all possible—to discourage Mario Cuomo. *Fortitude* is one of the four cardinal virtues. "He has the knack of not giving up," St. John's basketball coach Lou Carnesecca, who coached Cuomo in freshman baseball and was a referee in intramural basketball games in which the future governor participated, told me. "He's a very strong-willed person. He's not gonna yield too much to pressure," Carnesecca rightly said. "He has the ability to get out of himself more than anyone else."

The children in Cuomo's polyglot neighborhood learned to play ball before they learned to speak each other's languages. "We just played ball; we didn't have to talk much," recalls Artie Foster, Cuomo's boyhood friend. Cuomo's love of contest grew rapidly, and his talent at baseball and basketball was soon evident.

"He always wanted to win," Foster said of his childhood buddy. "So did we all. But that was the way we played—no sense horsing around—why not win?" Foster said that Cuomo's competitiveness was especially evident on the basketball court. "You dive in, jump for the ball—that's where you can see someone who is really competitive." Foster said Cuomo "was solid" and would "use his bulk to get in" to the basket. "Sometimes," Foster related, "I thought he was a little too pushy, but always competitive."

Cuomo found another attraction in sports: escape. Playing games occupied the mind. "To play ball," he recalled years later, "was to suspend for a while the arduous and frustrating task of looking into every situation for some ultimate purpose. It was to use all of one's strength, all of one's being, in a single exciting episode—the game, which had a beginning, a middle and an end, all in one day—and for as long as it lasted, there was no need and little temptation to puzzle about deeper meanings."[2]

Cuomo had both talent and the desire to compete before he entered an organized sports program, but the man most responsible for developing young Cuomo's athletic skills and nurturing his competitiveness was Joe Austin. Austin is a South Jamacia resident who worked for the Piel's Brewing Company and devoted his life to building youngsters' character through sports. Mike Lee, a local sportswriter, dubbed Austin "a one-man athletic association." Austin "does more actually every day for youngsters regardless of race, color, or creed, than anyone else in Queens," Lee wrote in 1949. "If you're a boy and want to play baseball [in the spring and summer] or basketball during the fall and winter, Joe asks nothing other than [that] you follow orders and work as a team player—and most of the expense for equipment, uniforms, etc., comes out of Joe's modest pocket."

During the late 1930s and the 1940s, at a time when most whites were just beginning to become aware, through the accomplishments of such superb athletes as Jesse Owens and Joe Louis, of the fact that blacks could compete successfully with whites in sporting events (and when most whites were not eager to see that happen), Joe Austin was developing young baseball and basketball players of all races and ethnic backgrounds in South Jamaica. "There was one fellow in Queens County," noted a 1950 sports column on the success of black Brooklyn Dodgers Jackie Robinson and Roy Campanella, "who, most of the time at his own expense, with no publicity, chose players for their ability, not their color. . . . a man who rendered more than lip service to their race."

Mario Cuomo played on the Austin Celtics in both baseball and basketball for about six years. "Whatever good happened to me," Cuomo wrote in 1964, "I'm aware of the debt I owe Joe because the hard competitiveness and principles of fair play that he always tried to instill are as much a part of his alumni as any of the training they received at home or at school." "This guy really helped him—made him a ballplayer," Frank Cuomo says of Austin's impact on his brother. Cuomo never forgets what Austin did for him and other kids from the area. In 1964, when Cuomo was a young lawyer, Austin was hospitalized for an operation. Cuomo heard about it, Austin told me, and sent him a personal check for a hundred dollars. Since Cuomo has reached high office, he has invited Austin and some of his former teammates to several social functions.

Cuomo's desire to compete was insatiable. While an undergraduate at St. John's, he showed up at ten-thirty in the morning for a Celtics game that wasn't scheduled to begin until one in the afternoon. "I was up all night studying for an exam," he explained to Austin, "and if I went to bed now, I wouldn't have gotten to the game."

Once the Celtics basketball squad won a game with only four players. One of them was listed in the box score as "Matt Dente." It turns out that this was actually Cuomo. In order to play as much as possible, Cuomo played under different names for different teams. Using such aliases as Glendy La Duke and Lava Libretti, as well as Matt Dente, Cuomo displayed his baseball and basketball talents in a variety of leagues.

He played during the early fifties against top-flight basketball competition. His team enjoyed certain advantages when playing at home. These included "their" timekeeper and "their" referees. With their man controlling the game clock, the final minute of a game could go on for a near eternity if the home team was behind. Cuomo recalls a game against a team that included a fellow who was six feet four inches tall and one of the best college players in the country until he was implicated in the point-shaving scandals of the early fifties. The game was played on Cuomo's team's home court, with their referees. Cuomo was guarding the former college star, and in the process, he said: "I hit him, I kneed him, I clawed him, I tackled him—I did everything short of indictable assault, and I wasn't very far from that. But 'our' ref didn't call any fouls on me. Instead, he kept calling them on the other guy. I think he had called four on him by late in the first half. Finally we were standing next to each other when somebody else was shooting a foul and this guy turned to the official and yelled, 'Hey, ref, aren't you gonna call another foul on me?' 'Why?' the ref asked. 'Because I'm perspiring all over this SOB Cuomo!' "[3]

During his first two years at St. John's Prep, Cuomo concentrated on his studies and participated only in intramural athletics. There was plenty of competition available even on that level. St. John's emphasized physical fitness. "The school offered every kind of intramural sport, from basketball to Ping-Pong," recalls Cuomo's classmate Joe Mattone. "And everybody in the school had to climb twenty-foot ropes in the gym, no matter who you were—unless you had a letter from your doctor excusing you."

After Father Cotter suggested that he try out for the varsity basketball and baseball teams in his junior year, Cuomo quickly demonstrated his ability to play on the interscholastic level. He was a frequently used substitute in basketball and a standout outfielder in baseball. During his senior year the "Little Redmen" finished third in the Metropolitan Catholic High School basketball tournament. Prior to the final game, the St. John's coach chose another player to represent the school in the halftime foul-shooting contest. But when the time came, the coach indicated a bit of indecision. Cuomo saw his chance and leapt up to volunteer. In the contest he made thirteen of fifteen shots to win the 1949 *Brooklyn Eagle* trophy.

In the spring of 1949, St. John's Prep won the baseball championship of the Brooklyn Catholic High School Athletic Association. Mario Cuomo hit .350 for the Little Redmen that season and was chosen as the second team left fielder on the All-Brooklyn CHSAA All-Stars.

When Cuomo moved across the street to St. John's College the following year, it was on an academic, not an athletic scholarship. He always had an underlying desire to be a star athlete, but he was never a "jock" in the popular usage of that term. The fact that his scholarship was not tied to participation in sports was to be important in giving Cuomo the freedom to do what he wanted with both his academic and his athletic careers.

Cuomo's competitive spirit was evident at other St. John's campus locations in addition to the gym and the ball fields. A fad swept the campus while he was there of playing an Italian game called *amore.* It was played by two people, each of whom would cast out a number of fingers. Each contestant would guess what the total number of fingers would be, and shout out his guess. If one player thought the other would put out two fingers, he might cast out three fingers and yell *"Cinque!"* Cuomo and his friends were in the habit of noisily playing this game in front of the cafeteria. They liked to dominate the scene, which they usually did.

Cuomo was adept at throwing fingers out part of the way. If a player put out two fingers all the way and another part of the way, he could claim to have had either two or three out. He would

shout either "I had that *out!*" or "I had that *in!*"—whichever would
make him the winner. This was standard procedure on the part of
those who played the game to win, and Cuomo was one of the best
at the half-finger trick. The game became so popular that leagues
were organized. Cuomo made the finals in one league, but was
defeated by another student, Nick Siletti. Mario refused to admit
that he had lost. "No, no, you cheated," he insisted.

Although Cuomo was not a scholarship athlete, hopes were
high that he would become a valuable addition to the first-class
sports program at the college. Those hopes were never realized.

Opinions differ on whether Cuomo would have made the freshman basketball team at St. John's. He surely intended to try, but
his way was blocked when he broke his wrist shortly before try-
outs began. Thereafter, he confined his collegiate basketball to
intramural leagues. It must be understood, however, that the nature of intramural basketball at St. John's was markedly different
from what it was at most colleges. Cuomo had no difficulty finding
worthy competition. The number of first-rate basketball players
who entered St. John's greatly exceeded the capacity of the varsity
squad, which was among the best in the nation. It was no disgrace
not to make the varsity. "St. John's was such a powerhouse in
basketball," in the only slightly exaggerated view of Cuomo buddy
Nick D'Arienzo, "that there were many people who were not on
the team who probably could have made any other college basketball team." St. John's intramural director Anthony Sarno agrees:
"I had an intramural program that had more varsity potential than
a lot of colleges get in a lifetime. . . . We put on a good show, and
it was very popular, because the students realized that at any other
school these fellows would have been on the varsity."

The intramural games were played in the college gym at noon.
Students took them very seriously. In order to play one had either
to go without lunch or swallow it all in a couple of bites. Most of
the players competed with a high level of intensity, none more so
than Mario Cuomo. Everyone who played in or watched the intramural basketball games has a story to illustrate Cuomo's furious
competitive nature. "I remember him in intramurals," Lou Carnesecca told me. "Oh, God Almighty. You couldn't take him prisoner. He was that kind of a guy." Sallese remembers watching
Cuomo battle "almost to the point of fisticuffs" with Carnesecca
over a call the latter had made as referee.

Jim Starkey's introduction to Mario Cuomo came on the intramural basketball court. Cuomo's team got a rebound and started a fast break down the court. Starkey picked out an opposing player to try to block. It was Cuomo, and he kept coming at Starkey at full speed. "I realized that this guy was determined to get to the basket, and he was *going* to get to the basket, whether he had to go over me, through me, or any other way," Starkey told me. "I decided to get out of the way. But that's indicative of how Cuomo was: determined, single-minded, competitive, with a great desire to win."

"He was a competitor—a very *stiff* competitor," Nick Sallese recalls. "He was not averse to giving you the knee or the elbow, or sticking out the foot for you to trip over." "You didn't fool around with Mario," Tony Sarno says. "He got you under the boards in basketball and you hadda compete with him. He's some kind of man. He had that *strong* determination." Wherever there was a contest, Cuomo competed all-out. He played a "skins versus shirts" basketball game "like his life depended on the outcome."

Cuomo used sports as a way to "blow off steam." The more intensely he played, the more completely that goal could be accomplished. Once during his senior year, he played a lunch-period intramural game that ran so late that he decided not to shower or change before class, but just put on his senior academic gown over his shorts. He was caught by one of the priests, who did not approve of such attire.

In his senior year Cuomo's team, the Shafts, finished second in the Intramural Invitation Tournament and he was named one of the top three intramural all-stars.[4]

Cuomo's wrist healed in time for him to play on the freshman baseball team. He had an excellent season in the spring of 1950, batting .360 and playing an outstanding defensive game in the outfield. He was expected to become a mainstay on the varsity nine the next year, although a sophomore- and junior-studded St. John's team had made it to the College World Series the year before. Coach Frank McGuire needed a catcher, and he decided that Mario Cuomo was well suited to work behind the plate. McGuire had another player in mind for center field. The obstinate Cuomo had a different opinion. "*Nobody* can talk him into doing *anything—no*body," his brother Frank testifies. Cuomo still hoped to be the next Joe DiMaggio, and one could hardly play that role with a mask and a chest protector. "He thought it would be a disservice to himself and to the team, 'cause he wasn't a catcher," Carnesecca says.

When McGuire had two close friends trying to make the team, he followed a practice whereby they would either both make it or both be dropped. Cuomo was not aware of this policy, and when he threatened to quit, he was startled by McGuire's response.

"You're going to quit?" the coach said.

"Yeah. I'm not going to break my fingers trying to catch."

"Well, I understand that Joe Repice is your friend."

"Yeah, what of it?" Mario asked.

"Well, if you quit, I'm going to drop him from the team," McGuire told him.

Cuomo's sense of justice was outraged. "How could you? I have an option to quit. You're punishing my friend for nothing, because you can't get your way with me. That's a helluva thing to do."

McGuire called Repice over and told him the situation. "Your friend Cuomo wants to quit. I told him I didn't want him to do it."

Repice discussed the situation with Cuomo. They agreed that they were both outfielders and would either make the team as such or not play at all. "Screw him; I'll quit, too," Repice said.

McGuire was not about to start letting players tell him where they would and would not play. The coach reiterated his demand that Cuomo catch. "The hell with that," the strong-willed sophomore said. "I'm not catching." According to some accounts, Cuomo proceeded to tell McGuire what he could do with his catcher's mitt.

Within a few weeks it was evident that Cuomo's not playing for the St. John's varsity was the team's loss, not his. "As the schedule progressed," wrote a sports columnist for the St. John's campus newspaper, *The Torch*, "it became apparent to most observers—at least to this one—that a Cuomo with one arm was a distinct improvement over the present outfield." Cuomo's outstanding season for the Austin Celtics in the summer of 1951 (when he was a unanimous choice for the Queens Alliance All-Star team) attracted the attention of Ed McCarrick, a scout for the Pittsburgh Pirates. In August Cuomo was offered a bonus to sign a contract with the Pirates organization. It was an offer the single-minded nineteen-year-old DiMaggio fan could not refuse, a dream come true.

But the scout and the Pirates officials were not the only ones who needed to be convinced that major-league baseball was Mario

Cuomo's destiny. By this time he and Matilda Raffa were keeping serious company. After a date one night several months before, when they were, at least in Matilda's opinion, not yet serious about each other, they had had a conversation on the Raffa stoop before she went inside. Mario told her that he loved baseball. "I remember the look on his face," Mrs. Cuomo told me, "when I said I'd never marry a baseball player. He looked at me with this funny look, as if I'd slapped him."

Baseball players in the early 1950s could become heroes to young boys across the nation, but none of them counted their salaries in the millions and few made even a respectable living. And then there was the travel, particularly in the minor leagues. It was an idyll that Matilda Raffa failed to appreciate. "What girl wanting a family would marry someone like this?" she asked rhetorically. "It'd be like marrying a nomad—it would be so unstable."

Convincing Matilda that he could love both baseball and her— and that she could learn to live with both baseball and him—was only part of Mario's problem. The other difficulty was his parents. Immaculata Cuomo was afraid that Mario might hurt himself, but her objections were only minor. Her husband was another matter. "Pop, I've got a chance to play professional ball," Mario told his father. Andrea Cuomo was less than impressed. Playing games was all right for kids, but that was not what he had in mind as a career for his brilliant son. Was *this* what he had sent him to school for? Andrea would not agree to Mario's signing.

Mario was downcast, but an aspect of his competitive spirit is, as Carnesecca puts it, his "stick-to-itiveness." He will not give up. A family friend talked to Andrea and told him what a great opportunity it was for Mario. The father relented, but only on the condition that professional baseball not interfere with his son's education. Pirates general manager Branch Rickey praised the senior Cuomo for his stance and made a commitment that Mario would train and play only during school vacations until he had completed his degree.

The deal was concluded at Cuomo's grocery store in August 1951. "In order to beat the morning rush of business," McCarrick said, "the signing took place in the room in the back of the store." There, at a little table with provolones and salamis hanging from the ceiling above, Mario Cuomo signed a contract to play for the Pirates' Salisbury team in the Class D North Carolina State

League. The two-thousand-dollar bonus he received for signing
eventually found its way to Matilda Raffa's ring finger, where it
still resides.[5]

                                    Cuomo spent ten days at the Pi-
rates' spring training camp in De Land, Florida, during the St.
John's spring break in 1952. At the end of the semester, he reported
to the Brunswick (Georgia) Pirates of the Class D Georgia-Florida
League. At that time scout McCarrick sent an assessment of
Cuomo to the Brunswick manager, Mickey O'Neil. Several weeks
later McCarrick sent Branch Rickey a three-page report on the
organization's prospects on the Brunswick team. McCarrick's two
reports contained several perceptive observations on Mario
Cuomo's personality, as well as his athletic abilities.

McCarrick began his report to the Brunswick manager with an
evaluation of the new player's physical abilities: "I think Cuomo
has the tools to go all the way if the best can be brought out in him.
He runs very well and should steal a lot of bases. His arm is average
major league and he can cover a lot of ground in the outfield. He
has fine power and is very strong physically. . . . He is a fine hustler
and competitor."

Far more intriguing was Ed McCarrick's analysis of Mario
Cuomo as a person. "If he lacks anything, it is a realization on his
own part of the fine potential he has," the scout stated. "Sometimes, I think he has a slight inferiority complex and needs to be
told frequently that he has the goods." "Like all bright fellows,"
McCarrick continued, "he is sometimes moody and different than
the ordinary person. It takes some time to get his confidence and
to know the warmth that is in him. When you break through that
barrier, I'm sure you will like him very much."

In his July report to Rickey, McCarrick called young Cuomo
"potentially the best prospect on the club" and said he "could go
all the way if he improves his hitting to the point of a respectable
batting average. He is aggressive and plays hard." "He is not an
easy chap to get close to," McCarrick noted, "but [he] is very well
liked by those who succeed in penetrating the exterior shell."
Cuomo was the sort, the scout added, "who will run you over if
you get in his way."

Ed McCarrick's job was to assess baseball talent, but it is obvious that he was a sagacious judge of the whole person. His discern-

ing insights about Mario Cuomo stand the test of time. There can be little doubt that Cuomo's consuming desire to win stems at least in part from "a slight inferiority complex," however unjustified such a feeling may be. The real opponent in all his competition is himself—or his self-image. "I think he had an intense competitive spirit," Bernie Babb told me, "but most of the time he was competing against himself, striving for perfection. He's so intense about *every* thing he does." Several of his friends labeled Cuomo a "perfectionist," one who "always gives a hundred ten percent," and "got the most out of his talent."

A person with some self-doubts seeks periodic, if not constant, reinforcement. He "needs to be told frequently that he has the goods." One seeming way to overcome self-doubt is to engage in contest after contest, proving your worth time and time again. The physical opponent that one runs over if he gets in the way represents internal doubts that must be mentally run over whenever *they* get in the way. Victory over external competitors can be a way of beating back the internal demons, whatever their source, that lurk within us.[6]

"For a couple of months I was in heaven," Cuomo has said of his season in the minor leagues. In his first game he went one for three, with a run scored. The occasion was marred only by the local paper listing him in the box score the following day as "Buomo." The typesetter was more successful in the descriptive account of the twi-night doubleheader: "Matt [they were, it will be remembered, in a region where there weren't many Marios] Cuomo made his first appearance with the Pirates last night. The new center fielder held down the garden spot in good fashion. He made one especially outstanding catch in the opening game." Shortly thereafter, the *Brunswick News* reported that "Matt Cuomo seems to be rounding out in pretty good fashion. The new Brunswick centerfielder covers the middle section of the garden unusually well and he proved on a couple of occasions last night that he has a mighty good throwing arm." Cuomo went three for nine in his first three games.

"Matt" Cuomo's reputation as an aggressive, hotheaded young ballplayer was soon confirmed in Georgia. An umpire threw Cuomo out of one of his early games for arguing a double-play call. The new center fielder apparently did not take into consideration that his ejection could have been most costly to the team, which was shorthanded at the time. Late in June the catcher for the Albany Cardinals blocked Cuomo from the plate and tagged him out as he tried to score. Cuomo's temper flared and he suggested to the opposing player that they meet in private that night or the next morning, to settle their differences. It was presumed that the future attorney had in mind something other than a meeting of the minds, and the catcher offered to duke it out with Cuomo right after the game. Fortunately both young men had cooled off by that time. After singling in an August game, Cuomo called time and returned to argue with the plate umpire, who promptly ejected the New Yorker. Accounts of the incident varied, but Cuomo maintained that the umpire had verbally abused him while he was at bat and he had returned to object.

The most notorious flare-up of Cuomo's temper in the 1952 baseball season came in a game in Tifton. While Cuomo was at bat, the opposing catcher uttered an ethnic slur. Cuomo was so angry that he swirled around and punched the catcher. The only problem was that the catcher was still wearing his mask. The only resultant damage was the assailant's bruised knuckles. "That's not hot-tempered," the governor said more than three decades later, "—that's stupid."[7]

Cuomo's professional baseball career seemed to be off to a great start. He was hitting .353 in mid-season and had just been slated to move up to a Class B team. The night before he was to leave the Brunswick club, Cuomo crashed into the outfield fence while trying to catch a fly ball. He tried to continue playing but finally doubled up on the field. A doctor worked on him for fifteen or twenty minutes, and he was able to leave the park under his own power.

He was back in the lineup a few days later, but he had injured his wrist and was unable to hold the bat right. The club management told him that he had to play anyway, because his batting average did not matter. It was game experience that he needed. The injury resulted in a drastic drop in his average.

Bouncing one's head off the wall is not advisable, but Mario Cuomo's cranium was to suffer worse abuse before the 1952 Georgia-Florida League season had gone much further.

Although not yet engaged, Mario and Matilda were very serious by the time he left for Georgia. She was wearing his ring on a chain, but she was somewhat worried about his going so far away. She wrote to him every day, but went several weeks without receiving a letter in return. The Raffas were staying at their summer home at Lake Hopatcong, New Jersey, and Matilda would go all the way to the post office every day, only to be disappointed. "I'll never see him again! I'll never go out with him again!" she cried to her mother and younger sister and brother.

One morning Matilda's mother came down and told her that she had had a dream about Mario the night before. "There's a good reason why he's not writing to you," Mary Raffa told her daughter. "A ball hit his head. I saw him [in my dream] hit his head and the ambulance came. They put him on a stretcher. He's in the hospital."

"Oh, come on, Ma," Matilda said, "You don't have to go out of your way to make up excuses for him." Mrs. Raffa had liked Mario right from the start, and was "always in his corner," Matilda explained to me.

An hour or two later, the long-awaited letter from Georgia arrived. Mario had indeed been struck directly in the head by a fastball and knocked unconscious. Baseball players did not wear batting helmets in those days. He had to be removed from the field on a stretcher, and was hospitalized for a couple of weeks and unable to play for nearly a month. How his future mother-in-law, who spoke little English, probably did not know where Georgia was, and knew nothing about baseball, could have had this vision is one of the things that Cuomo told me he doesn't understand and would rather not think much about.

The beanball had produced a blood clot that gave Cuomo piercing headaches that persisted through his years in law school and into his early days of practicing law. The clot finally dissolved, and he has had no trouble from it for about thirty years.

When Andrea Cuomo heard of the accident, he said, "I no senda you to college to play baseball. You go to law school." While his father's opinion was of some importance to him, Mario Cuomo was noted for his obstinacy. He would make up his own mind about his career.

Cuomo wanted to carry on with his professional baseball career, but a doctor told him that if he were hit again, there was a good chance that he would not recover. There were other considerations as well. Young Miss Raffa still did not aspire to become a baseball wife—or a widow. In any case, after his season had been interrupted by his crashing into the fence, Cuomo had been something less than awe-inspiring at the plate. Another Joe Di-Maggio he no longer seemed likely to be. He had not yet learned how to hit a good curve ball. After his hot start Cuomo's batting average plummeted in the wake of his wrist injury. In 81 games for the season as a whole, Cuomo wound up batting .244, with 10 doubles, 10 triples, 1 home run, and 26 runs batted in. In 254 at-bats, he struck out 56 times. These statistics were hardly glamorous, but Cuomo was an excellent fielder and base runner, and there was hope that he could regain his preinjury batting form. The Pittsburgh organization still considered him to be a good prospect. Management wanted to move him up in the minor-league system, and assigned him to Waco, Texas, for the 1953 season.

There was, finally, the growing realization on Cuomo's part that while baseball could answer his desire for competition, it could not meet his other requirements. "I guess I never really wanted to play baseball badly enough to make good," he told me. "It was fun, but I needed something more." Of course there was team spirit, but it was increasingly difficult for a bright, socially concerned young man to see helping a baseball team as a fulfillment of his obligation to work for his fellowman. Sports could satisfy some of his personal needs, but that was never enough for Mario Cuomo. "I spent the next winter thinking a great deal about playing ball and how much I enjoyed it," Cuomo recalled many years later. "Perhaps because I enjoyed it so much, the old instincts made me uncomfortable. There had to be more to life than playing ball. I felt I had to do something else. I didn't know what, but I knew—I thought—that I had to look beyond center field for it."

The Pirates held on to the rights to Cuomo, in hopes that he would decide to return to the game he loved so much. They assigned him to one farm team after another in the late fifties—Jamestown, Salem, Dubuque, Batavia—but he never played professionally again. The Pittsburgh organization did not officially give up on Cuomo until 1965, when there was no likelihood that a successful thirty-three-year-old attorney would decide to restart a minor-league career.[8]

* * *

When Mario Cuomo returned to St. John's for his senior year in the fall of 1952, his professional sports career was over, even though he was not yet certain of that. But neither his love for sports nor his hunger for competition were anywhere near an end.

As a minor-league player on a college campus, Cuomo was even more of a celebrity than he had been before. But intramural director Sarno remembers young Cuomo as being much more modest than were many other star athletes who passed through the campus. He may have seemed arrogant to some, but few remember him as seeming self-impressed. And, for all his combativeness, it was constantly clear that he never wanted to hurt anyone. Underneath Cuomo's competitive exterior he was, in fact, a *gentle* man. His struggles were not intended to inflict harm on anyone. They were in part a contest with himself and in part a means of establishing a pecking order.

When pecking orders are being established, the challenge is always for the top spot. There is no point in competing with clearly inferior rivals. So it has always been with Cuomo. As I have previously noted, he loves to be the underdog. He feels comfortable when he must come from behind. As his later career would demonstrate on several occasions, he liked nothing better than a contest in which he faced seemingly hopeless odds. The underdog *must* work harder, and Mario Cuomo is never happy unless he has plenty of work to do.

He doesn't know how to act when he is the favorite. It makes him uneasy. The prime case in point is his 1986 reelection campaign. There was no question from the start that Cuomo would win by a huge margin. Early in the campaign, press assistant Dick Starkey sent the governor a memo quoting New York Mets' manager Davey Johnson as saying at the beginning of that year's baseball season, "We're not gonna win; we're gonna dominate." Starkey told Cuomo that the same expectation existed for his reelection. This made Cuomo most uncomfortable. The strategy for a front-runner is to sit back, not work very hard, not debate. All of this went completely against Cuomo's grain, and he began to act irrationally. He later described his campaign (which he won by the largest margin in the history of New York governors' races) as "a disaster."[9]

Here we have another reason—not quite unconscious, but perhaps semiconscious—for Cuomo's reluctance to enter the 1988 presidential race. Had he entered the chase when he withdrew, early in 1987, he would have been at least the cofavorite with Gary Hart. Had Cuomo jumped in after Hart's withdrawal, he would have instantly become the heavy favorite. That is not a position he likes to be in. He knows that he is not at his best in such situations and has a tendency to make mistakes when he is ahead. If, on the other hand, he were to enter the race in the spring or summer of 1988, he would start facing the proverbial "tough row to hoe." His "work would be cut out for him." He would then be completely in his element. And he would be even happier than he would have been had he played center field in Yankee Stadium.

Friends are stumped when asked for examples of how Cuomo relaxed in college. "You mean that didn't involve competition?" responded Bernard Babb with a laugh. "I'd be hard-pressed to think of anything that didn't involve sports or competition of some kind." He has never been happy "recharging his batteries"—unless it could be accomplished quickly.

As they grow older, many men who are athletic enthusiasts turn to less demanding sports, such as fishing or golf. But these endeavors are too sedentary to suit Cuomo. "Sports" with too little action have never appealed to him. His brother Frank says that Mario often asks him when he is going to take him out fishing again. Frank says, "Anytime." But Mario never takes him up on the offer. The reason is clear from Fabian Palomino's description of one fishing trip the Cuomo brothers did take. They went out on a boat and after about twenty minutes, Frank caught a fish and said, "Well, that's the first one."

"What do you mean, 'the *first* one'?" Mario inquired.

"Well, the fish are running," Frank replied.

"I see how it's done now," Mario said. "Can't we go back? I can't spend all day out here, you know."

Mario Cuomo has no more use for golf than he does for fishing. When he became secretary of state, Cuomo hired Al Levine as his administrative director. Then he found that Levine was a golfer, and told him he had never hired a golfer before.

"Al," Cuomo asked, "what's your handicap in golf?"

"Well," Levine replied, "I play to an eight or a nine."

"What? I shouldn't hire you! I'd feel better if you had a handicap of twenty-five or thirty!"

Golf, like fishing, is too slow and relaxing for Mario Cuomo. These sports can, of course, be competitive, but they seem to him to be closer to the cardinal sin of *sloth* than to the virtue of work.

"I never played baseball again after I got married," Cuomo said to me. "It was constant work—a little softball for a couple of years, then I stopped even that until I became secretary of state." But the urge never died. Palomino says that each spring he would take out a bat and swing it wistfully.

Never able to resist a challenge, even in his mid-fifties, Cuomo is ready to play basketball at the drop of a hat. In 1986 a businessman in his late thirties from Buffalo was at the Executive Mansion for a barbecue. The man, dressed in a white cashmere sweater and white duck pants, stayed after most of the guests had left. At about 11 P.M. he started suggesting that Canisius College's basketball team was great.

"Ah, St. John's is *much* better," the governor said.

"Well, if you think St. John's is so good, I'll play *you* in basketball."

"Naw," Cuomo said, "it's the end of the day, and the end of a busy week, and I'm tired."

But the other fellow kept it up. He said he was going to go back to Buffalo and tell everybody that the governor was afraid to take up his challenge.

"Well, you're younger than I am. How many points will you spot me?" Cuomo asked.

They continued the discussion until the governor agreed to play without getting any points. He just couldn't allow the challenge to go unanswered. He went in and got a pair of sneakers for the younger man to wear and proceeded to play an aggressive game. Cuomo kept his opponent from getting inside, and the other fellow couldn't hit from the outside. The governor wound up trouncing him.

"To tell you the truth," Cuomo told Palomino, "I was prepared to cheat, but thank God I didn't have to."

"I had to play," the governor explained to friends later, "or he would have gone back to Buffalo and said I was afraid to play him."[10]

One could not help wondering as 1988 dawned how long the

Great Competitor could refrain from entering the biggest contest of them all.

The governor often jokes about "cheating" to win games, but his brother Frank says he (Frank) was quoted out of context when a reporter printed that he had said Mario cheats. Frank Cuomo says he *did* say that, and it is accurate, but only up to a point. "If you were playing pool," Frank told me, "Mario wouldn't drop one of his balls into a pocket. But he might suddenly and loudly cough while you were taking a shot." "He doesn't exactly cheat" when playing basketball, a friend says, "but sometimes he adjusts the score a bit." In short, in a game he will get away with anything he can, without flagrantly violating the rules. This "cheating" should in no sense be taken as an indication that he would as an officeholder have any propensity toward "cheating" the public. That would be impossible for someone with Cuomo's character. He just likes to win.

"Just liking to win" can cause problems, though. A little aggressiveness in a politician can be an asset. But too much can be, well, too much. "Cuomo loves a fight and pounces on anything that moves in print or in person," columnist Mary McGrory accurately said in 1986. This, George F. Will noted later that year, "is not altogether bad." Cuomo "also is intellectually quick and combative," the conservative commentator pointed out, "qualities that can cause slower and thinner-skinned journalists to call him thin-skinned."

Cuomo's boiling point seems to have risen in recent years, but through his adult life it has been reached on many occasions. His 1977 campaign for mayor of New York was a particularly hot one. When a rival politician at a meeting in a Brooklyn high school called him a liar, Cuomo went after him. "With both hands," according to an account the man gave to a *Newsweek* reporter, "he [Cuomo] grabbed me by the chest and flung me through the swinging doors." Aides—in this case, perhaps, "seconds"—separated the combatants, and after he had cooled off, Cuomo apologized and the two shook hands.

Although both men dispute their accuracy, published reports say that when Governor Hugh Carey reneged on a promise to support Cuomo in 1977, the candidate went in and angrily complained to the governor that he felt betrayed. As Carey started to get up from his chair, Cuomo is said to have raised his voice and ordered, "Sit down, Hughie, or I'll knock you right on your ass!" The governor sat down.

Other examples of Cuomo's short fuse burning down are plentiful. Several others will be found in later chapters, but a few might best be mentioned in the present context. Once during a parade in which he was marching, Cuomo saw someone along the sidelines holding an obscene poster. He left the parade to give the man a piece of his mind. During the 1985 legislative debate over a mandatory seat-belt law, he labeled opponents of the bill "NRA hunters who drink beer, don't vote, and lie to their wives about where they were on the weekend." He quickly realized that the statement was unfair as well as unwise and called it "the blunder of the universe."

Cuomo has a disturbing tendency to view everything that happens as part of a personal contest. When someone criticizes him, he not only gets angry, he often tries to get even as well. He is noted both for trying to figure out who among his staff were the sources of unattributed comments in news stories and for making personal telephone calls to reporters and columnists who make statements he thinks unfair or inaccurate. Those who cross him are likely to be given a cold shoulder for some time, but friends and Albany reporters say he returns fire rapidly and does not hold grudges for long. His reputation for lasting vindictiveness is, in fact, largely unfounded. Many people who supported Ed Koch against Cuomo in the 1982 primary, for example, were given positions on the governor's senior staff.[11]

Mario Cuomo's competitiveness was most evident in his athletic career, but, as we have just seen, it carried over into other areas of his life. We shall see it again and again in the pages that follow. It is clear that one of the factors that most attracted him to the law was the chance to meet an opponent in verbal combat. Indeed, the law was for him a way to translate his competitive urges from the physical to the intellectual realm and, at the same time, to add the possibility of helping others to a much greater extent than was the case on an athletic team. He loved the clash of minds in the courtroom. "The real high," he told a reporter in 1977, "is the excitement of the trial or the oral argument. You're totally immersed. You don't feel anything. It's like spraining your ankle in the middle of a ball game and not knowing how badly hurt you are until the time-out is called."

Mario Cuomo has always loved to win debates, and he usually does. But even when he does not, he is unlikely to say so. "The guy is amazing," Frank Cuomo says of his brother. "He's right much more than he's wrong. But, then again, I've never heard him admit it when he was wrong." As a young lawyer, Cuomo saw cases as contests to be won. "I could see he was a keenly competitive type." Fabian Palomino has said. "He would talk about 'winning cases'— 'How many you won?' " Cuomo liked to point out in the old days, Palomino told me, that he had lost only one case.

When someone says he's too combative, the governor often lays it to his long experience as a practicing attorney. "Matilda says at dinner on a good day I sound like an affidavit," he told Anthony Lewis in 1986.

When he began to help wronged citizens in their struggles with the city government, Cuomo again saw it as a contest. His preoccupation when he represented the "Corona 69" in their struggle to save their homes (see Chapter 6) was "seeing how he could formulate a case that would win." "I'm going to beat them [the city]—one way or another," he said frequently during the Corona dispute. Plainly he had succeeded in identifying the cause of the aggrieved citizens—and doing good, as his religion and his conscience required—with his own need to experience victory.

While the law with its adversarial system and its opportunities for helping others went a long way toward fulfilling two of Cuomo's greatest needs, politics finally offered an even greater opportunity to combine his passions. It was, in fact, an almost inevitable next step for someone with Cuomo's blend of competitiveness and conscience.

Cuomo has often made the connection between the competitive desire and politics explicit. When he decided not to give up his seemingly hopeless 1974 quest for the Democratic nomination for the lieutenant governorship, Cuomo explained it this way: "I have never walked off the field in the eighth inning in my life." And he made a most revealing statement when a friend pointed out to him in 1977 that his 1974 loss had been something of a blessing in disguise, since he had subsequently been appointed secretary of state, a position in which he was able to accomplish much more.

"What's lieutenant governor?" the friend asked.

"Elected," answered a still chagrined Cuomo, making it clear that while he wanted to do good, he also wanted to *win*. Appointed office gave him an opportunity to satisfy the Christian part of his motivation, but not the competitive part. Only elective office could meet both needs.[12]

Cuomo knows perfectly well that the only way he can reconcile his desire for victory with his religious imperatives is to keep constantly in mind that "the joy of winning is the joy of having an opportunity to do the good." He is just as much aware of how often he fails to live up to this objective. His diaries are replete with such instances:

"Doug Ireland and the *SoHo News* ran a piece headlining a quote from me: 'The people around the Governor [Carey] are cowards and phonies and you can tell them I said so,'" Cuomo wrote on April 24, 1981. "I regret it; it makes me uncomfortable even to think about it. . . . I reacted in irritation and made an intemperate statement. Sometimes I think we learn very slowly, if at all. I'll have to try harder on this as on so many other things."

June 5, 1981: "Yesterday afternoon at the AFL-CIO convention I mentioned at the beginning of my remarks that I was surprised Carey could say he didn't know what I was doing. I also made it clear that I was annoyed; I shouldn't have. The *Daily News* ran a headline 'Cuomo: Carey Doesn't Appreciate Me,' which had a whiny quality I didn't like. One cheap shot in reply to another cheap shot makes two cheap shots . . . nothing good!"

"The press came in to see me in my Capitol office shortly after I arrived in Albany," Cuomo wrote on April 6, 1982, "and I was testy—especially with Fred Dicker. That's not helpful, because the press reads testiness as weakness, and they're right."

Just before the 1982 general election, Cuomo took up one of his favorite roles, that of self-critic, and analyzed a tape of his most recent debate with his Republican opponent, Lew Lehrman. "I didn't like my performance," Cuomo wrote. "I looked too hard, too negative, at times arrogant. I was trying hard not to reveal my anger at the increasingly distortive campaign he's been running, . . . but I failed."

It is odd that someone who is so constantly and so harshly self-critical finds it well-nigh impossible to tolerate milder criticism from others.

On August 29, 1982, Cuomo wrote: "It's a tough business. It's especially difficult to avoid reacting emotionally to what you know are deliberately false charges and believe are pretenses. There is so much you'd like to say in response—but there's usually not the opportunity, and if there is, it's not always covered by the media. It's a real test of belief and of whether under pressure you will forget who and what you are and make the effort nothing more than an exercise in egoism."

There is the danger—one might accurately say the devil—that lurks within Mario Cuomo, constantly threatening to destroy the delicate balance he has carefully crafted between his passion for personal victory and achievement on the one hand and his obligation to serve humanity on the other. *Egotism*—the sin of *pride*—is the enemy against which his guard must never be let down.

Cuomo directly confronted the issue of his competitiveness in a March 1982 diary entry: "I don't like hearing from people: 'You're a fighter; very competitive; everything is a challenge to you; you must win for the sake of winning. I think [your son] Andrew is like you.' I hope he's not! And I hope I'm not. The political power one wins is good for the good it can do. The acceptance is good for the political power it gives. . . . Losing, not having the acceptance that gives the political power, is being denied the chance to do good. . . . I'm so sure this is true that it's hard to live with the reality of my departure from it."

Depart from the ideal he often has, but at least Mario Cuomo is aware of his departures and of the need for a larger objective than personal triumph. Many other politicians are motivated by the need to win untempered by the duty to serve.

Knowing one's faults is good; curing them is better—but of course far more difficult. Mario Cuomo's greatness as a historical figure may be determined by the degree to which he is able to rise above the sort of petty actions that have led to his being labeled, with whatever justification, "mean," "vindictive," "authoritarian," and a "bully." George Will has wisely suggested that if a man of Cuomo's abilities brawls with the press, he "should do so not from pique but only for sport." The *New York Times* put it well in an editorial just before Cuomo's 1986 reelection triumph: "Ordinary politicians play hardball. The Governor, with his immense talents, should be extraordinary."[13]

It is time for Mario Cuomo to make hardball a part of his past.

In his youth Cuomo's inability to hit a curve ball and his being hit in the head by a fastball both contributed to his decision to move beyond baseball. By the 1980s he had become a master at hitting political curve balls. But the high, hard political pitch aimed at his head remains the greatest danger he confronts. He has the agility to get out of the way of such intentional beanballs. If he ever learns to do it consistently, he may well become unbeatable.

"Sometimes it feels like you and me against the world," Helen Reddy sang in a 1974 song written by Paul Williams and Ken Asher. Surely there have been times when Mario Cuomo—like most of us—has felt this way. For him the problem has long been to find a way to take the competitive spirit enunciated in those words and make the "you" as inclusive as possible. In that way, personal victories can take on a larger meaning that is in keeping with the religious imperative to do good for others.

The degree to which Cuomo identifies his own triumph with the common good is evident in what he wrote a few days after he defeated Koch in 1982: "It wasn't Mario Cuomo—most people don't know a whole lot about me—it was the message we were delivering. Even when only vaguely perceived, it's the little guy against the big guy; it's the underdog against the favorite. . . . it's 'us' against 'them.' And 'us' won!"

The point here is not the validity of Cuomo's analysis of the meaning of his victory, which I think is largely correct. It is rather what it shows about his psychological—even spiritual—need to link his own success with larger causes.

Winning is extremely important to Mario Cuomo. It is one of his greatest passions. He craves victory in everything he does. Yet he would never endorse the maxim of another noted Italian-American competitor, the late football coach Vince Lombardi. "Winning isn't everything," Lombardi maintained. "It's the *only* thing." For Cuomo, winning *is* essential, but it certainly is *not* the *only* thing. "Again today," he wrote in his diary during the 1982 gubernatorial campaign, "I was reminded that perhaps the greatest danger of all in a campaign like this one is forgetting why you are doing it—or at least why you should be doing it. The temptation is to measure everything as though victory is more than the most important thing—it is the only thing."[14]

Because of his religion and values, Mario Cuomo can fully enjoy winning only if it means victory not for himself alone, but for others as well. To find his place in the world, he needed to find a career in which he could immerse himself in the thrill of contest and taste the delights of victory, but at the same time meet his obligation to serve others. Baseball did not provide such opportunities. The law would come much closer, particularly if he could use his legal skills to help the underdog. In the end, though, it would take another, fully public, career to enable the very private Mario Cuomo fully to blend his passions for competition and service.

5

FAMILY

F AMILY" is the central metaphor
that Mario Cuomo employs to indicate the sort of interdependent
relationship and mutual responsibilities that we all have in a society. During his 1982 gubernatorial campaign, Cuomo searched for
a way to describe his fundamental political and social philosophy,
which he had been developing throughout his life, and which was
then under frontal assault from the Reagan administration. The
concepts of government and society that he enunciated in that
campaign were not new. He had been saying the same sorts of
things for many years. But in the Reagan era it was essential to find
a new way to express the need for cooperation. "I found it,"
Cuomo recounts, "in the most extraordinarily obvious place; I
found it in the idea of 'family.' That concept described as well as
it can be described by me the indispensable importance of sharing
benefits and burdens, the notion of communal strength and of
obligation to the whole."

Cuomo first used the term "family" to illustrate the interdependence or mutuality about which he had long talked in a
September 1981 speech at the New York State Fair in Syracuse.
"Family" serves as a more readily understood expression than
others Cuomo has used, such as "synergism." He continued to use
the term throughout the campaign and used it as the core of his
widely acclaimed 1983 inaugural address:

Those who made our history taught us above all things the idea of
family. Mutuality. The sharing of benefits and burdens—fairly—for the
good of all. It is an idea essential to our success.
And no family that favored its strong children—or that in the name
of evenhandedness, failed to help its vulnerable ones—would be worthy

123

of the name. And no state, or nation, that chooses to ignore its troubled regions and people, while watching others thrive, can call itself justified.

We must be the family of New York—feeling one another's pain; sharing one another's blessings, reasonably, equitably, honestly, fairly—irrespective of geography or race or political affiliation.

His most basic values are expressed in the concept of family: "our need to share and protect; even our need for one another's concern." The philosophy behind the symbol of society as a family grew out of Mario Cuomo's own family experiences and out of his religious values. He does not recall any direct connection between his use of the term "family" in a larger, inclusive sense and that of Pope John XXIII twenty years earlier, but whether conscious or unconscious, the connection between his philosophy and that of the gentle, loving, elderly pope of the early 1960s is clear.[1]

The establishment of Cuomo's own family in his years in law school and as a young attorney helped to nourish his philosophy of interdependence that he would eventually call "family." During that period of his life, many aspects of his character blossomed, and it provides us with an excellent opportunity to see the extent to which Cuomo as a young man practiced what he now preaches about family life.

Before we move on to Mario Cuomo's establishment of his own family, it is well to specify the values and characteristics he had learned from the family in which he grew up.

Cuomo cannot separate the influence his mother and father had on him. "They didn't do anything separately," the governor told me. "I never had talks with my father. I never had talks with my mother. There was no difference in them. When you saw the one, you saw both. They were always in the store. . . . My relationship with the two of them was the same." It is certainly true that Mario Cuomo saw much more of his parents together than do children whose mothers are at home and whose fathers work away from the home. I believe it is possible, though, to distinguish between the influences of Andrea and Immaculata Cuomo on their youngest child.

Although Mario spent a great deal of time in his early years by himself, because his father worked in a setting connected to the home he also saw a lot more of his father than the typical child does. Andrea instilled basic values in his children, mostly by example rather than by lecture. This in itself had an impact on Mario. His notion that the good person's responsibility is to set an example, not to judge or condemn others, can be directly traced to the way Andrea Cuomo instructed his children.

Andrea Cuomo's dedication to his family inspired Mario to try to act in a similar fashion. But Andrea's devotion to his family was expressed through his work to advance them. Since he worked all the time, he had little time to spend with his family in recreation and none in vacations. He finally began to spend time at play with his grandchildren after he retired from the grocery business, but prior to that time he worked almost constantly. In all of these respects, it is apparent that Mario is the proverbial chip off the old block.

It is clear that Mario Cuomo acquired the work ethic from his father. "You work, then you can enjoy," Andrea used to say. But Mario never stops working; his work *is* his enjoyment. The same seems to have been true of his father, at least until his retirement.

Andrea Cuomo not only worked hard, he also refused to give up. He understood that pessimism or negativism is the greatest sin. His perseverance has often served as an inspiration to Mario in times of difficulty. Cuomo might paraphrase the Beatles to say, "In times of trouble, father Andrea comes to me—*Don't* let it be."

Toward the end of his 1982 gubernatorial campaign, Cuomo found himself exhausted as he wrote in his diary. "I couldn't help wondering what Poppa would have said if I had told him I was tired or—God forbid—that I was discouraged." Mario thought in particular of an incident that had taken place just after the family had moved from South Jamaica to Holliswood. They returned from the store after a terrible storm one night to find the forty-foot blue spruce in their new front yard uprooted and leaning all the way to the road ten to fifteen feet below.

The Cuomo boys were city-bred. "Frankie and I knew nothing about trees," Mario remembered. "We could climb poles all day; we were great at fire escapes; we could scale fences with barbed wire at the top—but we knew nothing about trees. When we saw our spruce, defeated, its cheek on the canvas, our hearts sank. But not Poppa's."

Andrea Cuomo was not the sort ever to give up. "He was stronger than Frankie and I and Marie and Momma all together."

They all stood in the rain for a few minutes while the head of the household thought. Then Andrea declared: "O.K., we gonna push 'im up!"

"What are you talking about Poppa? The roots are out of the ground!"

"Shut up," Andrea said, "we gonna push 'im up, he's gonna grow again." He had no doubts. In his way of thinking, will could always overcome adversity.

He got rope out of the house and tied it around the top of the tree. Frank pushed from below, while Andrea and Mario pulled the ropes from the top of the hill. Once the tree was upright, Andrea dug out a muddy hole around its base, so that the roots would sink deeper. Then they all shoveled mud onto the roots and moved large rocks on top to steady the tree. Finally, still in the pouring rain, Andrea drove stakes into the ground and tied ropes from them to the tree. Satisfied with the job, he proclaimed: "Don't worry, he's gonna grow again."

Father knows best. The spruce stands majestically in front of the house to this day, nearly forty years after it was saved by a diminutive Italian-American man whose vocabulary did not include "surrender."

Andrea Cuomo may have been as important a source of his son's dedication to selflessness as were the teachings of the Church. *"He never did anything for himself, period,"* the governor emphatically said to me of his father. Mario has tried his best to follow this course.

He has also adopted from his father a strong sense of compassion and honesty. His "father was a very compassionate man—one of high integrity," Mario's brother-in-law Ted Vecchio points out. "This is what he [Mario] grew up with, and it must have rubbed off on him." When Andrea refused to join in black-market sales during World War II, or to pay off the cops who brought Mario in for driving without a license, he was teaching valuable lessons in a code of personal ethics.

Mario picked up other qualities from his father as well. "His father was very athletic in his own way," Joe Mattone recalls. When Andrea was in his fifties, Mattone saw him demonstrate his strength by standing on one leg and holding the other straight out for three minutes. "My father was tough," Frank Cuomo told me. "You could not argue with my father—you did not argue with Andrea Cuomo. You had respect for him—and I think Mario

learned even more of that respect than I did. He didn't go away
in the service, he wasn't exposed to the things I was. He was
always living at home until he met Matilda and they started keeping company and he got married—that's the first time he really left
home."

Mario Cuomo's feelings for his late father are evident in many
ways. I found it revealing to watch his reactions as he listened, I
think for the first time, to the words of Dan Fogelberg's song
"Leader of the Band." We were on a helicopter somewhere over
Connecticut, returning to Albany from a bill-signing ceremony on
Long Island. It was the summer of 1987, six years after Andrea
Cuomo's death. The governor put on a tape someone had made for
him. The first song was Fogelberg's tribute to his father. As the
music began, I told Cuomo what it was about. He listened to
Fogelberg's words:

> His hands were meant for different work
> And his heart was known to none
>
> . . .
>
> And he gave to me a gift
> I know I never can repay
>
> . . .
>
> My life has been a poor attempt
> To imitate the man
> I'm just a living legacy
> To the leader of the band
>
> . . .
>
> And Poppa, I don't think
> I've said, "I love you," near enough

A lump moved noticeably in the governor's throat at these lines.
When the song was over he said quietly, "That's very powerful."

Cuomo often mentions the accomplishments of his parents. "If
I run," he wrote in his diary before beginning his 1982 gubernatorial campaign, "I will be a long shot, but so were Momma and
Poppa." His best speeches have centered around references to
their rise. Some cynical critics might question Cuomo's sincerity
in such statements, but I believe that he is truly in awe of what his
parents and others of the immigrant generation achieved. The
odds were certainly against his parents. Their struggle is part of
the source of Mario's strong identification with the underdog.

From his mother, Mario Cuomo derived other qualities. One,

plainly, was her wit. Some people, even among the governor's friends, think that he may put words in her mouth. One friend suggested to me that Cuomo "does a Finley Peter Dunne with his mother." The reference is to the late-nineteenth- and early-twentieth-century American humorist and journalist who created a character named "Mr. Dooley" who was forever uttering gems of wisdom and insightful remarks in a thick Irish brogue. But family members insist that the sagacious comments Mario attributes to his mother actually emanate from Immaculata Cuomo's fertile intellect.

The examples are numerous. One of the best was Mrs. Cuomo's 1984 comment that Walter Mondale reminded her of polenta, a mushy Italian peasant dish. When a reporter asked Immaculata Cuomo about Mario running for the presidency, she said: "I tell him, 'Don't worry about it. Take-a your time. You got a lotta time. In time, another pope is born.' "

Then there is the famous story of Immaculata's continuing interest in seeing Mario become a judge. Throughout Mario's political rise, his mother persisted in bringing up the subject. He told her that he had been chosen as secretary of state.

"Oh, that'sa nice. When you gonna be judge?" Immaculata asked.

A few years later Mario became lieutenant governor.

"That'sa nice," his mother said. "When you gonna be judge?"

Then in 1982 Cuomo was elected governor. "Ma, I'm the governor," he said.

"That'sa nice. When you gonna be judge?"

"Whattaya mean, Ma? I'm the *governor!*"

"Stupido! Stupido!" Immaculata said to her son. "How long is governor?"

"Four years, Ma."

"How long is supreme court judge?" the old woman asked.

"Life, Ma."

"Who's stupid, me or you?"

Mario Cuomo often refers to "Aristotle's rule for success: decide what you want to do and do it." "Actually," he says, "it was my mother's rule for success. But, as I once told *New York Times* reporter Mickey Carroll, 'No one would listen unless I said it was Aristotle.' "

Immaculata Cuomo is a tower of fortitude and wisdom. These traits have had a perceptible effect on her youngest son. One example of her strength came in May of 1987, when a burglar broke into the Holliswood home she has occupied by herself since the death of her husband. She heard the man trying to get in the door of her bedroom, which was chained. She had the presence of mind, first, to yell, "Matthew, I think somebody is in here." Frank's son sometimes stays with her, but was not there at the time, as she well knew. She also put a chair under the doorknob. Her daughter asked her why she didn't call the police, 911.

"Because I had to sit on the chair," Immaculata replied.

"But Momma," Marie said, "when you got up from the chair, why didn't you call the police?"

"Because when I got up from the chair, he was gone. Why did I need the police then?"

After it was all over, Immaculata felt sorry for the burglar. "The poor man, I scared him."

It seems highly likely that Mario Cuomo drew from his mother his willingness and courage to go against many of the expectations for Italian-American males (and all other American males) in religion, education, and sexual conquest.

Mario is very attentive to his mother. He calls her frequently and has her to the mansion often. He always jokes, though, that Frank is her favorite. Frank is a very different person from Mario. As Frank says, "We're two different people, my brother and I. ... We look alike, maybe—other than that—[we have very little in common]."

Frank greatly admires his brother, and is deeply proud of his success. Yet at the same time there is a controlled, subdued resentment. "It's never, 'He's my brother,' " Frank said to me. "It's always, 'I'm his brother,'—'Really, can I have your autograph?' " Once Frank said to me: "I've gotta write a book someday—called *Reflected Glory.* " He points out that he has derived no benefit from his brother becoming governor. "I didn't gain a governor," Frank said when Mario was elected, "as far as I'm concerned, I just lost a brother, because now I'm not going to get to talk to him as often as I could [before]."

Mario is well aware of the fact that Frank has had "all the bad luck in the family—except for his wife, Joan—a wonderful good break. Joan is a beautiful lady. They're very happy together." "But he's been very, very good to me," the governor says of his brother. "He knew nothing about politics. He couldn't care less. He's got nothing good from politics, just abuse."

Frank told me that Mario is "so completely different when he's with the family and not with outsiders. He reverts to being *Mario.*" This brings up an important point. It will be recalled that the outlook of the southern Italian *contadino* was narrow. He usually believed not only that one's family came first, but that nothing was owed to anyone outside the family. Strangers were, as a rule, not trusted by the people out of whom Mario Cuomo's forebears arose.

It has often been charged that Cuomo himself maintains this characteristic. "Mario Cuomo trusts no one completely who isn't a member of his own family," one former associate of the governor has insisted. He is said to engage "outsiders" easily, but to offer his trust only rarely. If true, this would be a negative aspect of Cuomo's family emphasis. And it cannot be denied that he chose his son Andrew as his campaign manager and most trusted adviser during his first term. The charge seems greatly exaggerated, however. Most of the governor's other top aides—except for Fabian Palomino, who has almost become family—are people that he did not know long, if at all, before they were appointed. Some of them were close to Governor Hugh Carey, with whom Cuomo had had a bitter split, and others backed his rival Edward Koch in the 1982 gubernatorial primary.[2]

Matilda Raffa Cuomo believes that it was destiny that brought her together with her husband. When she graduated from Midwood High School in Brooklyn, where she had been a first-rate singer and head of the color guard, she was accepted by Brooklyn College, Hunter College, and Columbia. Her older brothers were very protective of her and did not want her to commute to Manhattan. They insisted that she go to nearby St. John's Teachers College, which she could reach via a short bus ride (or, as it turned out more often, be driven by one of her brothers). The Teachers College made use of the same building that the all-male St. John's College occupied, but at different times. The men's classes ended at 2 P.M. and the women took classes from 4 to 6 P.M. as well as on Saturday mornings. This enabled women who were already teaching (particularly nuns who in the Brooklyn Archdiocese were permitted to teach without college degrees but were required to pursue degrees) to continue to work at the same time they were attending classes.

St. John's College students who wanted to meet girls would

hang around the lobby after classes, waiting for the Teachers College students to arrive. Many of the latter, no less eager to meet members of the opposite sex, arrived an hour and a half or two hours early for their classes. The old college building's lobby was dominated by a huge clock and a statue of St. John the Baptist. The statue had a finger pointed into the air, so the older students attending college under the GI Bill dubbed it "the Finger." There Matilda Raffa and Mario Cuomo began meeting in 1951.

Since the Raffas lived in Flatbush, Brooklyn, and the Cuomos resided in Holliswood, Queens—and "Brooklyn girls never went out with the Queens fellows ordinarily," Matilda credits destiny with bringing the couple together. Had her brothers not forced her to go to St. John's—or had Mario not been involved in extracurricular activities that kept him at school in the afternoons—they never would have met.

During his high school years, Mario had been somewhat shy with girls, but he had become more socially active in college. He was now known as one who had an eye for beautiful women and served as the committee chairman who chose the queen of the ball at several college dances. Cuomo's own attractions were considerable: a darkly handsome young man with an athletic body and the reputation of an outstanding student and sports star. Still, he was hardly a "ladies' man" when he met his future wife. Mario was immediately taken with the shy, attractive young woman of Sicilian extraction with curly, reddish-brown hair. They met most days for coffee in the tiny, dingy St. John's cafeteria, which was the social center of the one-building campus. Then Mario began asking Matilda to go to basketball games. Anthony Sarno saw Mario waiting under the clock and statue every afternoon, and he finally asked what he was doing there every day.

"I'm waiting for my girlfriend," Cuomo replied.

"You better cut it out," Sarno warned, "or you might end up marrying that girl."

"What do you think I'm trying to do?" the already serious young suitor responded.

The Raffas were much better off financially than were the Cuomos. Charlie Raffa had started out as an unschooled laborer and carpenter who had risen to being a cabinetmaker who made supermarket fixtures (display cases, refrigeration units, and so forth). During World War II he did very well making life rafts for the navy on cost-plus contracts. He had his own plant and was well enough off to own a summer home and a boat at Lake Hopatcong, New Jersey. Raffa may not have been rich, but his children never wanted for anything.

Both of Matilda's parents took an instant liking to her new boyfriend, for many of the same reasons that she did. He was very serious. "We used to talk about philosophy," Matilda remembers. "I realized right away I could trust him. He wouldn't betray me or make me feel bad. He made me feel very secure." "There was this religious aspect about him," she told me. "I think that's what my mother liked—that she found him very stable and very sincere." "One thing I can tell you," Mary Raffa said to her daughter after meeting Mario, "is that he'll never hurt you."

One day Mario told his brother Frank that he had met a very nice girl and was going to tell his parents and bring her over to the house, but he was nervous about it. Frank encouraged him, and as it turned out there was no cause for worry. The Cuomos liked Matilda right away. Frank said she was "calm, smart, pretty—just the type of girl you want your brother to marry."

Talk of marriage was delayed by Mario's fling with baseball and by the expectation that he would soon be drafted into the armed forces. Because of deferments for scholarship students, Cuomo was not conscripted during the Korean War.

Soon after his graduation from St. John's, Mario and Matilda made wedding plans for June 1954, right after her graduation. The ardent young Catholic man gave his betrothed a lecture on the Church's teachings on birth control. The men of the two families met—unbeknown to the couple—to arrange the wedding in a scene that seems straight out of the Old World (or Hollywood). Charlie Raffa and his oldest son, Frank, met with Andrea Cuomo and his oldest son, Frank, to work out the dowry. Each family negotiated how much it would provide to help the new couple get a start in married life.

Dowry or no, the newlyweds soon found themselves in a financial tight spot. They were married on June 5, 1954, in St. John the Baptist Church in Brooklyn. They honeymooned for less than a week in Puerto Rico, and soon after their return Matilda found herself, as they say, "in the family way." This should not have been entirely surprising, given the engagement lecture against birth control, but for a young couple with little money, the news could not be taken as an entirely unmixed blessing. The expectant father was faced with the prospect of accepting assistance from his father-in-law, which his pride would not tolerate, or of dropping out of law school. Andrea Cuomo and Charlie Raffa met again and agreed that "Mario has to stay in school."

Matilda had obtained a teaching position at the Dutch Broadway School in Elmont. When she arrived in the fall, the principal discovered that he had hired one person for the job, but he would soon have two. He was very good to her all the same. The new Mrs. Cuomo was fortunate to have a position in Elmont, because in the New York City schools women were obliged to leave their jobs after five months of pregnancy. In Elmont she was able to keep teaching until a few weeks before her daughter Margaret was born in March of 1955.

Life was not easy for a family of three with the father in law school. At the time of their marriage, the couple had rented a furnished apartment because they expected Mario to be drafted when he finished law school. Fatherhood foreclosed that possibility during peacetime. They wound up moving in with Mario's parents in Holliswood so that Immaculata could take care of the baby while Matilda returned to her teaching job. She had to be the breadwinner while Mario finished law school. He did not like this situation, and very much wanted to bring in money himself. He started working part-time for his father-in-law, but the dean called him in and told him that he could not work at all if he wanted to keep his scholarship. Mario did manage to supplement the family income by sometimes staying up all night to write legal briefs, at a hundred dollars apiece, for a Brooklyn law firm. He also took a summer job as a bookkeeper for Charlie Raffa's company. His meager and sporadic income helped, but Matilda was the major source of family sustenance.[3]

Cuomo was an outstanding student at St. John's Law School, where, he says, he "found and fell in love with Our Lady of the Law." And love was the proper word. He calls his relationship with the law "an affair"—he derives almost sensual pleasure from it. "I found the beauty of the law's logic and power awesome," Cuomo says. In the law he found just what he was looking for—the guiding principle of "reasonableness."

Cuomo's reverence for the law was well summarized in the words of his hero, Thomas More, when he warned against cutting down the laws in order to get at the devil: "And when the last law was down and the devil turned 'round on you, where would you *hide*, Roper, the laws all being flat? This country is planted thick with laws from coast to coast—with man's laws, not God's, and if you cut them down . . . do you really think you could stand upright in the winds that would blow then? Yes, I give the devil benefit of law for my own safety's sake."

Law school demanded hard work and long hours, and Mario Cuomo liked nothing better, unless it was tough competition, which was also abundantly available in the law. He found the clash of minds as exhilarating as the throwing of elbows beneath a basketball net. But another side of him craved complete immersion in all-absorbing solitary work. Oliver Wendell Holmes said that the law "places its servitors in a black gulf of solitude more isolating than that which confronts a dying man." That was no drawback to someone who used to create a world of his own in the back room of his father's store, or when reading a book. Cuomo loved legal research and analysis. It was never a distasteful chore to him to dissect a problem and examine it from all possible angles. He could not bring himself quickly to accept even an obvious conclusion. The law was an arena where preparation paid off, and he was one to prepare and prepare—and then prepare some more. He was not only brilliant; he was also clever, creative, competitive, and the possessor of a magnificent memory. It was a combination perfectly suited for the study and practice of law.

At St. John's Law, Cuomo was a dean's list student, participated in the student assistant program at the United States attorney's office in the Southern District of New York (in which students assisted in representing the federal government in civil suits and criminal prosecutions), was the chairman of the student bar in 1954–55, helped to found a publication called the *Catholic Lawyer*, and was elected the "dean" of the Delta Theta Phi law fraternity.

St. John's Law School was not Harvard, but it did have a good reputation. It produced many judges, and in the years since Cuomo was there, it has become a fount of political leadership. Hugh Carey, Cuomo's predecessor as governor of New York, and John Deukmajian, the current governor of California, are both graduates of St. John's Law School. It was no mean feat to finish at the top of one's class at this institution. Mario Cuomo tied for that honor when he received his law degree in 1956.[4]

The dean of the St. John's Law
School, Dr. Harold F. McNiece, arranged for Cuomo to interview
for a clerkship with Judge Adrian Paul Burke of the New York
State Court of Appeals, the state's highest court. It was a high-
prestige, low-pay position, but Cuomo jumped at the opportunity
and was glad to get a $4,200-a-year salary.

After Judge Burke hired Cuomo, he told his senior law clerk,
Fabian Palomino, who was also a St. John's Law graduate, to take
the newcomer in hand and show him the ropes. "You'll like him,"
Burke told Palomino. "He's Italian, a former baseball player, and
basically he's a nice guy. He seems like a very warm person. You'll
get along with him well." That proved to be an understatement.
Palomino is a delightful character whose dark face is almost constantly brightened with a smile and whose love of food is evident
in his rounded proportions. ("I like to say to the governor: 'I could
lose weight; can you grow hair?' " Palomino told me.) He and
Cuomo hit it off immediately and became fast friends. They have
remained so ever since. Palomino is as close to an alter ego as
Cuomo has. He now holds the title of special counsel to the governor and is, Cuomo says, "the best lawyer I ever met."

Palomino quickly learned what sort of a worker Cuomo is.
During the summer of 1956, before he had met the new clerk,
Palomino received a telephone call from Judge Burke. "I don't
know, maybe you'll have to take this new law clerk into hand and
help him—guide him a little bit," the judge told Palomino.

"Why? Is there any problem, Judge?"

"Well," Burke said, "I assigned him a simple motion two weeks
ago and apparently he's still working on it. The research he's doing
is intensive, and I suspect it's going to be kind of a long document
whenever he writes it up. I think he's going way beyond what we
need."

When Cuomo showed up for work after Labor Day, he came
in with a stack of papers about fourteen inches high and flopped
it on the desk. After they were introduced, Palomino asked him
how he was coming with the motion.

"Well, I've done a lot of research, but I'm still at it," the eager
young clerk replied.

Palomino looked at what Cuomo had produced. He had "gone
through the whole history of writs from day one—the yearbooks

where they had recorded the decisions—all of these permutations
and slight variations, and he had gone all the way to bring it up
to date. He had sources that nobody would have consulted, except
maybe historians. He quoted what one author in 1738 or something had to say on prerogative."

"We get a thousand motions a year in here," Palomino told him,
"and you can't really spend all this time researching a motion."

"Gee, but you really have to know," Cuomo said.

Palomino explained that what the court needs to know is what
the existing law is, what exceptions and changes there have been,
and why those exceptions and changes were made. "You've got to
give it to them in a couple of pages," he said. "They don't have time
to read all this."

With some reluctance, Cuomo accepted what the senior clerk
told him, and cut his motion down to a more acceptable length.

The work at the Court of Appeals was hard, and it required the
clerks to be in Albany for significant portions of the year. By this
time the Cuomos had moved into a two-bedroom, third-floor walk-
up apartment on Francis Lewis Boulevard in the Cunningham
Heights section of Queens. "It was a sacrifice for me to live there
by myself all week," Matilda Cuomo told me. "He's up in Albany
and I'm alone in Queens with the two kids [a second child, Andrew, was born in December 1957, while Mario was employed at
the Court of Appeals] and no car. It was very rough. We really
struggled in the beginning, no doubt about it." She said she and
the children should have moved to Albany, but she chose not to
move so far away from family and friends. She had to depend on
her father-in-law to drive her to the doctor, to do her shopping,
and to play with the children.

While his wife was suffering in Queens, Mario was Br'er Rab-
bit in the briar patch in Albany. He and Fabian often worked from
eight in the morning to one-thirty or two the next morning. They
both had rooms at the old Wellington Hotel. The accommodations
were something short of luxurious. Bathroom facilities were available down the hall. Later Judge Burke arranged for them to get a
much better room at the Sheraton. Then he moved them again, to
the De Witt Clinton. There they saved money by eating supper
together in the hotel room. They found that the hotel's room
service was very slow, so they called from the court, placing their
orders for chopped steak, or whatever was cheapest on the menu.
Knowing that it would take about forty-five minutes for their

meals to arrive at the room, they took a leisurely walk back to the hotel. They also made a practice of requesting extra rolls and coffee with their evening meal. They would tell the room-service waiter that they would take care of the trays themselves. Then the next morning they reheated the coffee and ate the rolls for a free breakfast.

There were a variety of economies available for the struggling new attorneys. A friend of Fabian's in the Brooklyn district attorney's office told him about a place on the Bowery where they sold suits for ten dollars and twelve dollars each. He passed the word along to Mario, who thought it sounded great. Unfortunately the suits were out of style, "but if you buy dark colors, blacks and blues, then people will not notice them," Palomino points out. "So we used to go there and buy two or three suits at a time." The owner suggested that they should tip the tailor.

"You mean in addition to paying ten dollars for a suit, you want me to tip the tailor!" Cuomo asked. "Why?"

"Because I don't pay him!" the owner replied.

The two clerks were both talkers. They would stay up late into the night, if not to work, then to talk and kid each other. Their appetite for conversation was insatiable. When they were not in Albany, they worked in Judge Burke's district chambers in Manhattan, which were located in the Lincoln Building, across the street from Grand Central Terminal. The workload while they were in district chambers was not as heavy as it was in Albany, and they were often through by five or six in the evening. "We each could have gone across the street to Grand Central and gone home," Palomino said to me. "I lived in Brooklyn Heights and he lived in Queens. But instead, we walked all the way down Fifth Avenue and across 34th Street to Penn Station and got a train from there. That way we could talk more. It was that kind of a relationship."

Cuomo loved to debate almost any topic. "And when it came to debating," Palomino says, "he loved to win; he *loved* to win. We used to debate and I guess I was a little quicker than he was at times, and he would get upset, but he would not stop. He would keep it up." The governor's recollection of who usually won those debates, as one would expect, differs from his friend's.

Palomino was impressed with—and sometimes exasperated by—Cuomo's thoroughness. "Even though the answer was obvious and the obvious answer was the right one," he says, "Mario always poked into things, pulled it, twisted it every way he could to make sure that the answer was the right one." Fabian recalls one case in which they both listened to the arguments and were reviewing the records. It involved an attempt by the trucking industry to argue that a law limiting truck weights to three thousand pounds per axle should be interpreted as meaning three thousand pounds per *wheel*. It was, Palomino said, just a flier the industry was taking to see if it could reap a bonanza. He took the briefs with him that night when he took a bath. In about twenty minutes he yelled out to Cuomo, "Easy case!"

"What did you say?" Mario inquired, rushing into the bathroom.

"The opponents have to lose," Fabian said. "There is no way they can win this case."

"How can you say that?" Mario shouted. "The attorneys probably took months writing this brief, and here you are lying in the bathtub and in twenty minutes you say they've got to lose!"

"If you look at the law, you look at the policy behind the law, and you look at everything else, there is no way they can or should win," Palomino explained. "*That* is how I can say they must lose."

"Well, you should take more time. You should think about it more."

"What more is there to think about?" Fabian asked. "What would you suggest I think about?"

"Oh," Mario responded, "I'm sure a lot of things could occur to you if you thought more about it. The person deserves more than twenty minutes."

Palomino turned in his recommendation for affirmation, and the court agreed by a seven-to-nothing vote. This led Cuomo to realize that working fast might not always be wrong, but he persisted in giving cases a great deal of thought and examination.

In October 1956, a few weeks before the results of the previous July's bar exams were to be published, Cuomo went to Judge Burke and asked if there was any way that he could learn of his results early. He said he didn't think he had failed, but if he had, he wanted to disappear for a few days. The judge told him to ask Fabian, who knew some people on the State Board of Law Examiners. Mario went in and asked Fabian if he could find out.

"Sure," Fabian said. He sat with his feet on his desk, picked up the phone, and dialed a friend at the state board. He chatted with his friend for a few minutes, while Cuomo stood in front of the desk, his tension building. Finally Palomino said, "Look, Jack, we have a new law clerk here who took the bar in July and I'd like to get his results. His name is Mario Cuomo. He's in the second department." Palomino was silent while his friend looked for the score.

By this time Cuomo's knees were practically knocking. Fabian's friend got back on the phone and told him that Mario had received an outstanding grade. But Mario could not hear that end of the conversation, so Fabian said, "No, no, not the first department, the second department. Oh, you already checked that list? Yeah, that bad, huh? Well, listen, what can you do? That's just the way the cookie crumbles, I guess." Before he hung up, Fabian shot a quick glance at Mario, who was white as a sheet.

"I guess I have to tell you," Palomino said to Mario after ending his telephone conversation, "good or bad, I have to tell you." He paused a few moments longer and then smiled and said, "You passed—you did very well!"

Cuomo stared back with a strange look. "Are you *sure* I passed? Because if I didn't, I'll kill you!"

After much laughter in retelling this story, Palomino said to me: "All these people who say he has such a quick temper are wrong. I mean, if he didn't slug me then, you know it shows he's a man who has a great deal of self-restraint!"

Palomino remembers that the major concern of the judges on the Court of Appeals was their health. "They've got it made. They're in the highest club in the state; nobody can overrule their decisions. They get all summer off and sneak a little spring vacation, one at a time. So it's a great job. The big thing is to keep your health up." One of the consequences of their concern with health was that everyone who worked at the court was required to wear galoshes during the frequent Albany snowstorms.

This led to one of the things Palomino likes to kid Cuomo about. He tells him that the future governor's greatest accomplishment on the Court of Appeals was to devise a galoshes hook, fashioned out of a bent coat hanger, that enabled people wearing heavy coats to pull up the zippers on their galoshes without bending over.[5]

American ingenuity is boundless.

* * *

When he neared the end of his two-year stint at the Court of Appeals, Cuomo sent out dozens of applications to the best Manhattan law firms. A friend advised him to use his middle name, Matthew, as he had in Georgia. Cuomo spurned the advice. "I wasn't rejected," the governor told me. "I couldn't even get an interview." Only one Manhattan firm granted him an interview, and that was because one of its partners was a friend of Dean McNiece.

Here was a young man who had finished at the top of his class, had held a prestigious clerkship in the state's highest court, had excellent results on his bar exam, was noted as an extremely hard worker, and was stable, with a family. But he could not even get in to see the people in the Wall Street firms.

Cuomo says now that he did not think a great deal about the reasons for his rejection at the time, because he was too concerned with getting a job. "Only later did I begin to think about prejudice." Friends and relatives remember the reaction being more immediate. "I remember him being bitter," Frank Cuomo told me. "He was saying things like, 'I'm Italian. . . .' " "Any major Wall Street firm should've welcomed him with open arms, scoring the way he did on the bar, getting letters of commendation—that was extraordinary, really," Joe Mattone says of his friend. "But because of the way his name was spelled, they rejected him."

But Mattone made the interesting suggestion that the matter was a bit more complex than the major Manhattan firms simply rejecting all Italian-American applicants. "You could get the lesser jobs," he told me. "But if you were really a topflighter, and you were gonna push one of the WASPs out of a partnership, they didn't want you." It was okay to have an Italian or two in the lower ranks of a prestigious firm, but they wouldn't touch someone who was likely to become a junior partner in three years and a full partner before long. They didn't want any Italian stars in their firmament.

His rejection by the Manhattan law firms gave Mario Cuomo an unmistakable personal taste of discrimination. He had, of course, experienced some discrimination while growing up, but there had not been much in his multiethnic neighborhood, and the sense of "not fitting in" in his first years at St. John's Prep was rather amorphous. "I'd say it really was a blow to him," Mattone says. "I think it left a scar on him—the unfairness of the system—

and maybe he resolved to do what he could, when the time came, not to have that happen [to others]."

Be that as it may, Cuomo's already existing identification with outcasts was strengthened by his troubles with the Wall Street law firms. Those problems reinforced his propensity to join the cause of the outsiders. He became more suspicious of elites. It was about this time that he began to feel real remorse over his earlier embarrassment at his parents' language and customs. Ethnic pride began to replace ethnic shame. Cuomo is today, as Nat Hentoff has put it, "as manifestly proud of his roots as Alex Haley."

Throughout his legal and political career, Cuomo has remained rightly sensitive to ethnic slurs. He is an exceedingly tolerant man, but he will not tolerate prejudice or elitism. Once when Cuomo was a young lawyer in private practice, a wealthy, well-bred, white-haired, WASP patrician client named Earl Andrews took a liking to him because he was so bright and creative. He invited Mario to lunch at his elegant, understated private club. Once there, Andrews began to patronize Cuomo, referring to him as the "son of immigrants" and saying something to the effect of: "Isn't that nice. Even someone like you can make it to this great City, and eat with the most successful people." Then he said he thought he should order for Mario, because perhaps he wouldn't understand their club menu that well. Andrews ordered clam juice "with a clam in it."

"Do you know why I said, 'make sure you put a clam in'?" Andrews asked his guest in a tone of paternalistic instruction. "If you don't tell them to put a clam in, it may not be fresh clam juice."

When it came time to order the next course, the soup, Andrews told Mario to order for himself.

"Sir," Cuomo said to the waiter, "when you have a minute, I'll have the turtle soup—and would you please put a turtle in it."

Everyone at the table, with the notable exception of the host, burst into laughter. Andrews turned red and said to Mario, "You are mocking me." The waiter told Cuomo he had better leave, so he excused himself and walked out.

"Sometimes," Cuomo wrote in his diary in 1982, "I think the best thing about the past is 20 stories like the turtle story."

Cuomo himself insists that there is no lingering resentment from the ethnic discrimination he suffered. "I mean, I'm not maybe a typical case," he told a reporter in 1986, "but life has been so good to me and my family. . . . The idea of resenting anything makes me feel so guilty that it worries me. I mean, look what I've got."

And "what I've got"—among other things, the governorship of New York, immense popularity and respect, and a claim on the nation's ear and its conscience—represents not only an opportunity to do good and a personal victory; it is also in Cuomo's mind (as well as in fact) a triumph for Italian-Americans and for outsiders of all varieties. The governor's sister Marie articulated this aspect of her brother's success when she said to me: "The Italian-Americans have gotten bad names with so many different things. People pick up on that and ignore all the good things that have been accomplished by Italian-Americans. [In Mario,] Italian-Americans have someone to be proud of, even if they don't agree with everything he says. He has integrity and he's someone who makes us proud to be Italian-Americans."

And that explains the part of Mario Cuomo's makeup that led him to say early in 1986, "If anything could make me change my mind about running for the presidency, it's people talking about, 'An Italian can't do it; a Catholic can't do it.' "[6]

As it happened, the elite Manhattan law firms probably did Mario Cuomo a great favor by turning him down. His friend John Gerity points out that it is unlikely that Cuomo would take a position with a major firm today, because "he likes to be his own man, and to a certain extent that's something you have to give up if you're with a really prestigious firm." In a smaller firm, it is possible for an outstanding attorney to become the main partner in a relatively short period. Although it was not a decision he made for himself, when he wound up on Court Street in Brooklyn instead of across the East River in a Wall Street firm, Cuomo was in effect trading prestige for independence. He had unintentionally made a first-rate bargain.

In December 1958 Cuomo joined the Brooklyn firm of Corner, Weisbrod, Froeb, and Charles—the same firm for which he had written briefs while he was in law school. "Court Street" did not have the best connotations in New York legal circles. A 1975 piece in the *New York Daily News* summarized the general assessment of Court Street: "You should know better than to believe anything a Court St. lawyer tells you. Court St. lawyers are notorious. They are internationally known for conniving. Whenever you see an ambulance, you'll always see a Court St. lawyer chasing it." But the fifteen-member firm Cuomo joined was one of the oldest and best in Brooklyn. It had been established in 1837 and had as clients most of the prestigious institutions in the borough. It was basically a staid, business-oriented firm, but in a relatively short time Cuomo began to put his imprint on it, converting it more into a litigating firm. He brought Fabian Palomino and other outstanding attorneys into the firm. They did a variety of work, representing among others banks, municipalities, and contractors. Cuomo worked hard, as usual, and rose rapidly. He was made a partner in 1963 and soon came to dominate the firm.

By the early sixties the federal government was deeply into its urban renewal projects. Under the Title I program, Washington underwrote two-thirds of the cost of urban renewal projects in New York City. Handsome fees could be made quite legitimately in these condemnation cases, which were the speciality of one of Cuomo's partners, John Finn. Finn was extremely jealous of Cuomo and his superior talents. According to others in the firm, Finn tried to thwart Cuomo in any way he could. Cuomo handled some condemnation cases, but he did a wide variety of other work. He quickly developed a reputation for creativity and being able to find ways to win the most difficult cases. "When there was a hard one," Joe Mattone says, "they gave it to Mario."

As Cuomo's—and the firm's—reputation grew (the firm eventually came to be known as Corner, Finn, Cuomo, and Charles), other lawyers started bringing him their "impossible" cases, the ones they could not handle in a routine fashion. The defeated litigants in one action Cuomo won actually came back and tried to get him to represent them in a subsequent case. His forte was not as a trial lawyer but as an appellate lawyer. He was so good at it that eventually he stopped trying cases entirely and just specialized in appellate work. "Arguing an appeal or arguing a motion," says Sal Curiale, who worked in the firm in Cuomo's later years of private practice, "he had no peer."

He was a superb negotiator (a skill that would bring him to the public's attention by the late 1960s) and a good technical lawyer. In addition, he made a point of always being fully prepared for a case. He analyzed beforehand every possible question that could be asked—every conceivable weakness in his case—and prepared a response for each.

Cuomo's reputation for creativity was well deserved. No matter how impossible the case, he could always come up with something. Not that what he came up with invariably worked, but he could always think of something. Once he handled the appeal of a man who held up a liquor store and wound up killing the clerk when the latter unexpectedly came out with a gun. A relatively new law stated that if someone was killed in the perpetration of a felony, it was to be considered first-degree homicide, because the willingness to commit the felony is taken to be a willingness to kill to carry it off.

The case was hopeless, but Cuomo managed to come up with an argument. He asked the court how it could hold that in every case a person intent on committing a felony should be considered a willful murderer merely because someone was unexpectedly killed during the commission of the crime. "Suppose you had a situation," Cuomo said, "where you had a paraplegic in a wheelchair who had a neighbor and one night he thought the neighbor was out and he knew where the neighbor's wall safe was, so he went in to burglarize him. Well, the neighbor was actually in the other room and he comes out and dumps the poor helpless paraplegic out of his wheelchair and is about to bash his skull in with a candelabra. If he can reach in his pocket and pull out a gun and shoot the guy who's trying to kill him, would you say the poor, helpless paraplegic thereby forfeited his life?"

The judge leaned over his bench and said, "Mr. Cuomo, when you have a case with a paraplegic and a wall safe and someone trying to bash his head in, then you come to us and we'll answer the question. In the meantime, let's deal with *this* case!"

Cuomo had a deep reverence for the law, believing it to be the embodiment of reason and fairness. When an officer of the court did not seem to have the proper respect for the law or for fairness, Cuomo could become exceedingly angry.

He was noted, as Palomino put it, for "not taking any crap from judges." Cuomo was prepared, and he expected judges to be also. He also expected them to give him fair treatment and deal with him civilly. Once Justice Henry Ughetta of the state appellate court in Brooklyn found out what Cuomo did when he did not get the judicial treatment he believed he and his clients deserved. Cuomo was making an oral argument before five judges of the appellate division, and Ughetta, who had taken a liking to Cuomo, leaned over to talk to the judge on his left. Palomino thinks he was probably saying something like, "Listen to this kid; he's bright."

When Ughetta started talking, Cuomo stopped. The judge looked up and said, "You may proceed with your argument, counsel."

"I won't proceed with my argument until I get the undivided attention of the court," Cuomo declared.

Palomino, who was in the court waiting to present a case, says Justice Ughetta "turned red like a thermometer and said, 'Well, you *have* the undivided attention of the court. Proceed.'"

Mario resumed his argument, but moments later the judge, in a fit of anger, wheeled around his chair so that his back was to Cuomo. The young attorney waited a couple of seconds, then picked up his brief and walked out of the courtroom.

When he turned back around, Ughetta asked where counsel was. He was told that Cuomo had left. The judge declared that Cuomo had better come to see him within twenty-four hours.

Cuomo went to the judge's chambers the next day and Ughetta asked him if he was going to apologize.

"Judge, I don't think I owe you an apology," Cuomo said. "Do you know what you did to the system of justice, the appearance of it, when you turned your back? You are supposed to be disinterested. My client is entitled to a full hearing by every judge on the court. What you did was not proper, and I don't see how I can apologize. I didn't do it for myself, but for the system of justice and for my client. We are entitled to better treatment than that."

Justice Ughetta paused for a moment and then said, "I'll accept your appearance here as an apology."

Representing corporate clients could not long satisfy Cuomo's need to serve others. Within a few years of his joining the firm— and before the Supreme Court's 1963 decision in *Gideon* v. *Wainright* established the right of an indigent defendant in felony prosecutions to a court-appointed counsel—he was doing a good deal of pro bono work, representing poor defendants in criminal cases. On two occasions Cuomo represented convicted men appealing their death sentences. Both times he used all his resources to convince the court to commute the sentences. These life-and-death cases "made indelible impressions on me," Cuomo says. His later steadfast opposition to capital punishment is deeply rooted in his basic religious values, but his participation in the appeals of people sentenced to the electric chair certainly added to the strength of his principled opposition to the death penalty.[7]

* * *

By looking at his years in the private practice of law, it is possible to examine in some detail several of Mario Cuomo's basic characteristics. His attitudes toward work, money, and his own family developed more fully while he was a young attorney. Each is critical to an understanding of Cuomo as a public figure in his later years.

As he has in all his occupations, Cuomo the counsel saw hard work as the route to advancement. He is never truly happy unless he has reason to work almost around the clock. When he was a practicing lawyer, the seven-day work week was more common than the six-day one, and the five-day work week was unheard of. He often worked all night on a brief.

And he expected similar dedication from others. When Sal Curiale was working as an associate in the law firm in the early seventies, he had been working Saturdays and holidays for several months. Then one day he did not get into the office until 10:30 A.M. At noon he went to lunch and came back at one. He wrote these times into his daily work log, which the partners reviewed. The next day he came in and found a note in Cuomo's handwriting that said: "When one comes in at 10:30, it's a good idea not to take a whole hour for lunch—MMC." Curiale was astonished. "I'm working my ass off, you know—coming in weekends." But Cuomo's note "wasn't a joke."

Cuomo himself never went to lunch. He would have something like a pot roast sandwich at his desk, virtually inhaling it, so as not to waste time.

"Life goes so fast," Matilda Cuomo said to me. "I mean you have to smell the roses. I tell Mario that—at least tiptoe through them." But he leaves almost no time for smelling roses.

He would never take a vacation if he could possibly avoid it. In this, if in little else, Cuomo is reminiscent of Herbert Hoover, who tried desperately to avoid vacations entirely, and if obliged to take one would rush from one vista to the next, so as to see as much as possible in the least amount of time. In later years Matilda dragged Mario off to visit relatives in San Diego. Dick Starkey gave him a note advising him: "Grit your teeth and enjoy it." When Cuomo did go on a vacation after he was in public life, his staff heard from him even more than when he was in Albany. He was almost constantly on the phone. A real vacation would be one of the worst threats that Cuomo could face. "People say, 'I want you to get him away on a vacation to the Caribbean,' " Fabian Palomino told me.

"He'd go out of his mind if it was a couple of days that he was away from things he considers it his responisbility to fulfill." "It drove him *crazy* to be on vacation," Dick Starkey says.

Aside from sports, Cuomo has never had hobbies. Like everyone else, he needs recreation. But when one considers the meaning of the word—to "re-create" oneself—it can be understood that different people can accomplish the purpose of recreation at different paces. Cuomo can relax and recreate himself very rapidly. "The thing he can do is really relax and he can get his batteries recharged in a very short time," Palomino says. "It is a facility not many people have. . . . He can relax in a couple of hours as well as most people can in a five-day vacation." A portion of an evening spent telling jokes and stories about old times and old characters he has known will renew all of Cuomo's energies.

He does *everything* rapidly. It is as if his life were operating on a video recorder played at the fast-forward search speed. He sleeps only four or five hours a night, but he has always done so, his sister told me, very soundly. It seems that he sleeps the same way he does everything else: intensely. He is able to cram eight hours of rest into four or five hours of sleep.

Cuomo usually awakens at about five in the morning. He needs no alarm; his zest for life and work are sufficient to arouse him before dawn. It is normally his first task to brew coffee and sit drinking it in his study while writing his hopes and questions into his diary. At about six forty-five Dick Starkey calls from New York with an oral digest of the morning papers. By that time Cuomo's work day is already well over an hour old. It often does not end until sixteen hours later.

Once when I was riding with him from the Albany airport to the state capitol at about five in the afternoon, Cuomo saw many people heading home. "What do these people find to *do* at home all that time?" he asked in genuine curiosity. "How do they keep busy enough to stay up until midnight?" The comment was doubly revealing. In it Cuomo indicated both that he thought it was necessary for people to keep constantly busy and that everyone should stay up until midnight.

It seems clear that the possibility of having idle time is threatening to Cuomo. "That's the way he was brought up," his brother told me, "constantly working—work, work, work. 'I'll take a vacation soon,' [he keeps saying]. The trouble is, he always thinks there's another emergency." Sometimes, of course, an attorney or a public official faces genuine emergencies. But if there are none, Cuomo will create them in order to have something to keep him busy. "A constant," Dick Starkey told me, "including the secretary of state and lieutenant governor days—it was a sure thing—Friday afternoon at five-thirty or so, there was going to be some crisis, that the governor generated. We're going to be on the phone, and we're going to be running around until seven or eight o'clock. He *never* was comfortable with being able to sit back and relax and say, 'Well, let's take a deep breath.'"

Starkey told me that a joke among members of Cuomo's staff has long been: "My God, the summer's coming; the legislative session is over. What's Mario going to find to do to occupy himself and us?" But it is no joke. Cuomo always does create a campaign for the slack season. He'll find an issue and barnstorm around the state. "Whenever you thought there was a period of comparative relaxation, it was *then* that he would turn on the steam," Starkey says.

If members of his staff suggest that it is time for a vacation, Cuomo will say that *they* can go, if they want, but leave him out. "*You* wanna go on vacation? Okay, *you* go," Al Levine, who worked for Cuomo when he was secretary of state and on several occasions since, quotes him as saying in effect. "He puts a guilt trip on you." The implication is: "You wanna let me do all the work? Fine. Go ahead. I'll do all the work. *I'll* get it done. *You* go on vacation."

"The one great sin," Cuomo firmly believes, is "wasting existence." He will do anything he can to occupy his time, even if it's cleaning the oven. "I look forward to doing it," he wrote in his diary after his election in 1982. "Cleaning, arranging, working, catching up, making it neat, putting things in order. Never leave moments totally empty. If I can, I run. If I can't, I'll work." "If you're too tired to read or write or think, do something you're not too tired to do. The refrigerator. The leaves. The shoes."

Never leave moments totally empty. What does it say about someone if he is afraid to have unoccupied time? Cuomo is aware that there must be some meaning to his addiction to keeping busy. "Once in a while I think about 'why' and what a psychiatrist might say. But then, I'm usually shining the shoes when the question comes up, and I bury it with the fury of my strokes."[8]

I have no training in psychology or psychiatry, and I believe that the value of psychoanalysis from afar of public figures is severely limited. I would not venture to guess what a passionate desire always to be working may mean. Most Americans, brought up in a culture still infused with the work ethic advanced by the Puritans, see nothing amiss with a leader who thrives on work and challenge. It is a trait that many of our political leaders have had, particularly during periods of progressive reform and governmental activism. Others, usually those who have risen to prominence during eras of conservative retrenchment (Calvin Coolidge and Ronald Reagan come readily to mind), had no such love for work. It is, in any case, obvious that Mario Cuomo's "workaholism" is an important part of his makeup.

One of the more unusual qualities of Mario Cuomo is that, with the exception of a brief period in the years immediately after his marriage, money has never held any great attraction for him. Even in the period of his early practice of law, when he briefly had some interest in making money, that interest was at a much lower level than that of most young men on the rise. His friend Nicholas D'Arienzo stretches the truth—but only a bit—when he asserts that Mario was "never out to make money." The only error in that statement is the use of "never," but the period during which Cuomo was out to make money did not last long.

It is obvious that Cuomo set out to build a rewarding career. He tried to finish first in his class in law school, took a clerkship on the Court of Appeals, and applied to the top Manhattan firms. There are different sorts of rewards. Many of them are not monetary. He avidly pursued success in the law. But money was only briefly a measure of that success.

Coming from a relatively poor background can have varying effects on different people. Most of those who are bright and success-driven see money as their salvation. If lack of money was the cause of one's family's deprivation during childhood, it is reasonable to conclude that accumulating large amounts of money in adulthood is the best assurance that one's own family will not suffer similar deprivation.

Joe Mattone, Cuomo's good friend since prep school, is quite willing to say that his own motivation was precisely this. "I didn't like the idea of sleeping three in a bed, getting hand-me-down shoes," Mattone told me, remembering his youth. He saw doing well in school as a route out of poverty. Even making friends could be functional in advancing a career. "I think it differed for Mario," Mattone said to me. "My idea was to go out and make money; his wasn't. . . . I make no apologies for my goal, but I don't think it was the same as his." Cuomo had a desire, Mattone believes, "to be something that *he* felt was important."

But becoming a husband and a father produces responsibilities and challenges. Mario Cuomo was not the sort to shirk the former or shy away from the latter. The fact that the Raffas had considerably more money than the Cuomos was the major reason for Mario's pursuit of money in his early years of practicing law. On the responsibility side he felt a need to provide for Matilda and their growing family in a style similiar to what she had enjoyed before her marriage. And the financial success of Charlie Raffa constituted a challenge for Mario the competitor. He tried for a while to make money, in large part at least, just to prove to himself that he could do it.

Mario's father and his godfather, Rosario Cuomo, had decided to occupy their time after leaving their retail businesses by dabbling in home construction. They bought several lots in Holliswood and began building houses. Mario has always been a "kitchen man"—he loves to sit at the kitchen table, drinking coffee and talking—and he immediately fell in love with the kitchen of one of the houses they were building. With assistance from his father, young Cuomo was able to purchase a new, family-built Cape Cod house a few blocks from his parents' home. The house, which was eventually expanded to five bedrooms and a finished basement, was adequate, but far from luxurious. But it would have to be paid for. The purchase price of twenty-eight thousand dollars was a large amount for a house in 1958.

So to provide for his family and to demonstrate that he could do it as well as anyone else, Cuomo set out to make money in his first years in private practice. Even then, though, he was uncomfortable with the idea of making money. "I don't think he enjoyed charging people money for services," Mattone told me with a sense of amazement. "Most lawyers want their worth recognized. . . . [But Mario] didn't know how to negotiate a fee. . . . He could find a solution to a legal problem, but he couldn't negotiate a fee." "He never wanted to discuss money with clients," Curiale says. And when he became a partner, "he would never discuss salaries with his employees. Somebody else would always have to do that."

After he entered politics, money continued to be the one subject about which the usually loquacious Cuomo had difficulty speaking. He hated to ask people for political contributions. "It killed him—it actually killed him—to go to so many fund-raisers—to go and ask [for money]," Nick D'Arienzo told me. "It was so contrary to his personality. Every time he went, he really was in pain and he would say, 'This is my three hundred fourteenth'—he knew the number. I think it was like a nail in the cross; every fund-raiser for him was a nail that he could feel—he hated that."

Since he has been in public office, Cuomo has emphasized to staff members that he would not tolerate his political operatives putting pressure on his appointees to contribute to his campaigns. "If anybody approaches you and asks for a political donation for me, for my campaign, and you can't afford it, and somebody gives you the squeeze, I want to know about it. If you can't afford it, I don't want your money."

After years in which money for both personal and political needs was usually scarce, Cuomo was confronted with an odd situation in the wake of his victory in the 1982 gubernatorial primary. "A strange problem has developed," he wrote in his diary on October 28 of that year. "We have more money [in the campaign coffers] than we can spend—much more! I told [campaign finance chairman Bill] Stern today that I believe we have a moral obligation to tell people we will accept no more contributions."

Mario Cuomo comes by his aversion to asking people—whether clients or potential contributors—for money honestly. As in so much else in his life, this characteristic appears to be taken from his father. It will be recalled that when Andrea Cuomo sold his store he refused to try to collect the money owed him by neighborhood people.

Once he had made money—never huge amounts, but a comfortable living—for a few years, Cuomo realized that, at least for him, it wasn't hard to do. He had proved that he could do it, and he lost interest in it. The pursuit of money could not sustain him. As long as it was a challenge to be met, Cuomo's competitive nature gave him the desire to try and make money. But once he had done it, it was as if money had become an unworthy opponent. The sport was no longer there. He seemed to say to himself, friends indicate, "Is that all there is to it? So I made money—so? Now what else is there in this marvelous world we're living in?"

There is no question that, had he wanted to, Cuomo could have made—and still could make—money by the bundles. But he believed there must be more to life than accumulating money. And as a lawyer, he could see that all he seemed to be doing, as his sister Marie put it, "was making rich people even richer." That, he believed, was not what God had put him on earth to do.

After his brief early fling with making money, Cuomo became almost totally uninterested in the subject as it applied to him. "He has absolutely *no* interest in money," Al Levine says. "He knows what money can buy, [but] he has no interest in creature comforts." "I've never known him to treat himself to *any*thing," Levine told me. Cuomo adamantly refused, for example, to have any public funds spent for improving New York's Executive Mansion in any way that might be perceived as providing for his or his family's comfort. If structural work was needed to preserve the building for future generations, spending public funds was appropriate. But all other improvements in the mansion were made as a result of Mrs. Cuomo's fund-raising from private donors.

It is not that Cuomo *detests* money. "I wouldn't say that I spurned it," he told me. "I always provided well for the family. But we were never rich. Could I have been rich? Of course," he said matter-of-factly. "It's a question of where you apply your energies." Since his early days in private practice, Cuomo has chosen to direct his prodigious energies elsewhere.

When he entered public life in 1975 as secretary of state, Cuomo gave up his private law practice, although this was not required by law and no previous secretary of state had done so. He wanted both to avoid any appearance, however slight or unjustified, of conflict of interest and to devote all of his time to serving the public. It was not a decision that his wife endorsed. "It hurt me a little bit—and the children," Matilda Cuomo said to me of her husband's decision to abandon his law practice in favor of public service, "because we felt we had struggled so much, all of us. . . . We figured we had come to a point in our lives where we were going to make a lot of money" from Mario's senior partnership in the firm.

"I'm almost ashamed to admit that I feel I have deprived my family of so much," Cuomo wrote in his diary in 1980. "I don't blame Matilda for being a little resentful, especially since she knows others have done what I've done and still practiced law and probably gotten rich—legally." "She has never agreed fully with my decision to give up the practice and the income. I'm thinking that maybe I have to find some way to put my family—what's left of it—up higher." "She doesn't see it as a commendable effort to create no false image of conflict," he wrote on the same subject the following year, "she sees it as selfishness on my part." And, in a strange way, she is right. It is a central paradox of Mario Cuomo that since what he most wants to do is serve others, in him selflessness can almost be seen as a form of selfishness. But this is about the best form that selfishness can take.

Cuomo's "selfish" desire to serve others left him virtually broke by the time of the 1982 campaign. The family home in Queens had appreciated greatly in value in the rising New York real estate market, but when it came to liquid assets, the Cuomos were at "the bottom of the barrel." "I had nothing." The last twenty thousand dollars in cash that they had had been spent on their eldest daughter's education. "So there you are in public life," the governor said to me, "and what do you do? You have the children's college, weddings to pay for."

So Cuomo sold the only asset—other than his extremely valuable time—that he had: his diaries. He received an advance of something in excess of a hundred thousand dollars, which, as he says, sounds like a lot of money "until you take out fifty thousand dollars for taxes and you start paying tuition."

"I have great respect for what money can buy, for a person like me," Cuomo said in an interview. "It can buy you *freedom.*" He has the assurance that he could make a large amount of money if he wanted to. But "that was never really an objective for me. It can't buy us happiness; *but,* it could have bought us more *security.* If I'd spent more time on it, I would have been *freer.*"

Even today money does not flow freely in the Cuomo household. As the winter of 1980 approached, Matilda Cuomo asked her husband if they had enough money for her to buy a coat that year. "I felt so badly," he told Palomino. "We do have the money, but I felt so bad that she had to come and ask. She was the one to make the sacrifices."

Matilda Cuomo is certain that money has not been a priority in her husband's life. She points out that they both have many friends "who are very, very wealthy, who have done extremely well. But this has never been his criterion to be a success in life." That opinion seems to be universally shared by those who know Cuomo well.

"Some people can never be satisfied," Matilda Cuomo notes. "There's never enough" for them. It is that attitude that Mario

Cuomo has always rejected. Avarice is, after all, like lust, pride, and sloth, among the seven deadly sins. And it is one of Mario Cuomo's principal purposes in life to reject those evils.[9]

For a short time Mario Cuomo's objective was making money. Then it became helping others. Both goals required long hours of hard work. And that work—plus some play—took precious time away from his family during the early years of its existence. In those first years of marriage, Cuomo simply did not treat his new family in a way that would mesh with his later ideal of the family unit as the model for society.

It is not easy, as Matilda Cuomo found out, "to be with your family and be committed as [Mario] has been. . . . I understand that—that's why they have divorces and families break up. But people have to work at it harder. There are sacrifices to be made on everybody's account."

The Cuomo family ultimately expanded to include five children. Joining Margaret and Andrew were Maria, born in 1962, Madeline in 1964, and Christopher in 1970. As in most families containing a committed man, it was the wife and children of the Cuomo family who were obliged to make most of the sacrifices. If a father is out five nights a week, there is no way that he can pay as much attention to his children as would be desirable. "The day-to-day affairs of the family," Mattone says of the Cuomos, "were left up to the wife. You just can't be in two places at once." The children have understood—sometimes. "Why can't we go on a trip like so-and-so?" they often wanted to know. "I think, more than the kids, it was I who sacrificed," Matilda Cuomo told me. "I would have liked a lot more time being with him, traveling with him. You can't have that."

Time is the most precious commodity in Mario Cuomo's world. The ways in which he chose to spend some of it in the early years of his marriage may have been understandable, in fact commonplace, but they were not always commendable. The rest of Cuomo's career leads us to expect more from him than the commonplace.

A group of lawyers from Cuomo's firm and other Court Street firms developed the custom of going to a local bar, which changed names frequently, to "unwind" almost every night. Cuomo worked too much to join them very often, but did attend some of their sessions. Although some of them drank to excess, Cuomo never did. He nursed a vodka-and-tonic or two for the whole evening. But they sometimes stayed there arguing and talking—often about how they could do good if they had political power—for a couple of hours at a time.

There was nothing illicit about Cuomo's time spent at the bar. Women have always been attracted to him, and friends who were there say that women in the bar sometimes tried to pick him up. Whenever possible, he pretended not to notice. If they were too forward, he would tell them they were wasting their time.[10]

"There was a lot of hurt going on. It's not easy," Matilda Cuomo said of the early years of her marriage. He was working most of the time, and she was left with the children.

Cuomo "liked to give lip service to 'You work hard during the week, but you should take your weekends off and you shouldn't work late,'" Sal Curiale told me. "But that was all lip service, because he would be in the office seven days a week."

Under the circumstances, the best Matilda Cuomo could do was to insist that if her husband worked on Sunday, he at least had to be sure to be home for dinner with the family. "I would be very flexible," she told me. "If we weren't going to have it at one o'clock, we'd have it at five o'clock—and the kids knew this. So I would work with him and for sure we'd always have that Sunday dinner."

Even that was sometimes difficult, though. Curiale remembers working in the office on a brief with Cuomo one Sunday afternoon. The phone rang and Mario answered it. His end of the conversation went something like, "Um-hm. Uh-huh. Yes, Matilda. Okay, Matilda. Yes. Um-hm. Okay."

"What's the matter?" Curiale asked.

"It's Matilda's birthday, and we have company at the house. I have to go."

Curiale was incredulous. "And then he used to say, 'Well, you can get a lot of work done during the week and you shouldn't take the time off from your family.'"

When Cuomo was trying in the late 1960s to help sixty-nine families in Corona retain their homes (see next chapter), the litigants would show up at his house at any time on a weekend or at night. The ultimate affront may have occurred one Christmas Eve. A group of Corona residents arrived and sat down with Mario at the kitchen table to discuss the case. "They were in the kitchen and my kids were crying because they wanted to open their gifts, which was our tradition [on Christmas Eve]," Matilda Cuomo said to me. She finally had to whisper in Mario's ear, "Please tell them to leave. It's Christmas Eve!"

There are two things for which Cuomo has told Palomino he will never forgive him. One was the way he treated him in getting the bar exam results. The second is telling Matilda that he really didn't have to work as late as he did. (It remains to be seen whether any of the stories Fabian told me will be a third thing for which Mario cannot forgive him.)

One night Palomino was home at nine-thirty and Matilda called him to ask where Mario was. "At the office," Fabian replied.

"Tell me something," Matilda requested. "Does he really have to work so late?"

"Matilda," Fabian said, "the fact is that he is very gifted. He doesn't have to work that hard, but it is his temperament. As long as he has time, he's not going to let that time go unused. If he has time when a critical case comes up, he's going to sit there and look at it and ask questions about it. I'll tell you something: the answer that he gets when he spends all that time with it is the same answer he could have given you off the top of his head three weeks ago, if you asked him. But he's got to go through the process. But does he honestly *have* to? No."

The next morning Mario called Fabian. "What did you *do?*" he pleaded. "When I got home last night, Matilda said, *'Even Fabian* says you don't have to work that late—*even Fabian!*' "

After he became governor and Palomino became his special counsel, Cuomo started telling his old friend things like, "I spoke to Peg [Fabian's wife] this morning. I told her, 'You know, Fabian really doesn't have to work so hard.' Thank God the world is round and everything comes back!" Cuomo says, breaking up in laughter.

"It was very hard," Matilda Cuomo told me. "I would not have my daughter do that." "The whole thing is," she said, "he did have to work hard. I guess you could label him a workaholic in the sense that he felt he had to put in that much effort to do it right. I understood that he felt better; that he *had* to do it that way."

Cuomo worried greatly about the possible ill effects of his lack of time with his family. He made sure that the time he did devote to the children was "quality time." It should come as a surprise to no reader who has gone this far that Matilda says that Mario would not idle his time around the house. He would play ball with the kids, talk to them, and do his best to make up for lost time. He would join with the kids and his father to play boccie.

Palomino remembers being in the library with Cuomo once in the mid-1970s when he told him that Andrew was graduating from high school the following Sunday.

"Great," Fabian said. "How is Andrew doing?"

"You know, I really don't know," Mario replied. "I've been so busy running around the office for a long time—I really don't know. I haven't spent a lot of time with him in the last four years. I guess I've taken him to two or three ball games. Matilda made me take him."

Palomino says that Cuomo felt most guilty about being at work so much when Andrew was growing up. He tried to remedy the situation when he became lieutenant governor and Andrew went to Albany Law School. Mario insisted that Andrew live with him in his apartment at the Wellington. It was only then that father and son really got to know each other well. They have been very close ever since.

One suspects, in fact, that the governor's protective attitude toward his family (and toward Andrew in particular) stems at least in part from his desire to make up for earlier time he did not spend with his children. In any case, attacks on his family are, even more than ethnic prejudice, the blows that Cuomo finds it most difficult to let pass by. He has learned, in most cases, to deflect criticism directed toward him personally. But he cannot put up with attacks on Matilda, Andrew, or the other children. Political opponents and members of the media have found that this is the way to get Cuomo's dander up, so they do it whenever possible. This is the one form of fastball aimed at the head that he has not yet managed to duck.

Being protective of one's family is in no way a fault. It is a natural instinct, and up to a point is a most admirable quality. Harry Truman won praise in many quarters for defending his daughter Margaret against music critics. If Cuomo can manage to defend his family without seeming defensive, to react without overreacting, he can transform this political liability into yet another asset.[11]

* * *

It is clear that Mario Cuomo did not always live up to his ideal as a family man. It is equally clear, however, that he put a great deal of energy into compensating for the lack of time he spent with his family. And it seems that all of his children have turned out well. That is a testament to Matilda Cuomo's success as a parent, but it also indicates that her husband must have fulfilled his responsibilities as a father to a considerably greater extent than would be indicated by the record that would have been created by his punching a card into a time clock when he entered and left the home.

And his habits in this regard have improved over the years. Since he entered politics, Cuomo has tried to make it a practice to sleep at home every night, even if that means a midnight flight to Albany, and to have either breakfast or dinner with that portion of the family that remains at home on every day that he possibly can. "He really relishes the weekends here," Matilda Cuomo says. He has a great relationship with his youngest child, Christopher. They play basketball, fool around, and wrestle. Mrs. Cuomo is concerned that her husband will get hurt, since their son is six feet two inches tall and wears a size thirteen shoe.

Matilda Cuomo long ago became reconciled to her husband's work habits, and she adjusted the family to them. "There's a lot of closeness in our family, an awful lot," she told me. "I think politics can do that. We have totally absorbed the best that politics has to offer, because we are together more, we appreciate each other more. We feel a sense of purpose."

Cuomo says that it is impossible to understand him without understanding his relationship with his wife. "Matilda and I are the same age, same background, same school, same intelligence, everything," he points out. "It makes it difficult in a lot of ways because neither of us is a dominant figure. She doesn't do what Mario wants, and I don't do what Matilda wants. We've been fighting our way through thirty years of equality, which is difficult—but has somehow made for a very successful marriage."

"Matilda's as good at making policy as I am," Cuomo has said. "I will say that it has probably been hard for Matilda to be a political wife, although she never shows it. She is very supportive and works well with me. Still, I have to believe that somewhere in her psyche she knows that she could just as easily be the governor and I could be the husband of the governor." This attitude was demonstrated in the 1986 reelection campaign, when the governor aired television commercials featuring Matilda. These were the first in New York history urging voters to retain a first lady.

Cuomo's pride in and love for his children is manifest. Frequent comments in his diaries indicate his concern and affection for them. "Andrew hurt his back," he wrote in 1981. "He needed x-rays. He went to his sister Margaret. How lovely!" (Margaret Cuomo Perpignano is a physician.) "Madeline is 16 and beautiful. But 16," he wrote knowingly in 1980. "Chris did not get a good report card. He is bright but distracted in school, constantly in need of attention. I believe that he is still reacting to the inattention he suffered in the mayoralty and [lieutenant] gubernatorial campaigns. Matilda and I agreed we'll have to watch him more closely and pay as much attention to him as possible."

Cuomo is constantly aware of the danger that his career poses to his family. "All of this can be absorbing," he wrote in 1981. "It's not difficult to be consumed by the effort to serve and to win. Little wonder that there is such a high incidence of divorce and disorientation among the children of politicians. One could easily spend all one's time thinking only about the problems of the state and the next campaign. And too many days, I do." He realizes that he must alter his outlook, at least at times. "I'm not a single, unattached public servant. I can't devote myself totally to public service without abandoning other major obligations. I have a wife and children—two still at home, both badly needing and fully deserving my time, attention, advice and manifest concern," he continued. "I've tried to do the right thing by them, but too often I haven't succeeded. I'll have to try harder."

He believes, as does Matilda, that the family has come through its ordeals well. They have, he contends, "remained close, supportive of one another." The family has been through a lot—and its tribulations have not been confined to problems caused by Mario's workload. Family members have been robbed and attacked on several occasions. Margaret was accosted when she was fourteen and Maria when she was eighteen. In the spring of 1982, Matilda and Chris were accosted by two muggers. The Cuomo home has been burglarized twice, as has Immaculata Cuomo's house. Maria was nearly killed in a 1980 automobile accident. Charlie Raffa, Matilda's father, was beaten and left for dead by an assailant. His survival was miraculous, but he was left severely incapacitated.

And Frank and Joan Cuomo had a five-year-old son drown many years ago.

The Cuomo family has had its share of tragedy to go along with its remarkable triumphs.

Like his father, Mario Cuomo has talked about family more than he has spent time with his family. Andrea Cuomo worked all the time, as Mario does, but both had their ways of making it clear that they loved their families deeply.[12]

The fact that Mario Cuomo has not uniformly practiced what he preaches when it comes to family life does not mark him as a hypocrite. Rather, it marks him as a human being. Who, after all, *does* invariably live up to his or her own ideals? Cuomo's imperfections in this area may disqualify him for canonization, but they should not be seen as a detriment to his ability to exercise political leadership.

Not practicing what one preaches amounts to hypocrisy when it is consistent and intentional. In Cuomo's case, it is neither. His immediate family has sometimes suffered because of his desire to serve the larger family outside his home, the society. A politician who knows right from wrong, fervently preaches the former, and tries his best to live up to his preaching, should not be faulted too much for having failed at times to live up to his own highly demanding standards. It is better to occasionally fail fully to practice what you preach than not even to know what ought to be both preached and practiced.

6

CONCILIATOR

ALTHOUGH Mario Cuomo found the law much more fulfilling than baseball, he soon came to realize that he needed more if he was to satisfy his twin desires for competition and service. He sought new outlets for his energies. One route of service was to teach, and in 1963 Cuomo joined the faculty of St. John's Law School as an adjunct professor. He also began to join civic organizations and to seek legal battles in which he might accomplish more than simply making money for himself and for others who were already well-to-do. In the process he began to develop another of his talents, one that may appear to contradict his keen competitiveness. Cuomo discovered in the 1960s and early 1970s that he has an extraordinary skill at reconciling people who are in conflict and at finding compromises that can be accepted by both sides in a dispute.

"There is no substitute for the ancient and honorable art of negotiated compromise, not of principles but of implements," Cuomo said in a 1981 speech, "compromise that comes only after extended, honest, tedious—sometimes excruciating—dealings and exchange. And compromise that operates from the principle that the common good often requires at least a partial sublimating of what appears to be the individual good. Call it 'give and take.' "

"He has a remarkable ability as a conciliator—a peacemaker, someone who can find a suitable middle ground where none seems to exist," Margaret Swezey, a Citibank official in Queens who has known Cuomo in civic activities there for years, said to me. "Anyone who knows Queens knows what an impossible task Cuomo faced in the Corona and Forest Hills situations, but he did it." No matter how cantankerous or aggressive opponents in a case might be, Cuomo's former law associate Sal Curiale told me, "they'd go into his office and everybody would come out smiling, as if there was this 'I don't know why I disagreed with you—well, you never explained it to me' attitude." The spell might wear off later, Curiale said, but Cuomo had an amazing talent for reconciliation. "People couldn't help feeling like, 'Gee, this guy's right,' when they sat down with him and talked and laughed, and he told stories, or whatever." He would then say to the feuding parties, "What do you say we work it out this way?" "You came out of there feeling good, no matter how you felt when you went in," says Curiale.

Cuomo has strong values and high ideals, but he has always been a practical man. He appreciates that different people can have different views of things—and can be equally sincere in their positions. The first task in finding a way through an impasse is to determine what each of the two sides believes to be essential. "The facts generally suggest the solutions," Cuomo has said. "But first you must air the facts." The opposing sides in a dispute are likely to do a good deal of posturing. Some of the items that each claims are essential may not be. So if the mediator can find out what is really essential to each party, a solution can be fashioned by including those items and working out the others on which mutual agreement is possible. John Gerity sums up Cuomo's approach to reconciliation by saying: "Many times people think a solution is giving this person half of what he wants, and the other person half of what he wants, but it's not so much that as it is not denying to either side that which they really feel they require, [and] then making the solution up out of what's left over."

Cuomo often says that in most situations "the truth lies somewhere in the middle." On several occasions he has employed the image of finding the way between Scylla and Charybdis.* These references do not imply any simple "splitting of the difference." The best course may be much closer to one side than the other. In his report on the Forest Hills housing dispute, Cuomo quoted Edmund Burke's statement that "all government—indeed, every human benefit and enjoyment, every virtue and every prudent act—is founded on compromise." But there is a difference between

---

*This image provided Sal Curiale with his only opportunity to win an argument with Cuomo. When Curiale made reference in a brief to being "between Scylla and Charybdis," Cuomo said, "Oh, the two whirlpools." "No, you're wrong," Curiale said. "One was a rock and one was a whirlpool." They bet a dollar on it, and Curiale won. Thereafter, Curiale said, "he made me sorry, because every mistake I made, grammar, whatever, was corrected at every opportunity." MMC doesn't like to lose.

practicality and expedience. Cuomo never favors the latter. Similarly there is a difference between compromising in order to advance basic principles and compromising basic principles. Again Cuomo strenuously opposes the latter. He knows that it is impossible to completely satisfy both sides in a dispute. "But," he asks in a good summary of his view of conciliation, "can't we be helpful in at least defusing the situation? There must be some intermediate plan that will give something to everyone; that will at least reduce the roar to a grumble."

In situations where Cuomo is trying to bring conflicting parties together, he almost never gets angry, even if the opponents in the dispute start yelling at each other or at him. He understands that in the heat of the moment, antagonists are likely to lose their tempers (as he has been known to do when *he* was on one side of a conflict). But when his role is that of mediator, he generally remains above the fray and keeps calm.

The ability to mediate disputes may, in fact, not be such an odd talent to combine with an intense competitive nature. As long as one is not personally involved on one side of a controversy, compromising does not in any sense imply defeat. The one who drafts a compromise and persuades both sides to accept it can actually be seen as the victor over *both* of the original contestants. If the compromise solution helps those who were being crushed by government power and seems also to serve the public interest, the situation seems tailor-made for Mario Cuomo: the need for legal skills and reasonableness, identification with the underdog, the opportunity to taste victory and at the same time to serve others. It is small wonder that Cuomo found this sort of public law and mediation so much to his liking.[1]

By the early sixties Cuomo was itching for greater involvement in serving others, especially those in need. His pro bono work helped to meet this need, but he wanted more opportunities to help. At the same time, he had just read *The Divine Milieu* and his Church was beginning to encourage its communicants to leave the walls of the fortress and go out and try to ease the world's problems. Cuomo needed little encouragement in this direction.

Although Cuomo as yet showed no interest in politics, some of his activities in the sixties were the sort that might be expected of one grooming himself for office. In 1963 he was elected president of the Catholic Lawyers Guild of Brooklyn. Only thirty at the time, Cuomo became the youngest president in the group's history. Later he won a similar position in Queens. In 1964 the Brooklyn Junior Chamber of Commerce named Cuomo "Man of the Year" in the legal profession.

Cuomo also began to take steps that were a bit more out of the ordinary for the time. He became a prominent member of the Catholic Interracial Council and the Committee on Catholic-Jewish Relations in Brooklyn and Queens, and was a member of the board of directors of the Legal Aid Society. He was much sought-after as a speaker on a variety of topics. His oratory was already notable. After he addressed about five hundred people at a PTA meeting in Belle Harbor, Queens, in 1963 on the subject of "Equal Rights for Children," Cuomo was praised by the event's organizer as "the only speaker we have had so far who commanded such a stupendous standing ovation."

One of Cuomo's favorite speeches in these years was one saying it is possible to get to heaven in a Cadillac, but it is hard. In this modern-day version of the biblical message that it is easier for a camel to go through the eye of a needle than for a rich man to enter heaven, Cuomo told audiences that there is nothing wrong with becoming rich, but it carries with it an obligation to help the less fortunate. It's not wrong to seek the goods of this world, he said, as long as one keeps the proper perspective. When you rise in the world, be sure that you don't forget those you leave behind.

Teaching was one of Cuomo's loves and the law was another, so it was not surprising that he jumped at the chance to join the law faculty at his alma mater. He continued to teach at St. John's one or two nights a week until 1973. "After all these years," one of his former students—a Republican—said in 1984, "we still have a rapport. He never forgot his students. We always regarded him as very concerned with what happened to us later on. We always knew he was brilliant and had finished high in his class and clerked on the Court of Appeals. He was always a great guy."

Cuomo's ties to St. John's grew stronger when he was elected to the St. John's Alumni Federation board. His position put him in a difficult spot in 1965, when a bitter dispute broke out between the faculty and the university administration. The trouble began in March, when some two hundred faculty members walked out of a faculty meeting to protest inadequate pay and lack of faculty participation in the establishment of university policy. At the time, the university president, the Very Reverend Edward J. Burke, pledged that there would be no reprisals against the professors involved. The dispute simmered through the rest of the spring semester. In April the institution's board of trustees announced a plan to grant the faculty an important role in policy determination. Although some faculty members were displeased with the plan and with the lack of consultation with the faculty in developing it, the board's action seemed likely to defuse the tension.

Then in July 1965 the university named a new president, the Very Reverend Joseph T. Cahill. Within a few days, leaders of faculty organizations were accusing Cahill of "apparently backtracking" on the board's pledge that the faculty would have a say in determining policy. An uneasy truce prevailed through the fall, until just before the Christmas break, when President Cahill announced the dismissal of fifteen faculty members who had been active in the campaign for academic freedom. The number of fired teachers rapidly increased to thirty-one. The United Federation of College Teachers called for a strike to begin when classes resumed on January 3, 1966. Cahill said that the firings were the result of "unprofessional conduct" on the part of the dismissed faculty members.

Somewhere between eighty-five and two hundred—depending on whose figures one accepts—faculty members joined the strike at the beginning of 1966. Hundreds of students participated in temporary class boycotts. The dispute split various St. John's constituencies—faculty, students, and alumni—into bitter, warring factions. Even the school's chapter of the American Association of University Professors divided into pro- and antistrike factions that denounced each other. The former charged that the administration had at first barred priests from joining the AAUP, but then ordered them to do so in order to offset the power of the more militant United Federation of College Teachers and to flood the AAUP membership with administration lackeys and transform it into a "company union." Whatever the accuracy of that charge, a majority of the St. John's chapter condemned the strike, while the national AAUP censured the university for a "grievous and inexcusable" breach of academic freedom.

The alumni were also polarized by the dispute. The Alumni Federation quickly took a stand in favor of the administration. Before the strike even began, the directors and executive committee of the federation issued a statement saying they believed the administration's actions in "the separation of certain members of the faculty . . . were taken with the best interests of the student and faculty in mind, and not done out of vindictiveness or as a device to frustrate the reasonable right of expression." The Alumni Federation board, claiming to speak for thirty thousand St. John's alumni, then took out a full-page ad in the *New York Times.* The ad fully backed the administration, crediting President Cahill with "opening the windows to refreshing changes. The alumni directors argued that the administration had assured responsible academic freedom, but declared that "freedom without responsibility becomes license. The ad further contended that freedom of expression had been abused by some faculty, who allegedly made "misleading and unprofessional statements."

Some other St. John's alumni were outraged at the federation board taking the side of the administration and claiming to speak for all alumni. They called for a general alumni meeting to hear representatives of both sides. The meeting was held in mid-January. One of the questioners was federation board member Mario Cuomo, who, according to some who were present, clearly took the side of the administration. Other alumni who believed that the administration was in the wrong for firing professors without due process were upset with Cuomo's stance.

Cuomo himself is rather vague about the strike and his position on it. "I think I said," he told me, "I wasn't prepared to condemn the teachers because I didn't know why they had been fired; I wasn't prepared to condemn the administration for not telling us why they fired the faculty because I wasn't sure they weren't protecting the faculty from some kind of slander, by keeping it all private." Cuomo is usually most reluctant to rush to judgment. He recalls saying to others on the alumni federation: "I am one who needs to know facts in order to arrive at conclusions. Everybody's taking sides, for the administration, for the teachers—it's not that easy for me, since I don't know enough of the facts." To the faculty Cuomo believes he said something like: "If you have a legal right to have the reason disclosed, then you ought to go to court to fight for your legal right—if you really want it disclosed. The administration is warning you that if you go to court and you force them to disclose the reason, it's going to hurt some individuals, but if you want to take that risk, then go to court."

"That's my position as I remember it," Cuomo told me. "I

really didn't come down on anybody's side—I don't *think*. I was
not a big player in the strike."

Certainly taking a neutral, "wait-and-see" position is what one
would have expected of Mario Cuomo. It is equally certain that
Cuomo would like to think that he *did* take such a position. But
the haziness of his own memory on the topic combined with the
distinct recollection of others that he sided strongly with the administration leads one to believe Cuomo was not as neutral as he
now thinks he was.

St. John's suffered greatly as a result of the dismissals and
strike. It was threatened with loss of accreditation, lost many leading professors, and opened the 1966–67 academic year with a
smaller faculty and reduced enrollment. President Cahill finally
agreed in 1967 to submit the dismissals to binding arbitration, and
many improvements were made in the university over the next
few years. Faculty participation in decision-making was increased
and academic freedom was enhanced by the addition of non-Catholics to high administration posts and to the theology department.
The episode was, nonetheless, an unhappy one, and it left many
alumni unable to feel quite the same toward their alma mater.

Mario Cuomo was not one of them. He went on to become
president of the St. John's Alumni Federation. He seems puzzled
that anyone should feel strongly about the stand that he took.[2]

By the time he became involved
in the St. John's dispute, Cuomo had already begun his series of
battles on behalf of "nobodies" against the city power structure.
Those crusades would ultimately bring him to the public's attention and enable him to launch a political career. When he started
along this path, though, he apparently had no thought of entering
the political arena.

For a man noted for liking tough competition against heavily
favored opposition, a legal battle against Robert Moses was just the
ticket. For more than thirty years, Moses had been one of the most
powerful men in the nation's largest city. He was a master builder
of public projects—highways, bridges, playgrounds, housing projects, cultural centers, and, most of all, parks. His reputation was
enormous, and his influence even greater. What Robert Moses
represented—and what Mario Cuomo began to fight against—can
tell us a great deal about the state of American politics in the 1960s

and about how Cuomo's view of the public interest differed from
that prevailing at the time.

Robert Moses was a "man of vision"—*his* vision. He consciously built projects intended to emulate the ancient Romans.
He wanted *his* public projects to last as theirs did, so that *his* legacy
would be remembered and appreciated long after he was gone. But
Moses' vision included no real people. Of course all his efforts were
directed toward the creation of "public" works and "public"
spaces, but he plainly wanted to put his stamp on them. And his
view of the public is significant. "The public" or "the people" to
someone like Moses is something abstract. It is not only that it is
a faceless, undifferentiated mass; nor is it simply a case of the sum
being greater than the parts. To those who think the way Moses
did, "the public" is a sum *without* parts.

In this way of thinking, individuals do not matter in the slightest (except, of course, for *the* individual, to whom the public will
be eternally grateful for his bestowing of benefits on it). The public
interest or the common good can be achieved at the expense of,
discomfort of, and disruption of the lives of numerous individuals
who, in any realistic view, themselves constitute an important
portion of the public. Such thinking was behind much of the
"urban renewal" of the sixties. The interests of real people—especially poor and powerless people—rarely entered into the planning for these public improvements.

Robert Moses was a megalomaniac. All of his grandiose
accomplishments in public works were not sufficient to satisfy his
enormous ego. His consuming dream had long been to create the
ultimate urban park, the greatest in any city in the world—a project that would outdo those of the Romans. Such a park would be
worthy of the name "Robert Moses Park" and would be the greatest of the many monuments to himself that he would leave behind.

As early as the 1920s, Moses had chosen as the site for his dream
the Flushing Meadows in northern Queens. These three miles of
marshland had become a filthy garbage dump, to which all the
trash of Brooklyn was carted to be burned. In *The Great Gatsby* F.
Scott Fitzgerald called the place "a valley of ashes." Here, in an
area half again as large as Manhattan's Central Park, and located
very near the geographic center of New York City, Moses wanted
to create the world's greatest city park.

The power broker worked at his dream for decades, making use
of the 1939–40 New York World's Fair and many other projects

along the way as means of making improvements at the site. Moses saw in a second world's fair, this one in 1964–65, the opportunity to finally achieve his dream. He took the presidency of the fair in order to direct it toward his goal of a permanent park. To improve the area Moses employed his usual tactic of condemning any land that he wanted for a project. His arrogance was supreme. When *he* wanted land, he expected it to be condemned, and he didn't give a damn who had to be pushed off of it. It had always been so in Moses's long career. To clear the land for his improvements, biographer Robert Caro notes, Moses "evicted the city's people, not thousands of them or tens of thousands of them, but hundreds of thousands, from their homes and tore the homes down. Neighborhoods were obliterated by his edict to make room for new neighborhoods reared at his command." Or, to make way for the future "Robert Moses Park."

Among those who were in the way of Moses's plans for the fair and park were a group of scrap-metal dealers in the Willets Point section of Queens. They did not desire to be "improved" out of existence, and they hired an attorney named Michael Castaldi to fight the condemnation in court. Shortly thereafter, Castaldi learned that he was about to be named a judge, so he sought another attorney to work with him and take the case over when he was elevated to the bench. The person he asked to take this role was Mario Cuomo, who had then been in the private practice of law for about five years. Castaldi told Cuomo that he thought the case would be impossible to win, but the junkyard dealers very badly wanted to try. This was just the way to get Cuomo to take the case. He liked impossible odds.

Moses had his own high-powered legal retainers to eliminate any such obstacles as junk dealers. His chief lawyer for the World's Fair was Samuel I. Rosenman, former aide to President Franklin D. Roosevelt. Rosenman was, according to *New York Post* reporter Joe Kahn, "the lawyer for all these guys who tried to fuck everyone—you had to be suspicious when you saw he was involved." Everyone, it seemed, who had substantial power in New York City—bankers, construction companies, law firms, labor unions, architects, suppliers, and (for a time) the news media—was allied with Moses in the fair project.

Here was quite an opposition for young Cuomo and his junk dealers.

Moses began using his usual tactics to deal with his upstart

opponent. He threatened to end Cuomo's career if he stood in his
way. Moses "went to the partners in my firm," Cuomo told me,
"and said, 'You got to talk to this guy; he's just an obstructionist.'"
Cuomo did not budge. Finally he was summoned to Moses's headquarters, "the Arsenal," on the grounds of Flushing Meadow Park.
Surrounded by the upper echelon of his retainers, Moses explained
to Cuomo how important it was for the fair that the junkyards be
eliminated. He said he wanted to put a Little League stadium in
their place.

"You don't *need* a Little League stadium," Cuomo told him.
"You have Little League fields all over the place that nobody's
playing on."

"Well," Moses said, shifting arguments, "we have to get the
junkyards out of the way, because the whole *world* is coming to see
the World's Fair, and this is a blight."

Cuomo told him to put tall trees around the junkyards "and
pass a regulation that says you can't pile cars or scrap above a
certain height. Then nobody will see it, except from the air."

"No, that's not good enough," Moses insisted. "We'll pay them
generously."

"They don't want to be paid generously," Cuomo said, "because there's no place else that they can do this business. This
whole city is zoned against heavy industrial use. If you had another
location, it would be something else. But you're putting them out
of business. These are people who are war heroes, people who won
all kinds of awards for cooperating with the government—even
those who weren't in the service. These are people who are very
hardworking. They're not highly skilled; they're not commercially
mobile; they have limited abilities—they're very good at what they
do. You're trying to take away their livelihood."

"No. You've got to surrender," Moses demanded.

So they went to court. The opposition was not just the normally all-powerful Moses, but the City of New York. The city's
corporation counsel, Leo Larkin, handled the case against the
scrap dealers.

"I beat them," Cuomo says proudly. "They *couldn't* be beat—
but they were, in the highest court eventually, the Court of Appeals." Cuomo had managed to defeat all the high-priced opposition and to block the condemnation. His own price was not so
high, but he had great difficulty collecting it. "This was not a
situation where you got money in advance," he says. "I gambled

everything on *winning.*" That was fine with the scrap dealers, who expected to lose. "Once they won and they had to pay off, their attitude changed a little," Cuomo told me. His success enhanced his already considerable reputation as a brilliant young attorney, and he was soon being sought out by other groups in Queens neighborhoods who were, as a later movie would put it, "mad as hell and weren't going to take it anymore."[3]

Cuomo had shown that you *can* fight City Hall, that individuals do not have to surrender when the powers of the city make demands on them. At least they wouldn't have to, it seemed, if they had Mario Cuomo as their barrister.

The small Corona neighborhood in Queens was, in the early 1960s, a perfect example of the sort of "urban village" that southern Italian immigrants had created in American cities. It was a self-contained community of small, neat homes with grape arbors and fig trees in the yards. Its residents were almost all people whose families had been there for decades. They had neither the need nor the desire to leave. The people there spoke Italian. Everyone knew everyone else. There was almost no crime. Indeed, police records showed that not a single serious violent crime had been reported in Corona between 1960 and 1966.

Mario Cuomo understood the residents of Corona. "They were," he wrote in 1974, "nice, gentle family people. Simple, hard-working, law-abiding. A vanishing breed." The very feeling of these words set Cuomo off from most New York "liberals" of the time. By the late sixties most liberals had stigmatized lower-middle-class ethnics as ignorant, backward, racist warmongers. Cuomo knew better. He understood these people.

The picture-book life of Corona's urban villagers was first threatened in 1965 by the construction nearby of a massive complex of high-rise, concrete buildings intended to house twenty thousand people. The complex was the brainchild of Sam Lefrak, who in some ways might be considered a private counterpart of "public" builder Robert Moses. With Moses-like modesty, Lefrak named his housing complex Lefrak City. There are indications that city officials promised Lefrak that a new high school would soon be built in the area.

Also in 1965 the administration of President Lyndon B. Johnson began to push for the admirable goal of large-scale integration

of American society. The approach chosen was the scatter-site
program, whereby significant numbers of blacks would be inte-
grated into middle-class white residential areas by the building in
those neighborhoods of housing projects for lower-income people,
most of whom would be black or Hispanic. It was a wonderful
idea, but one whose attractiveness was directly proportional to the
distance one lived from a proposed site for such a project.

People who had never previously taken any interest in public
affairs were likely to become enraged—and publicly so—if they
learned that a "project" was to placed near them. "From the dark
recesses of the American soul," author and *New York Daily News*
columnist Jimmy Breslin has written of the effects of such scatter-
site proposals, "little men will appear, men you have never heard
of, and they will stand in front of the crowd and harangue and the
television lights will turn on them and the despair of the American
soul will rise with the sound of their voices."

The fear is of the outsider, the unknown, the different
—"them." "They" are likely to be black, but Mario Cuomo insists
that the problem is more one of class than of race—a clash between
working and nonworking people. He tries to understand the needs
and anxieties of both groups and to get them to understand each
other.

Washington, in any case, was determined to promote meaningful residential integration, and by 1966 pressure was increasing on
the new city administration of Mayor John V. Lindsay to find
spots in middle-class neighborhoods in the city for 7,500 units of
low-income housing. Some sites had already been chosen when
Lindsay took the city's helm. One of them was a four-and-a-half-
acre plot in Corona, which was slated to become the home of 509
low-income tenants. When the Board of Estimate (a body consist-
ing of the mayor, the City Council president, the comptroller, and
the presidents of each of New York's five boroughs) held a public
hearing on the proposed Corona housing project in late 1966, bus-
loads of angry residents of the area appeared to protest. Only a few
of the protesters were Corona "natives"; most were the new Le-
frakians, who did not want the poor anywhere near them and who
did want a new high school. The Board of Estimate obligingly
altered its plans and agreed to find another location for the housing
project and place a new high school on the Corona site.

The residents of Corona had no particular objection to a high
school being built on a vacant lot. But in November 1966 the local

school board received notice from the city's Site Selection Board that the planned school site would be expanded to twelve acres in order to accommodate an athletic field. This would necessitate the condemnation of sixty-nine Corona homes, effectively destroying the stable Italian-American urban village. The residents were irate when they learned of the expanded school plan and its consequences for them. In the early weeks of 1967, they hastily formed the Corona Taxpayers' Civic Association, headed by Nicholas Piazza, and sought an attorney to assist them. Corona is only about a mile and a half from Willets Point, and some of its residents knew the Willets Point junk dealers. When the latter learned of the threat to Corona, they said to their friends, "You oughta get this guy Cuomo; he's a miracle worker."

The Corona people came to Cuomo, who told them, "Never again."

"I had spent years on Willets Point," Cuomo explained to me, "and my partners were upset. I didn't make any money; I was fighting for a fee, even then, and I said, 'I *can't* do it again.' "

Then Cuomo made what he calls "a fatal mistake." He accepted an invitation from the Corona people to visit the neighborhood and have a cup of coffee with them. "These women sat around a table and *cried*, and told me stories, and I listened to them, and I walked through the streets, and I was hooked." The crusader in Cuomo could not resist an opportunity to help those who had been wronged and were in need. The competitor in him could not resist another fight with City Hall against impossible odds.

The residents of Corona were not people of means, but they were determined to save their community and they raised money through raffles, bingo games, and picnics. Matilda Cuomo says that they frequently gave her jars of homemade tomato sauce and all kinds of other foods. These were partly intended as payment for services for which they had no cash, and partly as peace offerings to Mrs. Cuomo, whose home the Corona litigants were constantly invading at all hours of the night and weekend.

The people of Corona had the immigrant's patriotism that gave them confidence that, in America, justice would prevail in the end. Surely, they thought, the city's political powers would listen to reason. They were mistaken.

Cuomo and his clients worked feverishly to find other suitable sites for a high school, so that they could present the Site Selection Board with sound alternatives to destroying the Corona commu-

nity. They found several, and went to City Hall in March 1967 for
a formal hearing before the board. The formal hearing, however,
turned out to be a formality, not a hearing. As Cuomo put it,
"Corona had come to be heard, but the board had not come to
listen."

The Site Selection Board for new city schools was a product of
the emphasis on centralization that was a goal of the 1963 revision
of the city charter. It consisted of the comptroller, the borough
president of the affected borough, and three appointees of the
mayor. This meant, quite simply, that the board did whatever the
mayor wanted it to do.

Apparently Mayor Lindsay did not want it to listen to the
arguments of the people of Corona. When they arrived for the
hearing, only one of the five members of the board was present.
The other four sent deputies. Cuomo and the Corona residents
spent hours arguing their case and presented mountains of statistics and briefs demonstrating why alternate sites were preferable.
When they were finished, the proxy board members took five
minutes before announcing their unanimous decision to go ahead
with the Corona site. They never looked at the briefs that had been
presented. One of the absent members had even sent along a written opinion, which obviously was reached without benefit of the
community's evidence.

The liberal city administration was displaying the sort of arrogance and contempt for common people that was beginning to
give liberalism a bad name and to cause those same common people
to begin to drift into the ranks of the conservatives. The people of
Corona could not believe what they saw that day at City Hall.
They dug in for a long struggle. Cuomo got a new hearing, at
which the two elected members of the board accepted the community's position, but the mayor's three appointees persisted in finding against the residents. Lindsay insisted that "the homeowners
made a poor presentation of their case," but a member of his
cabinet who attended the hearings said that was not so. "We were
all tremendously impressed by Cuomo's presentation," he said. "It
was lucid and thorough and compelling."

Cuomo moved the battle into the courts, where he was able to
hold off the condemnation for more than two years. In April 1969
the Court of Appeals ruled against him in a four-to-three decision.
Cuomo then took his case to Deputy Mayor Robert Sweet. The
attorney emerged from that meeting saying that he was confident,

because he believed that Mayor Lindsay had not been aware of the facts in the situation and "now that he has been informed, he's sure to do something for us." The *Long Island Press* was less optimistic. Pointing out that it was a city election year, the paper noted that politicians "tend to favor expediency over fairness. If the city suddenly reversed its position on the issue after three years, it could result in an embarrassing loss of face for the Lindsay administration."

The paper's assessment proved to be correct. In October 1969 the city completed condemnation of the Corona properties. Cuomo had run out of appeals. Now even if he could somehow get Mayor Lindsay to admit that a mistake had been made and to agree to reverse himself, the only way to undo the condemnation would be to get the state legislature to pass a special bill. This had never been done.

The outlook for the sixty-nine Corona homeowners was bleak in late 1969. "This looks like the end of the line for the tight-knit little Italian neighborhood," a *Daily News* article stated after the court approved the condemnation. But the "Fighting 69" did not give up easily. Their case had thus far attracted only minor city-wide publicity. That changed with the entrance into the cause of two flamboyant personalities.

Vito Battista, a state assemblyman from the East New York section of Brooklyn, was a bitter foe of the Lindsay administration. He saw in the Corona situation a vehicle both for the attraction of much media attention to himself and for lashing out at Lindsay. Battista was a crude publicity hound. Cuomo said that once when Battista was being interviewed in front of a television camera he charged that Cuomo was making over a hundred thousand dollars from the Corona homeowners. When the interview was over, an angry Cuomo (who was actually paid twelve thousand dollars for his several years of work on the case) said, "Vito, you know that's an outright lie. It's not true."

"I know," Battista said, "but when you get in front of the lights and get caught up in the excitement, it's hard to stop."

Such a person may be unpleasant, but he can be helpful to people who need to get their case before the public. "We were dead," one of the Corona 69 said. "He [Battista] rekindled the flame and got us fighting again."

Mario Cuomo did not, of course, give up any more readily than did the Fighting 69. After the condemnation he continued to call meetings to discuss what else might be done. Jimmy Breslin decided to tag along with his friend Michael Caponegro, a lawyer-politician who was a native of Corona, when he went to one of these meetings in November 1970. Breslin was struck both by the rightness of the Corona residents' cause and by the power and persuasiveness of their attorney. He immediately became a champion of both.

When they got to the meeting, Breslin asked Caponegro whether the Corona homeowners had anybody to help them.

"Nah, maybe some little local lawyer, but no heavyweights like us," Caponegro replied.

"You're sure? I mean, if somebody else has been working, and we're walking in here like big shots."

"Nobody that counts is here," Breslin's friend assured him. Then someone started to speak. Breslin asked who it was. "He's the little local lawyer they were using," Caponegro told him.

It took only a few moments of listening to Cuomo speak—"Smooth, connected sentences. Sentences with interesting words in them"—for Breslin to realize that he was "a heavyweight," albeit an unknown one—somebody who *would* count, before long. "I had not heard anybody speak like this in years," Breslin said later.

Within days Breslin had turned the Corona 69 into a cause célèbre. The liberal media suddenly discovered that a serious injustice was being carried out against a small, powerless community. The bandwagon on which Mario Cuomo and his clients had so long traveled alone was suddenly laden with cause seekers.

Breslin had entrée at City Hall. It now took only two weeks for Cuomo to get what he had been unable to obtain for three years: an invitation to present his case, including alternatives, to one of the mayor's top representatives. Cuomo soon convinced Deputy Mayor Richard Aurelio that a mistake had been made and that political as well as ethical considerations demanded that it be corrected. But the best alternative site for the school, a vacant area in nearby Forest Hills, had been designated as the new location for the scatter-site housing project that had been moved from Corona. Cuomo had long before devised a compromise solution, in case he could get the city administration to see the error of its ways but could not get the school moved to another location. For three years nobody in power would give him a chance to present his proposal. The idea was simple. The school could be built without athletic fields on site. They would be constructed in nearby Flushing Meadows-Corona Park (which had *not* been named for Robert Moses after all). This would save a majority of the homes. About twenty-eight houses would have to be moved to new locations in the neighborhood, but the community would be saved.

Here was a good example of a Cuomo compromise. It gave each side what it considered to be essential: preservation of the community, but not without some discomfort; and the new high school, but without on-site playing fields. Aurelio liked it, and sold it to the mayor. On December 2, 1970, Mayor Lindsay called a press conference to announce the Corona compromise—the Cuomo compromise.

The initial reaction was almost all favorable. One editorial called the compromise "a small miracle of civic wisdom. . . . the plan is not perfect, but it is equitable. It does not meet the specifications of those who have been demanding 'all or nothing,' but it does come to reasonable terms with the conflicting and legitimate concerns of the two sides." This was an excellent description of the elements of any Cuomo effort at conciliation.

The same editorial warned that "it would be a shame if political pique or intransigence by those demanding 'all or nothing' were to undermine the efforts of those who have tried to write a happier ending than the usual one." Unfortunately that is precisely what happened.

The chief culprit was Vito Battista. When the compromise plan was first explained at a meeting of the Corona homeowners, they were generally pleased that they had achieved far more than had seemed remotely possible a few weeks earlier. Battista himself was praised by the speakers as a helpful force in the struggle. He got into a heated argument with Breslin, whom he accused of "trying to take all the credit for this compromise," but he seemed satisfied with the compromise. Then when the meeting ended, the television cameras were turned on Cuomo, Breslin, and Caponegro, ignoring Battista. Being left out of the TV lights was the one fate that Vito Battista could not abide. Besides, he did not want to have his "cause" settled, and he thought that he had his adversary, John Lindsay, on the run. Battista persuaded some of the Corona homeowners that the mayor's agreement to the compromise was a sign of weakness. The agitator urged that the homeowners oppose the compromise, arguing that if they did, Lindsay would cave in. Cuomo saw it differently. He was certain that Lindsay had gone as far as he would ever be willing to go, and that opposition by the homeowners would lose the very real gains that had been made. Concerning the residents who followed Battista, Cuomo has generously described their opposition to his compromise as "a legitimate and difficult difference of opinion." His view of Battista's motives is less benevolent. "It's annoying how easy it is to play the 'big lie' game," Cuomo wrote in his diary, with reference to Battista, in 1972. "Just a little plausibility, a very big mouth, and a hungry group of media people are all that's needed." In another diary entry Cuomo said that Battista "has an amazing ability to paralyze the intellects of brighter people, maybe with decibels."

The unity that had marked the Corona community during four years of seemingly hopeless struggle dissolved after their limited victory. Battista and a few of the Corona residents began to suggest that there was a major scandal behind the compromise—that Cuomo and Piazza had "sold out" the homeowners. This was patently false, but Breslin was responding in kind from the other side. He warned the opponents of the compromise that if they did not stop fighting it, he would tell the mayor to bulldoze their homes. "I'm sorry I ever got involved," Breslin told a reporter. "It's a rat's nest. I used up all my credits in City Hall trying to help these bastards instead of myself. Now I owe favors."

Threatening phone calls and letters were received by both those who favored the compromise and those who opposed it. One anonymous broadside that was distributed by someone favoring the compromise described Battista as a "loud mouth publicity seeker who misleads people with his academy award performances." This was a defensible characterization, but the sheet went on to characterize three Corona residents who led the opposition to the compromise a "power-seeking alcoholic," a "sewer rat," and a "fugitive from the nut house." Although six or eight of the Corona families became very abusive of Cuomo, he seemed to understand their feelings and did not lose his temper with them.

The split of the community was tragic. Cuomo had found a way to preserve Corona, but his compromise became the pretext for outsiders to destroy the community and turn neighbor against neighbor. And the outcome remained in doubt. Mayor Lindsay's agreement to the settlement was only a first step. A bill still had to be gotten through the legislature authorizing the city to return the homes (of which it had become the owner since the condemnation was finalized) and to relocate them. Had there been no opposition from the residents or from Battista, this would not have been too difficult, but Battista arranged to trade his vote on the city budget and other bills for the opposition of Assembly Speaker Perry B. Duryea to the compromise bill. The bill died in committee in the state assembly in June 1971. Cuomo denounced Battista for his deal with Duryea. "It was outrageous, political, devious and cruel," Cuomo said. (His use of "political" in this context is instructive.)

Cuomo went back into the courts once more, working for further delays to keep the homes from being demolished until the legislature reconvened in January 1972. In the interim Lindsay worked with Cuomo to revise the compromise plan so that only four homes would have to be moved immediately. The revised compromise was put into a new bill, which the legislature finally passed and Governor Nelson A. Rockefeller signed in June 1972.

The Corona settlement was a remarkable accomplishment. It was not a case of a condemnation being stopped, but of one being *reversed.* This was the first time that an already accomplished New York City condemnation had been turned around. Cuomo was the first person who ever carried fighting City Hall to such a successful conclusion. Of course he did not do it alone. It is unlikely that he could have achieved his success without Breslin's intervention— or, in truth, Battista's. But the bulk of the credit for pulling off this near miracle rightly belonged to the tenacious attorney who kept up the fight against apparently hopeless odds for more than five years.

Cuomo summarized the larger meaning of the struggle in a letter he wrote to the Corona Taxpayers Association the day after Rockefeller signed the compromise bill into law:

It involved the integrity of the whole governmental system. A mistake was made. Everyone knew it. The question was: Would the System be big enough to confess and correct its own blunder? And the System did. And it did so not because it was forced to by vast political strength—we had none of that—it did so not because of the financial power of our group— because we were all practically beggars. In the end all we had on our side was the rightness of what we were saying. And in the end it was rightness that prevailed.

Just think about it: when is the last time that happened? Isn't it good to know it *can* happen?

When it was over, Cuomo advised those Corona residents who had backed his compromise to embrace their neighbors who had so bitterly fought them—and him. If the victory was going to mean anything, the old sense of community had to be restored. That's what they had been trying to preserve from the start.[4]

Cuomo had won one battle, but the Corona issue had become intertwined with another—the location of the scatter-site low-income housing project that had originally been planned for Corona. It had been shifted to a nearby site in affluent, largely Jewish, Forest Hills. By the time the Corona conflagration was being brought under control, the Forest Hills fire was threatening to do even greater damage—damage to the already reeling Lindsay administration, to race relations in the city, and to the city itself.

If ever there was an imbroglio that demanded the most skilled conciliator in the city, Forest Hills was it. The issues in Corona look simple when compared with those in Forest Hills. Here the question was no longer one of where to put a building, but of whether to try to place the poor in an upper-middle-class community.

If scatter-site housing was ever to be achieved in New York, Forest Hills seemed an ideal place to start. It appeared to be a basically liberal community. It went for John Lindsay in both the 1965 and 1969 city elections. Most of its residents—or their close forebears—had themselves experienced severe discrimination. "My ancestors did not break loose from the ghettos of Europe," the area's state senator, Emanuel Gold, said, "to have me lead the charge here in New York City to keep others in ghettos."

But that is exactly what some of Gold's Forest Hills neighbors seemed to be doing when they learned of plans to locate three 24-story low-income apartment buildings on a vacant eight-and-a-half-acre tract adjacent to the Long Island Expressway at 108th Street in Forest Hills. The plan to shift the housing project from the Corona site to Forest Hills had been hastily approved by the Board of Estimate in December 1966. The community had not been adequately informed of what was going on, so there was little opposition at that time. While the Corona struggle continued in the courts from 1967 through 1969, so far as the public could tell, nothing was happening on the Forest Hills proposal. In fact, it had been discovered that the subsurface soil was so poor that the cost of pilings to secure the buildings would bring the cost of the project far above the available federal subsidies. During these years of what proved to be deceptive quiet, officials were studying other building designs and working to get federal subsidy limits increased. The residents of Forest Hills were lulled into complacency by the inactivity. When Corona residents (and their attorney) suggested the 108th Street site as a logical alternative location for the proposed North Queens High School, many Forest Hills people protested. As Cuomo put it, they "doggedly charged Corona with a selfish reluctance to make its contribution to the commonweal. A year or so later their tune was to change."

Real trouble began in Forest Hills late in 1971, when excavation work was started at the 108th Street site. The Forest Hills Residents Association, launched by an angry real estate dealer named Jerry Birbach, led a torchlight protest march to the construction site in November. About three hundred people joined in the march. When they reached the site, some of them began throwing rocks, smashing the windows of the construction trailers. Others threw flaming torches. Then the chanting crowd went out on the Long Island Expressway and blocked traffic.

What was it that so alarmed these middle-class people that they turned to acts of violence? A one-word answer will suffice: fear. The fear, most of them insisted, was not of blacks, per se. It was of crime, which they associated, quite rightly, with the poor. If large numbers of poor people (many of them black) moved into Forest Hills, the residents believed, the results would be rising crime rates, declining schools, and a general deterioration of the area.

The principal target of the wrath of the Forest Hills militants was Mayor Lindsay. One of their favorite slogans was "Don't Let Adolf Lindsay Destroy Forest Hills." When the mayor held a fund-raising dinner in Queens, Forest Hills residents physically attacked those who came to contribute. Almost every guest "received at least one kick in the shins," the *Times* reported. Local citizens spat upon the mayor's car when he visited a nearby Queens community. Forest Hills people followed Lindsay to Florida, where he was a contestant in the 1972 Democratic presidential primary. Their loud protests were instrumental in producing a poor showing for the New York mayor.

As the Forest Hills situation deteriorated further, Lindsay became desperate to find a way out. "In deep trouble—bewildered really," as Jimmy Breslin put it, "—John Lindsay's City Hall turned to the one person in the city they felt had the temperament to work out a solution."

In May 1972, a few weeks before the state legislature passed the bill implementing the Corona compromise, Mario Cuomo got a telephone call from former Deputy Mayor Richard Aurelio. After several minutes of general conversation, Aurelio got to the point. Mayor Lindsay wanted to try the approach of an independent fact finder who could come up with a suggestion for resolving the Forest Hills mess. He would like Cuomo to give it a try. Cuomo did not think there was any need for a quick decision, but the next day the mayor called him and gave him an hour to decide whether to take on the task.

It is sometimes best for Mario Cuomo if he has to make a decision rapidly. As he said, he could have analyzed the question forever. Forced to decide almost immediately, he followed his instinct and accepted what seemed certain to be a thankless task. Cuomo said that Owen Moritz of the *Daily News* told him that he was certain that whatever report Cuomo made would leave "everyone unhappy and me despised. He said it would definitely hurt my 'political' prospects." The almost universal impression was, as Cuomo said at the time, "that there is no chance of personal gain to the man in the middle and, therefore, there is no good reason for assuming this posture." He wondered whether things were that bad. "Is it naive to believe that someone just might want to do this thing because it's a right thing to do?"

Surely Cuomo, as usual, had to convince himself that he only wanted to do it because "it's a right thing to do." But it is never so simple. A few hours after he accepted Lindsay's offer, Cuomo says, "I thought about the staggering complexity of the problem; it was even worse than Corona. I thought about the problems it would present at the office—and elsewhere. I even thought about my reasons for saying 'yes' and that got very complicated." By problems "elsewhere," Cuomo presumably meant at home, where his decision to take on another impossible task—without staff or pay—was unlikely to be welcomed. But what of his reasons for accepting this burden? He *did* want to "do good," but by this time he seems clearly to have been bitten by the political bug. Common sense and most of his friends might tell him that this assignment was no way to start a political career, but Cuomo's instinct told him something else. (He would find himself in a similar situation a decade and a half later, when common sense, his friends, and political strategists told him that he could not run for the presidency by not running. Cuomo's instinct would win that contest, too.)

Cuomo's position in the Forest Hills controversy was different from those he had held in the Willets Point and Corona disputes. Now he was a mediator. His task was not to assist those fighting City Hall in blocking the project, but to find some middle ground that both sides could tolerate. That position in the middle was not easy for Cuomo. "I'm more and more convinced I'd rather argue than arbitrate," he wrote shortly after getting involved in the Forest Hills mediation. "I'll have to resist the temptation to be an advocate so long as I'm in this role," he wrote in his diary after he accepted the appointment. "It's much easier being an advocate. The restraint and patience required of the middleman in our situation are hard virtues to cultivate." But they were necessary virtues for one who was beginning to harbor hopes of becoming not merely a politician but an extraordinary politician—one who would use his office to advance the common good.

As others had warned, Cuomo soon found himself the target of militants on both sides of the dispute. Both at home and at his office, he received many anonymous, abusive telephone calls. When the Corona people held a celebration dinner with Cuomo, Lindsay, and others at Jeantet's restaurant early in July, about 150 Forest Hills people showed up and nearly caused a riot. Had they been able to get at the mayor, the mob might well have pulled him limb from limb. Lindsay prudently stayed inside. Police officers asked Cuomo to go out and talk to the crowd. "There was a lot of pushing and shoving," as Cuomo recounts the incident, "and some stupid kid—for no reason—leaned over a circle of people surrounding me and slapped me in the face. I grabbed for him but was stopped. I'm glad I was; I'm not sure what I might have done at that instant."

Cuomo set a target of completing his investigation and reporting his recommendations in six weeks. It was an ambitious goal even for someone who worked as hard as Cuomo. The fact that the mayor supplied him with no budget and no staff was not particularly troubling to Cuomo. "I believe it would not have been too useful to have a staff even if one could have been supplied," he wrote in his diary. "The relay time to get the information from the staff to me would have been a problem." The major reason why he was just as pleased to do without a staff, though, was simply that he liked to do things on his own: "Then too, there's nothing like doing your own research for developing a command."

By being completely open to both sides, Cuomo gradually overcame some of the suspicion that his investigation was a "setup" for the mayor. In fact, Cuomo had had frequent and sharp differences with Lindsay in the past, and had taken the position of mediator only on the understanding that he would be completely independent and free to make whatever report he found to be indicated by his findings. He used the technique with each side of pointing out the facts that supported the other side as well as those that backed their own position. This added to the suspicions of the disputing parties. "Every night as we sit through these meetings," Cuomo wrote, "I argue both sides of the case. That has an unsettling effect on many of them; no one is less to be trusted than a man without a position." Eventually, however, Cuomo's "devil's advocate" approach began to create a "psychology of compromise."

As with other examples of Cuomo's compromises, he did not set out simply to split the difference, but instead to try to give each side what it believed to be essential. Even more, though, he wanted to find a solution that would be best for all concerned. He understood from the start that the stakes in the Forest Hills struggle were extremely high. If the project was completely killed, as the Birbach group desired, the whole concept of scatter-site housing might die with it. Worse, federal housing assistance of any kind would be seriously threatened. "If Forest Hills does not get built," Cuomo wrote in June 1972, "then the entire country may say 'It won't work.' By virtue of the the federal requirement that we build in middle-income non-racially-concentrated areas, if projects are not built in places like Forest Hills, the result will be to dry up the supply of housing funds entirely." Cuomo was well aware of the fact that many people in the administration of Richard M. Nixon would not be adverse to finding an excuse to slash housing assistance.

So it was clear to Cuomo from the outset that the project must not be scrapped. On the other hand, it would accomplish nothing other than spreading the ghetto if the project drove all the middle-class whites out of the area. There seemed to be little doubt that many Forest Hills residents would flee if the project was built on its planned scale. Accordingly, cutting down the size of the project might help to achieve its stated objective of integration.

Reducing the number of units in the housing project would help to reduce the fear on the part of its neighbors. "Is that a 'compromise' with principle?" Cuomo asked himself. "Not necessarily. The principle is the validity of serving the need of the low-income segment of our community. But that need is perhaps better served by a project that is acceptable to the community and assured of its cooperation." It was, moreover, clear that the only housing projects that ever achieved their objective of integrating the poor into a middle-class society were those that were sufficiently small that they did not become insular communities separated from the surrounding area. There was no point in that. "The present size of the project," Cuomo understood, "threatens the potential tenants themselves. As it now stands, this project's dimensions will make it difficult if not impossible to have any kind of meaningful assimilation. Thus for the sake of the low-income sector who will live in Forest Hills, this project should be reduced. The low-income sector will never accept this proposition nor even believe that it can be sincerely offered, but it is nevertheless clear to me that it's true."

To reduce the size of the project was not at all, in Cuomo's view, a step against those who would live in the project. Reducing the "threat" the project posed to the surrounding community would increase the degree of acceptance with which the new project residents would be met. And to the extent that large size made the project "an enclave," Cuomo pointed out, it would reduce "the chance for upward mobility, so even the project tenants themselves should want it smaller."

Cuomo concluded that the best solution for everyone involved was to cut the project from three 24-story buildings to three 12-story buildings, with 40 percent of the units reserved for the elderly (many of whom would be white) and the remaining 60 percent for low-income families (many of which would be black or Hispanic). This was a carefully reasoned position, which Cuomo believed to be in the interests of the poor and of the Forest Hills community. But he realized that "the suggestion of anything like 50 percent will be regarded by offhand observers as a simple cop-out. No one will believe that it was anything other than arbitrary." He was right. Most journalistic references to the compromise have ever since treated it as a simple slicing in half of the project, with no hint that there was long, torturous, and sound thinking behind it.

The key to "selling" the Cuomo compromise for the Forest Hills impasse was, from the one side, convincing blacks and their liberal champions that a reduced project would be beneficial to the poor themselves, because it would assure some racial and economic integration, whereas a larger project would become an independent community that would essentially be a high-rise ghetto. The key from the other side was to persuade middle-class whites that improving the living conditions of the poor would be in the self-interest of the middle-class whites. This was a tall order. Running away was not the answer, Cuomo told whites. They must help the poor to rise, he insisted, because the entire society is interconnected. If the middle class did not help to pull the poor up, it would be pulled down by the poor.

Although Jerry Birbach had threatened to sell his house to a black family and lead a white exodus from Forest Hills, Cuomo's numerous long discussions with area residents convinced him that "there will be *no* exodus if the compromise is adopted. Unfortunately, unless one has the kind of extraordinary exposure to the community and its thinking that I've had, there would be no way to know this. But I'm sure that these people are too tough to surrender, particularly since the project as reduced gives them a reasonable chance for success."

Cuomo's report was released late in July 1972. The *New York Times,* the *Daily News,* and the *Long Island Press* all wrote editorials urging the adoption of the Cuomo compromise. Queens Democratic Leader Matthew Troy, Representative Edward Koch, and the Anti-Defamation League of B'nai B'rith also came out in favor of the compromise. But Mayor Lindsay and Queens Borough President Donald Manes remained silent for three weeks. Lindsay announced his support in mid-August. This was far from the end of the matter, though. The Board of Estimate would still have to approve. In the meantime, opponents on both sides could be counted upon to attack the compromise.

Cuomo believed that both sides *should* be pleased with his compromise, but he knew that they would act as if they were not: "I'm sure that once the community is told of three 12's they will probably be surprised that this much of a reduction was recommended, but instead of accepting it, their experience as businessmen and bargainers will tell them to demand more." He further realized that a person who affects a certain posture for bargaining purposes can become locked into that position. "What is initially in part a

pose then communicates itself and feeds on itself and eventually
the illusion becomes reality," Cuomo wrote the day after a stormy
City Planning Commission hearing in September 1972. "Yesterday the hundred or so Forest Hills residents who screamed and
stomped, cried and shouted, believed what they had earlier pretended to believe."

The Board of Estimate met at the end of October 1972 to make
a final decision on the Forest Hills project. Mayor Lindsay sent a
stand-in. Jerry Birbach and other members of the Forest Hills
Residents Association put in personal appearances. So did a number of professional liberals. The two groups spent nearly twelve
hours going through what amounted to the script of a theatrical
production. None of them indicated that they wanted any part of
a compromise. Lindsay-bashing was the favorite sport of the day
(although there were also a number of boxing matches, including
one that began when one woman took and started to eat another's
banana and the latter jammed it into the former's face). The only
person to say anything nice about the absent mayor was city coun-
cilman Alvin Frankenberg, a Liberal party member from Queens.
"For trying to provide housing in a city that cries out for housing,"
Frankenberg said to a rising chorus of boos, "he [Lindsay] is called
a Hitler. What has come over our liberal Jewish community that
it has buckled under to the Jerry Birbachs?"

When the play was finished, the vote was taken and everyone
but Percy Sutton, the distinguished Manhattan borough president, who is black, voted in favor of the Cuomo compromise.
Sutton, who had suffered verbal abuse from the Forest Hills crowd
all day, eloquently expressed his dismay at what he had seen in the
confrontation. He said that many of the things that he had seen in
the meeting room that day reminded him of Mississippi in the
1960s or, he added pointedly, Germany in the 1930s. "This is a sad
and evil period here in America today," Sutton said. "A period in
which those in the very highest places give comfort and support
to the ugliest sentiments of humankind."

Sutton closed with a declaration of social responsibility that
precisely paralleled the position that Mario Cuomo had often
taken. "We who, through strength or luck, made it out of the
depths of poverty must not condemn those who are left behind,"
Sutton said. "We do not have the right to rejoice in our good
fortune and then look back and say, 'Not you. Not *you.*'"

Sutton's last comment was directed particularly against a black woman who had startled the crowd by speaking against the project. She turned out to be a middle-class property owner from Queens. "If you try to put any low-income housing projects in that fine middle-class *black* community of St. Albans, Queens," she declared, "you'll get a lot bigger crowd down here than you got from Forest Hills. Nobody wants those people." This statement lent support to Cuomo's argument throughout the controversy (and since) that the real problem is one of class much more than it is of race. Many middle-class blacks with whom Cuomo talked during his fact-finding in 1972 said they were afraid of low-income projects because they would bring crime into their neighborhoods. "It's clear to me," Cuomo wrote of the Forest Hills resistance, "that the objection is to crime and deterioration and not color. The coincidence that most of the lower economic class are black is what produces confusion." The most important division, Cuomo insists, is between working and unemployed people. Many of the latter are black, to be sure, and he would not deny that racism adds to the difficulty. But he staunchly maintains that class is a more significant factor than color in creating hostility toward the poor.

That being the case, the job for well-meaning middle-class people like himself was not to strike up "correct" poses on international and domestic racial issues, but to try to improve the lot of the underclass. One step in that direction was to try to persuade people in middle-class neighborhoods to give the poor an opportunity for a better life. This burden must fall on the middle-class, Cuomo once told his sister-in-law, Joan Cuomo, less than half jokingly, because "you can't put poor families in with the very rich. The very rich don't talk to *each other*. The middle class will say 'Good morning' and go out and sweep the street, and fix their lawns, and if you put them [the poor] there, it will work out."

Perhaps so, but convincing middle-class people that such an outcome was possible was quite a chore. Mario Cuomo proved to be one of the rare individuals who can occasionally make some headway. The most laudatory—but I think essentially accurate—assessment of his achievement came from Cuomo's sometime friend, Jimmy Breslin:

But everything really is about race and class. The real question is whether we are ever going to be able to live together and keep turmoil at a minimum. And in my time in my city I have seen few men who had the ability to walk toward this kind of trouble, put a strong hand into it, and then with deep intelligence and compassion, but always with that strong hand, hold onto the situation and turn it slowly, painfully, skillfully, always making certain not to inflame. And, in the end, actually improve the situation. Make gentle the soul of man. Even a little. Only a few in a lifetime. One was Bobby Kennedy and he is gone.

Breslin's unstated point, of course, was that Mario Cuomo is another such person—and he is still with us.

During the all-day circus of the Board of Estimate hearings on the Forest Hills compromise in October 1972, Representative Benjamin Rosenthal, Democrat of Queens (whom Cuomo described at the time as "one of the exceptional politicians who have not lost their integrity"), predicted that the scaled-down project would succeed and in ten years people would scratch their heads trying to recall what all the trouble in Forest Hills had been about. This appeared to be naive optimism at the time, but it proved to be accurate. The Cuomo compromise worked. The Forest Hills project turned out to be a success. Jerry Birbach did sell his house in 1973, when he moved to Cuomo's neighborhood of Holliswood. But the people who bought Birbach's home in Forest Hills are white and have lived there without complaint ever since. No exodus of whites from Forest Hills took place. And when Mario Cuomo ran for governor in 1982, Jerry Birbach voted for him.[5]

That would appear to qualify as a successful mediation under anyone's standards.

The community disputes in which Mario Cuomo became involved from the early sixties through the early seventies (and there were many others that I have not gone into here) exposed some of the flaws in the thrust of sixties liberalism. Cuomo made reference to these problems at several points in the diary he kept during the Forest Hills mediation. Those who demanded that the full-scale project be built and who insisted that the Forest Hills residents were racists, pure and simple, had developed "the crusader's intolerance," Cuomo said. After he released his compromise proposal, several "liberal" organizations issued a statement condemning it and the mayor. "Like so many other allegedly 'liberal' pronunciamentos," Cuomo noted, "this one appeared to be primitively absolutist. It referred to the compromise as a 'kissing of the feet of the Forest Hills racist.' I can't believe that's a fair or even intelligent appraisal."

Cuomo agreed with a friend that the real bigotry "is with the so-called liberal who demonstrates a remarkable inability to appreciate any part of the arguments made by the 'middle class.' " Here, in fact, was the crux of the matter. "Liberals" were deserting the middle class, making no attempt to understand its concerns. Surely some of the stands taken by middle-class Americans in the period were wrongheaded, but the proper response to such perceived errors in judgment was to try to persuade the people who had made them that there was a better way. Instead, most "liberals" just severed their relations with the "reactionary" middle class and began to throw brickbats at its members.

In the sixties many liberals were slipping more and more into an abstract view of a public interest without a living public to compose it. Centralization of decision-making—achieved in the revision of the New York City charter in 1963—was a means of removing the troublesome real people who could get in the way when experts and politicians were trying to advance the interests of "the people."

It was Mario Cuomo's genius to see the mistake in this way of thinking at a time when most liberal Democrats were moving more deeply into this erroneous approach. But unlike so many others who began in the sixties (most of them, incidentally, much later in the decade than he) to react against a liberalism run amuck, Cuomo did not reflexively swing to the opposite extreme. He knew that the liberals' goals remained desirable and should not be abandoned because some of their means—and some of the creed's practioners—had gone astray. There was, in any case, at least as much error on the other side. The dangers of total decentralization were as great as those of overcentralization of decision-making. "Community control" would mean that virtually nothing in the way of public interest needs would ever be met, because each community would resist any burden it was asked to bear.

Cuomo's insistence on a middle course on the issue of centralization was typical of his thinking. "The polar positions are the easier ones to take," he said. "They have the virtue of simplicity and sometimes even of passion." But, he believed, they were usually wrong.[6]

Mario Cuomo remained a liberal—or, as he would have it, a "progressive pragmatist"—because he understood the need for an active government to serve, as he would later put it, as a "balance wheel" to help those unable to help themselves. At a time when other liberals were jumping off the deep end and their enemies were trying to drown them, Cuomo made an attempt to throw them a life preserver. He worked to restore common sense to the liberal approach and, most of all, to bring real, working, middle-class people back into the thinking of liberal intellectuals—and back into the liberal Democratic political coalition, from which they were defecting in growing numbers as they came to believe that they were no longer welcome there.

During his dealings on Corona and Forest Hills in the early seventies, Cuomo repeatedly came up against government power that seemed incompetent, out-of-touch, dishonest, muscle-bound, or all of the above. "As a young lawyer, I learned a great disdain for politicians," Cuomo told me. "I got myself in situations where I was on the side of people against government. . . . The neighborhood groups that I represented—and, really, I learned—'disdain' is not too strong a word—for the political system, government, politicians." His disrespect for most politicians grew, but simultaneously, so did his realization of the possibilities of using political power for good ends.

At one point in 1972 when he had run into an obstacle, Cuomo wrote in his diary, "Of course, since I had no political authority or base, I was in no position to make demands." The desirability of having political authority was becoming ever clearer. The more Cuomo saw of what political power could do—for ill or good—the more he began to see it as the duty of those who would try to use it for good to seek it.

When, late in 1972, Cuomo expressed frustration at the seeming inability of politicians to see and act upon "simple truths—inescapable ones," he briefly fell into his old disgust with the political system: "But then this has been true for so long that it seems hardly worth the effort to attempt to change it." He quickly caught and rebuked himself. " 'Hardly worth the effort . . .'—what grim words. I'm sorry I said them. I must be tired. They're bad words—weak, self-pitying, surrender words," Cuomo said. "It *is* worth the effort; there's no choice but to make the effort. That's what it's all about—it's climbing mountains without ever reaching the top, hoping, despite the slips and slides. That in the long run you're getting closer. And knowing, at least, that you're trying to get closer. It's the trying that counts."

The Catholic could not pass up the opportunity to make this world a better place. The competitor could not refuse the challenge: "The game is lost only when we stop trying." The conciliator could not resist the chance to have more power to bring people together and solve problems.

"It seems to me here, as in most similar situations, the only safe route past Scylla and Charybdis is somewhere between them," Cuomo wrote at the end of his published diaries from the Forest Hills mediation. "What's needed is a sturdy ship and a sound navigator."[7]

Plainly it would not be long before Mario Cuomo offered himself to some electorate as that sound navigator.

7

NATURAL

POLITICS was *not* in Mario Cuomo's blood, as it was in that of, to pick one example, members of the Kennedy family. Andrea Cuomo could not understand someone "going into politics." It wasn't a job. His son stood to make much more money—and hence to provide better for his family—as a lawyer. When Mario told his father that he was going to enter politics, Andrea said, "Mario, I brought you up to be honest. Now what happened?" To the senior Cuomo's way of thinking, most politicians were at best shady, and at worst sleazy, lying thieves.

His son's view of politicians in the late 1960s and early 1970s was not much different. Mario Cuomo had seen the law that he loved being interfered with and defiled by judges chosen for their political affiliations. He had seen politicians and government crushing the interests of ordinary people. He noticed that in each of the struggles in which he became involved in that period, "the eventual solution was basically generated not by government, but by people outside of government." "I had seen politics at its worst," Cuomo told me. "Integrity appears to be something of a rare commodity in politics," he wrote in his diary in 1972, "and when present it's normally a burden." Many people, he said, had "concluded that politicians are inveterate liars and, therefore, one can safely believe as fact anything that contradicts a 'political' statement." After watching the displays of both sides—and most of the middle—at the Board of Estimate hearing on the Forest Hills compromise, Cuomo recorded in his diary: "No Profiles in Courage would be written on this day."

But perhaps the difficulty lay not in the nature of politics and government themselves, but in the people who entered the field.

"I started to realize," Cuomo told me, "that maybe the problem was that people who wanted to improve things thought that politics was inevitably corrupt." The government needed better people in it, Cuomo concluded. He saw in politics "always the extremes and the pandering to simplistics," and he rebelled. "I refuse to believe it must always be so," Cuomo wrote in October 1972. "There is an intelligent balanced alternative that this town will understand and respect if it is properly and honestly articulated." And who better to articulate a balanced, honest view than Mario Cuomo?

Entering the political arena himself came to seem to Cuomo almost a moral obligation. "Involvement in politics is not demeaning but is demanded—by common sense, by self-interest, by religion, by love, by God," Cuomo declared shortly after launching his political career. He had had some success in helping the powerless to battle against government from the outside, but how much more might he be able to accomplish from the inside? Here was the ultimate opportunity to fulfill his religious need to participate in this world and try to improve it. Public office, as Cuomo sees it, provides a chance to serve others. It comes down, he says, to something we are usually afraid to talk about: love. Love is giving, not taking, and when you are in government you can give of yourself to help other people. You may not be able to do a great deal to improve the lives of others, but even if you can do so to a small extent, you have accomplished something and made your time on earth worthwhile.

"I'm very much taken with the obligation to try," Cuomo told a reporter in 1975. "Maybe that's because I for so long stayed out of the system and took shots at it . . . and excoriated John Lindsay, Nelson Rockefeller, Bob Moses and everybody else. I spent 18 years in lawsuits fighting these people," he continued, "and then at the same time going around to churches and synagogues making speeches about your moral obligation to get involved. I reached the point where I felt like a hypocrite taking shots at the establishment. Nothing is easier than that."

"There's an awful lot worth doing," Cuomo contended in 1975. "Anyone who tells you that you can't work with the system is talking nonsense. Government can change for the better."

It is to be expected that most people would greet with considerable skepticism such an explanation of why a person decided to enter politics. In Cuomo's case, however, I think it is an accurate—

but only partial—explanation. His other major reason for entering politics was his love of contest. Much more than either sports or the law, politics was a field that offered a full scope for both the Catholic and the competitor that together constitute Mario Cuomo. Here, more than in the other endeavors he had tried, one could both win and serve—one could, in fact, win *in order to* serve. Winning in politics could be seen as not just for the self, but for others. In politics and government, one could work and compete, teach and preach, serve and help. It was the natural career for Mario Cuomo, even if neither he nor those around him had fully realized it earlier.

"Something happened," Matilda Cuomo says of her husband in the early seventies. "I never would have believed it—that he would get fully into politics." She told me that it was "a shock" to the family when Mario came in and said that he wanted to go into politics. His reason seemed to be the notion that "maybe I can do something worthwhile."[1]

Of course Mario Cuomo is not unique in having chosen to enter politics for the right reasons, even if on occasion he acts as if he thinks he is. Idealism and the desire to improve the lives of others have been the initial motivators of many people who have decided to go into politics. But in one important respect Cuomo does differ from many of the others who entered politics with similar goals. He did not begin seriously to consider running for office until he was forty years of age. Those who enter political combat when they are considerably younger— as do most people who are attracted to politics—usually have not yet firmly established their values. They are still sufficiently pliable that they begin to make small accommodations with the system as they find it. They compromise their ethics a little here, their ideals a little there, in order to win. How, after all, can they ever accomplish anything if they do not attain office?

By the time Cuomo decided to seek political office, his four decades of nonpolitical life had solidly shaped his value system. He was quite willing to compromise, but he would not be compromised. That is to say that he never insists on accomplishing everything at once. He is an incrementalist, not an absolutist. But there are certain fundamental principles on which he refuses to compromise. Put another way, Cuomo is flexible, but not pliable. "Political prudence" has never been for him. He has insisted on being candid about his beliefs, whether they were politically popular or not. "If I'm in it only to get elected, and so surrender all my principles or compromise my positions on things I really believe in," he asks, "what's the point of my getting elected?"

Many people involved in politics would say that such a position is naive. But there are times and situations in which a "politics be damned" attitude is the best politics of all. That may not have been quite the case when Cuomo began his political career in the 1970s, but it seemed more and more to be the case in the 1980s, as a cynical American public sought someone who could restore its shattered belief in politicians and government. That is just what Mario Cuomo has tried to accomplish from the moment he entered politics.

Even before Cuomo gave any serious thought to seeking office, others had identified him as a person whose gifts were sufficient to make him what we can now see as the equivalent of the Robert Redford character in a later movie. In terms of raw political potential, Mario Cuomo was as much "The Natural" as was Redford's character in terms of raw baseball potential. One of the first to realize this was Congressman Hugh Carey, who as a fellow alumnus of St. John's Law School came to know Cuomo well. When Carey first ran for Congress, Cuomo helped by writing speeches on aid to education. Then when Carey thought about running for mayor in 1969, he tried to persuade Cuomo to join his ticket, perhaps as a candidate for City Council president. Cuomo wouldn't hear of it. He told Carey, "No, you don't want me. I don't have any money, and I'm not a particularly good politician." Carey continued to talk up his St. John's friend, anyway. "I got a genius nobody knows about," Carey told Jimmy Breslin during their mutually unsuccessful 1969 campaigns. "He's a law professor at St. John's. Brilliant sonofabitch. Mario Cuomo. I begged him to run with me. Nobody knows him. The first time they ever hear of him, they'll be right there in his hands. But I just couldn't talk him into running."

But the seed had been planted in Cuomo's mind. Breslin and Jack Newfield of the *Village Voice* nurtured it in the early seventies. Both saw Cuomo as someone with the potential to become another Robert Kennedy—a leader who could reunite the poor and the middle class in a Democratic political coalition: the "urban populist," the *new* liberal, the Great Liberal Hope.

Before the next city elections four years later, Cuomo would give serious consideration to entering the race—but not for city council president. Cuomo, who had received much favorable publicity as a result of his roles in the Corona and Forest Hills disputes, and had turned down a couple of city commissionerships (including the chance to become the city's first taxi commissioner) Mayor Lindsay offered him, thought about starting at the top. He began testing the waters for a 1973 run for mayor of New York City. It was not a job that looked all that pleasant to the Queens attorney. "I don't envy the mayor's position here," Cuomo wrote in his diary while he awaited John Lindsay's decision on the Forest Hills compromise. "What an obscenely difficult job he has!" But Mario Cuomo is the sort of person for whom obscene difficulty holds its charms.

Cuomo was in no sense a conventional politician. He did not rise through the regular political system. He was not active in a Queens Democratic club. He had flirted with the club system as far back as the early 1960s, when he debated the issue of federal aid to parochial schools before the Tenth Assembly District Club in Queens. Cuomo favored such aid, but most of the people in the club opposed it. "It soon became apparent," Cuomo told me, "that there was no place there for me. I had no interest, really, in the club approach to politics." So in the estimation of the regular leaders, Cuomo had not "paid his dues." Still, those leaders were in some respects the political equivalents of baseball scouts, and the Ed McCarricks among them could not resist trying to sign a Natural when they discovered one. If Mario signed this time, though, it was going to be on his terms. What he sought was not a cash bonus but an opportunity to change the way the game was played.

Now that he was ready to become a player in the game of politics, Cuomo wanted to see it as clean—or at least as potentially clean. This was easier for someone who had not come up through the club atmosphere, New York's political version of the minor leagues. Those who had traveled that route could never convince themselves that politics could be a way to serve, a vocation second only to the religious life. But Cuomo now wanted to see politics as it *should* be and, he hoped, *could* be, not as it was. Despite much evidence to the contrary and many disappointments along the way, Cuomo has continued ever since to insist that politics can be a noble profession, one concerned not with graft and corruption but with improving society and making people's lives better.

It is no coincidence that Mario Cuomo's entrance into politics occurred at the time of growing public mistrust of government and politicians, resulting largely from the lies of the Johnson and Nixon administrations. The damage done to American democracy by Vietnam and Watergate was substantial. Major repairs would be needed to restore the system. When Cuomo was first considering running for office early in 1973, the Watergate scandal was just beginning to become public. When he did run for the first time, in 1974, the impeachment proceedings against Richard Nixon were underway. Nixon's resignation came in the later stages of Cuomo's first campaign.

Vietnam and Watergate turned most people more strongly against politics. Those disruptions seem to have had the opposite effect on Cuomo. As the reality of American politics fell ever further from the ideal, Cuomo felt the call to try to reverse that direction. "Today, when perhaps the most dangerous enemy of effective democracy is the cynicism of that vast public whose alert and intelligent involvement makes democracy work," he said in 1975, "should we not avoid anything that feeds that cynicism unnecessarily?"

Mario Cuomo's fondest hope when he entered the political arena is summed up by a statement he often makes: "Someday I want to hear a mother say, instead of 'My son, the doctor,' or 'My son, the lawyer,' I want to hear her proudly say, 'My son (or daughter), the politician.' "[2]

There's a dreamer for you.

After the Forest Hills settlement in the fall of 1972, people other than Carey, Breslin, and Newfield began to mention Cuomo's name in conjunction with citywide office. *Newsday* City Hall columnist Edward O'Neill suggested in early December that Cuomo "could appear on a ticket fashioned by Rep. Edward Koch, the Manhattan reformer who aspires to mayoral greatness." By early the following year, it was becoming clear that if Cuomo ran for any office, he, too, would aspire to mayoral greatness. In early February 1973, a political columnist described him as "the darkest dark horse of them all," but did not rule him out.

The first constituency Cuomo had to win over if he hoped to become mayor was the occupants of a Cape Cod house in Holliswood. Matilda Cuomo thought her husband was crazy to imagine that he could win. She and other members of the family also worried about the effects a defeat would have on Mario. How badly would he be hurt if he failed? One day early in 1973, family friend Bernard Babb got a message that Matilda had telephoned. He returned the call and asked, "What's going on?"

"Will you talk my husband out of doing such a stupid thing as running for mayor?" Matilda pleaded.

When Babb phoned Mario, the latter said: "I can't talk now. Lindsay's coming on. He's got an eleven o'clock press conference and he's going to announce whether he's going to run."

John Lindsay declared that he would not seek another term—one that he was quite unlikely to win—and Cuomo was ready to jump in. He told the press that Lindsay's departure should "put an end" to rumors that a Cuomo candidacy would be a "Lindsay ploy" to divide the vote.

Although he had not risen through the normal political channels, Cuomo believed that as a virtually unknown political novice with no money of his own, he needed the help of Queens County Democratic Chairman Matthew Troy, Jr., if he hoped to get on the ballot. He did not yet understand that the way for a person like himself to win was to run *against* the political bosses, not to seek their backing.

Cuomo was impressed that Troy had immediately come out in favor of the Forest Hills compromise. "He's always been a good friend and proved it again today," Cuomo wrote of Troy in his diary at that time. Troy indicated to Cuomo that he would back his candidacy for mayor. Cuomo was at this point politically naive enough to take Matty Troy at his word. He now says that he did not trust politicians in general, but believed that Troy was an exception. Cuomo had even told some Queens Democrats at the time Troy was being considered for the county leadership post, "One thing about Matty Troy—he'll always tell you the truth." It was only later that Cuomo realized that, as he put it in a conversation with me, Troy was "one of the great liars in political history."

The potential candidate had put together a small organization to explore the possibilities and had found a few dozen backers with sufficient financial resources to gather a small fund with which to start the campaign. Money had to be a major consideration for

Cuomo. He was not in a position to say, "Oh, if I lose half a million or a million, what the hell? I've got it; I might as well use it."

Such Cuomo enthusiasts as Adam Walinsky, a former associate of Robert Kennedy and a longtime activist in New York politics, organized a series of breakfasts in the various boroughs of New York City to seek political and financial support for a Cuomo mayoral candidacy. The crowds in Queens, Brooklyn, and Manhattan, where the three breakfasts were held, were large, influential, and friendly.

Although Cuomo was well received at his Manhattan breakfast, he was viewed with considerable suspicion by many sophisticated Manhattan "liberals." They knew what Italian homeowners from the outer boroughs were like. They were ignorant, conservative bigots. The Manhattanites had just seen one in the last election. Mario Procaccino had won the Democratic nomination for mayor in 1969 as the champion of law and order and the small homeowner. Fortunately, as the Manhattan liberals saw it, the voters had reelected the upper-class liberal John Lindsay. Now, however, there was another Mario from across the East River who wanted to be mayor. There was no need to listen to him. Right-thinking people already knew that Cuomo did not dismiss out of hand the fears and complaints of the middle class. He admitted that crime was a legitimate concern. "We have been reduced to the primitive state of worrying not so much about the quality of life as we are about its very preservation!" Cuomo wrote in 1972. How, "liberals" asked each other, could anyone like that be trusted?

But Cuomo's abortive 1973 candidacy was not one of simpleminded "law and order." Hardly anything is simple to Mario Cuomo, and from the start of his political career he rejected all simplistic solutions. Ed Koch, the erstwhile liberal whose weather vane turned with the conservative winds of the Nixon years, promised voters in 1973 that he would be tough on crime. When Koch and Cuomo appeared together at Matty Troy's club in Queens Village early in 1973, Koch gave the simple answers that frightened members of the middle class wanted to hear. When it came his turn to discuss crime, Cuomo leaped right into all the complexities behind the problem.

"You've got all these blacks and Puerto Ricans down in South Jamaica, where I was born and raised," the likely candidate said, making it clear from the outset that he would not shy away from the racial dimension of the crime issue. "You think they're *all* bad because they're the ones coming up here mugging and raping you and breaking into your houses. And you're saying, 'We don't want them in our neighborhoods. We don't want them anywhere near us. Leave them where they are. They should all die.'

"Well, the net result of that attitude is their poverty will get worse and they'll produce more muggers and rapists. The truth is *we can't get far enough away from them to be safe,*" Cuomo told his startled audience.

"Okay. The liberals come and tell you that it's our moral obligation to help those people because we oppressed them—the blacks anyway—for 400 years. That's what John Lindsay told you, right? However, here in Queens, how can I tell my father that? . . . He never punished a black or hurt a black or enslaved a black. If you tell him about his 'moral obligation,' he won't know what you're talking about. Here's what you have to say to my father: Whether you love them or not, whether you have an obligation to them or not, is between you and God. When you go to confession on Saturday, talk to the priest about it. But unless you do something about where they are now, how they live now, they will continue to come into your neighborhoods and mug and rape.

"Where are you going to go next?" Cuomo inquired after a pause. "Wyandanch? Then where? Montauk? You know what's going to happen? In time they'll be three miles away from Montauk and your daughter is going to get caught because next is the water and it's all over. You can't run forever. You have to find ways to break up segregated neighborhoods. And most of all," Cuomo said, his voice rising and his fist hitting the table, "you have to find ways to get them jobs. Real jobs. And that, in part, means electing people who will really do that. Remember, we have to do this because we love ourselves, not because we love them. In the end, the only thing that works is self-interest."

It was a powerful speech—and a sensible one. Cuomo had taken on the assignment of being a missionary to his own people. But while Cuomo may have been a Natural, the environment of Matty Troy's club was closer to Hobbes's view of the state of nature than to Locke's. The audience was not eager to find ways to break up segregated neighborhoods. The "Me decade" was dawning, and enlightened self-interest held less appeal than unalloyed (and unenlightened) self-interest. Cuomo's message apparently made some of Troy's lieutenants uncomfortable. How would their troops in the field respond to what Cuomo was saying? Wouldn't it be safer to give them a simple "Knock the dirty bastards over the head" message?

Matty Troy's support for Cuomo began to waver. There is no way to be sure that Cuomo's speech at Troy's club was the reason, but it is likely that it was. Some of the boys preferred another Mario, one much closer to the Procaccino mold: Representative Mario Biaggi of the Bronx. Biaggi (who was himself indicted and convicted on a political corruption charge fourteen years later) would take a "tough" law-and-order stance undiluted with much of Cuomo's concern for the root causes of crime. In mid-March 1973 Troy abruptly canceled a meeting of the Queens Democratic Executive Committee that had been scheduled to endorse Cuomo.

A few nights later, while Cuomo and his supporters were preparing for the campaign at his headquarters at the Pan Am Inn, word arrived that Troy had changed his mind and decided to back Biaggi. Cuomo and his campaign workers were shocked at this "double cross" by a man Cuomo considered to be a trustworthy friend. Although it had been apparent for some time that Cuomo intended to run, he had not yet said to his backers that he definitely would. Troy's duplicity got him angry enough to say, "The hell with it; we'll go!"

It seemed to be a situation that would be to Cuomo's liking. Without the organization's support, he would be a very long shot. It would be the sort of David versus Goliath contest that could get all his competitive energies running at top strength. The next day they were to get out the nominating petitions. Dick Starkey, who was working on Cuomo's precampaign, went to the law office at 32 Court Street. While Starkey was there, Cuomo began thinking aloud about how the campaign could be financed. There would be neither money nor manpower available from the Queens Democratic organization. Cuomo said he could ask the head of a large construction company his law firm represented to give a big contribution. "But," he said, "we want to raise the fee that he pays us each year. If I ask him for a campaign contribution, I won't be able to do that." Cuomo had to be concerned with making ends meet at the law office and at home. Such considerations quickly led him to conclude that he could not run at that time without organization support.

A few days later Cuomo spoke at a Jackson Heights, Queens, forum for mayoral candidates. "I am not running and may never run for mayor," the wounded former near-candidate declared.

"Politics stinks," Cuomo said, his disappointment allowing disillusionment temporarily to overcome his idealism. Calling for "common sense and integrity" in politics, an angry Cuomo bowed out
of the race, saying that a leading Queens Democrat (presumably
Troy) had told him that he was naive. "You tell the people what
they want to hear," Cuomo said the party leader told him, "then
when you get in office you do what's right."[3]

That was not the way Mario Cuomo was going to seek office.
He would speak his mind and maintain his integrity. If the voters
didn't agree with him, he would just have to defer getting elected
until he could convince them.

The Troy double cross was a bit-
ter experience for Cuomo, but he remained determined to remake
New York politics in his image of what it ought to be. The next
time it would be easier to persuade Cuomo to run. His next opportunity for public service came in the fall of 1973, when Queens
Borough President Donald R. Manes appointed Cuomo to be
Queens' first ombudsman to the state Public Service Commission.
Cuomo saw his role as that of a watchdog "who would articulate
consumer complaints" to the PSC. It was a nonsalaried office,
making Cuomo a true public "servant."

The PSC ombudsman position was a step in the right direction
for Cuomo, but he sought greater opportunities for public service.
When he had resisted the urgings of Walinsky and others to run
for mayor in 1973, Cuomo says he worried that saying no might
be a selfish act—that maybe he should be willing to serve in order
to give something back to society. Now Walinsky tried to talk him
into running for governor in the 1974 state elections. "I have no
qualifications for governor," Cuomo objected.

"Well, then, run for lieutenant governor," Walinsky said.

"But to be lieutenant governor, you have to be equipped to be
governor," Cuomo contended.

"Ahh, it really doesn't work out that way," insisted Walinsky.

Cuomo was persuaded, but says that he was a reluctant candidate. He now maintains that he was a "lousy candidate" because
he didn't see a rationale for him to become lieutenant governor. "If
I wasn't qualified to be governor, how could I be lieutenant governor, the whole presupposition of which is 'you could be governor'?
The notion that 'probably you won't' wasn't good enough for me.

It didn't have integrity. I kind of sensed that. As a result, I was a lousy candidate."

Perhaps it is to some degree true that Cuomo was not fully convinced in 1974 of his readiness to be lieutenant governor. But the idea that his heart was not in the race seems more a retroactive explanation for his defeat than an accurate reflection of his attitude at the time. Cuomo was the first Democrat to announce his candidacy for the 1974 lieutenant governor's nomination, and all the evidence indicates that he very much wanted to win. Cuomo is not the sort who enters a contest without the firm intention of emerging on top.

This time Matty Troy told Cuomo from the start that the Queens organization would not support him. Cuomo's lack of ties to the club system meant that Troy's boys thought him undeserving. But Cuomo persisted—not the action of a man who thought himself unready for the office. His approach showed him to be unfamiliar with political intrigue and uncertain as to the best way to win office, rather than unsure of his qualifications. Cuomo endorsed Howard Samuels for governor. Hugh Carey, who was also seeking the gubernatorial nomination, recalls asking Cuomo, "Why did you do that? Don't you know that Samuels is running against me and that he has already said that he wants [State Assemblyman Antonio G.] Olivieri for lieutenant governor?"

"I know that," Carey quotes Cuomo as saying. "But Samuels said he is really for me and that he will give me money for my campaign after the convention."

"Mario, how can you do that?" Carey asked. "He is treating you like a mop—putting you in the closet and buying you with a promise of money for your campaign."

Cuomo's recollection differs significantly. He told me he wanted to support Carey for governor and had talked media wizard David Garth into working for Carey. "But then Carey screwed me at the convention," Cuomo charges. "He stayed away from me at the convention. I tried to find him, but he made a deal with the leaders, which I didn't know. They would give him the twenty-five percent of the [delegate] vote that he needed to get on the ballot without petition, but in return he would have to stay away from me or any lieutenant governor candidate. He made the deal, but he never told me. He expected me to remain loyal to him. I kept saying, 'Hughie, why don't we do it as a team?' But he never told me he had made a deal. So I wound up going with Samuels, and

Hughie called up and said, 'You're screwing me—you're going with Samuels!' I said, 'Boy, you've got some nerve!' "

Cuomo went to the 1974 New York State Democratic Convention at Niagara Falls thinking he had the support of most of the party leaders for the official endorsement for lieutenant governor. Brooklyn Democratic Chairman Meade H. Esposito was a strong Cuomo supporter. But when he arrived at the one-time honeymoon capital, Cuomo learned that the party bosses intended to leave him at the altar. State Democratic Chairman Joseph F. Crangle, it seemed, had achieved a premature consummation of the party's marriage with the Queens attorney and then called off the ceremony. Whatever remained of his political virginity gone, Cuomo decided to fight for his honor by trying to bring off the marriage against the wishes of Crangle and Troy.

Crangle had made a deal in the early morning hours to give the endorsement to state legislator John J. LaFalce, who like Crangle came from Buffalo. Cuomo's friends told him not to go onto the convention floor, because he would not get more than 1 percent of the votes and would be humiliated. "Get the hell out of here," Jimmy Breslin advised Cuomo. "At least preserve your dignity." Cuomo said that he had his wife and daughter there and would not quit. "Well, I can't stand to watch," Breslin declared, and he and Mike Caponegro caught a plane back to the city.

Party leaders suddenly suggested that Cuomo run for the United States Senate instead. Troy delivered the offer in person.

"You mean that I'm not capable of running for lieutenant governor because I haven't 'served' enough," an incredulous Cuomo responded, "but it's okay for me to go for senator because you know I'm going to lose. No, there's something else going on here, too. You're afraid I might hurt you. How can I hurt you? The only way would be for me to go to the convention and make an anti-boss speech. But I'm not going to do that because I *sought* the support of the bosses."

Cuomo knew both that the task of running against incumbent Jacob Javits, a New York institution, for the Senate would be a nearly hopeless one and that two other Democratic aspirants, Allard Lowenstein and Ramsey Clark, were better qualified than he was to serve in Washington. The bosses didn't know what to make of the latter argument when Cuomo made it. What politician ever declines a nomination because he thinks others are better qualified?

The other candidates were grateful to Cuomo for turning down the Senate offer. "I remember Al Lowenstein hugging me and kissing me," Cuomo told me, "when I said, 'Hey, I can't run against you guys for the Senate. You guys are much better for it.' " Cuomo rejected the advice of his friends and decided to go to the convention floor as a candidate for lieutenant governor and "take my beating."

Then Lowenstein pleaded with the Kings County leader, Meade Esposito, for a chance to address the Brooklyn delegation on behalf of his own Senate candidacy. Esposito agreed to gather his delegation in a caucus room and give Lowenstein ten minutes to talk. Al Lowenstein *never* talked for only ten minutes. He could spend an hour discussing the merits of the menu at Morrison's cafeteria, his favorite eatery. As was his wont, Lowenstein launched into a one-man filibuster that did not end until nearly an hour later. In the meantime, out on the floor, the voting for lieutenant governor was beginning, and Brooklyn was not present. When Matty Troy and Joe Crangle noticed that the Brooklyn delegates were absent, they became alarmed. Being intimately familiar with normal political dealings, they quite reasonably feared that some scheme to which they were not parties was afoot. "That guinea bastard is trying to screw us!" exclaimed Troy, referring to his Brooklyn counterpart, Esposito.

The only thing to do when you think you have discovered a plot against you is to counterplot. The frightened duo of Troy and Crangle pulled LaFalce, who otherwise would have easily won the endorsement. They said, "We'll show 'em. We'll go with Krupsak." Mary Anne Krupsak, a Polish-American state senator from Canajoharie, a small community between Albany and Utica, was attempting to become New York's first female lieutenant governor. It is interesting to note that some of the party leaders who offered the Senate endorsement to Cuomo made the same offer to Krupsak. They also suggested that she might run for attorney general or comptroller—anything but lieutenant governor, where she would be coupled with the party's candidate for governor and might pull the ticket down. Now Crangle and Troy changed their minds. It occurred to them that there was a good chance that putting a woman on the ticket might turn out to be a stroke of genius that would secure the liberal vote and take advantage of the gathering wave of feminism. In any case, it would at least upset the scheme that they imagined Esposito was hatching. They didn't even bother to consult with Krupsak. She had achieved considerable support on her own, but not enough to win. Her endorsement would come as totally unanticipated manna from heaven. (Well, maybe heaven isn't quite the best image for a setting dominated by Troy and Crangle.)

When the sudden word came down that it was to be Krupsak, not LaFalce, the Queens delegation went into an uproar. They refused to swallow a second deal in less than twenty-four hours, this one for an upstate woman. They rebelled and supported their hometown man, Mario Cuomo. On the first ballot none of the candidates was able to win the requisite 50 percent of the votes, but the reinvigorated Cuomo forces were hard at work on the floor. Walinsky, Victor Gotbaum (head of District Council 37 of the American Federation of State, County, and Municipal Employees), and Jack English (Democratic chairman of Nassau County) wooed delegates. Cuomo gained strength on the second ballot and won on the third, with 65 percent of the votes.

By this time, Breslin and Caponegro were back in New York, downing drinks. Breslin called Niagara Falls to get the sad details and was flabbergasted to learn that his man had won. That evening Cuomo returned from dinner at Como's restaurant to his hotel room and found a telegram from Breslin's wife, Rosemary: "Mario—Congratulations. Don't mind Jimmy. His old man was the first guy off the *Titanic.* "

As it turned out, however, Cuomo had miraculously navigated through the icebergs at the convention only to be inundated by a tidal wave in the primary. The "bruising battle" over the endorsement left the party seriously divided. Both Krupsak and Olivieri secured the 25 percent of delegate support that assured them of spots on the primary ballot that would finally determine the party's nominee. Howard Samuels, who had won the convention's endorsement for governor, initially declared his neutrality in the three-way contest for lieutenant governor. This appeared to some to show a lack of leadership on Samuels' part, and about a month after the convention, party leaders persuaded him to endorse Cuomo. This angered the supporters of the other two and helped to undermine Samuels' own hopes in his gubernatorial primary contest with Hugh Carey. In hurting Samuels the endorsement did nothing to help Cuomo.

Like many outsiders, Cuomo seems to have thought that the insiders were more powerful than they actually were. He did not yet realize that in New York, with its long tradition of independent progressive politics, the party endorsement can be a curse rather than a blessing. This has especially been the case since 1972, when a citizen campaign for George McGovern routed the party organization and won almost all of New York's seats at the Democratic National Convention. It is often better for someone like Cuomo to campaign *against* the officially endorsed choice of the party rather than to have that endorsement oneself. In 1974 Cuomo had the appearance of being the handpicked candidate of the party bosses. Such an identification can be deadly in New York. It would take three years and a few more defeats before Cuomo came to appreciate this fact.

The 1974 primary was Mario Cuomo's first experience as a full-fledged candidate. It proved to be less than encouraging. There was, for instance, an elaborately catered fund-raiser on Long Island, with tents on a spacious lawn. Everything was perfect—except that no one showed up. "We spent about ninety thousand dollars [on the entire campaign]," Cuomo told me. "And I didn't know what I was doing."

He didn't really like campaigning. His sister-in-law Joan recalls putting up posters for him at a Long Island Railroad station before he was to arrive in 1974. When he got there, "the object was to shake people's hands as they got off the train," she told me. "He couldn't do it."

"These people worked all day," the candidate said. "Now it's six o'clock at night. Why do they have to shake hands? They're tired; they want to go home."

Joan Cuomo says that Mario "didn't want to *impose* on them." "They're tired," he kept saying. "They don't want to be stopped by some nut in the street running for office. They couldn't care less." Cuomo later said that when campaigning in 1974 he often felt as if he were loitering.

When he could be persuaded to stop people, Cuomo was not content just to shake hands and identify himself and the office he sought. He always wanted "to stop and answer questions and make people really understand his positions," his sister, Marie Vecchio, remembers. "In those few minutes, he tried to educate the individual, then and there." As a result, the candidate was habitually far behind his schedule.

He arrived late at a teamsters picnic near Rochester. By the time he got there, much beer had been consumed. "You don't expect me to tell those guys to put down their beer glasses and quit the softball game to listen to me make a speech. No way," Cuomo said to one of his aides. "Sometimes," he told a reporter, "I wonder why I'm doing this. I ask myself where I get the nerve to think people should listen to me."

Cuomo tells a story illustrative both of his discomfort with politicking and the public attitude toward politicians in the Watergate year of 1974:

"Some of my staffers came to me at one point and said that I had to get out and do more handshaking, hot-dog eating, and so on.

"That's not my style, but I said okay. We went to the Rockaway Boardwalk. I figured I'd give it the Lindsay-Kennedy touch, so I hooked my finger in my jacket, slung it over my shoulder, and walked up to four ladies sitting and knitting at about 116th Street.

"Looking at the lady with the straw hat, I said, 'Good afternoon, ladies. I'm Mario Cuomo, the official designee of the Democratic party for lieutenant governor.'

"Ms. Straw Hat, still knitting, said, 'So?'

"It shook me but I was determined and kept on, 'The lieutenant governor is second in importance only to the governor. If something happens to the governor, the lieutenant governor assumes his seat,' " Cuomo continued.

"Ms. Straw Hat looked up [and] asked briskly, 'See those nails sticking up all over the boardwalk? A person walks there, the nails make goddamn bloody feet. What will you do about the goddamn bloody feet?'

" 'Madam,' I said, 'that does not come under the state's jurisdiction. It is really up to the mayor to do something.'

"Ms. Straw Hat, still knitting, turned to the others and said, 'See—another phony.' "

Nor could Cuomo arouse much interest in 1974 among leading Manhattan liberals. Neither *New York Post* publisher Dorothy Schiff nor Alex Rose, head of the Liberal party, would even agree to meet with him. "I suppose," Cuomo told a reporter a few years later, "they thought it would be a waste of time to talk to some crude Italian Catholic. After all, they were liberals." It is true that there aren't many Marios in the South, but neither are there many Marios among the Manhattan elite.

Despite all these difficulties, whenever Cuomo spoke before an audience in 1974, it was obvious that he was a Natural. "It became clear to me," says Dick Starkey, who served as Cuomo's press secretary in that campaign, "that he had this extraordinary charisma. When he came before groups, he had a great gift for relating to them. . . . He was just *good* at it—a natural." The trouble was simply that so few people were exposed to Cuomo in 1974. He toured the state, but nobody paid any attention to him. "His speeches weren't panned," as Starkey remembers it. "They were ignored." It was frustrating to both candidate and staff. "Here was a guy with all this communications talent," Starkey says, "but nobody was hearing it. . . . I *knew* that the wit he had was gold, as far as the media were concerned, if I could only get people to understand that he was entertaining, that he had wit as well as substance. He deserved much more attention, just for entertainment value." But if you are unknown and without money to finance a campaign, no one pays any attention to you—unless you attack somebody. Starkey told Cuomo that he could easily get him on radio and television if he attacked somebody. But that was not Cuomo's style, so the campaign continued to operate far from the television lights.

Virtually ignored, Cuomo could do little but hope that his very obscurity might be an advantage. Having never held public office was likely to be a plus in the wake of Watergate. (Being tagged as the choice of the party bosses, of course, was just the opposite.) "If you gave the voters a choice between a group of candidates and 'none of the above,' " Cuomo told a reporter late in the 1974 primary campaign, " 'none of the above' would win with 56 percent of the vote. Right now, I'm 'none of the above,' but it's a role that requires exquisite timing." He said that if he campaigned harder, he might get only 46 percent. Of course he was joking, but not entirely.

The nature of Cuomo's opposition in 1974 made the race particularly difficult. His two opponents for the Democratic nomination for lieutenant governor, State Senator Krupsak and Assemblyman Olivieri, were not the ideal opponents for Cuomo. Olivieri was a Manhattan liberal who won the endorsement of the New Democratic Coalition, New York's most potent liberal political organization. With two Italian-American males from New York City competing for much the same constituency, Krupsak had the advantage, although Cuomo later said "she would have won head to head anyway. She was a better candidate." Krupsak's gender was also a plus in 1974. The women's movement was decidedly on the rise at that time. "There was an enormous surge of grass-roots outpouring," Krupsak told me. "My candidacy was the right time and the right place—and I had all the right credentials. I was really the best-credentialed person of all the candidates at that time." Krupsak says that it was an extraordinarily clean and decent campaign on the part of all three candidates.

During a televised debate with Olivieri in August, Cuomo said that if he had been a member of the state legislature he would have voted against the 1970 bill that eased restrictions on abortions. Olivieri voted in favor of the permissive abortion bill, which was enacted into law. He said that he was personally opposed to abortion, but believed that others should have freedom of choice. This, of course, is precisely the position that Mario Cuomo forcefully adopted a few years later; but he clearly rejected the argument in 1974. Cuomo even came out during that campaign against the sale of contraceptives. Small wonder that many observers considered him the most conservative of the three Democratic candidates.

Cuomo continued to pick up endorsements from party leaders, but with little name recognition, less money, and the taint of being seen as the bosses' choice, he fell behind Krupsak. At the beginning of August, Samuels launched what some described as a "rescue operation" for Cuomo. As it turned out, though, Samuels needed a life preserver himself. Being tied to a sinking Samuels helped to drag Cuomo down, although it is unlikely that he could have won either without Samuels's support or if Samuels had won himself.

Cuomo carried New York City, but as he puts it, "I got murdered everywhere else. Nobody had ever heard of me. I was a New York City ethnic." Krupsak finished first with 44 percent of the statewide vote. Cuomo was a distant second at 32 percent. It was both the Watergate year, when being "antiestablishment" was popular, and a time in which feminism was a motivating force capable of outpolling candidates who were little known. These two factors were especially important in producing Krupsak's victory over Cuomo, because most voters tend to see women as more trustworthy than men and because the image of being the candidate of the bosses, always harmful in New York, was particularly damning in a Democratic primary election held only six weeks after Nixon's resignation.

Accepting defeat never comes easily to Mario Cuomo, but he had learned a great deal in 1974. For a first campaign it was, despite its many problems, generally well done. The greatest error had been the strategic one of trying to run with the party bosses instead of against them. But those who had seen the candidate were highly impressed. As Dick Starkey says, "That campaign was a wonderful dress rehearsal for later campaigns."[4]

Now that Cuomo had been fully exposed to political struggle, there could be little doubt that other campaigns would follow before long.

When Hugh Carey, who defeated Samuels in the Democratic primary and won the governorship in November 1974, offered Cuomo the position of counsel to the governor, a highly influential post with great power, Cuomo turned it down. Carey said that Cuomo was "the outstanding intellect in the Democratic party," and continued to try to find a spot in the administration that his St. John's friend would take. For a time Cuomo insisted that he could not afford to take any post in the new administration. Then he relented, saying, "I'd be a colossal hypocrite to have said all the things I did when I was campaigning across the state and then refuse to accept an appointment." Given his pick of a wide variety of cabinet posts, Cuomo made the surprising choice of secretary of state. The recently defeated political newcomer saw the position as an opportunity waiting to be seized. The fact that it *was* an opportunity was not apparent to less keen observers than Cuomo. The office had been a low-profile one, handling such tasks as registering corporations, providing training programs for firemen, and regulating barbers and nonsectarian cemeteries. It had usually been seen as a sinecure to be given to some party worthy who desired a title with little work or responsibility.

But Cuomo realized that there were great opportunities in this appointive office. In fact, Jerry Brown had just used the position of secretary of state in California to build himself up to the point where he was able to win the governorship in 1974. The possibility of taking a previously meaningless, anonymous position and transforming it into a highly visible office with great political potential was not lost upon Mario Cuomo. When he was named secretary of state, Cuomo was accurately described by Associated Press Albany correspondent David Shaffer as "a quietly ambitious man with a greater awareness of what the job can do for his political career and a greater willingness to work hard at it."

Before he accepted the position, Cuomo made sure that Carey was willing to allow him to expand the scope of the office. In announcing his selection, Governor-elect Carey said that Cuomo would be "a major member" of his cabinet and "a key figure in our efforts to make government sensitive to public needs. Cuomo, Carey said, would be assigned as a troubleshooter when difficult problems arose and would be a close special adviser to the governor. Cuomo declared at the time of his appointment that, unlike his predecessors, he would cease the private practice of law while he held the position of secretary of state. This move was neither required by law nor approved by Matilda Cuomo, but Mario believed that he must work full-time at his new job if he was going to serve the public properly and build a personal reputation that would enable him to win elective office in the future.

"I gave up a law practice in which I earned $66,000 last year, and I had other income, for this job at $47,800 a year," Cuomo told a newspaperman early in 1975. "But I feel that the state is entitled to all my ideas, whether they come to me during working hours or while I'm at home shaving. If someone has a second job, some of his thoughts will be on that job even while he is working on the first one."

Although he very much wanted to experience the joy of political victory, Cuomo had entered public service principally for the purpose of serving the public. As important as winning was (and is) to him, it has never been for him the end in itself that it is to many politicians. For him the real test began *after* an office was won. In 1974 he had not won, but he found himself with an opportunity to serve at least as great as that he would have had if he had been elected lieutenant governor.

Cuomo entered public service a few months after Richard Nixon's resignation had brought public respect for politicians to a new low, so one of the new secretary of state's general goals was to do all he could to rehabilitate the public's confidence in government. He suggested that many in the media and the public tended "to overplay Watergate" and forget the good people in politics. He set out to identify himself as one of those good people. As one close associate of Governor Carey told a reporter, "Mario could become the conscience of the administration."

Cuomo's first assignment as Governor Carey's troubleshooter was to investigate a nursing-home scandal. His report charged that Bernard Bergman, a well-connected Manhattan nursing-home en-

trepreneur, ran homes that both mistreated patients and cheated
the state by inflating Medicaid bills. But Cuomo found that this
was far from unusual. A number of "syndicates" existed, he said,
each owning chains of nursing homes that it operated solely for the
purpose of making as much money as possible. His report stated
that there was "widespread and intolerable abuse of service, massive profiteering, administrative inadequacy, legislative deficiency,
and political impropriety, if not corruption." Cuomo recommended the appointment of a special prosecutor to investigate the
nursing-home business in New York.

The new secretary of state quickly moved on to a crusade
against abuses by lobbyists trying to influence state legislators. He
said that the laws regulating the conduct of lobbyists were inadequate, but that he intended to start enforcing those laws while he
sought the enactment of stronger provisions. The lobbying law
then on the books, Cuomo noted, had been applied only once in
the sixty-nine years since its enactment. Cuomo proposed legislation that would strictly prohibit lobbyists from giving any sort of
gifts to legislators. He would not permit lobbyists to buy lunch or
drinks for legislators, or even to give out such items as calendars
and memo pads as Christmas presents. "Why should *any* gift or
payment be permissible?" Cuomo asked a stunned assembly Committee of Ethics. "Is it essential to our system that a lobbyist have
a cocktail party for legislators or others whom they seek to influence? Will their opportunity to make an intelligent presentation
be minimized if they cannot take a legislator or agency head out
to dinner? Are these things done for any purpose other than to seek
by the subtle workings of 'good will' or a friendly predisposition
to help produce a statute or rule or decision that will affect large
numbers of people, some of them no doubt adversely?"

Cuomo's testimony must have left many legislators feeling the
need for a drink, even if they had to buy it themselves. And his
recommendations went further. The secretary of state also urged
the prohibition of any lobbying in private ("corruption grows in
the dark," he said) and requirements that all paid lobbyists register
with his office, itemize the areas in which they planned to lobby,
and provide memos on all conversations they held with legislators.
This was the beginning of a quest by Cuomo to improve the ethical
standards under which New York officials and lawmakers—and
those who tried to influence them—operate. He noted that the
public had adopted a cynical attitude toward politics and govern-

ment, and that strong ethics legislation would help to restore some of the lost confidence in leaders and institutions. Cuomo's quest continued through his efforts as governor to obtain passage of a tough ethics law regulating the conduct of both legislators and members of the executive branch.

In fact, the 1975 legislative battle over Cuomo's proposed lobbying bill distinctly foreshadowed his struggle as governor in 1987 with the legislature over an ethics bill. Already in 1975 legislators—particularly Republicans in the state senate—and lobbyists were complaining of Cuomo's "holier-than-thou" attitude. They believed him to be just another politician, but one who was trying to build an image for being more honest than others. There is no question that Cuomo does have a tendency toward self-righteousness, but there is nothing calculated about his honesty. He does not see himself at all as "just another politician." He believes he is on a mission to improve politics and government. If he can do that, it just may be that he *is* holier than most of us.

In any case, the Republican-controlled senate derailed Cuomo's lobbying bill in the 1975 session by seeking to take enforcement out of the secretary of state's office and put it in the hands of a legislative committee. Cuomo and many Democrats denounced this plan. "They didn't amend the bill," Cuomo said of the Republicans in the state senate. "They devastated it. It's just a joke. It's like the guy who said to his girl, 'I'll marry you, provided I can go out with the boys when I want to and I can get up and go to work when I feel like it.' That's the kind of proposition they're making. It's a non-bill."

The lobbying bill died in the legislature in the 1975 session. Cuomo did use the old law as it never had been before, though. He levied eight-thousand-dollar fines on lobbyists who failed to file on time. The next year Cuomo tried again to get a tough lobbying bill through the legislature. Once more senate Republicans sought to place enforcement in the hands of members of the branch of government involved: the legislative and executive branches would each police their own members. "That," Cuomo declared, "would be inane—sort of like having two foxes in two chicken coops."

The state was faced with a severe fiscal crisis when the Carey administration took power. Cuomo set out to save even more in his department than was required by the Division of Budget. Within weeks of taking office, Cuomo recommended a $3.5 million cut in his own department's budget. He eventually reduced the State

Department's budget by 40 percent. Then, in 1977, he initiated "zero-based budgeting" in his department, requiring each of the managers under him to justify each expense, not on the basis of the previous year's expenditures, but on demonstrable need. This enabled him to cut his budget by an additional $400,000, while increasing productivity. He did so by offering new employees the "opportunity" to work for lower salaries than his Republican predecessors had paid, by staff reductions (accomplished almost entirely through attrition), by eliminating duplication of services, and by vastly increasing the use of computers in the department's varied operations. He also saved money and increased the impact of his department by creating a "guerilla-type strike force" of sixty inspectors who moved from one area of the State Department's jurisdiction to another, giving saturation coverage to uncover violations.

This was the sort of record that could distinguish Cuomo from the image of big-spending liberal Democrats that had become entrenched in the minds of many voters, particularly upstaters. ("Upstate" as it is used in New York is an imprecise term by which many residents of New York City mean everything outside the city limits. More generally, it encompasses the entire state north of Westchester and Rockland counties; that is, everything except New York City, Long Island, and the suburbs immediately north of the city.)

Upstate New York had long been a Republican stronghold. "Democrats from New York City don't often think of the towns and villages," Cuomo said a few months after he became secretary of state. "And the people in the towns and villages think you're New York City-oriented. So how do you convince them you're not? You have to show up." And that is just what Cuomo began to do. He used his appointive state office to travel around upstate areas, getting himself known and letting the people see that he, though a New York City ethnic, was concerned about their problems. This upstate exposure was to be critically important to Cuomo's later success in statewide elections.[5]

As secretary of state, Cuomo was able to pursue some of the issues and use some of the skills he had developed while representing people outside the government. He sought both to protect neighborhoods against unscrupulous real estate agents who engaged in blockbusting tactics and to provide for the slow integration of neighborhoods by revoking the licenses of agents who refused to rent or sell to blacks in "white" areas. Cuomo moved to "prevent the exploitation of middle class neighborhoods by people whose greed is greater than their desire for racial harmony." He made use of a 1975 court decision giving the secretary of state the power to bar real estate agents from soliciting business in neighborhoods where blockbusting was being attempted. The usual procedure was for avaricious brokers to try to get business by panicking homeowners with stories that blacks or Puerto Ricans were about to "take over" the neighborhood. Cuomo issued countywide nonsolicitation orders for Kings (Brooklyn) and Queens counties. "What I did in those two counties," he said, "was to order that real estate brokers can no longer solicit—that is, can no longer aggressively try to induce people to sell. The reason for going countywide is that when you put a nonsolicitation order on a local area, you stigmatize it. People figure that particular area must be slipping. This way we may be able to avoid that stigmatization."

At the end of 1976, Cuomo used the power of his office to regulate the real estate industry in order to revoke the license of a real estate company in Manhattan because the firm would not rent to blacks. The black newspaper *Amsterdam News*, which had been sharply critical of Carey for selecting Cuomo instead of Basil Paterson for the position of secretary of state, praised Cuomo in a lead editorial headlined "Bravo Mario!" The paper said Cuomo had shown "the kind of guts long needed in New York to help get this city back on the right track as a place of equal opportunity where the law is enforced equally for all people. . . . It has never been done before because no Secretary of State holding office prior to Cuomo has had the guts to do it. And therein lies the hope and beauty of Mr. Cuomo's action."

Hugh Carey was well aware of Cuomo's talents. The new governor soon developed a simple approach to the most vexing problems that came before him: "Let Mario do it." One of Cuomo's most noted talents was that of conciliation. Carey made use of this skill of his secretary of state to deal with several tangled disputes.

In June 1975 residents of Co-op City in the Bronx, the "largest middle-income housing development in the world," protested a 25 percent rent increase by embarking upon the biggest rent strike in American history. More than 80 percent of the fifteen-thousand families in the huge apartment complex joined the strike. Seven months later Carey asked Cuomo to begin to look into the problem. By May 1976 Cuomo had come up with a compromise whereby the tenants would take over management of the complex for six months, so that they could determine whether they could run it more efficiently, as they claimed, and whether the rent increase was necessary.

State Housing Commissioner Lee Goodwin had not been included in Cuomo's negotiations. She opposed his plan, insisting that the rent hike was necessary. Cuomo went ahead and presented his report to the governor late in June 1976 and declared that if Carey did not act on it quickly he would withdraw from negotiations. Governor Carey accepted the Cuomo proposal, and Goodwin resigned her office, saying that the plan did not meet "economic realities," because the old rent levels were not sufficient to maintain the buildings. Despite this note of disharmony within the Carey administration, Cuomo's compromise brought the thirteen-month rent strike to an amicable conclusion.

Cuomo's Co-op City agreement was something far short of a final solution. He never claimed that it was anything more than a temporary end of the thirteen-month impasse and an opportunity to work out a lasting solution. He noted that about 25 percent of the sixty thousand residents were black and that almost all of the families, whatever their race, were "middle class—that is, working people—not poor enough to be on welfare, not rich enough to be worry-free. Co-op City," Cuomo pointed out, "therefore, is prototypically the strength of this embattled city—working people of mixed color and religion living civilly and decently with one another." Some way for such people to maintain their homes within the city must be worked out, Cuomo believed, in order to save New York.

Soon after the Co-op City compromise, Cuomo received a new mediation assignment. In May 1974, prior to Carey's election, a group of Mohawk Indians occupied a 612-acre tract of state-owned land at Moss Lake, near Eagle Bay, north of Utica. The site was part of the Adirondack State Park, which was constitutionally required to remain "forever wild." The Indians claimed the land under provisions of a 1794 treaty. The situation was potentially explosive. Two people in passing cars had been hit by gunfire a few months after the Indian seizure. If the state proceeded with plans to remove the Indians, the likelihood of a violent confrontation was high.

It was a natural assignment for Cuomo, and Governor Carey gave it to him in the summer of 1976, more than two years after the occupation began. Representatives of the Mohawks of the Six Nations Confederacy had the same initial reaction to Cuomo that most others have had. "We were quite impressed with Mr. Cuomo and the way he carried himself," said Kakwirakeron, the Indians' spokesman, after their first meeting with the secretary of state. "He gave us the impression that he is an honest and straightforward man."

Within a few months Cuomo had worked out a proposal to move the Indians to a site in St. Lawrence County, outside the park, and set up an Office of Indian Affairs under the secretary of state's jurisdiction. But new problems arose and the dispute simmered on. Cuomo announced a new agreement in March 1977, only to have a court decision against the state's legal action to evict the Indians upset the process once more. An agreement to move the Indians to a five-thousand-acre site in Clinton County was finally reached, however. The great concilator had done it again.

Cuomo had become a sort of utility man on Carey's team. "I play shortstop, second base, pinch-hit," he said early in 1977. "I don't think I have any real identification other than as someone the governor can use from time to time." The designated hitter had not yet been introduced into the American League, but Mario Cuomo's role as secretary of state in the Carey administration amounted to a governmental equivalent of it.

The position as Carey let Cuomo develop it was a good one. He was even able to create the state ombudsman's office he had dreamed up during the Forest Hills dispute. A toll-free number was provided for New York residents who had any sort of problem with the state government to call for assistance.

Cuomo found his work as secretary of state to be rewarding. It was, by his own estimation, the best job he held prior to becoming governor. He found, as he had hoped, that government could be improved, albeit only at a glacial pace. "I have a feeling that we have been able to do some good things," Cuomo told a reporter at the end of his first year in office, "not terribly dramatic but nevertheless good." What he was able to accomplish, Cuomo said during his first year as secretary of state, "makes me feel like I'm doing something worthwhile."

Feeling that he was "doing something worthwhile" has always been the *sine qua non* of Mario Cuomo's existence. But if he could do some good as secretary of state, perhaps he could do more in an elective office. And of course an elective office would provide the opportunity to do something else that is essential to Cuomo: win.

His prospects for winning elective office seemed to be improving. Cuomo was gaining much more publicity than he ever had before. He got along well with people in the media, and favorable stories about him began to appear all around the state. Those in positions of influence were impressed by Cuomo's intelligence, energy, commitment, and ability to communicate. The fact that he was a Natural was becoming more widely known. By 1976 it seemed that someone was pushing him to run for every important office that came up for election. Jimmy Breslin and Norman Mailer tried to persuade Cuomo that he would be the best Democrat to run against United States Senator James L. Buckley in 1976. The secretary of state was flattered but had no interest in trying to go to Washington at that time.

But other elections were appearing on the horizon. In 1977 all New York City offices would again be up for grabs. Cuomo's name began once more to be mentioned as a possible mayoral candidate. Others thought he was better positioned for a statewide race in 1978, perhaps attorney general or comptroller.

For his part, Cuomo kept insisting that he had no intention of running for anything. But he continued to take steps that increased his visibility at the same time they served the public. Late in 1975, for instance, he began a newspaper column made available to papers around the state. It provided useful information about the services available from the State Department, but plainly it also served the function of spreading publicity about the secretary himself. And during the 1976 legislative session, Cuomo again fought for a law to restrict the activities of lobbyists. No such law was passed, but through his efforts, Cuomo demonstrated to the voters once more that he was on the side of the angels.

Few observers believed that Mario Cuomo, the man Carey's secretary, David Burke, called early in 1977 the governor's "legal theologian," who "has a vision of what goodness in government ought to be," would not soon find his way back into the struggle of elective politics. The only real questions were when he would run and for what office.[6]

8

LOSER

T HE TWELVE MONTHS
between mid-November 1976 and mid-November 1977 were
among the most significant in Mario Cuomo's political career.
During that year he was offered the state party chairmanship and
turned it down; was talked into running for mayor of New York
City, got into a runoff for the Democratic mayoral nomination,
and lost the runoff; developed a reputation as a poor campaigner,
someone who is prone to make costly mistakes, and a "loser";
defied the advice of almost all of the political experts by staying in
the general election as the Liberal party nominee for mayor, and
as such added another defeat to his record. It would not seem to
have been a very positive year, and when it was over many political
insiders thought Cuomo would never be able to win a major political contest.

In fact, the early fall of 1977 marked the low point of Cuomo's
political career. But in October and November of that year, he was
already beginning his rise from the ashes. During his lonely campaign as the Liberal candidate for mayor, Cuomo started for the
first time to follow his own political instincts, disregarding the
experts and defying the party leaders. In this mode he felt much
more comfortable and rapidly found his proper place in political
combat. By late 1977 Cuomo was on course for a successful political career. Early the following year a newspaper analysis called
him "everybody's favorite candidate for some office." Governor
Carey was soon summoning him to help a state ticket in deep
trouble by becoming Carey's running mate as the candidate for
lieutenant governor.

* * *

After his election as governor, Hugh Carey decided to dump Joe Crangle from the position of Democratic state chairman. To replace him Carey chose Bronx Democratic Chairman Patrick J. Cunningham. About a year into his tenure, Cunningham was indicted on an accusation of selling judgeships. While he was under indictment, Cunningham stepped aside as active chairman but did not resign his position. He expected to be exonerated and wanted to return to his duties. In November 1976 it appeared likely that the last of the indictments against Cunningham were about to be dismissed (as, in fact, they were in late December of that year). In the meantime, however, Carey had decided he did not want Cunningham, with his tarnished reputation, heading the state Democratic party as preparations were made for Carey's 1978 reelection campaign.

As chairman during the reelection cycle, Carey needed someone with a reputation for absolute integrity, someone who did not seem to be just another political operator, and someone with an ability to work out compromises. The résumé of Mario Cuomo matched Carey's new job description perfectly. But Carey was aware that Cuomo would be most reluctant to take the assignment, so the governor tried to force Cuomo into a position where he would not be able to refuse the proffered chairmanship. The governor's staff leaked to the press the story that Cuomo would be the new party chairman. "We put Mario in a box," one of Carey's aides gloated at the time they leaked the story.

Mario Cuomo does not like boxes, at least not those into which others place him. "He [Carey] leaked the story, thinking that I wouldn't be able to say no," Cuomo told me. A reporter called Cuomo to tell him about it and said to him, "Well, it's going to be in the paper tomorrow, so I guess you'll have to take it."

"Yeah? You watch," Cuomo told the newspaperman.

The decision was not in fact so easy for Cuomo. There were many good reasons for rejecting Carey's offer. The party chairmanship was not the sort of position Cuomo liked. It offered few opportunities for innovation, and its occupant would have far less independence than Cuomo wanted. The party chairman was expected to be the governor's man to a much greater extent than was the secretary of state. Nor was the party chairmanship a sufficient opportunity to serve. It was straight politics, trying to get your side elected, not directly trying to help the people. That would be fine for Cuomo's competitive urge, but not for his conscience.

"I wouldn't want to do it," Cuomo said to me. "It's not my kind of thing. It wasn't my role in life, not something I'd be comfortable with—raising money all the time."

A number of observers of the Albany scene agreed with an analyst who wrote that making Cuomo the party chairman "would be a waste of a man who is obviously meant for better things."

And, while we are on the subject of money, another major obstacle was that the Democrats in New York did not pay their chairman a salary. It was one thing for Cuomo to give up his lucrative law practice for the $47,800-per-year-post of secretary of state. It was quite another for him to do without income entirely. He may have been well suited for a monastic life, but he had a wife and five children who needed to be fed, clothed, sheltered, and educated. Because of the Carey administration's disclosure program for public officials (which Cuomo administered) and Cuomo's own scruples, it was not possible to solve the income problem by giving Cuomo a simultaneous appointment to a high-pay, low-work state job. He would not be prohibited from practicing law while chairman, but Cuomo has never liked to divide himself between public and private employment and, in any event, he could not earn very much in private practice at the same time he devoted sufficient energies to the party chairman's duties. Directing the reelection of the governor would be a full-time job. Another possible solution to the monetary problem would be to have some of the party's well-heeled adherents establish a fund from which Cuomo could be paid to serve as chairman. There would be nothing improper about such an arrangement. The more affluent New York Republicans paid their state chairman an annual salary of fifty-seven thousand dollars. But Cuomo still would not like such an arrangement. He would feel that the donors "owned" him and that his independence was compromised.

The most important reason for Cuomo to reject the party chairmanship was what accepting it was likely to do to his political career. It was a rare feat for a party official to be elected to public office. Cuomo had already suffered to some extent from the appearance of being the bosses' candidate in 1974. He had since rebuilt his reputation as a "nonpolitical" politician and a man of great integrity. Taking over the single most political position a Democrat in the state could occupy was very likely to destroy once and for all Cuomo's standing as "Mr. Clean"—and so also to wreck his chances of being elected to high office. This certainly is not to say that Cuomo would have engaged in corruption as party chairman. His entire career indicates that there was virtually no chance of that. But the public perception of a party chairman as a scheming politician of at least questionable ethics was one that even Cuomo might never be able to dispel if he ever became associated with that image in the public mind. The party chairmanship, as Gannett Albany reporter and Cuomo friend Woodie Fitchette noted when Cuomo was considering it, had "been a ticket to oblivion or worse in years past." "Considering the image politics has in the public mind these days, anybody who has served as a state party chairman is going to have a hard time getting elected to anything," the AP's Albany analyst quite rightly pointed out.

There were, however, important considerations to be weighed on the other side. Cuomo loves challenges and he believes almost anything is possible. Becoming state Democratic chairman and trying to prove that it was possible for someone in that position to be "untouchable," completely honest, and effective might be one way to begin to restore some public confidence in political institutions and politicians.

Tempting as Cuomo might find such a challenge, though, it was not likely to outweigh the reasons for refusing the offer. A more important reason for giving serious consideration to accepting the chairmanship was that the consequences of a refusal might well be as damaging to Cuomo's political future as being saddled with the political image of taking the job. Rejecting the job when the party seemed to need him—and when Carey had gone public with the offer—was likely to be seen by many (not least among them Carey himself) as ingratitude and a public humiliation of the governor. The result might be a falling-out between Cuomo and Carey that would be of sufficient magnitude to end Cuomo's political career.

The decision Cuomo had to make late in 1976 was a momentous one that might determine whether he would have a political future. It was a genuine dilemma, since either way he chose might lead to personal disaster for him. Although he now remembers rejecting the offer almost out of hand, Cuomo appears actually to have agonized over it for several days.

"I would have some real troubles taking the job and I am making that clear to the Governor," Cuomo said on November 18. ". . . The job does not pay a salary and I have no outside source of income. Something would have to be worked out and I am not sure what it would be. . . . But by the same token, something must also be done about the party and I am not sure there is an alternative now."

About a week later a published report indicated that, in return for helping Carey by taking the chairmanship, Cuomo wanted Carey to assure him of the lieutenant governor's slot on Carey's ticket in 1978. That position was already occupied, of course, by Mary Anne Krupsak, but it was thought that she might vacate it to take a job in Washington with the incoming administration of Jimmy Carter.

The negotiations finally broke down and Cuomo refused to accept the chairmanship. He says that Carey "was ticked."

"You made me look bad," the governor complained to Cuomo.

"Why'd you leak it?" Cuomo asked. "I never said 'yes' to it. I'm not a chairman."[1]

Indeed he is not, and in retrospect it is clear that the decision not to become one was not only the right choice, but one that enabled Cuomo to proceed down a route that would eventually lead him to high elected office.

That was far from certain at the time, though. Carey began to shut Cuomo out of his inner circle of advisers, and it seemed possible that Cuomo's rejection of the chairmanship might hurl him into the same political oblivion that acceptance was likely to have done—only the rejection seemed likely to accomplish the dismal end more rapidly.

But the party chairmanship dispute soon proved to be merely another episode in the roller-coaster relationship between Carey and Cuomo. It seemed that every time Carey got angry with Cuomo and began to freeze him out, some new need arose to make Cuomo appear indispensable to the governor. Such a need arose within a few months of Cuomo's refusal to take the state chairman's job.

In 1975 and 1976 New York City teetered on the brink of complete financial chaos. The possibility that the city would go into default was the greatest crisis facing the Carey administration in its first two years. Intervention by the state, which placed the city's finances under the direction of a newly created Municipal Assistance Corporation headed by financier Felix G. Rohatyn, saved the city from default.

The impression was widespread, however, that Mayor Abraham Beame was not up to the job of directing New York through this serious crisis. Rohatyn was among those who believed that Beame's "managerial weaknesses" made him unsuited for the mayor's office in a time of financial crisis. Leaders of both the Democratic party and the New York establishment hoped to find someone who could defeat Beame in the 1977 election. The one candidate who seemed a good bet to outpoll the mayor was Bella Abzug, a congresswoman noted for her large hats and her left-wing stances on almost all issues. In the opinion of most city and state leaders, the displacement of Beame by Abzug would be going from bad to worse. "Bella coming in scared the hell out of everybody," Herman Badillo, who had lost the mayoralty runoff in 1973 and would run again in 1977, said to me, "because a lot of people in the establishment may have been worried about me being mayor, but they were absolutely *terrified* of Bella being mayor." The establishment leaders feared that that situation might well cause the complete financial collapse of the city. From this perspective, finding a candidate who could head off both Beame and Abzug seemed imperative.

What Rohatyn, Governor Carey, and others sought was a "good government" candidate who could rally the forces of reform, obtain the Liberal party endorsement, and have a good chance of toppling Beame in the Democratic primary. Governor Carey's first choice for mayor was Congressman Ed Koch, who had been forced to drop out of the 1973 mayoral election early because of a shortage of campaign funds. But polls indicated that Koch could not win.

The demographics of New York City pointed toward an opportunity for a candidate of Italian ancestry. Estimates in the early 1970s indicated that there were some 1.7 million Italian-Americans in the city, making them the largest ethnic group, followed by approximately 1.5 million blacks and 1.2 million Jews. A couple of facts that were discussed early in this book are important in understanding the potential political impact of Italian-Americans in New York City. One is their practice of most often staying put in their urban villages. This meant that as other groups moved to the suburbs the potential political power of people of Italian heritage increased. But another part of that heritage was a general disinterest in politics.

Italian-Americans voted in fairly high percentages in general elections, but their interest in politics was for the most part insufficient to lead them to participate in substantial numbers in primaries. In heavily Democratic New York City, the primary is usually the election that really counts. The achievements that might be possible if the huge Italian-American population of the city could be made more politically active were perceived by several politicians in the mid-seventies.

Among Italian-American politicians in New York City, three names stood out in 1977 as mayoral possibilities: Congressman Mario Biaggi, Deputy Mayor John E. Zuccotti, and Secretary of State Mario Cuomo. Biaggi, who had lost in the Democratic primary in 1973, was unlikely to attract much support from reform elements. Either Zuccotti or Cuomo seemed a more alluring prospect for the "good government" folks who were desperately searching for a "white knight" to embrace.

Believing that Koch was unelectable, Governor Carey decided to push Cuomo as his candidate for mayor. Carey "turned to me as a possible winner more than as the best choice for mayor," Cuomo told me. He says that he was "very reluctant to do it," because he had no "rationale" to be mayor. He says now that he was not convinced that he was ready to be mayor—or that he was better for the job than were the other likely candidates. He attributes his ultimate defeat to these factors.

As was the case with his 1974 race for lieutenant governor, I think there should be no question that Cuomo is sincere in his belief that his uncertainty about his preparation to hold the office led to his defeat. And, also as in 1974, this factor probably was of some real importance. But in neither instance do I think Cuomo's hindsight on these losing campaigns is twenty-twenty. He *did* want to become mayor, although he went through much soul-searching in the process of reaching his decision to run. And there were other reasons for his defeat in the 1977 primary. Those other reasons were, in my opinion, far more significant than was any uncertainty in his mind over his readiness for the job.

A full analysis of the 1977 mayoral campaign is essential both to an understanding of Mario Cuomo's subsequent career and to assessing his reluctance to seek the Democratic presidential nomination a decade later. The 1977 primary campaign was the last one he conducted on the advice of experts rather than on his own instincts and beliefs, and the last one in which he was identified as the "establishment" or "party bosses'" candidate. And his agonizing over whether to run in 1977 almost eerily foreshadows the course he was to follow ten years later concerning a run for the presidency.

It does not appear that Cuomo was as reluctant a candidate in 1977 as his later recollection indicated. When Ken Auletta of *New York* magazine asked him about the possibility in July 1976, Cuomo said: "Personally, I would enjoy the opportunity. My wife, Matilda, would not. If she says no, I will say no." He said that he planned to have a heart-to-heart talk with his wife after the Democratic National Convention later that month. Asked later about the outcome of that exchange of views within the family, Cuomo reported that it was still not resolved. He and Matilda had had long discussions, he reported, and "she wants to think about it." This account appears to show that the reluctance to run for the city's highest office was not on Mario's part, but on that of his wife.

But Cuomo agonized: *To run or not to run? That is the question.* David Garth was one of those who had "scouted" the secretary of state as a Natural. He urged Cuomo to run for mayor. "Mario Cuomo was a friend and he is the only guy I have asked to run for office," Garth says. "We talked about it for three or four months." Cuomo kept weighing the alternatives. Garth got tired of waiting, and finally presented Cuomo with an ultimatum. He must have an answer, or he would go with another candidate. Cuomo said he would not run.

Ed Koch had asked Garth to "do" him. "I thought he was a good congressman," Garth says, "but I didn't think he had a chance to be mayor." After Cuomo made his apparently final decision against running, Garth called Koch and said, "Okay, you're a twenty-to-one shot, but we'll make the best shot we can."

With Mario Cuomo, though, no decision—no decision against running, at any rate—is ever final. In March 1977 Cuomo cited as a reason why he would like to be mayor that it is generally believed to be an impossible job. "That's the kind of challenge I like," Cuomo accurately said. These do not sound like the words of a man who really did not want to be mayor.

By early 1977 the mayor's race seemed to be taking shape. It was not a shape that pleased either Governor Carey or the financial and opinion leaders of the city. The Liberal party, whose sole proprietor, Alex Rose, had recently died, was in disarray and seemed likely to endorse Republican State Senator Roy M. Goodman of Manhattan for mayor. It was widely believed that a joint Republican-Liberal candidacy could do for Goodman what it had done for

John Lindsay in 1965: elect him. Carey certainly did not want a Republican in Gracie Mansion. On the Democratic side Manhattan Borough President Percy E. Sutton announced his candidacy in January. Although there were some circumstances under which Sutton, a black, might win the Democratic nomination, it was almost certain that he could not win a citywide general election. Ed Koch was next in line to declare his candidacy. Although he was entirely acceptable to Carey and most of the city establishment, Koch at the time seemed a very long shot. Other likely candidates for the Democratic mayoral nomination included Mayor Beame and former Congresswoman Abzug, both of whom are Jewish, Congressman Herman Badillo of the Bronx, who is Puerto Rican, and possibly Congressman Biaggi. Other names, such as Urban Development Corporation chairman Richard J. Ravitch, former Manhattan Democratic chairman Edward N. Costikyan, and former City Club chairman Joel Harnett were floating about in mayoral discussions, but none of them were taken very seriously.

Carey believed that the election of any of the leading candidates—Beame, Abzug, Goodman, or Sutton—would make it all but impossible for the city to get back into the bond market and refinance its debts. That was essential both to saving the city from default and to aiding his own reelection effort in 1978.

A further complicating factor in the mayoral contest arose in February when the state legislature passed a bill setting June 7 as the date for primary elections. If the election were held that early, there would be little time for any of the lesser-known Democratic candidates to mount a challenge to Beame and Abzug, whose name recognition far outdistanced that of their potential rivals. Nor would a June primary date allow enough time for a Democratic-Liberal alliance to develop behind one of the candidates, thus heading off Goodman's hopes for the Liberal nomination.

At the end of February, the Liberal party refused to endorse Koch. This convinced Carey that Koch was not going to be able to win. Carey apparently concluded at this point that Cuomo was the best bet to accomplish all the feats he needed from a mayoral candidate: win the Liberal party endorsement, gain the confidence of the bankers who were overseeing the city's finances, win the support of the middle-class voters of the outer boroughs, energize the Italian-American population, inspire people with his vision and oratory, and as a result of all this prevent the election of

Beame, Abzug, or Goodman. Other factors favoring Cuomo were that he had carried the city in his unsuccessful 1974 quest for the lieutenant governor's nomination and that he lived in Queens, which by 1977 had the second-largest population of the five counties that comprise New York City.

But if Cuomo were going to have a chance, he would need time to become better known to the city's electorate (and to the bickering group that had inherited the leadership of the Liberal party). To provide that time, the governor vetoed the June primary bill, in effect pushing the primary back to September. Carey insisted that the veto did not indicate that he was joining an anti-Beame coalition. And in truth he was not. He had long ago been one of that coalition's founders, so there was no need to join it at this late date.

All that remained was to convince Mario Cuomo—and Matilda Cuomo—that he should enter the race. A well-orchestrated campaign of newspaper editorials and phone calls from political, financial, and opinion leaders started pressuring Cuomo to enter the race. The statements and developments of the several weeks that ensued will sound familiar to anyone who followed Cuomo's Fred Astaire steps around the question of the presidency in 1987.

When Nat Hentoff asked a leading political figure with ties to both the regular and reform factions in New York's Democratic party why Cuomo was being pressured to run for mayor, he was told: "Because it's time for a mayor with character. In an emergency, you go for class. All Cuomo has to do is declare. Once the electorate gets to know him, he can't lose." Early in 1977 the ultraliberal Ramsey Clark called Cuomo "an unusually wise, sensitive, strong man who'd be effective in just about any public office. Mario knows himself. He is his own person." And from the party leadership, Matty Troy chimed in after Carey's delay of the primary with: "The delay gives Carey time to work on Mario. He will put tremendous pressure on him to run. And Mario is so far above the other candidates. . . . He will have broad-based support and come across like the 1965 John Lindsay—apolitical."

Editorialists and columnists praised Cuomo as "just about every Democrat's favorite candidate" *(New York Post)*, a man with "impressive credentials . . . high intelligence, a hard, realistic view of what needs to be done to save New York, a reputation for almost zealous candor, and a capacity to inspire" *(Daily News)*, and "a singularly thoughtful and truthful public figure so hooked on self-respect he would find it impossible to sell out" *(Village Voice)*. It was said that it "could be the job needs him more than vice versa" (White Plains *Reporter Dispatch*).

For his part, Cuomo kept insisting that he was not a candidate for mayor. He said that many people were urging him to run and promising to work for him or make contributions to his campaign, but that he was giving "no encouragement" to those who were advocating his candidacy. He insisted that the offers of assistance "have no more impact on me than the universal rejection of 1974." All sorts of people kept after him: "Declare! Declare now before it's too late. You'd be the only candidate in the race with class." "No, no, I'm not running," Cuomo said again and again. But for all his disavowals, Cuomo consistently refused to be, as he put it, "Shermanesque" about the race. He never says never, he noted. "Conditions could change," he pointed out. "The world changes, everything changes. I'm not being coy. I have a great sense of mutations."

"Why don't I get up and endorse somebody who's running and put an end to it?" Cuomo asked rhetorically in an interview with Nat Hentoff.

"Because you're not enthusiastic about any of them," Hentoff suggested.

"No I'm not," Cuomo said. "That bothers me too. Who the hell am I not to be enthusiastic about even one of them?"

"It could be you're an intelligent man," the writer answered. "Nobody has made much sense yet."[2]

All one would need to do is change a few names and insert "president" wherever "mayor" appears, and this whole scenario would precisely duplicate Cuomo's struggles with the question of the presidency a decade later. This may have been part of the reason for his reluctance to embark on a 1988 national campaign. It looked *too* much like the 1977 mayor's race, and of course he remembers all too well the disappointment he suffered then. Surely he would not want to repeat that experience on a much larger scale in 1988.

The apparent similarities between Cuomo's situation in 1977 and in 1988 are instructive, but they can be misleading. I suspect that he has been misled by them himself.

If Mario Cuomo began his quest for mayor in 1977 with people around New York saying many of the same things about him that people around the nation were saying about him with regard to the presidency ten years later, but he wound up losing in 1977, might not the same thing happen if he ran for the presidency in 1988? Cuomo probably feared this, since he attributes his 1977 loss to a lack of readiness and felt the same way about the presidency a decade later. But if he was mistaken about the causes of his defeat in the mayoral primary, there was no reason to expect that his defeat would be repeated in a presidential contest. And I believe that his interpretation of his 1977 loss is at least very incomplete.

A major reason for his defeat, as I shall detail shortly, was his continued linkage to the party leadership. Cuomo *is* independent, but appearances usually count for more in politics than does reality and to be an effective campaigner one must also *appear* independent. That was not the case in 1977. Cuomo *was* his own man, but he *seemed* to be Governor Carey's "puppet."

And one of the strange features of the support that arose for a Cuomo mayoral candidacy in 1977 was its diversity. It is a highly unusual occurrence for the *Post* and the *Voice* to applaud the same politician. Being all things to all people, or at least many things to most people, can be either a source of enormous political strength or a fatal weakness. What it proves to be in a given instance depends upon the politician and whether he asserts control over his campaign and defines himself or lets others create him in their own image. One of the principal reasons that Cuomo lost in the 1977 primary was that he failed to control his remarkable across-the-spectrum appeal and instead let others project conflicting images on him. Despite the apparent similarities between his position prior to entering the race in 1977 and his reluctance to run for president in 1988, this was a mistake that Cuomo would never repeat. And since he took control of his own definition and separated himself from the party bosses and experts, he has never lost an election.

If Cuomo's 1977 defeat was more the result of strategic errors, a case of mistaken identity in that he was wrongly perceived to be a puppet of Carey and the establishment, and a case of blurred identity resulting from his failure to assert control over his followers and campaigners in order to give the voters a clear understanding of what he stood for, there is no reason to expect that similar problems—or similar results—would obtain in a Cuomo presidential campaign.

* * *

In late March and early April 1977, Cuomo's resistance to running for mayor began to weaken. Suddenly his "no" became an "I don't think so, but . . ." Friends told reporters that the secretary of state was not out of the running, that he was "reassessing his position," and that the odds had changed from ten-to-one against his running to fifty-fifty. Other candidates were reported to be ready to pull out of the race if Cuomo got in. It was said that Goodman might beat Beame but would be "slaughtered" by Cuomo. As the pressure increased, Cuomo had a long session with the governor on Holy Thursday, April 7. "Carey didn't nail him to the wall or put him on the rack," a person who knew what transpired at the meeting said, "but he leaned on him. My sense of Thursday's meeting is that Mario is resisting a little bit less." The next morning the *Daily News* printed its special editorial listing Cuomo and John Zuccotti as the two best candidates for mayor. "The conditions should be created that will encourage him to enter the race," the *News* editorial said of Cuomo.

Since it was Good Friday, Cuomo was in church and unavailable for comment on the *News* editorial for most of the day. When Nat Hentoff caught up with him late in the day, it was apparent that Cuomo was nearly ready to jump into the race. There was, he said "no fixed change, but there are all kinds of turbulences at work now." The secretary of state told Hentoff that he thought Matilda was beginning to change her attitude. "She now is almost convinced by people she's been talking to that the good I may be able to do for the city could justify depriving the family."

If Matilda's resistance was overcome, it would be up to Mario. And he indicated late on Good Friday that he was leaning heavily in the direction of running. "It depends on whether I really would have a chance to do some good," he told Hentoff. "Then it would be worth making the effort." After a pause he added: "I think a sufficient chance exists."

Cuomo sought to escape a bit from the mounting pressure and make a final decision in some isolation by taking his family on a rare vacation over Easter weekend. They went to the Amish country in southeastern Pennsylvania. "I like the Amish," Cuomo explained to his friend, *Daily News* columnist Pete Hamill, a few days later. "They are a kind of 'WASP' Hasidim. And besides, they have restaurants there where you can get all you can eat for five-fifty.

On the second day, they were barring the doors to my kids," he joked.

"But we were also there because last week was a lot of turbulence. The *News* editorial. Pressure from the governor and other people. And time was running out." It being Easter rather than Ramadan, Cuomo went not to a mountain but to the hills of Pennsylvania to meditate on his decision.

While he was in Pennsylvania, Cuomo received a call from David Burke, Carey's secretary. Burke said, "You really ought to reconsider this. It is very important. You have a moral obligation."

"Let me think about it," Cuomo answered. "Maybe I'll change my mind. I'll talk to Matilda while we're here."

That, in all likelihood, was the main purpose of the brief vacation. From the first mention of the possibility, Matilda Cuomo had been against her husband running for mayor. Once he had been persuaded that he ought to run—and "ought" is the operative word in Cuomo's case—she had to be convinced. Among the Amish she relented.

"The fact is that my wife, Matilda, did not encourage the decision to run," Cuomo told Hamill. "She went along with it. She originally felt that it would ruin the family, that I would never be around, that I would be consumed by the effort first of running, then of governing the city. But a lot of people talked to her. I said I would go along with what she decided.

"In the end, after various people had talked to her, some of whom had been asked to talk to her by Governor Carey, she began to understand the opposite argument. That is, if I were mayor, I would be regularly attacked, pushed around by many competing forces. In a way, as mayor, you are besieged. And where would I go for help, for consolation, for peace? To the family. So she began to understand that in some odd way, the family was likely to get stronger, not weaker."

When Cuomo returned to New York on the Wednesday night following Easter, he received several phone calls telling him to go out and get the first edition of the next morning's *Daily News*. On its front page was emblazoned a huge headline saying that Cuomo would run for mayor. Carey was using the same leaking technique that he had employed five months before when he tried to force Cuomo to take the party chairmanship. There was a large difference this time, though. Cuomo did not want the party chairmanship. By mid-April 1977 he *did* want to be mayor, no matter what his memories later indicated. It is true enough, I think, that he did not want the job as desperately as some others did, but he had been convinced that it was a fitting challenge and a worthwhile opportunity for service.

Cuomo told me that he went into the 1977 campaign "halfheartedly." As I did with his similar statement about his 1974 race, I question the full accuracy of that assertion. It is not that he is trying to be deceptive, but I believe that after Cuomo has lost a contest he seeks an explanation. In that process his memory of his state of mind before and during the campaign is somewhat altered: *If I lost,* he tells himself, *it must be because I didn't really want to win. I didn't campaign well. In fact I was lousy. My heart must not have been in it. I knew that I wasn't really ready for the job. I shouldn't have let others talk me into it.*[3]

In fact, Mario Cuomo's 1977 defeat is readily explicable without resort to any assertion of halfheartedness on his part.

Mario Cuomo's biggest handicap in the 1977 Democratic mayoral primary was not his own feelings about the race, but Hugh Carey. Ed Koch was absolutely right when he said "the worst albatross Cuomo had was Carey." In fact, however, Cuomo's apparent ambivalance about entering the contest made the Carey problem worse. It made it appear from the start that Cuomo was Carey's "stooge" or "puppet." From the moment of his entrance into the race, Cuomo was seen as less than independent. Press reports spoke of Carey's "behind-the-scenes" actions and his "manipulation." The governor acted in a very heavy-handed manner, but also seemed to do several flip-flops on the Cuomo candidacy, at times denying that he was sponsoring Cuomo, at others threatening those who did not support the secretary of state.

Before Cuomo even made the formal announcement of his mayoral candidacy (which he delayed in order to take advantage of free air time in the hope of gaining in recognition), Governor Carey was telling leading figures in both the Democratic and Liberal parties that he would support Cuomo through the general election on the Liberal line, even if he lost the Democratic primary. His intention was to strengthen Cuomo's chances of getting the Liberal nomination, but Democrats were outraged at the suggestion by the leading officeholder in the state that he might desert his party in the general election. Mayor Beame described himself as "dumbstruck" by the governor's position. Carey then said that he would fight his own party leadership if it opposed Cuomo's nomination. But the governor backed off slightly on his pledge to support Cuomo on the Liberal line. Carey said if one of the other candidates won "overwhelming support" in the Democratic primary, he would "not ignore the will of the people."

Carey's clumsy attempts to dictate the party's choice were extremely harmful to Cuomo's prospects. Other candidates had little difficulty in portraying the secretary of state as Carey's "puppet"—a term they used again and again. Koch immediately predicted that Cuomo would have the "blessing of the establishment—the banks, press, and unions." Cuomo was obliged to spend much of his campaign denying that he was the "establishment" candidate, controlled by the governor, and trying—often in vain—to convince people that he was his own man. In fact, Cuomo was probably just what most New Yorkers who sought an independent, progressive, intelligent, and inspirational leader wanted, but they never realized what his qualities were, because he appeared to be Carey's tool.

After the early harm Carey inflicted on Cuomo's campaign, he kept out of the way until the last week before the primary. Then he appeared again as the proverbial bull at the china shop door. Before we go on to that stage of the election, however, we must turn to the other major flaws in Cuomo's campaign.

Carey's interventions were a problem that was to some extent beyond Cuomo's control, although he might have been able to demonstrate his independence to a greater degree. There is some question about how much he *wanted* to show his independence at this point. It appears that Cuomo still had not abandoned the idea that party leaders and political experts had the power to determine the outcome of elections. He collected more endorsements and raised more money than any of his opponents. As he had in 1974, Cuomo in 1977 ran with the party leaders when it presumably would have been to his advantage to run against them.

This was a strategic mistake, and a very costly one. Unfortunately for Cuomo, it was not the only major strategic error of the 1977 primary campaign. The city was in the throes of a deep financial crisis and it was badly split along ethnic, racial, class, and ideological lines. There was a kind of tribalism in the Democratic mayoral primary. Each major group had its candidate. What was

needed was someone to bring New York together. That was a role
for which Mario Cuomo was perfectly suited. He would later
speak of "the politics of inclusion." But in 1977, still somewhat
unsure of himself in the political arena, Cuomo deferred too much
to the advice of others whom he presumed knew more about politics than he did. Instead of preaching a politics of inclusion in the
1977 primary, Cuomo allowed himself to be persuaded to join in
the politics of division then rampant in the city.

Cuomo's basic error in 1977 was not, as he seems to think, in
letting others talk him into running, but in letting others persuade
him of *how* he should run.

Given a candidate whom many different constituencies found
appealing and one who was willing to listen to the advice of "experts," there was bound to be a battle among different factions
over just which facet of the candidate should be pointed toward the
public. A large part of the story of Mario Cuomo's defeat in the
1977 Democratic primary is about contending factions struggling
to control the image of the candidate, when he should have been
defining himself and controlling his followers.

Three drastically different images of Cuomo were put forward
in 1977: establishment candidate, "urban populist," and outer-borough ethnic. On some issues two of the groups would unite against
the third, but on others a different configuration would emerge.
The inevitable result was utter confusion on the part of the public
as to *who* Cuomo was and *what* he stood for. The candidate remained a blur that the public could never quite bring into focus.

Governor Carey, some of the party leaders, and some of
Cuomo's campaign workers left the public with the impression
that he was the candidate of the political establishment. Although
it was Carey and company that pushed Cuomo the hardest to enter
the race, the notion that he was their puppet was never accurate.
As he had demonstrated a few months before with the party chairmanship, Cuomo would not allow himself to be pushed into something against his will. Nor would he be beholden to anyone,
including the governor. He would remain his own man.

But the public can readily be forgiven for its inability to understand this in 1977. In certain respects Cuomo did not act like an
independent leader during the primary campaign. If the Democratic establishment did not control him, it seemed at times as if
the other two factions backing his candidacy did.

The urban populists were those who saw Cuomo as the new

Robert Kennedy. They included Jack Newfield, Adam Walinsky, and Jimmy Breslin. Their goal was to create a biracial alliance including the middle class and the poor, both black and white. This was an admirable goal as far as it went, but the champions of this strategy believed that they needed a target against which the wrath of these often conflicting middle- and lower-class groups could be directed. In bringing together a portion of the society that had been at each others' throats, the urban populists would widen another division. The idea was to turn "ordinary folk" against "the establishment." To the extent that this faction of Cuomo backers succeeded in placing their imprint on Cuomo, his image would contrast sharply with that created by Carey's interventions. How were voters supposed to tell whether Cuomo was the establishment candidate or the antiestablishment candidate? On different wavelengths they were receiving contradictory signals.

Sharply different in outlook from the urban populists, but also opposed to the establishment, were the outer-borough ethnic homeowners such as those with whom Cuomo had worked in his prepolitical days. These were the middle- or working-class sorts whom the urban populists hoped to make part of their alliance. The only trouble was that many of the homeowner group wanted no part of a multiracial alliance. One of them who considered himself a demographic expert and worked with Cuomo's campaign actually produced a document showing how it was possible to win the primary without black votes, Hispanic votes, or Jewish votes. Of course this concept in no way reflected Cuomo's thinking or that of his urban populist backers, but it shows the wide variance among the different groups supporting his candidacy.

The urban populist faction did not approve of the racial attitudes of the outer-borough homeowner faction, but the latter did represent part of the alliance they sought to form. And the urban populists had few if any blacks in their alliance. They had to start somewhere. Their point of agreement with the outer-borough ethnic homeowners was opposition to the establishment, the Manhattan elite, the most convenient symbol of which was the despised former mayor, John V. Lindsay. Accordingly these two factions united in talking Cuomo into running against Manhattan.

Garth's firm had found through polling late in 1976 that there was strong resentment in the four outer boroughs against Manhattan. People in those parts of the city agreed by a margin of more than two to one with the statement that "Manhattan officials don't understand the problems faced by most New Yorkers." Garth was gathering this information for Koch, and would soon be grooming *him*, to the extent possible, as an antiestablishment candidate. But the sentiment in Garth's poll was well known to Cuomo's supporters.

The outer-borough strategy, endorsed by the urban populists as well as the ethnic homeowner group, essentially red-lined most of Manhattan from the outset. This was a terrible mistake, in both practical and philosophical terms. It was true enough that much of the Manhattan elite was suspicious of someone with Cuomo's background, but with his brilliance, his compassion, his vision, and his ability to communicate, Cuomo was just the person to break through the prejudices of liberal Manhattanites—as indeed he did in later years. The votes that could have meant victory in the 1977 primary were needlessly written off at the outset.

The outer-borough strategy was even more tragic from a philosophical standpoint. Cuomo was working his way toward his "family" concept of society, and this necessarily meant practicing an inclusive politics. He should never have agreed to a strategy that amounted to orphaning the people of one of the boroughs from the family of New York City. The object of his campaign should have been to unite, not to divide. One of Cuomo's favorite metaphors for society, in addition to that of a family, is a mosaic. No matter how one paints the glass, it is impossible to create a mosaic of New York City without Manhattan. But he was persuaded to try just that in 1977. Throughout the primary campaign Cuomo shunned the liberal-chic organizations and beautiful people of Manhattan and tried to win without them.

The reason that Cuomo was susceptible to the argument that he should run on an outer-borough strategy must be sought in his own experience, which was almost entirely in Queens and Brooklyn. The Manhattan establishment, through its leading law firms, had rejected him; why shouldn't he now reject them? As he had sat in his Court Street law office, looking out past Manhattan toward New Jersey, he must often have thought of what a social chasm the East River was, separating Brooklyn and Queens from Manhattan. The temptation must have been too great to resist when people to whom Cuomo ascribed political wisdom told him that running against Manhattan was the way to get elected.

So Manhattan became the enemy and Cuomo's campaign headquarters were set up in the friendly territory of Rego Park,

Queens, far removed not only from the Manhattan elite, but from the media so essential to a successful campaign. This was intended to be symbolic of the campaign turning its back on Manhattan, and it worked—but not to Cuomo's ultimate advantage.

Some of those engaged in Cuomo's campaign pleaded with him to try to win over Manhattan rather than use it as his foil. Cuomo's brilliant pollster, Robert Sullivan, argued that the intelligentsia, centered in Manhattan, would be the key to victory in the primary. Particularly in light of the city's financial crisis, Sullivan contended, people in all parts of New York—including the outer boroughs—were looking for a *mayor*, not a champion of local interests. It was a time crying out for a leader who could unify the entire city, which Cuomo could be, but he was making the mistake of following the advice of those who would have him be the divisive, mutinous general of only part of the city.

City University history Professor Richard C. Wade, who had headed George McGovern's virtual sweep of New York in 1972 and helped Carey's uphill battle two years later, also kept struggling against the outer-borough strategy. He argued that the way for Cuomo to win was to show himself to be part of the long New York tradition of independent progressive leaders. Many of the people who would be mobilized by such a campaign were the very ones being excluded by the outer-borough strategy. Wade had a hard time at meetings at the Rego Park headquarters. He was a known "liberal." To the outer-borough ethnics, that meant he was in favor of integration (which he was), and so was to be viewed with great suspicion. To the urban populists, Wade was also a "liberal." To them, that meant that he was part of the establishment and so not to be trusted. The whole setup had its weird aspects. The allies in the outer-borough strategy were in agreement in their opposition to the "liberal establishment," but they attacked it from opposite directions. The Newfield group charged from the left, while the ethnic homeowner faction laid siege from the right. The independent progressives in the campaign were caught in the middle. "I was trying to get him out of Rego Park without dropping him in Greenwich Village," Wade told me.

Although I do not think Cuomo has ever analyzed his 1977 campaign in quite the foregoing terms, he would not disagree with some of this analysis. He told me that he did not think the campaign was well run. "I never thought that theme selection was good. Gerry Rafshoon and Pat Caddell were involved, but they had just made a president and while they tried sincerely to make me, it wasn't the same as making a president. They weren't here all the time. It was kind of absentee control, and local control was split up between many people," he rightly said. "It wasn't a well-managed campaign. I didn't run it myself and left it to other forces to run it, and I think every once in a while I'd intrude myself in the process. It was a mess."

Small wonder that the public didn't know quite where Cuomo was coming from. It would not be correct to say that he didn't know either, but he was being pulled apart by conflicting advice. The lack of focus and contrasting images added to the impression that Cuomo was indecisive. The "Hamlet" charge had already begun to emerge when Cuomo appeared unable to decide whether he wanted to be mayor. The confusion of the primary campaign reinforced that negative impression. Just what Mario Cuomo is would become clear to the public only when he made it so by shaping his own image to reflect his reality, rather than allowing putative experts to define him as they saw fit. Rafshoon and Caddell should not have been trying to "make" Cuomo. He had already done quite a job of that himself.[4]

One day Mario Cuomo's great strength would be to stand firmly and attract others not only to his person but to his values and vision. That day had not yet arrived during the 1977 primary. Instead of acting as a powerful magnet himself, Cuomo at that time permitted himself to become like iron filings drawn to the opposing poles of magnets set up by his backers. Or, to shift metaphors, Cuomo's 1977 primary campaign was one in which he became a dog with three tails, each wagging him at different times in different directions.

The preceding paragraphs, though accurate, may give a somewhat misleading impression. Most campaigns are plagued by internal conflicts, and Cuomo's in 1977 was unusual only in degree. The lack of direction—or the excess of different directions—certainly weakened Cuomo's candidacy. Perhaps it doomed it. But despite all the problems, the campaign was not a total disaster. Its candidate, after all, was the Natural. That plus can offset a lot of minuses.

The Cuomo that became nationally known a few years later was evident in 1977, although sometimes one had to look hard to find him. The combativeness was certainly there. After *Times* columnist William Safire wrote that Governor Carey was arranging for "the late mobster Sam Giancana's friend, Frank Sinatra," to raise money for Cuomo's campaign, the candidate wrote the following response to Safire: "He [Sinatra] is a nice man with blue eyes and my wife, Matilda, loves him. If he is willing to help me, that article would make me run to him."

The general dismay at what one had to do to be elected to office was also evident in the 1977 Cuomo. About a month after the exchange with Safire, Cuomo's campaign arranged a "photo opportunity" for the candidate with Sinatra, who was filming in Manhattan. Cuomo showed that he was uncomfortable with the artificial behavior required for a media event. He said that the photographers should have been with him that morning when he visited the New York Foundling Hospital. When one of the photographers tried to explain why it was better for a candidate to be seen with Old Blue Eyes, Cuomo sighed.

The real Cuomo was also visible in 1977 in his insistence on speaking his mind without regard for political niceties. When a member of the *Times* hierarchy asked him why he thought Percy Sutton could not win, Cuomo replied: "Because there are more bigots than blacks in this city."

"The people in this town are *better* than that," the *Times* man declared.

"I know this city," Cuomo shot back. "I've lived here all my life. Where do you live?"

"Scarsdale," came the barely audible reply, which promptly ended the discussion of that topic.

Certainly Cuomo started off well behind Beame and Abzug in name recognition and hence in the polls. But throughout the early part of the campaign, despite the strategic mistakes, Bob Sullivan believed from the impressions he was getting from what he calls his "ersatz polling" that Cuomo would catch both of them, come in first in the primary, and defeat Koch in the runoff. Carey's role made Cuomo almost as much of a target for other candidates as was Mayor Beame. Cuomo never was the front-runner, but the idea that he was the establishment candidate often made him appear to be.

Being tagged as the front-runner and as the governor's boy was even more harmful to Cuomo's candidacy than a similar identification would have been to another candidate. Not only was it harmful to the voters' view of him, it was also harmful to his view of himself. He hated to be seen as anyone's puppet; it caused him anguish. And, as I have noted on several occasions, Cuomo hated to be the favorite in any contest. Given his lack of name recognition and experience, he probably should never have been labeled the front-runner, but he was and it made him exceedingly uncomfortable.

Cuomo just could not get away from the Carey connection. Even some of his supporters complained that people kept asking whether the candidate was subservient to the governor. "Is the Governor really some kind of Dr. Frankenstein?" Cuomo asked once when this question came up. "And I'm a monster with a stick in my neck that responds to his electrodes? That's a lot of baloney."

Although it seemed clear that Carey's embrace was crushing Cuomo, the candidate maintained that the governor's support was only a temporary hindrence and would prove beneficial to Cuomo in the long run. If this statement was anything more than a *pro forma* response to a reporter, it indicates that Cuomo still had not accepted the lesson that he needed to separate himself from those whom the public perceived to be "the bosses."

As the campaign moved into its final month in the dog days of August, Cuomo said that "law and order" was the main issue. That would make his outer-borough ethnic backers happy, but Cuomo sought to distinguish himself from the simplistic and conservative advocates of "law and order" by assailing Beame's call for restoring the death penalty. Cuomo called Beame's position "political garbage" and a "political cop-out." Beame's quick response showed how Cuomo's opponents turned all topics back to the question of his alleged lack of independence. The mayor asserted that Cuomo was "acting as a buffer for his boss, the Governor, who is also opposed to it [capital punishment] and who has put him in as his puppet candidate."

Cuomo told me that he doesn't know why he kept bringing up the death penalty question, which had no logical place in the mayoral race since the mayor has no say in either the capital punishment law or its implementation. "It's one thing to have the death penalty position which I did," Cuomo said to me, "but I kept bringing it up. I didn't like the idea, but I can't examine my motivation. But I know I brought it up more than I needed."

It has often seemed that Cuomo finds the temptation irresistible to say things that may be politically harmful to him.

The two issues of death and the governor became further intertwined in the last week of the first primary campaign. Carey suddenly plunged back into the race that he had kept out of for several
months. "It was in the crucial part when everybody was paying
attention that he came in and just stomped all over the campaign,"
in the opinion of Bob Sullivan. One of the best examples of the
damage Carey did was a comment he made while passing through
a barbershop in the Bronx. He was quoted as saying that he would
review his opposition to capital punishment if Cuomo won and the
crime rate did not fall. Carey's denials that he had said such a thing
were of little use. This was the worst sort of statement that a
backer of Cuomo could make. It indicated that Carey—and, perhaps, Cuomo—might compromise on a matter of principle in
order to achieve political gain. Fuzzy as Cuomo was in the public
mind in 1977, integrity and high principle were central to the way
people perceived him—not to mention to the way he was.

By this time Cuomo had suffered two other blows. In April
both the *Post* and the *Daily News* had encouraged him to run. In
August both endorsed Ed Koch. Cuomo had a great opportunity
to win their formal endorsements, but his interviews with the
editorial boards of both papers went badly. Mike O'Neill, managing editor of the *News*, liked Cuomo, but he was upset with the
candidate's refusal to go beyond generalizations to specific ideas
for dealing with the city's problems. Rupert Murdoch, the right-
wing sensational-press magnate from Australia who had recently
taken control of the *Post*, found Cuomo insufficiently conservative
for his taste. Murdoch, in any case, did not want to endorse a
candidate who was already close to being the favorite. His desire
was to find someone he could *make* mayor.

Murdoch found his man in Ed Koch. Murdoch told Koch that
he would endorse him if Koch would promise to appoint Edward
Costikyan as his first deputy mayor. The congressman from Manhattan's "Silk Stocking" district did not hesitate before agreeing.
The immediate result was a front-page editorial in the *Post* on
August 19, calling Koch the man who could get New York moving
again. The Murdoch-ordered editorial was not labeled as an editorial in the first several editions of the paper. That was quite a boost
to Koch, but much more was soon to come. Murdoch began bla-
tantly to slant his paper's coverage of the mayoral race. The *Post*
was suddenly brimming with favorable coverage of Koch and negative stories about Cuomo. The impropriety of Murdoch's actions

was evidenced by fifty *Post* reporters and editors signing a petition protesting the paper's biased coverage. Murdoch responded by saying anyone who did not like what he was doing was free to resign. Several did.

Cuomo felt that the *Daily News* and the *Post* had misled him—perhaps betrayed him. The *Times* had already endorsed him at the end of July. That paper expressed the hope that Cuomo would be able to stem the "savage tribalism" prevalent in city politics. It was a hope based more on a knowledge of Cuomo the man than on Cuomo's campaign that year. To no one's surprise the *Village Voice* endorsed Cuomo.

After a long discussion involving much disagreement at former Mayor Robert Wagner's home, the Cuomo campaign decided to accept a last-minute endorsement from Mario Biaggi. Cuomo really did not want the blessing of the "tough" law-and-order congressman, but the staff knew how tightly bunched the four leading candidates were, and successfully argued that any advantage that Biaggi might bring in the Bronx or elsewhere might prove to be the difference between making the runoff and finishing out of the money.

When the only endorsements that made any real difference were counted on September 9, Koch finished first with 19.8 percent of the vote, followed closely by Cuomo at 18.7 percent, Beame 17.9 percent, Abzug 16.6 percent, Sutton 14.4 percent, and Badillo 11 percent. An election with such widely scattered results was without precedent. The two survivors would have only ten days to divide up the more than 61 percent of the votes that had gone to those who did not make it past the first cut.[5]

The outer-borough strategy "worked"—and in the process made clear what was wrong with it. Cuomo carried Queens and Staten Island and ran about even with Beame in the mayor's home borough of Brooklyn. But Cuomo was far down the list in Manhattan, and thanks to the campaign strategy he had used, he would have a hard time winning over many of the large number of Manhattanites who had supported Abzug, Sutton, Beame, and Badillo.

The brief runoff campaign against Ed Koch for the Democratic mayoral nomination in September 1977 was the worst time in Mario Cuomo's political life. He later said that all the negative images of him as a campaigner "arise out of the runoff of '77 and ignore completely my history before that nine-day period and my history after it." It seems that Cuomo "cracked," at least to some extent, during that runoff. It is important to try to understand why he reached a low point in that period.

He had hoped to come in first in the primary, at least a few points ahead of the runner-up. According to the original Cuomo plan, that runner-up was to be Mayor Beame. Under those circumstances a runoff victory would be relatively easy. Instead, Cuomo had finished second and now faced Koch, who would have many advantages in the runoff. And the public would not be voting against Koch as many of them might have had Beame, the mayor whom many held responsible for the city's fiscal crisis, been the alternative to Cuomo.

The campaign was, as one of Cuomo's aides put it, a "nightmare." Some of the problems amounted to continuing fallout from the fission among his backers. Others were directly attributable to the candidate's own errors.

In the former category was the failure to appeal to the constituencies of the defeated candidates, particularly the blacks and Hispanics. Beame was unlikely to endorse Cuomo because the mayor was understandably angry at Carey for putting Cuomo up to defeat him. Abzug was much more likely to wind up on Cuomo's side, because she was hostile to Koch. Unfortunately for Cuomo, however, a large portion of Abzug's following was less likely to support him. She was the darling of the Manhattan liberals who had been excluded from the outer-borough campaign. Her endorsement was certainly worth having, and Cuomo did get it, but it was not as helpful as it might have been if he had been running on a different theme and strategy.

If most of the Beame voters went with Koch and at least a majority of the Abzug backers followed her into the Cuomo camp, the disposition of the Sutton and Badillo supporters became critical. Since it had been clear for some time that neither of these candidates was likely to make the runoff, some in Cuomo's campaign had been making preparations to appeal to black and Hispanic voters. Cuomo himself had asked Richard Wade to make him a list of people to call on primary night. Wade made a list, with phone numbers and such other useful information as spouses' names. The list began with Basil Paterson, Percy Sutton, Herman Badillo, and a lawyer who was close to Bella Abzug. Wade sent the list and assumed that it had been given to Cuomo. It later turned out that the candidate had not gotten the list on primary night. Whether this was an unintentional snafu or the work of elements within the campaign who wanted to try to win without appealing to blacks and Puerto Ricans is uncertain. In either case it was a costly mistake.

Cuomo did seek the support of black and Hispanic political leaders, but the contacts were botched. Immediately after the primary Herman Badillo told his supporters that he would meet with both Koch and Cuomo and see what they would offer to do for the Hispanic community. He met with Koch and his handler, David Garth, and "they said, 'Absolutely! We'll recognize the interests of the Hispanic community and we will make appointments of Hispanics at every level, including deputy mayor,' " Badillo told me. There had never before been an Hispanic deputy mayor in New York. Badillo then held a similar meeting at his home with Cuomo. "I couldn't get an answer from him," Badillo recalls. "He'd go around in circles. He said, 'I wanna be independent; I don't wanna be bound to anyone.' I said, 'Nobody's trying to bind you to anything, but I can help you with the Hispanic community and I have some influence in the black community. That can make the difference." But Badillo said that he must know what Cuomo as mayor would do for the minority communities.

"It must have gone on for three hours," Badillo said. Finally he called his wife down and told her, "I can't get a straight answer out of Mario. What the hell is he trying to say?" The discussion went on for another hour, but no satisfactory response emerged from Cuomo. "Anytime you want to come and talk to me, we'll sit and have a cup of coffee," Cuomo recalls saying to Badillo, "but I can't make a deal and give you jobs." Badillo went back to his supporters and said, "Hey, fellas, we got a clear-cut, no-baloney answer from Koch; Mario said he'd give me a cup of coffee." As a result, Badillo endorsed Koch and most of the Puerto Rican electorate (which at that time was probably more favorably disposed toward Koch than Cuomo anyway) voted for the Manhattan congressman. Koch later made Badillo a deputy mayor.

Why was Cuomo so reluctant to make any commitment on Hispanic appointments? Probably for the right reasons—that is, as he said, in order to maintain his independence. There was nothing wrong with what Badillo sought, as Cuomo later acknowledged. But Cuomo seems to have been placing legitimate concern for recognition of the needs of ethnic groups in the same category as making deals with political bosses.

He wouldn't deal with them either, although someone did talk him into having breakfast with Meade Esposito. Koch did considerably more than have breakfast. He visited Esposito, Manes, and Cunningham to gain their cooperation. Such cooperation did not come cheaply. Esposito demanded that Koch appoint one of his boys, Anthony Ameruso, as commissioner of the city's Transportation Department. Despite the fact that Koch's panel on appointments found Ameruso unqualified, he was given the plum. Ten years later Ameruso was convicted of perjury for lying about a large personal stake in a company to which he issued a license to run a ferry service.

Cuomo was obviously right—from a practical as well as an ethical standpoint, since the bosses no longer controlled many votes—in not making deals with the bosses. The issue was not nearly so clear with Badillo's request for assistance for the Hispanic community.

For a time it appeared that Cuomo would have more success in courting the support of black political leaders in the city. The Reverend Eugene Callender, pastor of the Church of the Master, a United Presbyterian congregation in Harlem, invited the candidate to attend services on the Sunday after the primary. Cuomo brought his whole family but refused to speak. Callender and the congregation finally prevailed upon him to talk for a few minutes after the service had concluded. He gave a moving extemporaneous speech in the finest Cuomo style (portions of this talk were quoted in chapter 3). Like most audiences that have ever been directly exposed to Cuomo, these black Protestants were won over by the values and vision of this Italian Catholic. It was probably his best moment in the nine days between the primary and the runoff.

Later that Sunday afternoon the black elected leaders met at the Harlem State Office Building to discuss endorsing one of the survivors of the mayoral primary. They decided to back Cuomo, but they wanted Percy Sutton to make the announcement the next evening. On Monday morning, however, State Senator Vander Beatty of Brooklyn announced that a group of black political and community leaders was endorsing Cuomo. This angered Sutton and some of the other black leaders in Manhattan, and Sutton declared that he now felt "no urgency" to endorse anyone. The next day Basil Paterson, Congressman Charles Rangel, and other

Manhattan black leaders endorsed Koch. It seemed that the outer-borough strategy now applied to blacks as well as ethnics.

At this point Cuomo's chances of winning were not good. If the Beame, Sutton, and Badillo voters all cast their runoff ballots for Koch, he was almost certain to win. Cuomo probably realized this, and he recoiled from his coming rejection. Carey's ardor for making Cuomo mayor cooled noticeably after the primary returns were in. Some of the governor's aides told reporters that Carey's objective in pushing Cuomo had been to prevent a Beame-Abzug runoff. Now that that goal had been achieved, the governor seemed to be drifting back toward his original preference, Koch. Cuomo began to think that he had been duped by Carey, *Daily News* publisher W. H. James, and *Post* publisher Rupert Murdoch. The latter two had defected to Koch before the primary; now Carey seemed to be following suit. (True to form, Carey swayed back in the other direction a few days later, claiming to support Cuomo "more strongly than ever.") Cuomo's sense of being an outsider turned sharply negative. He became irritable. His wonderful, persuasive verbal skills gave way to a style of slashing attack. When he becomes nervous, he speaks too rapidly and his voice loses much of its magnificent resonance. Cuomo's style during the runoff, Ed Koch said to me, "did not reflect his regular persona." "He came across very hard, uncaring—the zealot—and those are not the most charming aspects of his personality," the mayor said. "The aspects of his personality that are most liked are his warmth, his compassion, his good humor. He lost those in that ten-day period—and I think he would agree."

In those last days before his loss to Koch, Cuomo was reported to be frazzled, constantly behind schedule, yelling at his staff, and—at least according to what Koch heard—"sulking" to his family. Cuomo has never liked to lose.

The Cuomo campaign became negative during the runoff. (Koch was also being negative, but in other campaigns Cuomo has resisted a negative approach, regardless of what opponents were doing.) Cuomo countered Koch's charge that he was a "creature of the establishment" by asserting that Koch was the creation of David Garth and his media wizardry. Cuomo's television commercials during the runoff included sharp personal attacks on Koch. One portrayed the congressman as two-faced. Another Cuomo ad showed Koch's face dissolving into that of John Lindsay. Here was the outer-borough strategy at its worst. The attempt to arouse resentment against what Cuomo in the campaign called the "Manhattan arrangement" was nowhere plainer than in this attempt to link an opponent to Lindsay, who was assumed still to be despised by the residents of the outer boroughs.

The continuing struggle for the soul of the Cuomo campaign was visible in an internal battle over the Koch-to-Lindsay dissolve. On September 15, the Cuomo campaign said that it was withdrawing the commercial. The next day campaign finance chairman Howard Samuels declared that the decision had been made to continue to use the controversial ad.

The brief runoff campaign (which was interrupted by Rosh Hashanah, which the Catholic Cuomo observed by not campaigning and the Jewish Koch observed by visiting as many synagogues as possible) featured several debates. The most important of these was the first, on WNET—Channel 13, New York's public television station. Cuomo appeared to be arrogant, practically a bully. He acted as if he were in a courtroom. "I was much, *much* too tough in the debates," he told me. "I was much too aggressive, too much like the courtroom lawyer—courtroom prosecutor as a matter of fact—and people don't like that. That comes off as very hard on television. I heard about it over and over again." To many observers it seemed that Cuomo had brutalized Koch. Cuomo believes that Koch always seeks to portray himself as a victim, in order to swing voters to his side. Be that as it may, by his attacks Cuomo certainly helped swing the sympathies of many to Koch.

It probably did not matter that much. Without Manhattan, the blacks, or the Hispanics, Cuomo wasn't likely to win anyway. When the votes were counted, Koch won by a fairly substantial margin, 55 percent to 45 percent. Cuomo had won the ethnic Catholics, but not much else. Koch prevailed in Manhattan, and among Jews, Puerto Ricans, blacks, and the intelligentsia.

Mario Cuomo's political career appeared to be at an end. He was tagged a "loser." Most liberals were ready to dismiss him. They even said he was "not very bright."[6]

Fortunately for Cuomo, the old saying about the darkest hour being just before dawn is sometimes true.

Before we proceed to that dawn, however, some light must be directed at the darkest episode during the preceding night. Another consequence of Cuomo's failure to assert control over his 1977 primary campaign demands examination. Koch's status as a lifelong bachelor who did not seem to practice the *Playboy* philosophy had produced, over the years of his political career, the sort of speculation and gossip that usually follow men in such circumstances. There was absolutely no evidence indicating that Koch was a homosexual, but that fact did not deter the whispers. Aware of what had been hinted in the past and of the probability that the question would arise in one way or another during the mayoral race, David Garth arranged to have former Miss America and popular Democrat Bess Meyerson frequently accompany Koch during the campaign. Garth made sure that Koch and Meyerson were often photographed holding hands or kissing. She was an actress playing a role. Hints were dropped that Koch and Meyerson might marry some day. It was all staged, but through most of the primary campaign the Meyerson ploy worked well. The question making the rounds was "Are they lovers?" rather than "Is Koch gay?"

That the latter "issue" finally wormed its way into the campaign is hardly surprising. But the way in which it did raises perhaps the most troubling questions about Mario Cuomo that have come up at any time in his career.

It is clear, first of all, that some of Cuomo's supporters were active in spreading rumors that Koch's affectional preferences were not "normal." Handbills reading VOTE FOR CUOMO, NOT THE HOMO were put up around the city during the 1977 campaign. Of course a candidate cannot reasonably be expected to control all the actions of his more unscrupulous supporters. Cuomo rightly points out that there were people going around saying he was connected with the Mafia, but "I can't hold him [Koch] responsible for that."

Koch wrote in his autobiography, *Mayor*, though, that "it was clear that Mario was going to be doing nothing toward disciplining or dismissing those of his aides who participated in the smear. The way in which he did that was so clear and so heavy-handed that there can be no doubt of his complicity."

That may well be the most serious charge anyone has ever leveled against Mario Cuomo. He categorically denies it. "As to the so-called gay-baiting and the accusations against him," Cuomo told me in 1987, "I never made it, believed it, thought it—I threatened people in my campaign and said that if anybody else engaged in that it will kill me, it won't kill Koch. It will help him and get him the sympathy vote." Cuomo noted again that Koch had a skill for making himself appear a victim. He told his campaign workers that trying to spread the homosexual stories was not only unethical, it would also play into Koch's hand. Cuomo told them it was cheap and stupid.

During the campaign, Cuomo says, a group came in to see him and said they had "evidence on Koch." "I threw them out," Cuomo told me. This account is confirmed by others who worked in the Cuomo campaign.

It seems, though, that if Cuomo was forceful in denouncing gay-baiting, some of his followers decided that they knew better how the campaign should be conducted. This is unsurprising, since we have already seen much evidence that Cuomo's 1977 campaign was largely beyond his control.

Late in the general election campaign, people who were or had been associated with the effort to elect Cuomo took the quest to smear Koch to new depths. Michael Dowd, who had been Cuomo's campaign manager during the primary, but had since left the campaign and returned to his private law practice, arranged for a Queens private investigator to try to find out if the rumors about Koch's sexual preferences were true. At about the same time—a couple of weeks before the November election—Pat Deignan, who had taken over as Cuomo's campaign coordinator, sent Thomas Chardavoyne, Cuomo's Brooklyn coordinator, to meet with a "security consultant" named Bruce Romanoff. Chardavoyne said he was told that Romanoff was working on a story on Koch and that he met with him to tell him "the usual standard rumors." Romanoff had a different explanation of the purpose of the meeting: "He asked me to look into it [Koch's sex life], past and present, the whole thing. He said he'd heard there was a chance Koch had a few boyfriends."

When Geoffrey Stokes of the *Village Voice* told Cuomo of the activities of his present and former campaign workers, the candidate said, "That's awful. That's stupid. That's childish." "Oh, Christ," Cuomo said. "Holy Mother of God. I'm so . . . I'm so . . . *disappointed.*" He pointed out that Koch had been in Congress for fourteen years, "some of it when the FBI was doing things it shouldn't have been doing." He said that politicians are "the most scrutinized people in the world. . . . *Nothing* gets away unnoticed." That being the case, Cuomo said to Stokes, "I'm telling you there *can't* be anything there."

"I hope, I *hope* Mike [Dowd] made it absolutely clear to you that during the primary I said I didn't want it explored. And I *don't* want it explored, especially at the last minute."

There is no reason to disbelieve Cuomo's unequivocal declarations that he personally had nothing to do with the attempts to investigate Koch's private life or spread rumors about him. Koch himself now says that he accepts Cuomo's statements "that he had nothing to do with it and regrets that the incident occurred." Koch told me that Cuomo "undoubtedly was very wounded by my commentary [in *Mayor*], because he is an honorable person and felt unfairly charged." The mayor said it made no sense for him to "continue to harbor the fury" because Cuomo "is genuinely distressed it occurred and believes, and therefore I accept, that he had nothing to do with it."

"So," Koch concluded our discussion of the subject, "it's an incident I have wiped from my list of injustices, and I'm not an injustice collector. I was affronted by that, but I have wiped it from my mind and it does not interfere with my personal and professional relationship with him."

"Some people choose to blame me for the acts of my subordinates," Cuomo said to me. "I guess I could be like President Reagan and say, 'Okay, I'm accountable.'"

Unfortunately Cuomo *is,* at least to an extent, accountable for what happened. He *did* have something to do with it. Not with the hiring of private eyes and the attempts to spread false stories about Koch. (Some Cuomo followers had also hired what Koch calls a "renegade cop" to swear that he had twice arrested Koch—once following a "homosexual brawl" at his apartment and once for soliciting male prostitutes on the street. Some Cuomo backers tried repeatedly to get this story printed in the final days before the general election.) Although the candidate does not appear to have been connected with any of these reprehensible undertakings and has condemned them in no uncertain terms, he did help to create the whole atmosphere in which his supporters thought that such activities had a place in the campaign. Cuomo's responsibility begins with his lack of control over the campaign. A candidate whose primary campaign had been pulled apart by competing groups tugging it in different directions was less likely than one who was in firm control to be heeded when he demanded that subordinates not pursue the homosexual rumors.

But Cuomo's responsibility for the rise of the homosexual question goes beyond omission to commission. It was the outer-borough strategy that led directly to Cuomo's highly questionable insertion of innuendo about Koch and homosexuality into the campaign. The raising of questions about Koch's life-style was in fact part of the strategy to attack Manhattan. John Corry, who mentioned the charges in a preelection profile of Koch in the *New York Times Magazine,* said that he "knew for certain that it was very much on the minds of various ethnic groups in the Bronx, Queens and Brooklyn." The ethnics in the outer boroughs were presumed to be New York City's closest facsimiles to Okies from Muskogee. They were not likely to be favorably disposed toward a mayoral candidate they thought was gay.

Pete Hamill summed up the contrast that some of Cuomo's backers were trying to make between their candidate and Koch when he wrote just prior to the runoff that "the difference between Cuomo and Koch might come down to this: Cuomo is a family man from Queens who goes to church every Sunday; Koch is a bachelor who lives in Greenwich Village and champions secular solutions for most problems."

That some of his backers were pushing this contrast might be considered something beyond Cuomo's control. But the theme was too central to the campaign to allow the candidate to be excused. Cuomo, moreover, was clearly a participant in the implementation of the strategy. He, for instance, often referred to Koch as a "Greenwich Village bachelor." And Cuomo, who under his authority as secretary of state the previous year had implemented a policy of not allowing discrimination against gays in the issuance of occupational licenses under his department's jurisdiction and had during the campaign endorsed a proposed city gay rights bill, started late in the campaign to distinguish his position from Koch's. As Geoffrey Stokes put it at the time, "it was Cuomo who dipped his bucket into the well and drew it to the surface."

Shortly before the general election, Cuomo charged that Koch favored allowing homosexual teachers to "proselytize in the classroom." In a debate on Channel 13, the candidates were given an opportunity to ask each other questions. Cuomo's first inquiry was addressed to Koch. He asked whether the gay rights bill then before the City Council allowed a homosexual to teach homosexuality. "I have repeatedly, before every gay group—particularly the gay group that endorsed you and condemned me," Cuomo said to Koch, "—made the point that I am opposed to proselytization." In fact, there does not seem to have been any gay group that endorsed Koch and condemned Cuomo. The New York Political Action Council, a nonpartisan gay and lesbian organization rated Koch—along with Abzug, Badillo, and Sutton—"preferred," Cuomo "acceptable," and Beame "unacceptable." Cuomo's attempt to smear Koch as a man who advocated trying to convert school children to homosexuality was akin to saying, "I have taken a courageous stand against wife-beating and child molestation. Why haven't you?"

This was not Mario Cuomo's finest hour.

As he has done with other errors he has made, however, Cuomo was able to learn from the mistake of allowing himself to be persuaded to follow a negative strategy that ultimately led to his shameful performance at the Channel 13 debate. Such negativism never again appeared in another Cuomo campaign. One suspects that the strong stand he took against the press's probing into Gary Hart's sex life in 1987 may have been in part a reaction against the excesses of his own campaign in 1977. "I don't know whether Gary Hart sleeps with twenty-five-year-old women," Cuomo said to me. "And frankly I don't care. And I don't think the media had any right to ask him a question like 'Did you ever commit adultery?' "[7]

Aside from his improper use of the gay "issue," which was essentially a carryover from the mismanaged primary campaign, Cuomo was a new and very different politician in the seven weeks between the runoff and the 1977 general election. His decision to continue to run for mayor on the Liberal line, even without the Democratic nomination, was one of the most important he ever made. It was the turning point of his political career, although that fact would not be particularly clear until five years later.

Hugh Carey's earlier pledge to support Cuomo on the Liberal line even if he lost the Democratic nomination was soon deemed to be, in the Washington terminology of a few years before, "inoperative." Carey had come back to at least give lip service to Cuomo's candidacy during the runoff, but it was hardly to be expected that the Democratic governor—who would be seeking reelection the following year—would oppose his party's nominee for mayor. Carey told Cuomo to "get the hell out" of the race so that he, Carey, would not have to be embarrassed. Carey believed that withdrawal would be in Cuomo's interests; he *knew* it would be in his own interests. If Cuomo withdrew, Carey would not have to break his pledge and abandon him. The governor would then be able to back the party's nominee, who was the almost certain winner and was his original favorite for the position, without the stigma of breaking his promise to Cuomo.

Cuomo told the people the governor sent to ask him to step aside that he would be pleased not to honor his commitment to the Liberal party, if Carey or his emissaries could suggest to him an honorable way out. "I couldn't think of any," Cuomo told me, "and they couldn't think of any. I said under those circumstances I'm going to live with my commitment. I wasn't looking forward to taking a pounding through the whole general election, with no money, thinking there was no chance of winning."

Others also advised Cuomo to take the shortest pathway to the exit. "Pat Caddell called," Cuomo remembers, "and encouraged me to get out of the race: 'You'll lose by twenty-eight points.'" Other experts warned Cuomo that running against his own party would end his political career, as would yet another defeat, which seemed almost certain. He did not find this argument persuasive for two reasons: he was tired of heeding the advice of experts, and his political career seemed unlikely to survive if he bowed out at this point.

Cuomo decided to follow his own instincts—and his sense of honor and duty. The Liberal party had given him its endorsement on the understanding that he would remain in the race through the general election. Cuomo did not want to break his word and inflict harm on the party that had endorsed him. To do so, he thought, would be dishonorable; it would amount to selling out. The commitment that Democratic candidates made to run on the Liberal line even if they lost the Democratic nomination was one that most people in such circumstances in the past had not honored. But, as some of Cuomo's friends told him, "You're not 'most people.'" Sticking to his commitment would demonstrate that this was so.

Besides, this was going to be the sort of campaign that Cuomo could relish. No longer would he be burdened with the albatross of being "Governor Carey's handpicked candidate," the "establishment candidate," and the "front-runner." Now he was unquestionably the extreme underdog. Shorn of his large primary campaign staff, he and a few others could do battle against

massive odds. They would "have their work cut out for them."
Mario Cuomo could never resist an opportunity like that.

Although Caddell and others told Cuomo that he would be
crushed by a huge margin, Bob Sullivan disagreed. He told Cuomo
that he would lose, but by ten points or less. Sullivan was impressed by the fact that Cuomo wanted to go on, that he would not
give up. He believed that many others would also be impressed.
They would realize that Cuomo was no ordinary politician; he had
a real sense of himself that he respected and that called forth the
respect of others.

Sullivan's first postrunoff poll showed Cuomo trailing Koch by
25.5 percent. Other polls indicated that he was behind by as much
as 40 percent. But Sullivan insisted that Cuomo's position would
improve. He believed that Roy Goodman, who had barely beaten
Conservative nominee Barry Farber for the Republican nomination, would not be a serious factor and the general election would
become a rematch between Koch and Cuomo. That is just what
happened. People began to rally to Cuomo. They liked someone
who wouldn't give up. His dogged effort against seemingly impossible odds won Cuomo the respect and admiration even of many
people who voted for Koch. This campaign saved his political
career.

"In this town," Richard Wade said to me, "if they run you over
once, they'll run you over again and again and again. That's what
New York politics is all about. This town is rough that way—if
they run you over [and you don't fight back], they'll never respect
you again." By going on, almost by himself, Mario Cuomo won
back the respect of at least some New York political and opinion
leaders. He did well enough in the general election to prove that
he was "somebody." He would have to be reckoned with in future
election years.

Had Cuomo not run in the general election, or not run well,
he might have become a judge, but there would have been little
chance that he would ever have had another opportunity to win
high elective office.

A week after the runoff, Carey announced that he was ending
his support of Cuomo and giving his "full and enthusiastic endorsement" to Koch. The governor's exit from Cuomo's mayoral
campaign was as graceless as had been his entrance. At this point
Cuomo was essentially on his own, facing an apparently hopeless
task. He loved it. He was a far better candidate when he was

expected to lose than he had been when it looked as if he might win.

The change from the primary and especially the runoff was remarkable. Cuomo was at ease. He was like the baseball team that is twenty games out of first place in September playing against a team in the thick of the pennant race. He was "loose"; the tension was gone. Now he did things his way. With little professional advice any longer at his disposal, Cuomo fell back on his own ideas and instincts. He simply said what he thought. *He* was in control.

During the 1977 general election, Cuomo returned, for the most part, to his usual personality. His humor, which had lain dormant through the runoff, resurfaced. He wrote his own speeches or, more often, just spoke off the cuff. "I just went on the stump," he recalls. "We were very natural, very loose." Cuomo is almost always extremely impressive when he speaks extemporaneously. "Fighting back in '77, he was a terrific candidate," Bob Sullivan recalls. "He was really dynamite."

In mid-October Cuomo pointed out the reason for the change in his approach. He said that there had been an "extraordinary convolution of roles" since the runoff. During the primary and runoff, Cuomo noted, Koch had been seen as an "outsider," while Cuomo was thought to be the "establishment" candidate. In the general election whatever onus went with the latter status had attached itself to Ed Koch.

As a result of Cuomo's generally outstanding campaigning as the underdog in the general election, he was able to close the gap between Koch and himself to less than eight points by election day. The final tally found Koch just short of 50 percent, with Cuomo at 42 percent. Republican Roy Goodman and Conservative Barry Farber split most of the remaining 8 percent of the votes nearly evenly. The Neighborhood Preservation party was nothing more than 11,400 signatures that Cuomo's supporters had obtained before the primary to assure him of another line on the ballot. It was the idea of Cuomo's son Andrew. It was "on the right of the ballot and two lines down," Cuomo told me. "You had to have a flashlight to find it." Yet Cuomo got more votes on this hastily created extra line on the ballot than either Goodman or Farber won all told.

Cuomo's was quite a showing for someone on a third-party ticket. It was good enough that it rehabilitated his political reputation to the point where he was soon being mentioned as a formidable candidate for almost every major office in the state. It can even be argued that, despite all the chagrin of the primary, the final result of the series of city elections in 1977 was the best possible outcome for Mario Cuomo. The New York mayor's office is a political dead end (which fact may have played some role in Carey's pushing of Cuomo toward it, as he had pushed him toward the similarly fatal post of state chairman a few months earlier). Cuomo's chances for reaching higher office were probably enhanced by his good but losing effort. This may have been one of the facts in Matilda Cuomo's mind when she told me that she believes in destiny.

When I asked Cuomo what he had learned from his experience in 1977, his reply was brief: "Don't marry her if you don't love her."[8]

9

WINNER

MARIO CUOMO emerged from the events of 1977 a three-time loser. He had never won an election. There were a number of political observers and practitioners in New York who had placed him in the category of permanent losers. Liberal party leader Ray Harding summed up the opinion of many when he said, "Mario Cuomo can't go through a campaign without stepping on his dong at least once." Many New York politicos still stereotyped Cuomo as an outer-borough Italian, who *must* be conservative and narrow-minded. Incredible as it seems today, some believed that he was not intelligent enough to win an election. He was not handsome, did not come across well on TV, seemed to be a bully when he debated, and had no money (actually, his 1977 campaign ended with a debt in excess of two hundred thousand dollars). These were enough negatives for almost any politician to be written off. And had it not been for his comeback in the general election, Cuomo almost certainly *would* have been written off. But his stunning abilities to inspire people and articulate a vision of society as it ought to be had been sufficiently evident in those last weeks before his final defeat that a number of people believed that he could still be a successful candidate for high public office.

Losing in 1977 had been good for Cuomo in several ways. Avoiding the dead-end position of mayor was only one of them. Losing promoted in him a streak of humility that had not been especially evident before. Much of his apparent arrogance evaporated. He learned important lessons in defeat that probably would have remained unlearned had he won. He changed his speaking style, abandoning the aggressive, courtroom manner that he now realized was out of place in political oratory and debate. He had long been an effective speaker, but the type of speaking that serves well in one arena is not what works best in another. There is a large difference between explaining one's position before the Court of Appeals and addressing a television audience.

Cuomo made a quantum leap as a public speaker in the few years after his 1977 defeats. He learned to translate his values and ideas into simple language without diluting his message. He mastered the art of communicating with "ordinary" people on a high level. He never talked down to his audience. Instead, he added emotion to his speeches without reducing their intellectual content. In 1977 Cuomo had been trying to do in public what he had been trained to do in the courtroom: win arguments. In later years he has been less concerned with debating points and more interested in stirring people emotionally and getting them both to understand and to feel his message. His speaking became a warm blend of compassion and communication with which he could literally bring tears to the eyes of grown men.

As 1978 dawned, Mario Cuomo stood at the beginning of a five-year period of development from which he would emerge in 1982 as the most striking political leader of our time. He had gained a reputation as "Rocky" as a result of his never-give-up battle in the 1977 general election. But to political scouts and coaches, the most fitting sports analogy for what happened to Cuomo between 1978 and 1982 was the one given by Pat Caddell just before Cuomo won the 1982 gubernatorial election.

"In 1977," Caddell told a reporter, "he was very much like Sandy Koufax sitting on the bench of the . . . Dodgers. Everyone knew Koufax had great potential and a great fastball. But he had no control, no curve. And then, one day, Sandy Koufax had it all. He had the fastball, a curve that dropped off the table, and pinpoint control. He went from being an enigma as a pitcher to one of the most awesome pitchers of our time." Similarly, Caddell said, "Cuomo has gone from being a man who had a lot of potential but couldn't seem to put it all together to one of the most awesome candidates I've ever dealt with." It may not seem quite right to equate an Italian outfielder who was a Yankee fan with a Jewish pitcher for the Dodgers, but in fact the fit is nearly perfect. By 1982 Cuomo could hurl shutouts at opponents as readily as Koufax ever could.[1]

* * *

Following the events of 1977, relations between Governor Carey and his secretary of state were barely cordial. For his part, Carey thought that Cuomo had blown the great opportunity he had bestowed upon him and then turned unreasonably bitter when the governor did the only thing he could do—endorse the winner of the Democratic primary. Carey was also angry with Cuomo for staying in the mayoral race after losing the runoff. The governor felt that Cuomo had unnecessarily put him in an embarrassing situation. Cuomo reciprocated Carey's mistrust. He sincerely believed that the governor had betrayed him. Cuomo told me that Carey had said to him, "In politics it is different. No one ever takes seriously those promises."

Cuomo *did* take promises seriously, and found it hard to forgive Carey's breaking of such an important one to him. During the first half of 1978, Cuomo directed some pointed humor toward the governor. "Everybody asks me . . . what is Governor Carey really like?" Cuomo said at the annual Legislative Correspondents' Association dinner in Albany in May. "I'm not sure any more, but Dave Garth promises to have a proposal by next Tuesday." A bit later in the same talk, Cuomo told the audience that both he and Carey are eschatologists. "We trust in a hereafter, which I believe, or at least hope, I can enter without the governor's endorsement."

By the spring of 1978, the question of just what earthly office Mario Cuomo would next seek to enter was prominent in many minds besides his own. Some politicians still considered Cuomo to be a "loser." Others wanted nothing to do with him because of his reputation as a Hamlet. Meade Esposito told Cuomo he would not support him for any office. Esposito had begun referring to Cuomo as "Waltzing Matilda," because of his emphasis on his wife's role in his decision-making.

Despite these bears among established political investors, Cuomo's stock had risen sharply in the months since the 1977 election. The image of Cuomo that remained in the public mind was one of a man who refused to give up, instead battling valiantly against huge odds. "Rocky Cuomo lives," *Daily News* City Hall columnist Frank Lombardi wrote in amazement in May 1978, "despite the fact that Cuomo began as a contender and worked his way down to being a Rocky."

Everybody, it seemed, wanted Cuomo to run for something in 1978. Even the Republicans. Even Hugh Carey. With his surprisingly enhanced reputation, his New York City origins, and his wide-ranging travels to upstate communities as secretary of state, Cuomo seemed more than ever to be a natural for a statewide race. Voters of Italian ancestry accounted for about 30 percent of the statewide vote. Everyone, therefore, wanted an Italian-American on his ticket. Cuomo appeared likely to be the best vote-getter among the state's Italian-American politicians. And he had won about half of the Republican vote in the mayoral race, more than either Goodman or Farber, who had battled each other for the Republican nomination. Dispatches from upstate kept reporting that Cuomo's charm and intelligence were winning over "even rock-ribbed Republicans."

The New York Republicans put a different twist on an old adage: If you can't beat him, ask him to join you. Rather than risk being beaten with Republican votes by this man, several figures in the New York GOP tried to persuade Cuomo to take a position on the Republicans' state ticket, perhaps as the nominee for lieutenant governor. Cuomo was angry enough with Carey to give the proposal some brief consideration, but he decided that he was a Democrat and would stay one. "If I'd taken a Republican nomination, I would have been called a prostitute," Cuomo said. But he did also consider an independent candidacy on his Neighborhood Preservation party line. "Could I win [as an independent]?" Cuomo asked in May 1978. "Most definitely. Party labels are not what they used to be. The highest registration in this state is independent. If you are status quo you're considered prima facie deficient. The establishments are the Democratic and Republican Party."

One lesson that 1977 had imprinted on Mario Cuomo's mind was that he never again wanted to be the establishment candidate.

In addition to a decision on which banner to carry into the 1978 battle—a question he fairly readily decided in favor of the Democrats—Cuomo faced the more difficult decision of which office to seek. The possibilities were numerous: attorney general, comptroller, chief judge of the Court of Appeals—even governor. Bob Sullivan's polls suggested that Cuomo would be much stronger in 1978 than Carey. Sullivan and others urged Cuomo to challenge the governor, but he refused even to consider it. He said that it would take him two years to learn as much about being governor as Carey already knew. In any case, Cuomo said, he still felt gratitude to Carey for helping him in the past, and he would not run against him. "He had given me my first chance in '75," Cuomo said of Carey. ". . . I wasn't comfortable with the idea of running against the guy who had brought me in, whom I'd known for a long time, who for whatever things he had done that I disapproved of had been in many ways very good to me." Cuomo kept telling disbelieving people that he didn't believe in "getting even."

Sullivan was amazed. "I think the gratitude is erased when you get a sixteen-inch knife in the back!" he exclaimed.

The attorney general's race was in many ways the most attractive prospect. It became even more so when the five-term incumbent Republican, Louis Lefkowitz, announced in April that he would not run again. "Attorney general was the most natural thing for me," Cuomo said to me. "I was a lawyer, and I always felt an extremely competent lawyer." One problem with seeking this office was that Bronx Borough President Robert Abrams had agreed to support Cuomo for mayor the previous year in return for Cuomo's agreement not to run for attorney general in 1978. Since Cuomo expected to be elected mayor, it had seemed a cheap bargain for him. His 1977 defeat changed that, and he began to employ sarcasm to point out Abrams' lack of courtroom experience: "We need an attorney, not a general." By the time of the Democratic state convention in June 1978, Cuomo was ready to declare for attorney general. Some of his staff were in Albany, site of the convention, working to get him the nomination.

Then an unexpected development sharply altered Cuomo's course. Just before the convention, Lieutenant Governor Mary Anne Krupsak, who had been shunned by Carey for most of her tenure, decided to run against the governor in the primary. She said that he was inaccessible, did not care about people, and was unwilling to "fulfill his obligations." Carey, already suffering extremely low ratings in the polls, suddenly found himself with a gaping hole in his ticket. He was in real trouble. Although he did not get along with her, Carey would have preferred to keep Krupsak, because her defection was bound to hurt him even if she was unsuccessful in her challenge to his renomination. Carey was reported to want City Council President Carol Bellamy as a substitute for Krupsak. The one person he clearly did *not* want as his running mate was Mario Cuomo. But once more necessity was the mother of invitation. Carey was in desperate need of help with Italian-American voters, with the intelligentsia, with upstaters, with suburbanites, with Republicans, and with independents. The reborn Cuomo seemed likely to be more helpful with all of these constituencies than would any other potential running mate. In addition, Cuomo's joining the ticket would erase the negative of Carey's desertion of him the year before.

Carey reluctantly concluded that, once more, he needed Cuomo. He was not happy about it, especially after the fact when the media reported the episode as Cuomo coming to Carey's rescue. There was, moreover, a real question about whether Cuomo would be willing to run with Carey. Gratitude may have kept him from running *against* the governor, but lingering animosity might keep him from running *with* him. Cuomo's leading supporters were unanimous in their opposition to his acceptance of the lieutenant gubernatorial nomination. They argued that he would lose what he had gained in the 1977 general election. Once more he would be perceived as "Carey's handpicked candidate." They pointed out that he had never won an election on his own, and being elected as the bottom line on an entry with Carey would not solve this problem. And the job itself was poorly suited to someone with Cuomo's energy and interest in accomplishment.

As soon as Carey was convinced that he needed Cuomo, he sent his secretary, Robert Morgado, and David Garth to ask Cuomo to run. Meanwhile, the governor and his staff organized a large statewide telephone campaign to convince Cuomo that he should accept. Cuomo was flooded with calls from Democrats all over the state. Within less than a day, he was persuaded.

One important factor in Cuomo's decision was that his staff, though completely opposed to his acceptance of the nomination, agreed that a refusal from Cuomo three days before the convention would probably be a fatal blow to Carey's prospects for reelection. Despite his serious differences with Carey, Cuomo believed he would be better for the state than the Republicans would. If he was needed to save the state from Republican rule, Cuomo thought, he must accept.

(Many Democrats wondered a decade later whether the same argument might not apply on a grander scale with respect to their party's 1988 presidential nomination.)

Bob Sullivan was apoplectic when Cuomo told him by telephone that he was going to run for lieutenant governor. "I literally screamed," Sullivan told me. "I said, 'No, no; wrong, wrong, wrong! It'll drive you crazy; you'll go nuts! That's the worst job in the world for you!' " Cuomo, his friends and staff knew all too well, had a need to work hard and feel that he was making an important contribution. That hardly fit the lieutenant governor's job description. "I thought he would be the last person in the world that should be put in the job," Sullivan said.

Cuomo himself surely did not relish the opportunity to take over a largely superfulous office. But it was a wise move from a political viewpoint. If his presence on the ticket helped Carey win reelection, Cuomo would become Carey's logical successor. In the meantime, he could use first the campaign and then the office to become better known around the state and to learn all he could about being governor. Here two of Cuomo's basic characteristics were in conflict. He did not like to be in second place, and he did not like to be in a position that did not demand much work and had little responsibility. But he did desire to be fully prepared for anything he did, and the lieutenant governorship would, he thought, be an excellent apprenticeship for one who intended to become governor.

The hostilities between Carey and Cuomo had not ended. Instead, a cease-fire had been agreed to for the duration of a different struggle against a common enemy. It was rather like the alliance between the Soviet Union and the West during World War II. The prospects for a cold war between Carey and Cuomo after the 1978 electoral equivalent of V-E Day were large.

When the Albany convention ended, a party was held at the Executive Mansion. The governor, his family and staff, and the lieutenant gubernatorial nominee and his family and staff attended. Carey's people stayed on one side of the room, Cuomo's on the other. Some of those in attendance described the scene as one reminiscent of a reception following a shotgun wedding—which is just what it was.

Cuomo proved to be very helpful to Carey's candidacy. The governor trailed far behind his Republican opponent, State Assembly Minority Leader Perry B. Duryea of Montauk. Many New Yorkers had come to dislike Carey. Bob Sullivan, who was doing polling on the subject, says that "the mention of Carey made people foam at the mouth at this time." He did seem remote, and had developed a reputation as something of a flake. He was known as a great "party" man in a sense of the word other than the political one. In short, he did not seem any longer to be a very salable political candidate.

When Cuomo arrived in Syracuse early in the campaign, he was asked how, after the governor had betrayed him the previous year, he could now be his running mate. Cuomo answered that Carey had gotten himself into a terrible political bind in 1977, "first by endorsing me and then making a commitment he couldn't keep. I don't think the Governor is much of a politician," Cuomo told the assembled media representatives, "but I think he's a great governor."

"Carey went wild," Cuomo told me. "He called Garth and said, 'See, he's going to screw me. He's saying I'm not a good politician.' Garth said, 'You dummy—shut your mouth! This is the line we win with: "He's a lousy politician, but a great governor."' After a couple of weeks," Cuomo recalls, "Carey was saying, 'Yeah, I'm not much of a politician, but I'm a terrific governor.'" This argument was probably the most effective in Carey's uphill struggle for reelection.

Cuomo assisted Carey in many ways during the 1978 campaign. He wrote a pamphlet, *Let's Look at the Record*, that made a strong case that Carey was, in fact, a good governor. "We didn't want to run on Hughie's personality," Cuomo pointed out. And the candidate for lieutenant governor was an extremely good campaigner. Since voters in New York do not cast separate ballots for the position of lieutenant governor, candidates for that office campaign essentially for the gubernatorial candidate, not for themselves. "You give me Hugh Carey as a candidate, and I'm a very effective campaigner," Cuomo says. He contends that it is much easier, at least for him, to make a case for someone else than for oneself. "You're not as aware of his weaknesses as you are of your own—so you can fool yourself about a third party easier than you can fool yourself about yourself."

Cuomo's role in the 1978 Carey campaign amounted almost to that of campaign manager, and Cuomo was by this time a superb campaign manager. His experiences the previous year had convinced him that the supposed experts knew no more about effective political strategy than he did. In 1978—and thereafter—he had confidence in his own political instincts. He followed them as much as he could in the second spot on the 1978 ticket.

The contributions Cuomo made to Carey's reelection were significant. His popularity upstate was critical in cutting the usual Republican majority there. His ability to appeal to normally Republican voters was crucial as well in the suburbs. And Cuomo obviously helped win over some Italian votes that might otherwise have gone to Duryea, whose running mate, Representative Bruce

Caputo of Yonkers, was also Italian. The intelligentsia was beginning to discover Cuomo, and he helped win back many of them who had been prepared to desert Carey. When all of these contributions are taken into consideration, it appears likely that Cuomo made the difference between victory and defeat for Carey in 1978.

That, at any rate, is what many political observers were saying after the Carey-Cuomo ticket won the election. That such a notion was afoot enraged Carey. His marriage of convenience to Cuomo was necessary only until the election was over. Then Carey no longer found it convenient.[2]

Campaigning for the post of lieutenant governor had been fulfilling for Cuomo. It was a contest, and one in which his team started out behind. He was campaigning principally for someone else, thus freeing himself from the usual nagging questions about whether he was doing what he was doing for the right reasons. He enjoyed himself.

When the Carey-Cuomo ticket won, Andrea Cuomo was told his son was now lieutenant governor. The old man was puzzled. "Lieutenant?" he asked. "He went in the army?" Actually the senior Cuomo may not have been too far from the mark. Once the campaign was over, the unpleasant reality was that Mario Cuomo had gotten himself elected to a largely useless office in which he would have not much more scope for initiative than he would have had if he joined the army. His position was almost completely under the control of a governor with whom he was not on good terms. The job was one that could be made more meaningful by the governor, but Carey's resentment toward Cuomo meant that he was unlikely to enhance the duties or powers of the office. Besides, Cuomo was a potentially powerful figure. If that did not bother Carey, it did pose a threat to Bob Morgado, whom Carey, with his chairman-of-the-board style of governing, allowed to administer the government most of the time. It was in Morgado's interests to keep Cuomo away from the governor and, given Carey's attitude toward Cuomo by this time, that was not hard to do.

"The next years were, I guess, *the* most difficult that Cuomo ever had," Dick Starkey believes. I found no one close to Cuomo who disagreed with that assessment.

Lieutenant governors, like vice presidents, have outlived their usefulness by the time the polls close on election night. Their only real purpose is to be there in case tragedy strikes. As long as it doesn't, they serve no discernible purpose.

"You live in the shadow," Cuomo has said of the lieutenant governorship. "You are either a rival or an irritant. The frustration in being lieutenant governor is in having an office where you can't get it done." This was especially aggravating to someone like Cuomo, who lives to accomplish goals. "No matter how much Carey had embraced me and brought me in, I would still have had the frustration of knowing I couldn't get it done: it's not my thing, I didn't sign that bill. I'm not the lead person—that's the frustration."

"I didn't see a whole lot of him [Carey] once I became lieutenant governor," Cuomo told me. "It was quickly apparent that I was not invited to staff meetings. . . . Once or twice I said a couple of things that created problems because I didn't know what the plans were, since I hadn't been to staff meetings."

Carey did permit Cuomo to transfer the ombudsman's office that he had established in the Department of State to the lieutenant governor's jurisdiction. This, Cuomo thinks, was at least in part because Morgado and Carey wanted to keep Cuomo occupied far away from the governor's office. In any case, Cuomo had only a small staff and not nearly the size agency under him that he had had at State. It was boring and frustrating—although not to all of Cuomo's staff. When I was talking to him once in 1987 about his days as secretary of state, Cuomo said, "I'll show you something. He buzzed one of his secretaries and asked, "What was the best job we've ever had, of all the jobs I've ever done?"

"Lieutenant governor," she replied without hesitation.

"Better than secretary of state?"

"Yes, I think so," came the emphatic answer.

"You gave the wrong answer," the governor told her.

"Okay, bye."

"I'll have to try again," Cuomo said. "Lieutenant governor— what's she talking about? Must be because she had no work."

He buzzed another of his assistants.

"Yes, Governor."

"What's the best job we ever had?"

"Uh, lieutenant governor."

"Not secretary of state?"

"*No!*" she replied, as if Cuomo were saying something incomprehensible.

"You gave the wrong answer, too!" Then, to me and himself: "Why would they say that?" He buzzed the second secretary again and she gave her reasons:

"When you were lieutenant governor, it was a very small, intimate group, and everyone there worked there because they believed very deeply in you. It wasn't civil service employees.

"I asked about the *job.*"

"Well, I'm telling you my best job. I can only speak for myself."

"I'm asking you what was the best job for *me.*"

"The best job for you?"

"Yeah."

"Governor."

"Ahh, good-bye," said Cuomo, laughing as he gave up on the good sense of his staff.

The reason staff members liked the lieutenant governor years is not that they did not have much work to do. Anyone who didn't like to work would not be a long-term associate of Mario Cuomo. It was the sense of camaraderie of a small, dedicated crew under siege.

There is no way to keep Mario Cuomo from working hard. He will always find something to do. "There were enough things to divert him to keep him from going stir-crazy," Sullivan says. "It was a bad time for him. In real terms, probably he enjoyed himself more in the lieutenant governorship than he will admit. But it was because he was so creative in keeping himself busy. We [on the staff] were going crazy with all kinds of projects that he cooked up."

There probably has never been any greater proof of Cuomo's creativity than his finding things to keep himself and staff occupied in the lieutenant governor's office.

In the early part of the term, Carey ignored Cuomo. Later he began insulting him in public. When asked about his lieutenant governor, Carey gave such responses as, "He doesn't do anything." The governor's aides told members of the media that Cuomo's memorandums to Carey read "like term papers." Statements like these angered Cuomo enough that his streak of self-righteousness sometimes surfaced. Those who said such things, the lieutenant governor told reporters, were "people with no vision, who believe in the grubby deal, who make the arrogant assumption that there is a secret technique for running government."

When I asked him what he did as lieutenant governor, Cuomo's answer summed up his feeling about those years:

"Babbled a lot—spoke a lot; never missed a day presiding over the senate my first year. I did a lot of special assignments for the governor's office. I don't even remember the rest of it."

"Was the job fulfilling?" I inquired.

"No, it was not" was Cuomo's immediate reply.[3]

One of the projects Cuomo found to occupy his time during his internal exile on the third floor of the State Capitol was running President Carter's New York campaign in 1980. As the Iranian hostage crisis lowered Carter's popularity to dangerous levels and the challenge to his renomination from Edward Kennedy became more formidable, the importance of the March 25 New York primary grew. Many leading New York liberals were backing Kennedy; other top Democrats in the state remained neutral. Two of Carter's advisers, Pat Caddell and Gerald Rafshoon, had worked for Cuomo in 1977. They approached him about heading the Carter effort in New York.

"I went to Hughie and he said, 'Yes, go do it,' " Cuomo told me. "I said, 'Okay.' I went to [United States Senator Daniel Patrick] Moynihan and [State Assembly Speaker Stanley] Fink and the whole batch of others . . . and asked them all. Fink hesitated. I said, 'I won't do it if any of you have an objection to my being chairperson. I want everybody's acquiescence, if not support.' " Fink was thinking about running for governor and was unsure of how chairing the president's New York campaign would cut with the electorate. He didn't want to give Cuomo an advantage, but he wasn't at all sure that being identified with Carter would prove to be advantageous. Fink eventually agreed, and Cuomo became head of Carter's New York campaign.

The task, like all those Cuomo really enjoys, was not an easy one. Jimmy Carter had never been a particularly popular figure in New York, especially among the intelligentsia, for whom Southern accents are among the less acceptable "dialects." Ted Kennedy seemed to fit much more with most New Yorkers' notion of what a real Democrat ought to be. Cuomo disagreed on both counts. He liked Carter and he was less than enthusiastic about Kennedy.

Most of Cuomo's best friends were supporting Kennedy. But Cuomo identified with Carter in an odd sort of way. Both were highly intelligent progressive Democrats who were, at least to an extent, the victims of liberal bigotry. When New York (and other) liberals who were upset by Carter's rise in 1976 made such statements at their cocktail parties as "I could never vote for anyone with a Southern accent," it struck a jarring chord inside Cuomo. He heard echoes of his own crumbled applications hitting the wastebaskets of Manhattan law firms two decades before. Although he was distressed when Carter mispronounced "Italian" during his acceptance speech, Cuomo naturally identified with anyone who was the target of prejudice, perhaps the more so when a major source of that prejudice was his own longtime nemesis, the liberal elite of Manhattan.

One of the most important features of Mario Cuomo is his ability to universalize from his own experience so as to identify with the targets of unjust discrimination everywhere, whether that discrimination is based on race, ethnicity, religion, region, or any other factor. That is one of the reasons that many people who know Cuomo well do not think he would have much of a problem in a national campaign winning support in the South. Cuomo is so adept at universalizing from his experience, that he can identify his youth in South Jamaica with life anywhere he goes. He can tell an audience in Indiana, as he did in the summer of 1987, that his experiences were very much like those of a Hoosier, and not be laughed off the stage. Instead, the usual reaction is warm applause and a reciprocal sense of identification from the audience.

In addition to his feeling of kinship with Carter's suffering, Cuomo believed that Carter had been a much better president than many had given him credit for being. He was therefore eager to help him defeat the Kennedy challenge and win reelection.

But if Cuomo's motivation in taking over the Carter primary campaign in New York was principally the positive one of an attraction to Carter (as well as partly a means of advancing his own career and simply giving himself something exciting and worthwhile to do), it was also based in part on his differences from Ted Kennedy.

Cuomo told me that his opposition to Kennedy in 1980 was simply politics—that he felt an obligation to President Carter. Since 1980, he says his relationship with Senator Kennedy has been very good. "We—the whole Democratic party—owe Ted

Kennedy a great deal," Cuomo said. "He kept the liberal agenda alive during the darkest days of the early Reagan years. That's not to say I always agree with him. I don't always agree with *anyone*. I didn't agree with what he and Fritz Hollings did on the Murdoch situation [the insertion of a provision in the omnibus spending bill at the end of 1987 that forced Rupert Murdoch to sell his newspapers in New York and Boston]. But my own view of Ted Kennedy is very complimentary. I have never had any hostility toward the man," Cuomo told me. "In 1980, all my friends—Jack Newfield, Jimmy Breslin, David Burke, and many others—were with Kennedy. They asked me to be for Kennedy, too. I said, 'I can't. I've given my word to Carter, and that's it.'" Cuomo says that he fought a hard campaign against Kennedy in 1980 but never attacked him personally. Cuomo is, as I have noted previously, a moralist in the best sense of the term. He tries to live by a strict moral code himself, but he is quite tolerant of others. He says he never made an issue of allegations about Kennedy's life-style because he does not like to judge others.

Jack Newfield, a friend of both men, could not fully understand why Cuomo would not go with Kennedy in 1980. "It doesn't make sense to me," he said, because I think they have so much in common philosophically."

I think that's just it—or, rather, just the reverse of it. Cuomo and Kennedy *do not* in fact have that much in common philosophically. Both are "liberals" in some broad sense, and they agree on many specific issues. But they approach their somewhat overlapping political philosophies from different directions and the result is that they are different kinds of liberals.

Ted Kennedy was never an outsider. His is in important respects much closer to the liberalism of an earlier New York governor, Nelson Rockefeller, than it is to Mario Cuomo's brand. Those who are born into wealth and develop a concern for the less fortunate are apt to think that money is the answer to all problems and to operate under the assumption that it is available in unlimited quantities. Part of the reason for New York's fiscal crisis in the 1970s was that during his four terms as governor Rockefeller acted as if the people of New York had as much money as he did. Ted Kennedy, who grew up in superaffluence similar to that which surrounded Rockefeller, has always been close to the conservative stereotype of a "tax-and-spend liberal." Mario Cuomo, who even in 1987 had to borrow money to pay for his daughter's wedding, has never known wealth. His whole life has been spent in situations where the books had to be balanced. As a result, Cuomo is a pay-as-you-go liberal. He has at least as much compassion as do the elite liberals, but he understands that there are limits and that we must strive, as he often says, to do more with less.

With positive and negative motivations pushing him to Carter and away from Kennedy, Cuomo reassembled the team that had worked for him in 1978. He, his son Andrew, and Jerry Weiss (a Cuomo friend since law school) worked with Joel McCleary, who was sent in by Carter's people. As he remembers it, Cuomo and his team did a bang-up job. "You give me a candidate I believe in, like Carter, and I'm a tiger," Cuomo told me. "I knocked the crap out of Kennedy and his people."

Well, maybe so. But while Cuomo was knocking the crap out of Kennedy, Kennedy was knocking the crap out of Carter in the New York primary. The reasons for Kennedy's victory—such as the Iranian crisis and the Carter administration's foul-up on a United Nations vote calling for the dismantling of Israeli settlements on occupied lands—were certainly beyond Cuomo's control. Still, the bottom line was yet another political loss for Cuomo.

The New York primary was just a regular-season game, though, even if a very important one. The Democratic League Championship Series to determine the party's representative in the November World Series was to be played in Madison Square Garden in July. By that time Carter was assured of victory—unless the rules of the game were changed. That is just what some of the Kennedy forces tried to do. Up until this point Governor Carey had stayed out of the Carter-Kennedy battle, even though he was an old ally of the Kennedys. When Carey decided to make his move, he sent intermediaries to ask Cuomo to step down as Carter's state chairperson. Cuomo refused. Carey went ahead and shortly before the opening of the convention joined the call for an "open convention." That term meant that all delegates would be freed from their commitments and allowed to "vote their consciences." That was a euphemism for rejecting the sitting president from their own party. Carey was endorsing this goal (although not necessarily in order to benefit Kennedy; Carey is believed to have clung to the hope that a deadlocked convention might nominate him), and Cuomo openly opposed his governor on the issue. The Carter position, to which Cuomo adhered, prevailed and the president was renominated.

Mario Cuomo *(standing)*,
about eight years old.
*Photograph from the Cuomo
family collection.*

Andrea Cuomo in the
family grocery store in
South Jamaica, Queens,
which he opened in 1931
and operated until 1954.
*Photograph from the Cuomo
family collection.*

Mario Cuomo, about fifteen years old. *Photograph from the Cuomo family collection.*

Mario Cuomo while a member of the freshman baseball team at St. John's College. *Photograph from the Cuomo family collection.*

Mario Cuomo with friends when he was about twenty years old. *(Left to right, front row:)* Donald Harper and Mario Cuomo; *(back row:)* Nicky D'Arienzo and Phil Meyers. *Photograph from the Cuomo family collection.*

Mario Cuomo on his wedding day, June 5, 1954, with his brother Frank in front of the family store. *Photograph from the Cuomo family collection.*

Mario Cuomo celebrating at
a Corona reunion in 1974
the 1972 reversal of City
Hall's condemnation five
years earlier, in 1967, of
sixty-nine homes in the
Queens community.
*Photograph by Janie
Eisenberg.*

A kitchen man with two of
his passions: black coffee
and his daily diary.
*Photograph by Robert Karp,
New York Post.*

A decade of difference characterizes the relationship between Ed Koch and Mario Cuomo. *(Above:)* During the 1977 mayoral campaign, the strain of friendly rivalry is evident after an exhaustive debate in Bushwick, Brooklyn. *Photograph by Janie Eisenberg. (Below:)* Mayor Koch and Governor Cuomo share a moment of mutual success at the signing of the bill in August 1987 opening the New York milk market to greater competition. *Photograph by Joan Vitale, Mayoral Photo Unit.*

Mario Cuomo campaigning with his wife, Matilda, during the Labor Day parade in New York City, September 1982. *Photograph by Images Unlimited.*

The Governor and his mother at the Columbia Law School graduation in May 1985, at which he delivered the commencement address. *Photograph by Ted Kaplan, Governor's Office.*

Cuomo playing bocci in Harley Park, Queens, with the Senior Citizens Bocci Club during the 1982 campaign. *Photograph by Paul Caramuto.*

Higher mathematics at the offices of Federation Employment and Guidance Services, March 1987. *Photograph by José A. Rivera,* New York City Tribune.

Cuomo at a Christmas party for handicapped children held in the Red Room of the Executive Chamber of the Governor's Office, December 1987. *Photograph by Don Pollard, Governor's Office.*

The 1987 family portrait. *(Left to right, back row:)* Andrew Cuomo, Margaret Cuomo Perpignano, Bob Perpignano, Christopher Cuomo; *(front row:)* Madeline Cuomo, Mario Cuomo, Christina Perpignano, Matilda Cuomo, and Maria Cuomo. *Photograph from the Cuomo family collection.*

On October 25, 1987, the family gathered at Tavern on the Green to celebrate the wedding of Maria Cuomo to Kenneth Cole. *(Left to right:)* Andrew Cuomo, Kenneth Cole, Maria Cuomo Cole, Madeline Cuomo, Matilda Cuomo, Mario Cuomo, Margaret Cuomo Perpignano, Bob Perpignano, and Christopher Cuomo. *Photograph from the Cuomo family collection.*

Cuomo cochaired the New York Carter-Mondale campaign for the November 1980 election. (Cuomo showed when we discussed that campaign in August 1987 that he has some capacity for repressing unpleasant memories. He said, "I can't for the life of me remember who my cochairman was." It was Donald Manes, the Queens Democratic leader who committed suicide in 1986 after being indicted in the massive New York City corruption scandal. It had been necessary for Cuomo to have many dealings with Manes over the years, but the Queens boss had never been Cuomo's sort of politician. His role in 1980 is the sort of thing that Cuomo might just as soon forget, and I think he was entirely sincere in saying he couldn't remember.)[4]

Although Carey did support his party's national ticket in the general election, the very public split over the presidency caused relations between New York's governor and lieutenant governor to hit a new low. If Carey sought a third term in 1982, it was doubtful in the extreme that he would want Cuomo on the ticket with him. It was even more doubtful that Cuomo would agree to run again with someone with whom he was not on good terms for an office that he did not want to hold. The lieutenant governor began seriously to eye the state's highest office.

In the meantime, though, Cuomo had been associated with yet another loss as the Carter-Mondale cochair when Ronald Reagan won in New York as well as in the nation as a whole in November 1980.

Life in the beautiful office on the State Capitol's third floor did not improve for Mario Cuomo in 1981. He did get to serve as acting governor when Carey and Morgado left the state for ten days in February. This gave him more of a taste of what it would be like to hold the top spot himself. Michael Del Giudice, who served as Carey's chief of staff and was much friendlier with Cuomo than were Morgado and Carey, shared power with Cuomo while the governor and his secretary were on a trade mission to Japan. "We sort of had a good time during those ten days," Del Giudice told me, "—a few minor crises, nothing major. But it was sort of fun. I remember thinking at the time—I never told him [Cuomo] this—that you can have some fun in government as well as try to do good and take care of problems."

Cuomo quickly concluded from the experience that being governor was better than being lieutenant governor. "I enjoy the responsibility—however limited," he said. "Yes, it's better being Governor: it gives impact to positions; it improves the capacity to help." A few hours before Carey's plane reentered New York air space, Cuomo gave a speech in which he said, "During my term there were no tax increases, no loss of jobs, no strikes, no vetoes overruled and 90% good weather!"

But the clock inevitably strikes midnight for an acting governor. The cruel stepsisters would return from their travels and Cuomo would be returned to his cinders. The hope that the public might yet be persuaded that its glass slipper fit his foot perfectly was about all that he had to sustain him.

Cuomo was sufficiently disgusted with the role of lieutenant governor that he did not perform as well as an administrator of his small staff in that office as he had with the much larger Department of State. There he had been a superb administrator. Some members of his staff think Cuomo may have let his guard down just a bit in his frustration at his powerless position as Carey's unwanted second. Whether or not inattention played any role, Cuomo did suffer his worst embarrassment in 1981.

In late October of that year, Cuomo's friend and staff member, former Gannett political writer Woodie Fitchette, flew down from Albany to see Cuomo in the city and personally deliver some horrible news. It had just been discovered that the lieutenant governor's chief of staff, William D. Cabin, had placed several fictional names on the state payroll and pocketed the salaries himself. Cuomo had met Cabin during his probe of the nursing-home scandal in 1975. Cabin was an investigator of various forms of corruption for several state agencies before he joined Cuomo's staff. His credentials as an enforcer of the law appeared impeccable. Now it turned out that he was trying to see if he had learned enough from those he had pursued to succeed where they had gotten caught.

The arrow-straight Cuomo was stunned. "If this is what I think it is," he wrote in his diary that night, "it is a staggering blow—not because I'm personally culpable but because I'm responsible. And I should be. For years, I have been painfully aware of how vulnerable we are to the fates, to forces beyond our control, to the vicissitudes of life. Now, as I sit at my kitchen table writing these notes, feeling the impact of this development, it's difficult even for me to think clearly and to analyze the situation. What is apparent about it already—that Cabin simply added names to the payroll (forging my signature on the records sent to the comptroller), took the checks for them, and kept the money—is enough for me to know that once the public is informed, as inevitably it will be, he will be destroyed and I will be hurt, quite apart from the fact that I am totally innocent. I will have been a victim of my trust in this individual, my chief of staff. 'If you cannot choose a chief of staff who is honest, how can you hope to run the state?' I can hear it now."

Cuomo went straight to the Albany district attorney, gave him the information he had on Cabin's scheme, and asked him to pursue the case with dispatch. The evidence soon showed that Cabin had bilked the state of $178,000, nearly $130,000 of which had gone into his accounts, the remainder being withheld for taxes. When the state police confronted Cabin with the evidence, he immediately confessed. He told them that he was sorry that he had hurt the lieutenant governor, because "Cuomo was good to me."

Cuomo wanted to announce Cabin's crimes himself at a news conference, but the story was leaked to the press and Cuomo held Carey's office responsible. Carey was by this time convinced that Cuomo intended to oppose him for the gubernatorial nomination the next year. As a result, the hostility between the state's top two officials had become still greater. "They decided, for whatever purpose, that it was good to embarrass me with the Cabin story," Cuomo said more than two years later.

When he made his statement to the press, Cuomo forcefully argued that anyone looking at Cabin's résumé would have thought him a good choice for the job, that anyone is vulnerable to the misdeeds of seemingly trustworthy subordinates, that *he* had disclosed the incident and turned it over to the prosecutor, and that restitution of the stolen state funds was probable. The explanation was a good—and accurate—one, but the Cabin affair was a serious blow to a man who prides himself on his "hands-on" management style.

Fortunately for Cuomo, Cabin pleaded guilty and the incident quickly faded from the public's attention. It remained, though, as a useful weapon available to any opponent in the 1982 governor's race. (And, although David Garth had promised Cuomo's camp that Koch would not use it, the mayor asked in one of the debates the following summer, "How can he run a big government if he doesn't know who's on his payroll?") That was a major concern, because by the fall of 1981 little doubt remained that Mario Cuomo would soon be running for governor.[5]

* * *

Cuomo says that he had not entered politics with a goal of becoming governor. "Remember, I started the thing [politics] on one leg—never taking it seriously, or as seriously as I do now. I always had the feeling that I'd go back into private practice." But as he got more deeply into government, Cuomo says he began to understand "how important it was for some people who couldn't make it without government." He concluded that those who had told him in the early seventies that if he wanted to help people he must get into politics were right. He had an obligation as a Christian of mercy to try to get himself into a position where he could do the most good. The lieutenant governorship, quite patently, was not that position.

If Cuomo had had his doubts in 1977 about his qualifications to be mayor, that was not at all the case with respect to the governorship in 1982. When I asked if he had had any doubts about his readiness for the job, Cuomo's reply was emphatic: "Absolutely not! From the very beginning, I had a *strong* conviction that there's nobody on the scene that's as good for this job as I am, except, possibly, Stanley Fink. And I wasn't too sure about Stanley statewide. From what I knew about Stanley, he was extremely capable; I liked him a lot—honest, knowledgeable. But I wasn't sure he could do it statewide; I didn't know whether he'd go well in the north country.

"I was *convinced* that I was ready. I had been secretary of state; I had been lieutenant governor. I had been all over the state. I knew the jurisdictions and what needed to be done—I *knew* I could handle it." Cuomo didn't think that anyone else who was being mentioned could do as well as governor as he could. Koch's name was not yet being mentioned, but when the mayor did enter, it had no effect on Cuomo's conviction that he was best for the job. "There was no *doubt* in my mind that it would be wrong for him to try to be governor," Cuomo said to me, speaking of Koch. "He would've been a lousy governor—a very good mayor, but a lousy governor—it just didn't make sense. So, the logic was very strong, and as a result of that I was an extremely powerful candidate. I was a *tough* candidate—I never rested, and I didn't have to. I ran in the mornings, slept a few hours a day, and I didn't *want* to [rest]. I enjoyed every minute of it. It was hard—not every minute. Sometimes you're way behind and you get discouraged and the money is not coming in and you wonder whether you've imposed too much on your friends and family—'I've done it twice unsuccessfully already, now I'm doing it a third time. . . .' But, overall, I was absolutely convinced that I was better for the job, and therefore I fought with a vengeance."

The vengeance with which Mario Cuomo fought in 1982 was certainly reflective of his conviction that he was the best person for the job. But he was also, in part, motivated by the desire to prove himself where he had experienced the only major failures of his life: before the electorate. Cuomo's losses had been very painful for a man who had always been successful at everything he had ever done in life. He had *failed*, nakedly, before the entire public of the state. Some people were still calling him a *loser*. It was hard for a proud man—a fierce competitor who loved victory—to take. The 1982 governor's race represented his chance for redemption.

How the field for the race would shape up depended largely on whether Hugh Carey decided to seek reelection. Cuomo himself wrestled endlessly with the question of whether to run against Carey. Just after the 1980 election, Garth told Cuomo that Carey would run, wanted Cuomo to run with him, and expected to be on the national ticket in 1984. That would make Cuomo governor, Garth said, and he better start talking up Carey.

Cuomo was not sure what to do. He told Ed Koch in late 1980 that he would not run against the governor, "even though Carey will probably lose—and he is very vulnerable—I owe him too much and it wouldn't be right to oppose him."

"Somebody will," Koch responded.

Among those who were seriously considering becoming such somebodies were City Council President Carol Bellamy, Assembly Speaker Stanley Fink, and Attorney General Robert Abrams. One name that was generally *not* included among the potential Democratic gubernatorial candidates was that of Edward I. Koch. "I doubt he would ever run," Cuomo wrote of Koch in his diary in February 1981.

As Cuomo's people tried to drum up support for his possible candidacy, they repeatedly heard the refrain that he was a "loser," that he couldn't win anything on his own. Cuomo tried to console himself with historical analogy. "What would they have said about Lincoln," he wrote in his diary, "who lost 6 times before he won the presidency?"

Cuomo was on good terms with New York Court of Appeals

Judge Sol Wachtler, who was being prominently mentioned as a possible Republican candidate for governor. The two men greatly admired each other, and did not want to compete in an election. Wachtler made it clear to Cuomo that while he welcomed a chance to run against Carey, he would not want to run against Cuomo, in whose hands be thought New York would be fortunate to find itself. The two progressives from opposing parties had a long discussion at the annual Woodie Fitchette birthday celebration in February 1981. Wachtler encouraged Cuomo to run. "The only fear I'd have, Mario," he told the lieutenant governor, "is that Koch, despite his protestations, might come in the race against you in the primary."

"I'm not worried about that," Cuomo told Wachtler. "The last thing that would keep me out is fear of running against Koch." It seemed to Wachtler that Cuomo *yearned* for Koch to run for governor. A rematch, on what Cuomo now believed to be his home field—the entire state as opposed to just the city—would give Cuomo an opportunity to redeem himself and to obtain revenge for the most galling loss of his career.

The awkward possibility that the two friends might wind up opposing each other in the 1982 general election vanished when Wachtler decided in September 1981 that he simply did not want to go through what it would be necessary to endure to compete in a statewide race.

While he waited for the gubernatorial situation to develop, Cuomo continued to do what he had done since 1979: "Try to do as much good as possible in my role as Lt. Governor, on a day-to-day basis . . . even if it was a small good that was imperceptible to the public—so as to justify all our effort in achieving public office." He said that he believed that Adlai Stevenson was right when he said that "good government is the best political strategy."

But the practice of good government, especially if it was imperceptible to the public, was plainly insufficient as a political strategy. In March 1981, Cuomo set up a group of advisers to discuss a precampaign and to meet regularly to lay the groundwork. He was still reluctant to oppose Carey, but would not rule it out if Carey were to seem a sure loser for the Democrats. "I don't think I ever said to the group, 'No, I will never do it [run against Carey],' but I never said, 'Yes, I will,' either," Cuomo told me. "I don't think I could have brought myself to do it."

As he got ready for another campaign, Cuomo tried to achieve some perspective. "It is necessary in the hurly-burly and excitement of this kind of thinking," he wrote in his diary, "to remind yourself that the basic objective is not to win an election, or power, or fun, but to help improve the conditions of people's lives. It's not easy."

As 1981 progressed, Cuomo's relations with Carey deteriorated further. Cuomo remained unsure of the governor's intentions for the following year. "The Governor appears to have dyed his hair again and that's being interpreted as a sure sign he's running again," Cuomo recorded in his diary in March. "I'm sure he is ... but I don't know if it's for Governor, for President, for Evangeline Gouletas [a woman from Chicago with whom Carey had recently become involved] or for all three!" The answer came a few weeks later, when Carey married Ms. Gouletas. A series of embarrassing stories about his new wife's previous husbands came out the week after the wedding, and Carey's prospects for reelection continued to decline.

Although Cuomo now says that he never could have brought himself to run against Carey, if polls showed that Carey could not beat the Republicans but that he, Cuomo, could, he would have to consider it. But as his supporters got excited about the prospect, reality intruded on Cuomo. His father fell into a coma in June and died on July 1, 1981. For a time, he had to turn away from political concerns, but no politician who hopes to be successful can turn away for long.

Another New York mayoral campaign was underway in 1981, and Cuomo agreed with some of his staff that he should try to get closer to Koch so that he might hope to win the mayor's endorsement for governor the following year. Cuomo visited Koch in June and in August sent a letter to friends stating why he was voting for Koch. On a couple of occasions during the mayoral campaign, Koch made statements to the effect of "Cuomo would make a great governor." Cuomo found this encouraging, but realized that the mayor's opponent for the Democratic nomination was "named 'Barbaro' and I serve his present purposes well." Ed Koch was no fool. Saying nice things about another leading Italian-American politician might be helpful in his current campaign against Assemblyman Frank J. Barbaro.

Barbaro was not considered to be a major challenge to Koch's reelection. Yet he wound up winning 36 percent of the vote in the Democratic primary. Two other minor candidates combined for

4 percent, leaving the incumbent with 60 percent. It was an easy enough victory, but some political observers realized that if there was this much opposition to Koch among New York City Democrats, it was a clear indication that he would be vulnerable in a statewide race. Four out of every ten Democrats in the city had voted against the mayor when the alternatives were little known and woefully underfinanced. Little note was made of this important fact in the Cuomo camp in the fall of 1981, however, since there was at that point no expectation that Koch would enter the gubernatorial race. The mayor had, in fact, pledged during his reelection campaign that he intended to remain in Gracie Mansion for twelve years and then retire from politics.

The major concern among the Cuomo backers for the remainder of 1981 was with Hugh Carey. Cuomo feared that if he ran against the governor he would be portrayed as "disloyal" and Carey would make him out to be a "crybaby" and "another Krupsak" for turning on him. These, obviously, were not pleasant prospects.

Cuomo's spirits and hopes soared in October, when a fundraiser at which former Vice President Walter Mondale spoke brought in more than $250,000. This sum was sufficient finally to retire the remainder of the debt from Cuomo's 1977 campaign and to give him a start toward his still unannounced 1982 campaign. Koch attended the event and again said that Cuomo would make a good governor. Important as all this was, the most significant aspect of the Cuomo fund-raiser was the number of people who had been willing to pay $500 to help him, despite the fact that Governor Carey was discouraging participation and no one could be sure what office Cuomo would seek the next year.

The euphoria of the fund-raiser lasted for less than twenty-four hours. The following evening Cuomo learned of Bill Cabin's crimes. It was as if someone had suddenly pushed the DOWN button on his rising elevator. The momentum from the highly successful fund-raiser never got a chance to continue.

But Cuomo himself would continue. He learned in December that a survey conducted by Republican pollster Robert Teeter showed Carey losing to the Republicans by thirty points, but Cuomo running even with them. This was exactly what Cuomo had to hear to convince him that there was a rationale for him to oppose Carey. The state must be saved from a return to Republican administration, and Carey could not do it. Cuomo could.

By mid-December 1981, although he had not yet said so, Mario Cuomo seemed to be running for governor, whether Carey sought reelection or not. He met again with Koch just before Christmas and told him that he would not be Carey's running mate, thus making it clear to Koch that Cuomo intended to pursue the state's top office even if that meant opposing the incumbent. Koch later said that this worried him, because he believed that Cuomo was vindictive and "would seek to torture me and therefore the City for beating him in 1977." For his part Cuomo left the meeting "with the impression that Koch wouldn't be comfortable dealing with me [as governor] and would prefer a number of people—even a Republican—to me." Each man believed the other's ego was too large to permit a comfortable relationship between them should Cuomo become governor while Koch remained mayor.

In a year-end statement to the press, New York's lieutenant governor said that he would make his own decision concerning a race for the governorship, without consulting Carey. It was the strongest indication Cuomo had yet given in public that he was likely to oppose the man who had been both his benefactor and his tormentor.

As the election year of 1982 dawned, Cuomo decided that the time had come for him to make his move. Surely conditions would change, he wrote, "but I mustn't do nothing while I'm waiting for all the facts. What I'll do now is go forward even faster and harder with all preparations for the race. Things may change—let them. If I run, I will be a long shot, but so were Momma and Poppa."[6]

As Cuomo had anticipated, conditions changed rapidly in the early weeks of 1982. In mid-January Hugh Carey announced that he would not seek reelection. This opened the floodgates for other Democratic contenders. Cuomo's public statement in reaction to Carey's withdrawal praised the governor's service. In answer to reporters' questions, Cuomo said that he would make a formal announcement of his own plans in March. Mayor Koch said he had no interest in becoming governor.

That statement may have been more accurate than the events of the ensuing weeks made it appear. "I think the real issue in the '82 campaign for me was that I really did not want to be governor," Koch told me, "and believed I was giving up a lot and making a huge sacrifice." Ed Koch is the quintessential New York City person. "For me to be in Albany as opposed to the city of New York everyday—I would not enjoy it."

This, of course, sounds very much like Mario Cuomo's after-the-fact rationalizations of why he lost in 1974 and 1977: he lost because he didn't really want the job. In both cases, though, there is at least a kernel of truth in this explanation. Cuomo was not entirely sure he wanted to be mayor in 1977 and Koch was less sure he wanted to be governor in 1982. As fierce competitors, however, both men went all out to win once they got into the races.

Ed Koch got into the 1982 gubernatorial race for some of the same reasons that Cuomo had joined the mayoral contest five years earlier. A number of leading figures in the party and the New York establishment pressured him to run. Notable among them were Rupert Murdoch, who feared Cuomo's liberalism and wanted to "make a governor" as he had "made a mayor" five years earlier, and Bronx Democratic boss Stanley Friedman. The day after Carey's withdrawal, Koch left for an eight-day vacation in Spain. David Garth accompanied him. Murdoch and his *Post* started a "Draft Koch" campaign while the mayor was away. Murdoch kept up the drumbeat throughout Koch's vacation. His most interesting innovation was the printing in the paper of a clip-out coupon for *Post* readers to send in to indicate whether they wanted Koch to run for governor. The coupon, like a ballot in a dictatorship, had only one box to be checked: "Yes."

When Koch returned, he began to waver in his declaration of disinterest. Garth did a poll showing that the mayor was very popular upstate. But Garth and most other Koch advisers tried to dissuade the mayor. Garth warned that breaking his pledge to remain mayor would destroy Koch's aura of integrity, which was his most valuable political asset. Perhaps even more of a problem was that the mayor was unable to say *why* he wanted to be governor. When Garth asked him, "Why the hell do you want to run for governor?" Koch could not give him an answer.

There was, in fact, more to Koch's decision than the pressure and the polls. Two other factors were, I think, responsible for pushing him into the race. It was true enough that he did not particularly want to be governor. But he even more did not want Mario Cuomo to be governor. And while he did not want to *be* governor, Koch did want to *win* the governorship. At any rate, he wanted to win *something*. His massive reelection a few months earlier had completed the fulfillment of all of the goals for which he had aimed through most of his life. But the intensely ambitious man does not lose his ambition when he succeeds. He craves new victories.

Stories were circulating that Fritz Mondale had Koch high on his list of possible running mates for 1984. Living in Albany might for Koch be, as he had said repeatedly, a "fate worse than death," but living in Washington, while perhaps not on a par with living in Manhattan, could be tolerated if one were vice president of the United States. Even Albany might be put up with for a while, if it was just a stopover on the way to Washington. As Koch said in trying to explain away his remarks on life and death in the state capital, "Everyone has to die sometime." Death in Albany might be a prerequisite to rebirth on a national ticket.

At the very least, running for governor was something to do—another goal for which he could strive and keep himself occupied. And while he was making his decision on whether to run, Koch's father died, as had Mario Cuomo's father the previous summer, while Cuomo was struggling with *his* decision on the gubernatorial race. Although it does not appear to have been a major factor in the decision of either politician, these two sons of immigrants were both reminded just before they entered the 1982 governor's race of whence they came and of the opportunity they had to raise their fathers' names to the highest governmental position in the state of New York.

A month after his return from Spain, Edward Koch announced his candidacy for the Democratic nomination to become New York's next governor.

Most political observers thought that no one had a chance to defeat Koch in the Democratic primary. His entry led Carol Bellamy, Stanley Fink, and Bob Abrams to reconsider and, ultimately, to decide not to seek the governor's office. Almost everyone thought that Mario Cuomo would be crazy not to do the same. When a leading New York real estate developer told Sol Wachtler that Koch was the only person who could lead the state, Wachtler said, "What about Mario Cuomo?"

"He looked at me as if I had said, 'What about exhuming the body of Elvis Presley and running him?' " Wachtler recalls.

When Wachtler raised Cuomo's name with a leading New York financier, the instant response was laughter, followed by the explanation, "Mario Cuomo is, Number 1, unelectable, and, Number 2, I don't think he's capable of governing. The man just isn't bright enough. He doesn't have the intelligence to be a credible candidate—and certainly not to govern."

Such opinions were common. Cuomo had, after all, never won an election on his own. *Perhaps*—although it was doubted by many of the state's most powerful figures—*he would have a chance against Bellamy, Fink, and Abrams. But Koch—who are you trying to kid? Koch creamed him before, and he'll do it again.* Some early polls indicated that Koch would have a forty-point lead over Cuomo or any other Democratic rival. If Cuomo was determined to run anyway, most people in the political know concluded, it merely proved that he had a Quixote complex.

Mario Cuomo and a few of his friends and advisers had a different opinion. It was not that Cuomo had anything against fighting the good fight in a hopeless cause. He rather liked the Quixote role. But he also liked to win, and that's just what he expected to do against Koch.

I asked Cuomo whether Koch's entry was a blessing in disguise for him.

"I didn't even see the disguise," Cuomo replied. "I said at the time, 'This will make me a winner.'" Cuomo believed that the early polls actually indicated the opposite of what almost everyone thought they did. "I saw the polls and I said, 'This guy can't win,' because he never got above forty-nine percent against the field. That was at a time when he was the most popular politician in America next to the President and had no opposition, really. Who was Carol Bellamy? Who was Mario Kukimo? Who was Stanley Fink?"

Everyone in New York—at a minimum everyone who would vote—knew who Ed Koch was. "If he only got forty-nine percent at the very top of his game, before you started making the attack on him," Cuomo reasoned, "and if his entry is going to clear everybody else out and it's just you against him, it means that you're guaranteed to get attention after Labor Day. You're guaranteed to get television—they'll have to get a race and there's only the two of you."

Before Koch announced, Cuomo spoke to Garth and gave him a list of reasons why Koch could not win. Garth was impressed by Cuomo's reasons, many of which were similar to his own thoughts on Koch's prospects, and he went to Koch to advise him not to run. Koch got angry and complained that Garth had defected to Cuomo. Garth insisted that he remained loyal to the mayor, but that Koch should know that Cuomo had a very good chance to beat him. If Koch had not already decided to run, this was probably enough to push him over the edge.

Bob Sullivan was also convinced that his man could defeat Koch, even though his own polls indicated that Cuomo would start very far behind. Sullivan charted out just how the election would develop, and it wound up following almost exactly that pattern. "He looked like a long, long shot," Sullivan said of Cuomo, "but he really wasn't. I never felt that way. I think the governor [Cuomo] must never have felt it, either." Sullivan believed that Koch versus Cuomo for mayor was a tough call, but that when the office at stake was that of the governor, the strong advantage would be Cuomo's. Voters, this opinion analyst believed, looked upon the qualities that were needed to be governor as differing from those that served well in a mayor. As people really started to think about these two men as possible governors, they would turn more and more to Cuomo. Koch might seem appropriate as a mayor of New York City, but he did not fit the image of a governor in the minds of most people. Cuomo did.

Koch, in any case, was much more identified with New York City, both because of his position as mayor and his thoroughgoing "New Yorkness," than was Cuomo. To many people in other parts of the state, electing Koch would be tantamount to turning the state over to complete control by the city. The closer they came to the date of the primary, the more people in other parts of the state were likely to come to this conclusion. It was not simply the result of Koch's well-publicized faux pax on rural and suburban life. Some such statements were almost inevitable, given Ed Koch's total identification with the city.

On top of this Koch had antagonized large portions of the city's electorate. The very rhetoric and policies that had made him almost a cult figure among some white conservatives in the city and suburbs had made him anathema to minority groups and many unionists. Koch had, moreover, had many nice things to say about President Reagan and his economic policies. As 1982 progressed, the American economy did the opposite. It was not a good time to be identified with Reaganomics—especially if you were running in a Democratic primary in New York. Koch had further alienated a substantial number of Democrats by seeking and obtaining the Republican mayoral nomination in 1981, to go along with his Democratic nomination. The recent city elections had shown that

Cuomo could expect to start a two-person race against Koch with an anti-Koch base of about 40 percent of the city's Democratic voters. Then, by breaking his ironclad promise to continue as mayor, Koch antagonized even many of those who had supported him.

The attraction of redeeming himself by finally winning an election on his own had been a major reason for Cuomo to enter the race. Redemption by not simply winning but by defeating Ed Koch would be sweeter still. A couple of years later Cuomo told a friend that it had, of course, been great to be elected governor and to give the keynote address at the 1984 Democratic National Convention, but "nothing can ever be as satisfying as beating Ed Koch." The intense competitive spirit that had characterized Cuomo as a ballplayer animated him in his 1982 rematch with Koch.

But Cuomo tried to avoid running the sort of negative campaign that his 1977 effort had become. He skillfully played on the idea that Koch was a good mayor who should have kept his promise to stay in that office, but was perhaps not so well suited to be governor. The lieutenant governor wore two buttons during the campaign. One said CUOMO FOR GOVERNOR; the other, KEEP THE MAYOR MAYOR. This was a highly unorthodox approach, one that Pat Caddell tried to talk Cuomo out of. "That's stupid," Caddell argued. "You can never say any positive thing about your opponent." But Cuomo insisted that it would work, and in this campaign he was making his own decisions. The "two-for-one" idea that New Yorkers would be better off with both Cuomo and Koch in high office worked well—certainly far better than the blatant negativism that the Cuomo camp had employed in 1977.

Cuomo and some of his advisers had assessed the situation and expected to win, in substantial part because of his popularity upstate. Although Koch began the campaign with high approval ratings in that region, the Cuomo people did not expect that situation to obtain for long when upstaters became more exposed to the mayor's caustic city personality. The Cuomo camp waited eagerly for Koch to make a mistake that would turn more upstaters against him.

The only error in this assessment, it soon became clear, was in thinking that there would be any wait for Koch to make such a mistake. As it happened, he had already done the damage, but hardly anyone knew it. Just after his smashing reelection triumph

the previous November (and before he had shown any interest in
running for governor), Koch had done an interview for Playboy.
The interview was published in February, on the day after Koch
announced his candidacy. The mayor, who was said by Garth to
have been in an "I-don't-give-a-shit" mood when he did the interview, turned out to have delivered himself of a number of opinions
that were unlikely to play well in Plattsburgh—or even, for that
matter, in Patchogue, Pleasantville, or any other localities in the
vast regions of the state beyond the borders of New York City.
"Have you ever lived in the suburbs?" Koch asked his interrogator.
"I haven't but I've talked to people who have, and it's sterile. It's
nothing. It's wasting your life." The Playboy questioner then asked
if wasting time on the subways bothered Koch. "As opposed to
wasting time in a car? Or out in the country, wasting time in a
pickup truck when you have to drive twenty miles to buy a ging-
ham dress or a Sears Roebuck suit?" The mayor went on to say:
"Anyone who suggests I run for governor is no friend of mine. It's
a terrible position, and besides, it requires living in Albany, which
is smalltown life at it's worst. I wouldn't even consider it."

These comments produced one of the most rapid major shifts
in the public's opinion of a political figure ever recorded. In the
few days from just before the Playboy fiasco to just after it, Koch's
positive rating dropped by twenty-five points, while his negative
rating jumped by twenty-eight points. Garth had never before
seen anything approaching this fifty-three-point swing in a few
days.

Despite the Playboy disaster (and several other examples during
the campaign of the mayor's paucity of knowledge about or concern for the state's nonurban areas), Koch remained a heavy favorite. This delighted Cuomo. In his announcement of his candidacy,
Cuomo indicated that he was the underdog against Koch, as he had
been in their 1977 mayoral race. It was true enough that Cuomo
was the underdog in 1982, but he had certainly not started out as
such in relation to Koch in the mayoral race.

Another major difference between the Cuomo-Koch contests in
1977 and 1982 was that Koch was plainly the "establishment"
candidate in the latter year. Endorsements and contributions
flowed to the mayor like the silt of the Nile to the Mediterranean.
This occurred not only because Koch was expected to win, but
because he was noted for having a long memory and a penchant
for getting even. If he won, as almost everyone expected, Koch

would as governor be able to punish those who went with Cuomo; in the unlikely event that he lost, Koch would still be mayor and in a position to retaliate against those who failed to support him. "The movement of the political establishment to Koch continues, almost inexorably," Cuomo wrote in his diary at the end of February. "They are concerned about Koch as Mayor whether he wins or not as Governor, and few of them have the courage to take him on, although many of them will say privately he is doing the 'wrong thing.' It is a demonstration of the political system at its weakest. Survival—not the good of the government or the people it serves—but survival for the politician becomes the test." Mario Cuomo tried to get all the endorsements he could, but he should have had no objection to a situation in which his opponent was tagged as the establishment candidate.

The fact was, though, that even in 1982 Cuomo tried to attain the "insider" status that having Garth running his campaign and getting the backing of party leaders would provide. Although running as an outsider fit Cuomo's personality and background, he did so in 1982 more out of necessity than choice. As the insiders flocked to Koch, Cuomo picked up the "outsider" banner. He did what any wise politician does: he attempted to turn his liabilities into assets.

One important insider that Cuomo wanted to see come out for him was Fritz Mondale. He did not. In fact, Mondale's people did not even deny the rumors that Koch was under consideration to be the former vice president's 1984 running mate. "I talked to the Mondale people about that [later], when they asked me to help them," Cuomo told me. "I said, 'Let's be honest. You guys aren't *owed* a thing. I broke my back for you and Carter. I stood when nobody else did. I took a beating in my own state. You said you love me. And then came the [gubernatorial] campaign.' They said, 'Well, we didn't support Koch; we were neutral.' I said, 'Hey, you know what Dante said about "neutrality."' And in fact they *weren't* neutral—they had leaked all kinds of stories. 'Try to tell somebody else you were neutral.'" But Cuomo supported Mondale in 1984 anyway. "All of that is irrelevant," he told Mondale. "I'm going to support you anyway, because I think you ought to be president. But it's not because I *owe* it to you. I don't owe you a damn thing. I don't think you're particularly loyal."

Cuomo did understand at the time why Mondale did not come out for him when former President Carter did. "Mondale has not endorsed me despite what I did for him and President Carter in

'80 and what Koch did to them," Cuomo wrote in his diary in
August 1982. "Actually, while I was pleased when the President
spoke out so forcefully for me, I didn't expect Fritz to. From his
point of view it's too big a risk. . . . I'm sure they expect Koch to
win. A Koch who doesn't forget those who went against him could
be a real problem as Governor of New York for a presidential
candidate next year. I'm not surprised that Fritz regards discretion
as the better part of valor."

In 1974 Cuomo had suffered, at least to some extent, from being
the official choice of the party. He would not face that burden this
time. The June 1982 Democratic State Convention at Syracuse was
well stocked with people who either favored or feared Koch. The
Koch forces went into the convention talking about denying
Cuomo the 25 percent of the delegate votes he would need to get
on the primary ballot without petition. The underdog's address to
the convention was vintage Cuomo. The main theme was that
Democrats must remain true to their values: "The body of this
party will not long survive without its soul." Implicit in Cuomo's
words was the message that Koch was no longer a true Democrat.
"We are the party that rejects fear and offers hope," Cuomo told
the delegates. "We are supposed to be the party that would never
put a poll where our conscience ought to be." He enumerated the
basic concepts that Democrats "are supposed to believe. *Always*,
not just when it is convenient."

When the convention ballots were cast, Koch won the endorsement, but Cuomo received the support of a surprisingly high 39
percent of the delegates. This outcome was ideal for Cuomo: it
remained clear that Koch was the choice of the bosses, but
Cuomo's much-better-than-expected showing added stature to his
candidacy.

Of course Murdoch's *New York Post* did everything it could to
boost Koch, including publishing polls that showed him farther
ahead than did any other opinion surveys. Even the *Times*, which
had stayed with Cuomo through all three elections in 1977, came
out for Koch in 1982. A week before the primary, Hugh Carey
added his endorsement to the mayor's impressive collection.
Cuomo could not have found this development particularly distressing. The governor's blessing had proven to be more of a curse
to him five years earlier.

The reversal went beyond endorsements. As the heavy favorite, Ed Koch found it much easier to raise money. Cuomo had

outspent him in the 1977 primary and runoff, but in 1982 the mayor outspent the lieutenant governor by a margin of about two to one.

There was at least one other key reversal of roles between Koch and Cuomo from 1977 to 1982. Whereas Cuomo had seemed a divisive candidate in 1977 because of his outer-borough strategy, in 1982 he spoke constantly of the "family" of New York and the politics of inclusion. Cuomo was a man from the city who was extremely popular upstate. Koch, on the other hand, was so completely identified with the city that he was not seen as being capable of unifying the state. And Koch's rhetoric was often perceived to be racially and ethnically divisive. If Cuomo was saddled with being an anti-Manhattan candidate in 1977, Koch was seen as an antisuburban, antirural, antiupstate, antiminority, and antiunion candidate in 1982.

Manhattan liberals and minorities had not been strong for Cuomo in 1977, but in 1982 the only Democratic organization in the city that backed him was that of Manhattan. Manes of Queens, Esposito of Brooklyn, Friedman of the Bronx, and even Nicholas LaPorte, the Democratic leader of Staten Island, which, with its large Italian-American population, had been overwhelmingly for Cuomo in 1977, endorsed the mayor. But Cuomo was better off without them. Continuing the reversal from his earlier contests with Koch, Cuomo won the backing of the liberal New Democratic Coalition, many of the members of which had viewed him with much suspicion in previous years. In 1982 it was no contest. Cuomo won more than 70 percent of the NDC votes. It was most ironic that Cuomo, who had lost the mayoralty while running on an outer-borough, anti-Manhattan strategy, now found the party leaders of all the outer boroughs backing his opponent, while the Manhattan Democratic organization, in which liberals, blacks, and Hispanics were powerful, supported him.

There was, finally, the question of which candidate was the "real" Democrat. Koch questioned Cuomo's "loyalty" to the Democratic party in light of his having run against its primary winner in 1977. He asked Cuomo to pledge to support the winner of the gubernatorial primary. Cuomo, who again won the Liberal party's nomination, said he had no need to do so because he was going to *be* the Democratic nominee. The question of Koch's credentials as a real Democrat were more serious. He had welcomed Ronald Reagan to Gracie Mansion during the 1980 presidential campaign (while Cuomo was cochairing the Carter campaign in the state). The mayor had had nice things to say about some of Reagan's economic policies, and Reagan praised Koch's fiscal management of the city. In March 1982, while on a visit to New York City, the president indicated that he believed Ed Koch would make a great governor. Above all, there was the fact that Koch had sought and obtained the Republican nomination for mayor in 1981. And in 1982 Koch endorsed four incumbent Republicans for reelection to the state legislature. For all these reasons Cuomo was able to use the argument that his opponent was not a "real Democrat" to great effect in a primary in which only registered Democrats could vote. Koch's association with Reagan and the Republicans was especially harmful in 1982, because the very deep recession of that year had, at least for the moment, discredited Reaganomics.[7]

The circumstances surrounding the 1982 gubernatorial election put Mario Cuomo in a position to reverse the outcome of his earlier battles with Koch. The raw materials out of which an anti-Koch majority could be fashioned were available. But Cuomo would still have to prove himself, to show himself to be a desirable alternative to the mayor. "This race has been Koch v. Koch and now Koch is slipping," Cuomo said at the end of May. "But not enough for Koch not to still be the winner. In the time remaining, I have to tell people about Mario Cuomo."

For all the differences in context between the 1977 and 1982 Cuomo campaigns, the greatest contrast was in the candidate himself. This time Cuomo was self-assured. He *knew* that he would make a better governor than Koch would. He confidently determined campaign strategy on the basis of his own values and instincts, not the advice of putative experts. And since his son Andrew, in whom he had great confidence, was managing the campaign, Cuomo was less involved in the nuts-and-bolts decisions that should not be allowed to waste a candidate's time and energy.

It was not that the factions that had pulled apart the 1977 campaign were not still present and prepared to repeat the mistakes of the past. It was simply that Cuomo now had enough confidence in his own judgment to resist and control them. He kept the support of the factions that had backed him (perhaps "fronted" him would be more accurate) in 1977. But now he was the magnet and they the iron filings. "Some people are worried that I have alienated my 'base'—which they think is Catholics and homeowners," Cuomo noted in late April 1982. "Their analysis is that the Liberal wing [of the Democratic party] is mostly Jewish and it will vote for Koch no matter what and that therefore I ought to stay close to the center." Five years before, Cuomo would have allowed such advice to influence him. No more. "That's suggesting I place myself according to the polls," he continued. "It's easier for me just to place myself where I'm comfortable, issue by issue." This time there was no need for external navigators. Mario Cuomo's internal gyroscope set the course of the campaign.

That gyroscope directed its craft to the surface. "I get the sense that people are eager to find something to believe in," Cuomo wrote in May. "They badly want a cause. . . . My whole case is an affirmative one that is aggressively confident of our ability to help ourselves. Most people like that more than they like surrender."

Or, he might have added, more than they like slinging mud at an opponent.

Not only did Cuomo's gyroscope approach help him to follow the best course, it also provided a useful contrast to Koch's "weathervane." "We won't switch positions to succeed," Cuomo said. "I am different from him because I am a traditional Democrat, I don't waffle. I have specific ideas and a vision." Concerning his opponent, Cuomo said to audiences: "Can you think of one thing that Koch is speaking up for right now that isn't something a poll would say is popular?"

This line of attack helped to defuse the death penalty issue. In some cases it even turned it into a plus for Cuomo. "It is clear that my position [on the death penalty] will cost me votes," Cuomo wrote in March. But he refused to soften his stand. "My mother told me in 1977 to do what Koch does: 'He won and you lost because he supported the electric chair,' " Cuomo told listeners. His mother had suggested that he should say what people wanted to hear and then after he was elected, he could do what was right. Cuomo would have none of it. He insisted that the state must not "become like animals" and kill. The death penalty, he pointed out, was a simplistic answer to the complex problem of crime. "I don't want to fool you," Cuomo said to voters in 1982. "If the electric chair is what you want more than anything else, vote for someone else."

Everyone knew that the electric chair was favored by a substantial majority of New Yorkers. There could be no question that Cuomo's stand against the death penalty was unpopular. But he was showing himself to be a man of principle. *His stand for something unpopular was popular.*

That was—and is—the key to Mario Cuomo's appeal. It also was central to Ronald Reagan's appeal. Polls throughout the first six years of Reagan's administration indicated that a majority of Americans disagreed with him on many important issues. But they respected someone who stood up for what he believed. That this feeling was such an important base for Reagan's popularity goes a long way toward explaining why the Iran-contra scandal was so damaging to him. As is the case with Reagan, Cuomo's apparent integrity and willingness to stick to his beliefs attracts people to him, whether or not they agree with him on all issues.

(I hasten to add that Cuomo differs from Reagan in several crucial respects. *What* he believes is very different from what Reagan believes. Beyond that, however, is the vast contrast in their intellects. Cuomo is much more than a front man for the vision he articulates. He is a great communicator who is also a great thinker. Cuomo has considerably more substance to communicate than Reagan appears to have.)

Another possible reason that his stand against the electric chair was not as harmful to Cuomo's candidacy as some thought it would be is that those who favor the death penalty are perhaps less likely to base their votes on this single issue than are those who oppose it.

All of the factors that made the 1982 Cuomo-Koch clash different from its 1977 predecessor were evident in the first debate, staged by Rupert Murdoch early in July. The *Post* invited more than six hundred business and professional leaders to the Sheraton Centre Hotel in midtown Manhattan. Murdoch wanted them as witnesses while his champ delivered a quick knockout blow to the punch-drunk journeyman boxer from Holliswood. Koch was so confident that he skipped training sessions before the match. But he and his seconds got more than they had bargained for. Their opponent turned out to be another Rocky Balboa.

Cuomo decided to pass up breakfast in the enemy camp, and instead made a dramatic entrance moments before the debate was to start. Those supporters that his side had managed to slip into the mostly Koch crowd gave him a large ovation. Then the mayor won the coin toss to determine who would go first. "No wonder

he's for casino gambling," Cuomo cracked. The audience was beginning to swing to his side already. Cuomo was at his best in the
debate, self-assured, powerful, articulate, and extremely persuasive. Koch was, in the unanimous opinion of the assembled media,
creamed.

The *Post* debate was the turning point of the campaign. It
deprived Koch of his most important asset: his aura of invincibility
and inevitability. It "gave me credibility," Cuomo says. Newscast-
ers and columnists started to suggest that there was a slim possibility that Cuomo might win. Koch was thrown on the defensive and
showed that he (and/or Garth) was worried by immediately stepping up his negative campaign. In the next debate a few days later,
Koch tried to hit Cuomo over the head with Bill Cabin. It didn't
work. Polls showed Cuomo narrowing the gap to less than ten
points.

A great deal in this election depended on polls, and they varied
to an extraordinary degree. Murdoch kept publishing surveys
claiming that Koch was ahead by about twenty points. These were
probably intended as self-fulfilling prophecies. But Caddell also
showed Cuomo trailing badly late in the campaign. He and a few
other Cuomo advisers argued with the candidate during the final
week that he was far behind and must use heavily negative commercials for the few remaining days. Bob Sullivan, on the other
hand, insisted that Cuomo was very close and that using negative
ads would be a big mistake. Once again Cuomo took charge and
did what his instincts told him to do. "I think negatives would cost
me votes," Cuomo said, "because they disappoint expectations of
some of the people who prefer me. Moreover, I think the problem
I have continues to be that people don't know enough about me.
I don't want to fill that vacuum with harsh talk about my opponent."

It is interesting and somewhat disturbing to realize that
Cuomo's decision not to use strongly negative commercials seems
to have been a pragmatic one rather than a moral one: *They're likely
to backfire;* not, *They're wrong.*

Caddell, now sure that Cuomo would lose, suggested that Dick
Wade draft a concession speech for the candidate. "Why should I
do *that?*" Wade asked. "I've already drafted a victory speech."
Sullivan's polls indicated a Cuomo victory. The late movement
was heavily in Cuomo's direction, as Sullivan had expected it
would be from the outset of the campaign. As the election drew

near, people who had not previously made up their minds—and some who had—were likely to try to envision each candidate as governor. Koch simply did not fit the role; Cuomo did. (There were, though, voters who were in no position to know what role Cuomo fit. When a *New York Times* reporter asked an upstate dairy farmer a month before the primary what he thought of Mario Cuomo, he responded: "I think she's a strong lady." There aren't too many Marios in rural New York, either.)

Since Koch had much more money available, Cuomo could not match him in television exposure. Instead, the Cuomo camp relied on what he termed "more an old-fashioned campaign than a modern one." Large numbers of people had come to *believe* in Mario Cuomo. Their voluntary work for what they saw as a cause provided far more effective telephoning, handbill distribution, and get-out-the-vote efforts than the Koch campaign's money could buy. On primary day Cuomo's forces had some ten thousand volunteers, most of them union members, pulling out his vote.

Despite Sullivan's polls, Cuomo worried in the primary campaign's final days. He remembered 1977, and he knew many others did, too. "Four more days," he wrote in his diary on September 19, "for the prediction of Garth and others that I would 'step on my own toe'—commit a gaffe—to come true. Four days more during which I need to avoid a blunder, appear confident, cool, in control. Four more days to avoid lying or selling out so that at least we'll know we made an honorable effort." The image that Cuomo attributed to "Garth and others" was more refined than the one Ray Harding had employed, but the point remained that many political observers were waiting for Cuomo to crack, to commit a major blunder and, perhaps, stoop to tactics of dubious honor.

He didn't.

When the votes were counted, Cuomo came away with a victory margin of 52 percent to 48 percent. Even in the mayor's city, Cuomo was able to keep Koch's margin narrow. Koch took the suburbs, where his apparently antiminority, antiunion positions were more popular than they were inside the city limits, but upstate went to Cuomo in a waterfall. It was a stunning upset. "He had the money, the establishment, the media, the presumption of victory," Cuomo wrote of Koch, in words that could have been written about Cuomo five years before. "We were not supposed to win—and we did." Although Cuomo's emotional balance wheel prevented him from fully experiencing the ecstasy of his triumph, he was as close to that level of emotion as he ever gets. "It was an emotional victory," he wrote in his diary. ". . . It said: you can tell the truth, stand up to the power brokers and editorial writers and political leaders, and still win. It was Rocky, David, the last-minute field goal by the underdogs."

Mario Cuomo's victory over Ed Koch in 1982 was especially sweet for him because he had allowed himself to be placed on the other side of all those divides in 1977. He was far more comfortable as the underdog, with the establishment on the other side. That's where he should have been in the first place, but it had taken a string of defeats in the 1970s and Koch's vacuuming up of the political leaders in 1982 for him to realize this. "It wasn't Mario Cuomo," he went on, "—most people don't know a whole lot about me—it was the message we were delivering. Even if only vaguely perceived, it's the little guy against the big guy; the underdog against the favorite. It's nuclear freeze and ban the bomb; it's 'save the whales' and Peace Corps [all of which sounds suspiciously "Manhattan liberalish"]; it's 'us' against 'them.' And 'us' won!"[8]

Now that Mario Cuomo's "us" was inclusive of everyone except the "power brokers" and "political bosses," it deserved to win.

The thrill of victory could not long be savored. "Us" had another match scheduled about six weeks later. Though somewhat anticlimactic, the 1982 general election would be another difficult contest.

"It may be that because we brought down Goliath in the primary some people expect the rest to be easy," Cuomo wrote a little more than a week into the general election campaign. "It won't be." He was right.

The Republican–Conservative–Right-to-Life candidate for governor was closer to Getty than Goliath. Lew Lehrman was a political newcomer with a passion for red suspenders and what he termed "radical-conservative" economics who had made millions of dollars from a chain of drugstores. A firm believer in supply-side economics and the gold standard, Lehrman was prepared to spend as much of his fortune as was necessary to become governor of New York (and then, it was widely believed he hoped, Ronald Reagan's successor as president of the United States).

Lehrman had two major advantages: his money and the freshness of his face. In the general election Lehrman spent $13.9 million to Cuomo's $4.8 million. Although Lehrman had very strong beliefs, he was prepared to deemphasize them during the campaign in order to take on whatever coloration seemed most likely to help him win. Since he was unknown to almost all New York voters when the election year began, he could be created in whatever image appeared most desirable.

For nine days after the primary, Cuomo had no commercials on television, because he had no money. Lehrman was already deep into a media saturation the like of which had never before been seen in a New York gubernatorial race. As Cuomo put it, "There are more Lehrman commercials than there are daytime tragedies on TV." But as important as television was to Lehrman's campaign, his immense targeted direct-mail effort may have been of equal significance. Nine million items were mailed by the Republican candidate's workers. This enabled Lehrman's campaign to reach carefully selected audiences and hit hard on certain issues that he would not want to say very much about before the electorate as a whole. One mailing to people with Italian and Irish surnames viciously attacked Cuomo on "traditional values" issues: abortion, crime, and homosexuality.

Cuomo moved rapidly to unify the Democratic party behind him. This proved to be relatively easy, although Koch looked glum in a commercial he did endorsing Cuomo. Many of Koch's supporters in the party had been such only because of their fear of the mayor and their expectation that he would win. A good many of them were quite pleased to have Cuomo as their candidate.

He set as his theme "Jobs and Justice," and sought to link Lehrman to Reaganomics at a time when the national unemployment rate was breaking through the psychologically significant 10 percent level. Such a linkage should not have been very difficult to establish, since Lehrman is a true believer in the supply-side theory. But his packagers had created an image of him that neglected to say much about his economic theories. It was up to Cuomo and his staff to show the public where Lehrman stood on economic issues, a task at which they were at least partly successful. Lehrman had broken somewhat with Reagan, it was true, but only because Reagan was not thoroughgoing enough in his supply-side belief to suit an ideologue like Lehrman. "My opponent . . . not only likes Reaganomics," Cuomo correctly said, "he wants to go farther."

Lehrman realized his vulnerability in the midst of a Reagan recession that was threatening to become a Reagan depression. He decided not to have the president come to New York to campaign for him. What Cuomo was doing was portraying Lehrman as Reaganism without Reagan; that is, Reagan's policies without his magical personality. Even those in New York (and they were many) who still liked the president were becoming fed up with his economic policies. An election-day CBS News poll indicated that only 25 percent of New York's voters thought that Reagan's economic policies had helped the state, while 58 percent believed they had hurt New York. If the outcome of the election hinged on economic policy, Cuomo was certain to win.

Cuomo also managed to turn some of Lehrman's advantages part way around. The slogan "Mario Cuomo: Experience Money Can't Buy" underlined Cuomo's experience in government, Lehrman's inexperience, and the fact that the latter was, in essence, trying to buy the election. And Cuomo reminded voters of his opponent's inexperience by noting that "the state is not a drugstore."

Lehrman, believing that his television saturation gave him the upper hand, would agree to only two debates. The first one, sponsored by the *Post*, which was now pushing Lehrman, saw Cuomo return to the Sheraton Centre, scene of his great victory over Koch three months earlier. Unfortunately it also saw something of a return of the "old Cuomo" of 1977. Angered by what he considered to be Lehrman's low blows in his targeted mailings, Cuomo became too aggressive. The problem was certainly not as bad as it had been in 1977, but Cuomo's vanquishing of Koch in the summer had raised expectations. He did not live up to them in his first debate with Lehrman and in the process turned the Republican nominee into a sympathetic figure.

Cuomo knew what had happened and how dangerous it was for him. "I have lapsed back into a mode that's closer to '77 than to the primary this year—at least it's perceived that way." He also knew the solution: "What I have to do is get back to talking about my vision and hope and belief."

That, essentially, is what he did in the last three weeks of the campaign. But while he talked about hope, Cuomo was startlingly frank about the limits of what could be done. "What is the answer to crime?" Cuomo said in an interview with the *Daily News* editorial board. "There is none. But you can make the system better."

Lehrman's ads distorted this statement into Cuomo saying that "there's nothing we can do about crime." Knowing that he was behind, Lehrman went more harshly negative in the closing three weeks of the campaign. It had an effect. Sullivan found that Cuomo's lead was shrinking. A few days before the election, he showed Andrew Cuomo a graph with three different possible movements between then and the election. One of them would give Cuomo a fairly comfortable victory, another a narrow victory, and the third a narrow defeat.

The tightening of the race reenergized Cuomo's forces. Their last-minute television campaign was excellent. By this time most people expected Cuomo to win. "I have a feeling that Mario is going to win, because he's such a good man," Senator Daniel Patrick Moynihan said.

But Cuomo's staff was scared. They had a long meeting at which they tried to persaude the candidate that he must borrow money for a last-minute media blitz to try to counter Lehrman's aggressive TV ads. Cuomo had made a promise to Matilda that he would not go into debt personally this time. The staff and other Cuomo backers were almost unanimous in telling him that this was the smart thing to do—that the debt would be easily paid off after he won.

"Great," Cuomo told them. "You want to borrow? You go ahead and borrow money. *I'm* not borrowing money."

Then, while the argument was continuing around him, the candidate began staring at Andrew. He kept staring for two or three minutes, and then said: "Is that my shirt? Are you wearing my shirt? Where did you get my shirt?" While everybody else was discussing the future of New York, the candidate and his campaign manager–son debated whose shirt the latter was wearing.

(Cuomo did not borrow money late in the campaign. He later decided that he should have, that not doing so was the one major change he would make if he had the campaign to do over. By the end they had more money than they could use, but much of it came in too late to help.)

The election would, to a large extent, turn on whether voters decided that crime or unemployment was a greater worry. Most people proved to be considerably more concerned about unemployment than crime. Given Lehrman's heavy attack on the crime issue, Cuomo might not have won if that had become the critical question. That was a real possibility, since the Tylenol killings occurred in October, a New York City policeman was murdered shortly before the election, and President Reagan made a television address asking people to "stay the course" and let his economic policies have a chance to work.

The day before the election, Cuomo made the following entry in his diary: "An astrologist sent me a horoscope that said that I was going to die on election day. I don't know if she meant literally or figuratively. Just in case she meant literally, I think I'll vote early."

For a time on election day, it seemed that if the prognostication had been intended as figurative, it might be correct. Early voter samples indicated a dead heat. In the end, Cuomo won by 3.4 percent, 50.9 percent to 47.5 percent, with the remainder going to minor candidates. Although the win was not as large as Cuomo had hoped for, the size of the victory margin was in line with the norm for New York governors' races.

Cuomo did not enjoy the victory as much as he did the primary, in part, no doubt, because it did not contain the revenge factor that beating Koch did. But the joy of winning was also diluted by Lehrman's actions on election night. Around 10 P.M. Adam Walinsky (who had migrated from the political left to the right and was advising Lehrman) called Cuomo to ask for a deal. Lehrman would concede then if Cuomo would invite him over to his hotel to help establish him as the spokesman of the Republican party. Cuomo declined the offer, saying that State Senate Majority Leader Warren Anderson was the rightful spokesman for New York Republicans. As a result of Cuomo's refusal to deal, Lehrman did not concede. Cuomo waited until well after midnight before coming down (as the band played the *Rocky* theme) to make his victory speech. Lehrman had still not conceded.

Before going down to speak to his supporters, Cuomo had gone over to his mother in the hotel suite and said, "Ma—you've got a governor in the family!"

"So what?" Immaculata Cuomo, too tired to care who had won, replied.[9]

The key to Mario Cuomo's victory in 1982 was his championing of traditional Democratic values in the new form and new package of "family." Only two years after Ronald Reagan had been swept into the White House on a

national wave of reaction to excessive government and social programs, Cuomo boldly campaigned across New York as a believer
in affirmative government. While many other Democrats were
trying to accommodate themselves to the conservative era, Cuomo
refused to apologize for his party's commitment to the poor and
the role of government in dealing with social problems. Government has an obligation, he said just before the November election,
"to help those who are in need—people who are in wheelchairs
because they are born that way, people who are old, a pregnant
woman in Essex County that cannot feed a fetus, a child she is
carrying. . . ."

Cuomo's only apparent concession to the conservatives was to
indicate that some members of his party had gotten carried away
with taxes and spending. He would be compassionate and rely on
government to solve problems, but he would combine fiscal responsibility with social responsibility. But this was not in fact a
concession. Cuomo had never been a "money-is-no-object" liberal
of the Nelson Rockefeller–Ted Kennedy stereotype. He was always one to be very careful about money.

The values and programs of the Democratic party, Cuomo said,
were "a politics that raised up a whole generation . . . from poverty
to the middle class. Who is right, Hoover or FDR?" Lew Lehrman
made his answer as clear as Cuomo's, asserting that his election
would prove that the New Deal and its principles were dead. But
a majority of voters in Franklin Roosevelt's home state was not yet
ready to bury his legacy.[10]

Mario Cuomo may have been lucky that his gubernatorial campaign occurred at a time when the worst recession since the Great
Depression caused New Yorkers to be upset with Ronald Reagan's
economic policies. But his campaign theme was not determined by
that external factor. He had long and passionately believed in the
necessity of policies of social responsibility. He was a missionary
in the "me" era preaching a vision of what "we" could and should
accomplish as a family. His vision attracted enough New York
voters to give him an opportunity to try to put his political and
social faith in practice.

10

GOVERNOR

MARIO CUOMO had impressed many people during his 1982 campaign. He had a vision and the ability to communicate that vision to large numbers of people. Such abilities can win elections, as he had just shown, but it remained to be seen if their possessor was capable of being something more than a great speaker: a great—or at least a good—governor. He had been criticized in the past as someone who took positions on issues but had no potential for decision-making or running a government. Since he had never before won a political contest of his own, there was trepidation in some quarters that he might be one of those politicians who say on the day after the election, "Well, we won; now what do we do?"

No one who really knew Cuomo had any fear of that problem. He very clearly was someone who desired to win because he had goals he wanted to accomplish as a public official (although it is obvious that he also wanted to win because he wanted to win). Whether he would be able to accomplish many of his goals was a much tougher question.

Although knocking off the heavily favored Mayor Koch and being elected governor of New York had brought Cuomo to the attention of some observers around the country, it was the stirring statement on interdependence and responsibility that he made in his inaugural address that first created serious national interest in this previously little-known Italian-American politician from Queens. He did not expect it. No one on the governor-elect's staff except Cuomo's longtime assistant Mary Tragale even liked the speech. "I drafted what I thought was a piece of garbage," Cuomo told me. "It was so familiar to me and so trite and hackneyed." He says he "delivered it thinking it was going to bomb."

It was a bomb, all right, one that scored a direct hit on the self-centered ethic of Reaganism. The bomb proved to be of very high yield, so high that it is worth quoting at length. The new governor spoke of "what I hope will be the *soul* of this administration":

For more than fifty years, without dramatic deviation—whatever party happened to be in power—New York has proved that government can be a positive source of good. It still can be.

I believe government's basic purpose is to allow those blessed with talent to go as far as they can—on their own merits. But I believe that government also has an obligation to assist those who, for whatever inscrutable reason, have been left out by fate—the homeless, the infirm, the destitute—to help provide those necessary things which, through no fault of their own, they cannot provide for themselves.

Of course, we should have *only* the government we need. But we must insist on *all* the government we need. So, a technically balanced budget that fails to meet the reasonable needs of the middle class and poor would be the emblem of hypocrisy.

It has become popular in some quarters to argue that the principal function of government is to make instruments of war and to clear obstacles from the way of the strong. The rest—it is said—will happen automatically: the cream will rise to the top, whether the cream be well-endowed individuals or fortunate regions of the nation.

"Survival of the fittest" may be a good working description of the process of evolution; but a government of humans should elevate itself to a higher order, one which tries to fill the cruel gaps left by chance or by a wisdom we don't understand.

. . .

A society as blessed as ours should be able to find room at the table— shelter for the homeless, work for the idle, care for the elderly and infirm, and hope for the destitute. To demand less of our government or ourselves would be to evade our proper responsibility. At the very least, the government of this generation should be able to do for those who follow us what has been done for us.

. . .

We can—and we will—refuse to settle for survival, and certainly not just survival of the fittest! I believe we can balance our lives and our society even as we manage to balance our books.

. . . Those who made our history taught us above all things the idea of family. Mutuality. The sharing of benefits and burdens—fairly—for the good of all. It is an idea essential to our success.

And no family that favored its strong children—or that, in the name of evenhandedness, failed to help its vulnerable ones—would be worthy of the name. And no state, or nation, that chooses to ignore its troubled regions and people, while watching others thrive, can call itself justified.

We must be the family of New York—feeling one another's pain; sharing one another's blessings, reasonably, equitably, honestly, fairly—irrespective of geography or race or political affiliation.

. . .

Many of those in attendance said they had never heard such an inspiring speech. It literally brought tears to the eyes of hardened politicians. Well, not all of them. Hugh Carey said to his successor, "Classy, Mario, real classy." But then he gave Cuomo some succinct advice that was typical of the old politics beyond which the new governor hoped to move. "Don't believe anybody," Carey whispered.

Praise for Cuomo's address poured in from all over the country. Some of it emanated from unexpected sources. "Dick Nixon wrote me a letter about it and said it was an excellent speech," Cuomo recalls. The Nixon endorsement aside, a gubernatorial administration could hardly have a more auspicious beginning.[1]

On Saturday evening of his second week in office, the new governor had a family dinner at a Manhattan restaurant interrupted by a call from the state police saying that his secretary, Michael Del Giudice, was trying to reach Cuomo with an urgent message. Cuomo's first thought when he was informed that Del Giudice was calling was "Prisons."

He was correct. A prison uprising had taken place at the famous "correctional facility" at Ossining. Inmates had taken some forty prison guards hostage. The prison, familiar to gangster film fans as Sing Sing, was more than a century and a half old. Like almost all state prisons, it was severely overcrowded. The inmates considered conditions in the facility to be intolerable. Their action, they later indicated, was one of desperation intended to publicize the way they were treated and to demand improvements.

The prison uprising was a critical test for Cuomo. The campaign and the inaugural speech had convinced most New Yorkers that their new governor was a man with a magnificent mouth and a soft heart, but Lehrman's incessant hammering at the death penalty issue had left a question in the minds of some whether Cuomo might be *too* soft. *Yes, we know he's a smart, compassionate man,* people thought, *but is he tough enough? Can he make decisions? Can he deal with a crisis?* These questions awaited answers, and Ossining would go a long way toward providing them.

Prison insurrections constitute the greatest source of nightmares for most governors. This is especially the case in New York, where Governor Rockefeller's decision to send a small army of state troopers and others into the Attica prison in 1971 resulted in the deaths of forty-three inmates and guards. The specter of Attica hovered constantly over Cuomo and his advisers as they dealt with the Ossining crisis.

Cuomo's first reaction was that he would go to Ossining right away and work out a settlement. "I found it very unsatisfactory to be so removed and depending on sporadic reports," he told me. Cuomo has supreme confidence in his ability to mediate any dispute, and felt that he could do so in this one, if he could just get into a face-to-face meeting with the inmates. Staff members persuaded him that he was wrong.

"We've got to go through the negotiation process and deal with it," Del Giudice told Cuomo. "You're the last card, not the first card, in terms of dealing with this thing."

"Okay, you're right," the fledgling governor finally conceded.

Cuomo established a command center at the World Trade Center and for fifty-three hours his new team faced its trial by fire. The governor took all his meals in the office during that period, and slept a few hours on a conference table. The crisis management team advising him included Andrew Cuomo, who had joined his father as a dollar-a-year special assistant; Timothy Russert, the governor's counselor; Fabian Palomino, who had taken the title of special counsel; Lawrence Kurlander, the criminal justice coordinator; and Del Giudice. They kept a telephone line constantly open to Correctional Services Commissioner Thomas A. Coughlin III, who was on the scene at Ossining.

"I will continue to devote my entire attention to this emergency until it is resolved," Cuomo said in a public statement at the beginning of the crisis. "The first priority is the lives of the corrections officers. Second, however, we must be aware that the lives of potential hostages in prisons throughout New York would be endangered by any agreement that would unduly erode respect for the state's authority." From the start of his hostage crisis, Cuomo understood that, compassion for the individual hostages notwithstanding, he could not capitulate to the demands of the insurrec-

tionists without encouraging similar episodes. His hard head kept
his soft heart under reasonable restraint.

"He was very strong during that whole crisis," Del Giudice
said of his boss. "He was fantastic," agreed Kurlander. "He was
able to establish early on what his long-term and short-term goals
were. And he was then able to structure a course of action to meet
those goals. And he was very, very tough-minded." When the
question of possible amnesty for the hostage takers came up,
Cuomo told me, "I made a judgment early on: 'I will not consider
amnesty; and make that absolute. Don't hold out any hope for
amnesty.'" Some thought such an ironclad position on amnesty
was a mistake, but Cuomo was insistant. He would, however,
negotiate on lesser points in order to avert a bloodbath. The judgment that had to be made, he said, was " 'Can you uphold the law
and save the lives at the same time?'—or 'Can you uphold the law
without forfeiting those lives?'"

Cuomo decided at the outset that he would not meet with the
press during the crisis, to ensure that nothing he said would undermine the negotiations. And he refused to allow the rebellious inmates to go on television to state their grievances.

The prisoners wound up offering to release the hostages if the
governor himself would go on television and read their demands.
Cuomo refused, saying it would set a terrible precedent. The governor and his crisis team made a calculated decision to keep saying,
"We don't want another Attica." They knew, Tim Russert told
me, that the news media would be trying to fill up airtime with
something. The state's comments on Attica triggered repeated
showings by the television stations of footage of the carnage in
which that prison confrontation culminated. The Ossining inmates were watching the TV coverage, and the Attica tapes
"scared the living hell out of them," Russert says.

Since the prisoners' main objective was to air their grievances,
the governor's team allowed the press to move closer to the prison
walls and told the inmates to use a megaphone to state their demands. They did this at a few minutes to eleven on the night of
January 11, and all the TV stations carried the prisoners' statements on the eleven o'clock news. This enabled the state authori-
ties to convince the hostage takers that they had gotten what they
wanted. The insurrection ended peacefully, with all the hostages
being released unharmed.

After the successful denouement of the Ossining crisis, Cuomo was widely praised as a great mediator. As Del Giudice says, it was "a case where you had to apply practical thinking and not be an ideologue—you know, 'Bust up the prison; screw them,' or 'Let them have everything.' It was right down the middle in terms of balancing the decision-making." Cuomo's progressive pragmatism had met an important test.

Horrible as it obviously was for those directly involved, especially the hostages and their families, Ossining turned out to be a great break for the new governor and his staff. "It was a terrific learning experience," Del Giudice says. "The administration came together—it came together very strongly." "It was our first real test of governance," Cuomo said to me, "and it was a tough one—hard to imagine a more difficult one. So that was good for us from a morale point of view. It was certainly good for us from a confidence point of view—gave us a little credibility early on."

Having gotten through a life-and-death crisis in which forty or more lives were at stake, Cuomo and his inner circle had passed their sternest test before the administration was two weeks old. Any questions about Cuomo's toughness and ability to deal with a crisis evaporated with the Ossining settlement. Cuomo's "handling of Ossining showed he was a good field general," Albany lobbyist Victor Condello told Ken Auletta, "and not a vacillating Hamlet. He made decisions. It established him as a decision-maker instead of a scholar and an attorney."[2]

The venerable skyline of Albany is dwarfed by a group of white marble monoliths that are part of the Empire State Plaza. The "Albany Mall" has been described as a modern equivalent of the pyramids of Giza. The project reflects the outlook of its originator, Nelson Rockefeller. Constructed over a thirteen-year period at a cost of nearly a billion dollars, the plaza exhibits a colossal architecture that would not have seemed out of place in Stalin's Russia or Hitler's Germany. The message these monumental structures convey to the citizen approaching them is unmistakable: the insignificance of the individual before the power and majesty of the state.

Rockefeller's mall did not make a fitting symbolic home for Cuomo's family of New York. The nineteenth-century State Capitol, which sits in the shadows of the modern monuments to the state, provides a far more suitable abode for the sort of government that Mario Cuomo envisioned. The governor's suite on the second floor, with its ornate official office and the much smaller functional space where Cuomo actually works, retains the flavor of the historic figures who have occupied it.

The Empire State Plaza conveys another message, one shared by Rockefeller and a majority in the state legislature for many years. It is simply the notion that there are no reasonable limits to the resources of the state. For decades governors and lawmakers of both parties in New York had found the path of least resistance (and of greatest electoral success) to be to tax and spend almost at will. If there were no discernible limits, there was no need to make tough choices.

Those halcyon days ended about the time Rockefeller left for his brief stint as vice president of the United States. When Cuomo became governor, he faced a projected $1.8 billion deficit in the state budget. This chasm between revenues and expenditures was attributable both to the excesses of the past and to the Reagan recession, but its causes were of scant import; it had to be dealt with at once. Governors and state legislatures do not have the luxury enjoyed by presidents and members of Congress of being able to write hot checks on a continuing basis. The constitutions or laws of almost all states require balanced budgets. The state's fiscal crisis made it "easy to provide an agenda," Cuomo said to me. "It's called survival."

One might expect a Democrat who prided himself on compassion and said the sorts of things that Cuomo did in his inaugural address to propose a substantial tax hike as the most socially responsible means of closing the budget gap. Surely that would have been the normal approach in New York. But Cuomo was convinced that, given the state's already high tax rates and the increasingly competitive world market, increases in the three broad-based state taxes—income, sales, and business—would be counterproductive. He had pledged during the campaign that he would not raise any of the "big three" taxes, even though together they accounted for almost 85 percent of the state's revenues. "I said no all through the campaign," Cuomo recalled. "I want the business people in this state to believe me. So the credibility factor, and the fact that these are bad taxes that retard business development— these are all things that went through my mind."

"We're not thinking about income-tax increases," Cuomo told

U.S. News & World Report. "It's too easy politically, it's too devastating economically and, in the long run, fiscally.

"The most popular thing to do here would have been to say: 'We won't bother anybody but so-called rich people. We'll put a surcharge on the income tax.'

"But in the long run, that would have cost us jobs in this state, because it would have been a disincentive to investment. And in the end, the people would have been punished by that tax on the so-called rich. It would hurt the middle class and the people struggling to go from poverty to the middle class."

Mario Cuomo's first objective as governor would be to find a way to balance the state budget without raising any of the three broad-based taxes—and without cutting essential services. "The real challenge before us," he declared in his first State of the State message, delivered on the fifth day of his administration, "is to balance our books the way a family would—without abandoning our weak, without sacrificing the future of our young, without destroying the environment that supports us." The necessity, as Cuomo frequently puts it, was "to do more with less."

Few would dissent from this objective, but reaching it would be a tall order. Cuomo knew little about how state budgets were made. Michael Del Giudice did; he had been through the process for two terms with Carey. He was struck by Cuomo's starting point. "Well, let's first establish some principles," the governor said. "Give me some facts and we'll establish some principles."

"I remember thinking," Del Giudice told me, " 'Establishing principles—what's he talking about?' Because in the seven or eight years of making budgets [under Carey], we discussed the politics; we didn't discuss principles."

Cuomo said: "First of all, I want to be fair. So if we're going to cut expenditures, we'll have to raise revenues. I want to be able to say, 'We're doing half expenditure cuts, half revenue increases. . . . If we're going to do cuts, every agency has to be cut. There's not going to be somebody safeguarded—well, except for prisons." Having just been through the consequences of inadequate prison facilities, Cuomo was determined to increase what he calls his "defense budget." In the end he also proposed increases in spending for the homeless, day care, and a few other social programs about which he felt strongly, including $3 million for a new neighborhood crime-control program.

In outlining the principles upon which the austerity budget should be based, Cuomo said: "We don't want to just cut across the board either. I want to make logical cuts in each category. It's not a ten percent ax across the board." One of Cuomo's first actions as governor was to impose a hiring freeze on all state agencies. But he knew that would not be sufficient. He realized that people would have to be laid off if $900 million were to be cut from the spending side of the state ledger. "If we have to fire people, we have to fire people," he said. "That's an unfortunate part of a $1.8 billion crisis."

His was a budget, Cuomo noted, of "excruciating pain" and "extraordinary sacrifices." As he was working it out with his staff and Budget Director Michael Finnerty, Cuomo told a story of his father taking the family to a restaurant when he was a boy. Andrea spilled a bottle of wine on the tablecloth, but blamed Mario for it. Mario was crushed by this injustice, but when they got home, his father explained, "You're young and can take the blame." After finishing the story, Cuomo looked at his budget director, whose age was then thirty-eight, and said, "We'll call this Finnerty's Budget."

Cuomo's approach to the budget became a model for his actions as governor. He attacked problems in a very organized fashion— the premises, the problems, the principles, and the recommendations. Everything had to have a rationale. Once that had been established, Cuomo would use his other skills to communicate with the public and the legislature. He treated the legislature in a much more positive way than Carey had, and as a result was able to win a good deal of cooperation.

But the budget proposals Cuomo was making were tough products to sell. Assembly Speaker Stanley Fink believed the governor was mistaken in thinking that higher taxes would drive businesses out of the state. Providing good services is at least as important to businesses as is the tax rate, he argued. Fink faced growing discontent among Democratic members of the assembly, who said they were upset with Cuomo's "Republican budget." "I have to spend a lot of my time with my [Democratic] members defending a Democratic governor," Fink told Ken Auletta. Democratic Assemblyman Melvin Miller of Brooklyn (who became speaker in 1987 and in that position had a stormy relationship with the governor) complained that Cuomo's budget was indistinguishable from what a conservative Republican might have submitted.

In fact, Mario Cuomo was playing to a conservative Republican audience in his first budget. One of his major objectives, he said from the start, was to win a "hallelujah endorsement" right after Easter, in which editorials in the *Times,* the *Wall Street Journal,* and *Barron's* would praise him for eliminating the huge deficit without raising any of the "big three" taxes. By March Cuomo could hear the chorus of praise beginning to rise in the background.

Cuomo's desire for the approval of Wall Street and the city establishment raises important questions about him: Is he actually a conservative who talks like a liberal? Do his policies amount to Reaganism with a human face? Or, in seeking to win over the establishment by demonstrating fiscal responsibility, was the new governor simply following a practice similar to that favored by Franklin Roosevelt—tacking to the starboard for a while before darting off in the opposite direction? Reassuring conservatives can help to provide a base from which to launch more progressive actions. Cuomo has repeatedly maintained that it is necessary to have a sound economic base if we are to have the resources needed to help the poor. Such a belief does not indicate that Cuomo was following a modified version of trickle-down economics.

Cuomo believed that his proposed budget would be passed without many significant alterations. "I think, strategically, the strength of this budget is that you'll have pressure from all sides all at once," Cuomo said. "What happens when there is equal pressure on all sides of a container? Nothing happens. So I don't expect to see many changes—no dramatic changes."

The pressures developed rapidly, but they were not quite equal from all sides. During February large delegations of students, state workers, local politicians, and others who faced cuts under the governor's proposals descended on Albany. Many of them had legitimate grievances, but Cuomo said that all must share the pain.

In the end, Cuomo got most of what he wanted in the budget passed by the legislature. He did have to compromise on some points, but Cuomo believes compromise is a necessary part of getting things done politically. He accepted a quarter of a billion dollars more in spending—mostly on education and to prevent layoffs—than he had originally proposed. All sorts of nuisance and "sin" taxes were raised, spending was slashed, and the state budget was balanced. The "hallelujahs" were printed, and Cuomo was off to the start for which he had hoped.[3]

* * *

Sharing the burden was an admirable idea, and Cuomo gave the impression that his office was part of the sharing. Tim Russert announced that the Executive Chamber budget would be cut by 10 percent from what it had been under Carey. It was, and Cuomo called it a "clear signal that he was 'sharing the pain.' " But even in Mario Cuomo's government reality does not invariably match the public image. Early in 1984 the *New York Times* reported that the governor had put dozens of people who actually work in the Executive Chamber on the payrolls of other state agencies. In fact, therefore, Cuomo's staff was no smaller than Carey's had been.

If not smaller, though, Cuomo's staff was set up very differently from Carey's. The former governor's secretary, Robert Morgado, had controlled access to Carey and for many purposes had been the de facto governor. Morgado is described by one of Carey's staff as "the kind of guy if you crossed him he'd cut your balls off, but you wouldn't find out till tomorrow when you got them in the mail. I saw people ruined—pounded into the dust." Mario Cuomo did not intend to give any staff member that sort of power. Del Giudice, who became his secretary, would not control access to the governor. Nor would he or anyone else on the staff be given the powers of an unelected chief executive officer. Hugh Carey had seen the role of the governor as a sort of chairman of the board who could delegate executive duties to others. Cuomo has never wanted to be in such a position. He must be involved in everything that is going on within his jurisdiction.

Although neither the experiences of New York under Carey's somewhat detached style nor those of the United States under Ronald Reagan's extremely detached governance were particularly salutary, one of the chief criticisms of Mario Cuomo as an administrator has been that he does not delegate enough, that he is too much of a "hands on" executive. He would respond that the only alternative to having *someone*'s hands on the rudder is to allow the government to drift aimlessly. And who did the people elect? *That* is the person who is responsible, and his or her hands should be those that set the course.

Fine. But the person who steers the vessel need not raise the sails and swab the deck as well. Cuomo's critics maintain that he cannot delegate tasks. "If he were president," a member of the governor's staff—in no sense an enemy or detractor—said to me, "he would want to run everything. He would want to order paper clips; he would want to know who left what lights on someplace—because that's part of his nature. Is he going to sign all the checks himself?"

Cuomo and his defenders say such criticisms are based on a false impression of his mode of operation. He uses a "spokes of the wheel" setup in which he is in the center. He claims that he delegates a great deal, but keeps a close watch on what goes on. He relies on a monitoring process. "He gives you room," Tim Russert told me, "but he wants to know how you are doing and what's going on." "He's very much into testing," Press Secretary Gary Fryer agrees. "He'll test you."

New York's governor can joke about the charge that he cannot delegate. "They say I can't delegate!" he said to me in the summer of 1987. "You should have seen me delegate when I learned that Maria is going to get married in the fall. I said, 'Here, Matilda, it's yours!' Bobby Richardson never got a double-play ball out of his glove any faster than I delegated that wedding!"

Despite the jokes, it is apparent that the criticism on this point bothers Cuomo. "It is accurate to say I do a lot myself," he explains. "It is not accurate to say I don't delegate an awful lot. We've done more than most administrations, and that required more people and more delegation by me. So I do more, my people do more, I delegate more. The net result is we get more done." He contends that people make the charge that he does not delegate only because his style is more hands-on than what they are accustomed to. He knows details of various areas of the government. "They're surprised a lot of the time that I know so much." Cuomo maintains that his knowledge of what is going on in his government results from his extra work—the long hours he puts in—rather than from a failure to delegate. "These bags under my eyes are filled with information," he told me. "That's where I carry my information."

The fact is that Mario Cuomo casts a wide net. "What did I want to do?" he said in answer to my question about his objectives when he became governor. "I wanted to do *everything*." "The difference between me and a lot of other executives was that they pick one or two priorities and get identified with them. . . . But we do all these things simultaneously. I gave us the first seat-belt law; I gave us the first acid-rain law, the biggest environmental bond issue, the biggest mass transit program—over eight billion dollars for the MTA, the twenty-one-year-old purchase age. So it goes on and on, but we do it all simultaneously. I know that any one of these things could be a priority. The first time I talked about priorities was last year [1986]. I said education would be my priority this year, and it was."

As he recites the achievements of his administration, Cuomo makes the case that they prove that he delegates successfully. "If you can do all that and do it without delegating, they shouldn't make you president, they should canonize you." In view of the many accomplishments of his governorship, Cuomo insists, "anyone who says I don't delegate is paying me an absurd compliment."

Although Cuomo is extraordinarily popular all over the state of New York, few people would associate him with one particular accomplishment, such as they would Rockefeller with the state university system or Carey with saving New York City from bankruptcy. The reason, Cuomo's supporters argue with considerable justification, is not that he has accomplished little, but that he has done so much in so many different areas that no one achievement stands out above the others. "It's not by design so much as just by the nature of how Cuomo is," Gary Fryer says. "He's not a one-issue guy. . . . He is a guy who is eclectic in his views and he's also kind of eclectic in terms of his priorities."

Fryer notes that some political observers have contended that the trouble with Cuomo is that he has done too many good things. He would be better off, according to this argument, if he just did one or two. Although this sounds ridculous, Fryer thinks there is a certain truth to it. "While we're fighting on a legislative agenda that has eighty-five separate things in it that we want to get done, and the governor's pushing on all eighty-five, you could probably achieve an equal result—although less useful—an equal *political* result, by simply saying, 'Okay. Education's it this year. Forget everything else.' "

But Cuomo is constitutionally unable to follow such a course. Fryer says that every once in a while they will sit around at a staff meeting and the governor will say, "We need to concentrate on just a couple of things."

Everyone in the room responds, "Yes, Governor."

"We've got to make these points," Cuomo continues.

"That's right, Governor."

The press secretary told me that the entire staff knows full well that "the next day he'll be calling fifteen different people, leaning on them on fifteen different issues—going in all kinds of different directions. That's the way he governs."

One reason that Cuomo's multifront approach makes some observers uneasy is that it reminds them of the way Jimmy Carter started out his presidency. They are aware that Cuomo and Carter admire each other, and fear that if Cuomo ever became president he might turn out to be "another Carter."

Such fears are the result of oversimplification. Mario Cuomo, to be sure, shares certain characteristics with former President Carter. Both are highly intelligent, hardworking executives who have wide-ranging interests and a penchant for hands-on administration. But the fact is that Cuomo seems to share another characteristic with Ronald Reagan: the ability to move and inspire people. In New York that has enabled Cuomo to make effective use of his office as what Theodore Roosevelt termed (in reference to the presidency) a "bully pulpit." Cuomo has demonstrated his ability in New York to rally public opinion to pressure the legislature to move on a variety of issues.[4]

Mario Cuomo appears to combine some of the strengths of Carter with some of those of Reagan, while avoiding the most obvious weaknesses of each. A leader with (at least) Carter's intelligence and love of work and detail, and Reagan's ability to communicate, but without Carter's dullness as a public figure and Reagan's distaste for work, general ignorance of policy issues, and detached executive style, should not be seen as similar to either man. As president, Mario Cuomo surely would have weaknesses of his own, but they would not be those of either Carter or Reagan.

There are several other charges sometimes made against Cuomo as governor that are closely related to the assertion that he does not delegate. Among them are that he has a weak staff, that he is too loyal to longtime associates, that he does not give his trust easily to newcomers, and that he is reluctant to take advice.

Michael Del Giudice points out that it is to some extent true of all of us that we are more likely to put our trust in those we know well. Cuomo, his former secretary says, is no exception. But Del Giudice believes that those who contend that Cuomo has a more than ordinary propensity to withhold his trust from outsiders are usually those who have been unable to get close to the governor because he doesn't respect them or doesn't like them. In fact, Cuomo formed much of his administration from people whom he knew slightly or not at all. "He didn't have a choice when he came in," Cuomo's former speechwriter Peter Quinn said to me. "If he only took the people who supported him, he couldn't have had an administration." Almost every Democrat with important experience in the state government had backed Ed Koch in the 1982 primary. "Everyone was [with the other guy]," Cuomo said as he was choosing people for his administration. Cuomo knew Del Giudice, but had not been close to him. He did not know Tim Russert or Gerald C. Crotty, whom he appointed to the second-highest position in the Executive Chamber, counsel to the governor, and who later became his secretary. Both had supported Koch. Nor did Cuomo know Michael Finnerty, his budget director, or R. Wayne Diesel, the deputy budget director. The list could be expanded greatly with other Executive Chamber aides and state commissioners that Cuomo took in without prior friendship.

Not only is it not necessary for someone to be a friend of Cuomo's to get an important appointment; it is not even necessary that such a prospective appointee agree with the governor politically. If Cuomo finds a person with the proper management skills to run a particular department, but the person does not have the exact philosophy he would want to see followed in that department, he talks with the person. He asks something like, "Look, this is how I think the department should be run. Can you do it?" If the person says he or she personally disagrees with that approach, but is willing to adopt it and run the department efficiently, Cuomo will make the appointment. "I think he probably sees more ability in people than they see in themselves," Cuomo's friend John Gerity says. "He appreciates what people can accomplish."

A distinction should be made, Del Giudice says, between advice on matters of government and advice on political questions. Staff members have complete access to the governor, and he listens to their advice on issues of government. Cuomo is much less open to political advice. The reason should be apparent to anyone who has read the previous two chapters. Mario Cuomo's experience with political experts has not been of the sort that builds confidence in their judgment. He has reason to think that following the advice of experts contributed to his defeats in 1974 and 1977. In

1982 no one wanted him to run against Koch—no one, that is, except Fabian Palomino, Andrew Cuomo, Bob Sullivan, and a very few others. They proved to be right while the supposed experts were once again wrong.

There is another advantage to be gained by the governor's closeness to his son and to Palomino. Too many politicians surround themselves with "yes men" (and, occasionally, a few "yes women"). Andrew Cuomo and Fabian Palomino do not hesitate to tell Governor Cuomo when they think he is making a mistake. Having people who know the boss well enough to stand up to him around a political leader is invaluable. (Andrew Cuomo left the administration to enter the private practice of law before the governor's first term was over, but his father remains in frequent contact with him.)

Mario Cuomo has a wide reach in terms of talking via telephone with many people from various walks of life across the country whose advice he values. But, as Del Giudice puts it, Cuomo "doesn't have ten thousand 'close personal friends,' like a lot of politicians do."

On the question of excessive loyalty to his friends, Cuomo has demonstrated on a couple of occasions that anyone who is shown to have engaged in corruption will be ousted immediately. It is probably true, though, that Cuomo does not relish ruining the careers of people who work for him, as long as they are honest and hardworking. Rather than fire someone who meets those criteria but is ineffective in his position, Cuomo is likely to transfer the person to a less demanding post. The "loyalty" issue is, in any case, a no-win situation. A politician is almost certain to be castigated either for being too loyal or not loyal enough—and sometimes for being both.

There has been a fair amount of turnover in Cuomo's staff. "In 1984," Del Giudice told me, "we made a decision to get rid of people and make deliberate changes, because some people were not working out. We changed about a dozen people—and he's done the same thing now in '87. Every two years he takes a look at who is doing well and who is not doing well and makes changes. That's a sign of strength, not weakness." A bureaucracy that does not change is one that creates a climate in which mistakes, incompetence, and corruption are likely to germinate. Changing people can help to bring in the fresh air that will prevent such infections. "You just get that recharging of energy, drive, ideas," Del Giudice

320

MARIO CUOMO

says. "Otherwise people become stale. You don't want stale people; they make mistakes."

One reason that some people leave Cuomo's service is that few can keep up with his pace for more than a few years. "You have to take all the vows when you work for him," Bob Sullivan said to me. "Poverty, chastity—chastity because you don't have time for anything else." But most of those—including Del Giudice, Russert, Quinn, and former Press Secretary Martin Steadman—who have left for greener (that is, more lucrative) pastures continue to express nothing but admiration for their former chief. They remain in awe of his intelligence and capacity for work.

A notable exception is William Stern, who skillfully directed the finances of Cuomo's 1982 campaign. "Quite frankly," Stern told me, "my view of Mario's character is quite negative, after a long association with him. My opinion of Mario's character changed after I got to know him well." Stern declined to be specific about what he found wrong with Cuomo's character. He has, however, harshly criticized Cuomo's policies, particularly what Stern sees as massive spending increases. "We're living off an economic boom in the region that we had nothing to do with creating," he contends. Stern also charges that Cuomo has a "dismal" record of "business as usual—big spending [and] taking care of the boys." Not even Stern suggests that Cuomo himself is less than completely honest himself, but he does believe that Albany is filled with politicians who are "in government to make money for themselves," and he insists that Cuomo has "no stomach" for cleaning up the mess.

Since Bill Stern seems to be more negative about Mario Cuomo than anyone else who has worked closely with him, it is worthwhile to explore the reasons for his falling out with the governor. Stern's relationship with Cuomo dates from the 1977 campaign, when he met with candidate Cuomo to decide whether to make a donation to the campaign. When he wrote a check after the meeting, Stern made it for a lesser amount than what he had indicated. Cuomo asked him why, and Stern said, "Because you only answered nine out of my ten questions right."

Stern became the finance chairman of the 1982 campaign, but he had said all along that he did not like or trust politicians, and had no desire for a public position himself. After the election he changed his mind. It appears that Stern expected Cuomo to give him a position of great authority in the administration, as a sort of economic czar. This did not happen. In fact, Stern found himself as head of New York's Urban Development Corporation reporting to Andrew Cuomo, not to the governor, and with Fabian Palomino sent over for a few months to get him started. This seems to have led Stern to feel a sense of betrayal. The governor placed more and more people around Stern, boxing him in. In the opinion of Peter Quinn, the reason for this was that "Cuomo figured this guy's brilliant, but he's a nut."

According to Palomino, Stern concentrated on saving small amounts of money administratively, but he was not moving on major projects. Another difficulty arose when newspapers began to suggest that Lucille Falcone, the UDC's general counsel, had been given the position because she was dating Andrew Cuomo. All concerned insisted that this was not the case, but she resigned in order to end the speculation.

Palomino told me that one of the major problems with Stern was that he did not understand reasonable disagreement. "If you disagreed with Bill, you became his enemy," Palomino says. "He liked everything to be his way." As a result, he fired several top employees. In one such instance an employee made a complaint to the governor's office and asked to have her case reviewed. Cuomo told Palomino to look into it, but Stern refused to give him the woman's file. The governor finally had to tell him to send either the file or his resignation.

Then Stern had a feud with Thomas F. Galvin, the head of the New York Convention Center. Stern accused Galvin of incurring excessive staff expenses, inefficient handling of contractors' bills, and inadequate investigation of possible safety problems at the Convention Center. "Stern went to the newspapers," Cuomo told me, "and said, 'You ought to check Tom Galvin's income tax returns.' And I let him know exactly what I thought of that. I thought it was cheap and mean. I think that hurt him when I told him. I think at that point the relationship started turning around. He's been very unhappy ever since. I can't explain it all."

The governor's siding with Galvin in the dispute completed Stern's sense of betrayal. His thinking probably went something like: *I made this guy governor. He wouldn't have been governor without me* (which is probably true), *and he turned around and stabbed me in the back.* Stern quit—or was fired from, depending upon who tells the story—his post in 1985, and began taking public shots at Cuomo's running of the state government. Beyond the notion that he had somehow been betrayed, Stern seems to have come to the disquieting realization that Cuomo is more "liberal" than he had thought. After he left the administration, Stern told *Time:* "Mario believes in government activism. That means spending rather than cutting."

"I don't have any negative feelings toward him," Cuomo says of Stern. "I don't like what he says about me, but overall I remember how good he was to me and to my family. I remember how hard he worked for me, how honest he was. He kept the books in 1982, and other people had a lot of trouble with campaign contributions that I haven't had, and that's because he kept the books."[5]

While some people have contended that Mario Cuomo's appointments to his staff and to cabinet positions have not been of consistently high quality, the only complaints about his judicial appointments have been partisan in nature. That might not seem unusual. What makes it so is that the partisan complaints come from Democrats upset with their governor's *lack* of partisanship in selecting judges.

Cuomo startled Democrats on his third day in office by appointing Richard D. Simons to a position on the Court of Appeals. Simons was regarded as a distinguished jurist, but he was a Republican. "The party is not relevant" in the selection of judges, Cuomo declared. Editorialists, members of the bar, Republicans, independents, and even some Democrats praised Cuomo for his sensitivity to his responsibility.

But as far as partisan Democrats were concerned, one Republican appointment was quite enough of a genuflection before the altar of evenhanded discretion. A variety of circumstances gave Cuomo the opportunity by the end of his first term to appoint all seven members of New York's highest court. He chose three Democrats, three Republicans, and one judge not registered in either party. This was too much for some Democratic bosses to swallow. Particularly galling to such party leaders was Cuomo's decision to elevate Republican Sol Wachtler to the post of chief judge. Queens Democratic boss Donald Manes was apoplectic. "That's not the way you do things," Manes huffed. "If you're a Democrat, you appoint Democrats!" Partisans such as Manes began to feel about Cuomo's scrupulous appointment practices the way disgruntled Republican spoilsmen did about President Rutherford B. Hayes's filling of offices in the late 1870s: He's "the type of man who, if Pope, would have felt called upon to appoint a few Protestant cardinals."

The selection of judges solely on the basis of ability, without reference to party or even ideology, is a principle about which Mario Cuomo feels very strongly. The Court of Appeals, in particular, must have the best people on it, he maintains, because it is a person's last resort. A statute might be bad, or the police might make a bad arrest, or a lower court might make an error in the law. The Court of Appeals is the last chance in the state to right a wrong. When Cuomo was a practicing attorney, he saw a number of cases decided not on their merits, but on the basis of partisanship. This outraged a young man who had a deep reverence for the law. So did facing people on the bench who clearly did not deserve to be there but had received politically motivated appointments.

But Cuomo's firm belief that judges should be selected only on the basis of merit is grounded on more than his own experience in the courts of those not so chosen. He is convinced that a truly independent judiciary is essential to maintaining the balance of power in the American system of government. The use of ideology or party affiliation as criteria of selection endangers that judicial independence, in Cuomo's view. He told a 1986 convention of the American Bar Association that while the Reagan administration was not the first to seek to appoint judges on an ideological basis, its effort "is a particularly emphatic one. The 1984 Republican convention urged that judicial candidates should give evidence of fealty on key social issues."

His comments, Cuomo said, were aimed "not at individual nominees but at the system as a whole, which is politicized." He contrasted the Reagan approach (which he noted was similar to Franklin Roosevelt's efforts on the other side in the 1930s) with his own judicial appointments in New York. He said that he named judges to the New York Court of Appeals "on the basis of their scholarship and experience, without knowing where they stood on such issues as the death penalty."

"Everyone would agree," Cuomo told the 1986 ABA convention, "that it is patently wrong to commit a judge explicitly to a conclusion before he or she has read the record." But that, in essence, is what the right-wingers in the Reagan coalition seek to do. The Founding Fathers "designed a system that tried to immunize the Court from the changing moods and passions of the people," Cuomo stated. If a prospective judge has a high intellect, integrity, and a good judicial temperament, the governor of New York argued, it does not matter what he thinks "when he's thinking politically." The sort of judges Cuomo wants to appoint would keep their political thoughts separate from their judicial decisions. "Under our system, cases should be decided in the courthouse. They should not be decided in the Oval Office or the Senate chamber," Cuomo remarked.

By practicing what he preaches on judicial selection, Cuomo created an outstanding Court of Appeals in New York. In addition to elevating Wachtler (who had served twelve years as an associate judge before Cuomo named him to head the court) and appointing Simons, Cuomo chose Judith S. Kaye, the first woman ever to sit on New York's highest court in its 140-year history; Fritz W. Alexander II, the first black to serve on more than an interim basis; Stewart F. Hancock, Jr.; Vito J. Titone; and Joseph W. Bellacosa.

"I have sought to shape not just a good court but an excellent one," Cuomo said after making his seventh and final appointment, "a court of strong and intelligent jurists who bring competence and commitment to every case and dispense justice based on reason, logic, and the accumulated experience reflected in the law. We now have an excellent court, a court that will fill the important balancing role in our governmental trinity and that will stand as a strong argument for the merit selection of judges."

One would expect the man who appointed an entire court to praise it, but Cuomo's assessment of the New York State Court of Appeals is echoed—indeed, amplified—by many legal observers. Hank Henry, the executive director of the nonpartisan Committee for Modern Courts, told the *Wall Street Journal* in 1986 that Cuomo's appointments "have uniformly been outstanding." The Cuomo Court, as it might well be called, has become probably the most influential state court in the nation. It has taken the lead among state courts in stepping into the breach left by the United States Supreme Court in the area of individual liberties. The New York Court of Appeals has taken the attitude that the federal Constitution provides the minimum floor of protection of civil liberties, and greater protections may be added by applying the state constitution. In its 1986 decision in *People* v. *P.J. Video,* the court decided in a six-to-one ruling that a local magistrate had violated a section of the state constitution in issuing a warrant for police to seize adult videotapes from a store. The United States

Supreme Court had rejected an argument in the same case based
on the Fourth Amendment of the federal Constitution. In basing
its decision on provisions of the state constitution, the New York
Court of Appeals protected its decision against being overturned
by the United States Supreme Court. It did the same in the spring
of 1987, in the case of *Patchogue-Medford Congress of Teachers* v. *Board
of Education.* The court in that decision used the same section of
the New York constitution, which provides protection against
unreasonable searches and seizures, to invalidate random drug-
testing of public employees.

The "renaissance" of the New York State Court of Appeals
with its Cuomo-appointed judges has been admired by jurists ranging from the liberal Justice William Brennan to the conservative
Justice Antonin Scalia. Few murmurs of dissent—other than those
of some Democratic politicos—can be detected among the praises
being sung for Cuomo's court appointments.[6]

In most respects Mario Cuomo
has been a remarkably open and accessible governor. At the outset
of his administration, he allowed journalist Ken Auletta to sit in
on almost everything that was happening in the Executive Chamber. The resulting two-part, more-than-you-ever-wanted-to-know
New Yorker article provides a wealth of information about Cuomo
and his government as it settled in.

His openness has also been shown in the numerous town
forums he has held around the state. In the early years of his
administration, Cuomo held one such forum a week for stretches
of two months at a time. The forums often lasted for several hours,
with the governor discussing issues and problems with his con-
stituents. Those who have only heard Cuomo deliver formal
speeches—and are deeply impressed with his oratory—often do
not realize that he is even better in an off-the-cuff setting. He is a
masterful performer at such question-and-answer sessions, com-
bining an extraordinary knowledge of a wide range of policy issues
with a charm and wit that win over the vast majority of those in
attendance.

Cuomo does a monthly radio call-in show, broadcast on local
stations throughout the state, on which anyone who can manage
to get a call through can speak directly to the governor and talk
about whatever is on his or her mind. He handles callers with a

blend of seriousness and humor that wins the admiration of all but the most hostile. Cuomo also devotes a good deal of personal attention to the mail he receives, appears regularly on television interview shows, and meets with the press more than any New York governor in memory.

During Cuomo's first few years in office, the press was absolutely in love with him. It was one of the longest and most passionate honeymoons between the press and a politician that has been seen in modern America. Reporters were fascinated by him. The state was in deep trouble, and Cuomo dealt with the budget deficit forthrightly. He had to tell many of those who had backed him in the campaign, such as the Civil Service Employees' Association, that times were tough and he would have to ask for sacrifice even from those who had been so good to him. The Albany media were amazed to see a politician who was willing to tell some of his most important supporters that he would have to lay their people off anyway. They were also wowed by the contrast between Cuomo and Carey. Not only was the new governor much more active and involved than his predecessor had been, but he also seemed to be a "regular guy"—a stable person. Carey had developed the reputation of being a flake.

As Gary Fryer paraphrases the early attitude of the New York press toward Cuomo, it was: "Oh, Christ, I didn't think there was anybody like this around. He's so smart; he's so thoughtful. He's real—he's got depth. What a guy! He's really got charisma." A good deal of this initial reaction was based on the new governor's intellectual prowess, but the emphasis of the early stories was mostly on Cuomo's personality: *Boy, is he nice. Boy, is he smart. Boy, is he exciting. Boy, is he funny. Boy, is he nice to me—he's accessible. I call him on the phone in the mansion on Sunday morning and he talks to me for an hour. I can't get off the phone. The guy is great—he asked me for ideas. He's really interested.*

But there is another side to the coin. As accessible as Cuomo is in many ways, he is not one to go out on the streets and "press the flesh." There are a couple of reasons for this. Part of it is that, since 1984, Cuomo has been, as Fryer puts it, "the Bruce Springsteen of politics." He is too much of a celebrity to be able to take to the streets without being mobbed. But, while true, that explanation does not go very far. Even before he became a superstar, Cuomo didn't like to roam the streets campaigning. The most important reason for his distaste for such activity is that he considers it to be phony. He never completely got over the feeling he had in his early campaigns that shaking hands with strangers was intruding on their privacy. He much prefers debating issues to kissing babies. He is an introspective intellectual, and believes his time is better spent discussing ideas or reading than it is smiling in front of cameras on street corners.

In keeping with the fact that Cuomo has so much substance behind his personality, the reaction of New York reporters to him has changed over his years in the Executive Mansion. They became accustomed to Cuomo's engaging personality and magnificent oratory. As the national media were swept off their feet by Cuomo from 1984 onward, in a duplication of the phenomenon among the New York media in 1983 and 1984, the New York press corps became somewhat jaded in its assessments of Cuomo as a personality. Instead, they began to focus on his substance. They are in most cases just as impressed with the governor as they were at first, but in a different way. They have gone beneath the veneer and gotten to the real object. When they did so, respect began to replace infatuation. *This guy works like a dog; he's one of the smartest people I've ever run into. He's willing to do unpopular things. He stands up for what he believes in. He has unquestioned integrity. He's real. He's not perfect, but he's a hell of a politician and a hell of a leader. He's accomplished a lot.*

Cuomo prefers this more realistic assessment that focuses on the person behind the image. He knows that he is more substantial than most politicians, and it bothers him when people focus on his persona.

The process through which the New York media—and much of the public—went with Cuomo during his first years as governor, Fryer suggests, is much like that of falling in love. At first, it's: *She's so beautiful. What a personality. She's so much fun to be with. She's so charming!* As the relationship evolves, though, it is likely to become: *Well, she's not always so charming. She can be a real pain in the ass at times. So, maybe she's not perfect, but now that I know her so well, I really love her.* The relationship becomes more solid as it becomes less ecstatic.

Fryer's analogy is a good one. Both the New York media and the public in the state have developed a more mature attitude toward Cuomo. But this does not mean that they are any less impressed with him than they were in 1983. He has, in fact, become ever more popular as his time in office progressed. Statewide

opinion surveys conducted by the Marist Institute for Public
Opinion in June of each of Cuomo's first four years in office found
his approval rating among New Yorkers rising from 57.0 percent
in 1983 to 59.0 percent in 1984, 69.6 percent in 1985, 70.6 percent
in 1986, and 77.3 percent in 1987. In January 1988, an almost incredible 85.3 percent of those polled agreed with the statement, "Governor Cuomo is a good leader for New York State." As New
Yorkers' feelings for their governor moved from the passionate to
the rational, more and more of them joined in the admiration.[7]

                                           But what, specifically, did Mario
Cuomo accomplish in his first years as governor? His soaring rhetoric sometimes raises expectations beyond what is reasonable. De-
tractors charge that he talks more than he fights for meaningful
change. In a narrow sense this may be true, since Cuomo does see
inspiration as a major part of his job as governor. And his achievements, though in many cases important, are plainly less dramatic
than the vision he offers in his speeches.

The fact is that Cuomo does not believe that he can bring about
the millennium. He believes in incremental improvements. Government, in Cuomo's view, can and should serve a meliorative
function. If it fulfills its proper role, government can help see to
it that, little by little, people's lives get better. The accomplishments he lists as the most important of his first years as governor
illustrate Cuomo's approach.

When he was lieutenant governor, Cuomo had been one of the
first politicians to begin talking about the impending crisis of
aging and decaying public facilities. He noted these problems in
the late 1970s and warned of their seriousness well before "infrastructure" became a household word. (Actually one doubts that
even today there are many households in which it is commonly
heard.) One of Cuomo's first objectives as governor was to persuade the public of the urgency of rebuilding the state's roads and
bridges. Political experts tried to convince him that he could not
get the people to approve a large bond issue for such a mundane
purpose. Typically, Cuomo disagreed, trusting his own instincts
and trusting in his own persuasive abilities.

Cuomo dubbed his proposal the "Rebuild New York" bond
issue. The voters in 1983 were asked to approve a $1.25 billion
bond issue to make improvements and repairs in already existing

structures. The results would not be readily visible. Most observers said that Cuomo had little chance of winning. He pushed forward anyway, staking his political reputation on the outcome of the vote. Andrew Cuomo and Tim Russert ran a campaign, using free publicity, to convince the voters of the desperate need for infrastructure repairs. The governor himself spoke on the issue whenever possible, and they won.

An insignificant accomplishment? Well, repairs have no dramatic impact, but the tragic collapse of a bridge on the New York State Thruway in the spring of 1987 reminded people of the possible consequences of not repairing and modernizing public facilities. Few people are impressed every time they cross a bridge by the fact that it does not collapse. There is no way to measure how many lives are saved by performing needed maintenance and rebuilding. This is the sort of achievement that Cuomo likes. It does good without being flashy. It points up one of the most important differences between Cuomo and many another politician. He is willing to expend political capital to achieve improvements, even if few voters will notice them and there seems to be little political gain to be had by pushing them. Cuomo is like the building contractor who puts extra materials into the foundation and frame of a house and is told by others that this is foolish, because prospective home buyers will not be able to see the results of such expenditures. "Put your money where people can see the results," such builders advise. Most politicians follow a corresponding approach, but Cuomo is willing to spend where there is need, regardless of how visible the results will be.

Another way in which Mario Cuomo differs from most politicians is that he insists on keeping his campaign promises. (This is another similarity between Cuomo and Jimmy Carter, who made a serious effort as president to live up to his campaign pledges.) He told his staff late in January 1983 that he could not believe that "the *Times* and then the *News* said right out that what Cuomo said in the past doesn't count. They're campaign promises." Cuomo was aghast at the casual notion that there must be a large difference between campaign rhetoric and government policy. He said that it was essential for his credibility and the credibility of government "to prove consistency." Fabian Palomino says that to Cuomo "it is the most important thing in the world that he does what he said he was going to do."

Most of Cuomo's campaign promises were worth keeping, but

he insisted on keeping even those that were mistakes. There was, for instance, an abandoned state mental hospital on Long Island that the Carey administration had decided was an ideal location for a prison. Millions were spent remodeling the facility for prisoners. The prisoners were moved in, despite some vocal protests from a local civic group. When Cuomo spoke before the group during his 1982 campaign, a woman got up to say that there should not be a prison in the area. Cuomo said that he agreed with her and if he was elected he would empty it out and there would be no more prison there. He should not have made such a statement, and there is little doubt that if he had it to do over again he would not say it. But he had made a commitment and he kept it. In the midst of his own rapid expansion of prison facilities, Cuomo closed this perfectly good prison on the Nassau-Suffolk border. Stupid? Sure. Wasteful? Of course. But for someone intent on restoring faith in the integrity of government, keeping promises is more important than other considerations.

If Cuomo's campaign statements occasionally go awry, his instincts are much more often correct. He made another pledge before a Long Island civic association during the 1982 campaign. Cuomo said that if he was elected he would not allow the opening of the Shoreham nuclear plant owned by the Long Island Lighting Company (LILCO). At the time, that was an unpopular position to take. In 1982 a substantial majority of Long Island residents favored the nuclear facility, which they saw as a wonderful way of reducing their electric bills. But public opinion on this issue has swung dramatically. Cuomo took the position that a nuclear power plant on Long Island constitutes an unacceptable danger to public safety because there is no way that the huge population of the island could be quickly evacuated. Del Giudice urged Cuomo to retreat from his unpopular position. "Trust me," the governor responded. "Opinion's going to turn on this. Their case is not there." He was right. Even before the 1986 disaster at the Soviet nuclear plant at Chernobyl, most Long Islanders had come to agree with their governor. *After* Chernobyl, normally proutility Republicans joined in the fight against Shoreham. Cuomo proceeded to push for legislation to make LILCO a public utility, a position that is also endorsed by most residents of the region the utility serves.

Principle is what is at stake in keeping campaign promises. It is similarly at the heart of the crime issue. Mario Cuomo has built a strong record in fighting crime. As I noted earlier, his own family has fallen victim to criminal activities several times. Despite having felt the effects of crime very close to him, Mario Cuomo's stand against capital punishment has remained steadfast, and he knows that many people reduce a politician's stance on crime to the simplistic question of whether he is for against the electric chair. "Crime control—I'm in trouble, because I'm against the death penalty; I gave clemency," Cuomo said to me early in 1986. "At least in the public perception I'm in big trouble. The truth is I have a very strong criminal justice record, but I'll never be able to convince anybody." But he keeps trying. When he spoke to a police union convention in Albany early in 1986, for instance, he departed from his text to say: "I know what people say. 'This mushy-headed liberal Cuomo, who read a book once.' These macho guys who want to burn people, fry them. I know how you feel." He told the police officers that he favors life imprisonment without parole as an alternative to the death penalty. "I'd say, 'That's it, Charlie, you're going to be by yourself for a hundred years." This little sermon elicited an ovation from the congregation of enforcers of the law.

One of the major accomplishments of Mario Cuomo's first term as governor was an unprecedented program of prison construction. He instigated the building of more prison cells than anyone else in the history of New York. In his first four years in office, he expanded the capacity of the state prison system by 27 percent. When Cuomo came into office, there were about twenty-nine thousand inmates in New York prisons; by 1987 he had added ten thousand more. And in the first budget he submitted for his second term, in 1987, Cuomo proposed the building of two more new prisons with facilities for fourteen hundred more inmates.

Some who place themselves on the left think that an emphasis on prison construction disqualifies a person from being labeled a liberal. The notion that it is incongruous for a liberal to want to put criminals in prison is an unfortunate legacy of the warping of the meaning of *liberal* in the late sixties and early seventies. Being liberal *does* entail having a respect for civil liberties and the constitutional protections of the rights of the accused; it should *not* imply an abandonment of values, utter permissiveness, or an unlocking of the cells of those who pose a clear danger to society. On the issue of criminal justice, as on so many other points, Mario

Cuomo is a liberal who defies recent stereotypes. He is a common-sense liberal.

Despite his initial difficulty in winning support from black and Hispanic voters in 1977, Cuomo as governor has become increasingly popular in New York's minority communities. Significantly, his popularity seems to be greater among the people than among black and Puerto Rican political leaders. Some of the latter think that Cuomo as governor has not done enough for them personally, even though they gave him strong early support against Koch in 1982.

Cuomo's personal experience with ethnic prejudice gives him a genuine bond with minority populations. And growing up in a changing neighborhood meant that Cuomo frequently played basketball with blacks. This, too, gave him a different prospective from that of an upper-middle-class youngster growing up in a lily-white suburb. It is clear to all that he has no tolerance for intolerance. He does not "pander" to blacks, but condemns racism in any form. When black racist and Muslim minister Louis Farrakhan came to New York for a 1985 rally at Madison Square Garden, Cuomo denounced him as an advocate of "ugly and divisive and wrong and hateful" ideas.

The governor did get himself into a difficult situation during his 1986 reelection campaign when he said that Puerto Ricans came to New York with no skills and some of them preferred welfare to low-paying jobs. Cuomo said that his remarks had been taken out of context. His point, he said, was that many people—including his own parents—had come to this country without money or skills, and what was needed was more jobs paying decent wages.

One reason for Cuomo's generally good relationship with the state's Hispanic population was evident on a trip he made to a devastated area of the Bronx. One resident got up to a microphone and tried to tell Cuomo about his problems, but stumbled repeatedly because he knew so little English. He finally said something to the effect of, "Governor, how I would love to tell you this in Spanish, so you would understand me. I know you don't understand my English."

"Go ahead, say it in Spanish," Cuomo said, "but say it slowly—*despacio.*"

The man, who had appeared to be ignorant when he was speaking in English, began to relate his troubles in eloquent Spanish.

The governor's Spanish response was not quite so eloquent, but it was clear to the Hispanic crowd that he truly understood what the man had said to him in Spanish.

Following the late 1986 attack by white youths on blacks at Howard Beach, Queens, Governor Cuomo met with a group of black leaders who demanded that a special prosecutor be appointed. The Queens district attorney had not been able to proceed with the case because victims of the attack refused to cooperate with his office. Cuomo met with the black leaders for six hours. Those present said it was another demonstration of his mastery of mediation skills. "I wish you could have seen it," Basil Paterson said. "He doesn't deal with you as governor. When you're dealing with him, arguing with him, he is Mario Cuomo more than he is governor. He is dealing with you on a one-on-one basis, personally. I've never seen that in any other high government official. . . . It's something to see. And it worked."

Saying that it was the only way to "see that justice was done," Cuomo appointed a special prosecutor, Charles J. Hynes, to handle the Howard Beach case. He also told the black leaders that he would draft a state civil rights law that would make it a specific crime in New York to deny anyone's civil rights. Cuomo indicated that he thought the real need was to address the underlying causes of racial tension, which he identified as "conditions of deprivation—economic deprivation, basically. In the long run, the best thing you can do to deal with these tensions is to strengthen our education system, strengthen our economy, provide more people with a chance to work." He went on to hint that a climate in which such actions would be accepted might be returning: "You said it in the 60's and it was popular. You said it in the 70's and early 80's and they dismissed it as mushy-headed liberals." But he was saying it in the second half of the eighties.

As governor, Cuomo continued to advocate the same approaches to racial problems as he had in his first years in politics. In the spring of 1987, he asked businessmen to launch a major training program for young people in minority groups. As he had so often in the past, Cuomo emphasized his belief that what was right was also in the self-interest of the businessmen. He said he hoped that they would help out of "love," but if that did not move them to act, self-interest ought to.

"You want to talk about racism in terms that are going to get to your pocketbook?" Cuomo asked those in attendance at the 1987 breakfast of the Association for a Better New York. "The majority of the work force in this country in the 21st century is going to be minority. Now one out of two of them is being raised in poverty. What kind of work force are you going to have? Who are going to be your sophisticated people who will out-think the Japanese and the West Germans? How are you going to make it without them?"

The governor listed a number of programs that his government had started to help members of minority groups to get ahead, but he said that a large opening was available for corporations to lend a hand.[8]

In the area of job growth, Mario Cuomo's years at the helm of New York have been very good ones. Employment in the state increased by nine hundred thousand jobs in his first four years in office. He readily admits that the national economy played an important part in aiding the success of New York recovery. "Anyone who denies that is just kidding," Cuomo said to me. But he added: "I like to think we cooperated with our good fortune and did our part well. There would not have been this kind of luxury where we could spend our budget and do all those things if it had not been for a good national economy."

The booming economy in New York, whatever the mix of its causation, enabled Cuomo to take some of the steps that did the most to raise his popularity to dazzling levels. He took office at the bottom of a severe national recession and rode the ensuing recovery for the next several years. Over a three-year period, he joined with the legislature to cut state taxes by $3.2 billion. By itself, that would have gone a long way toward enhancing his popularity. But the economic boom enabled Cuomo to increase spending substantially while concurrently cutting taxes. Despite the beginning of a gradual 1 percent lowering of the top state income tax rate from 10 to 9 percent, revenue from that tax leapt from $8.2 billion to $12.6 billion in the first four years of Cuomo's administration. State spending from the general fund (excluding federal aid and a few categories of revenue designated for specific uses) grew by more than 40 percent during Cuomo's first term. This was considerably more than twice the rate of inflation. At the same time, Cuomo was able to move from the budget he inherited, with its projected $1.8 billion deficit, not only to a budget technically balanced in cash terms, which is legally required in New York, but to annual state budgets that are in fact balanced in terms of generally accepted accounting principles. This was a significant departure from past practices in New York, where budgets had long been seriously unbalanced in GAAP terms. He even began to reduce the state's accumulated debt, from 10.2 percent to 8.4 percent of state personal income.

It is axiomatic that a majority of people in almost any situation will favor government spending but oppose the taxes needed to pay for it. That being the case, the most popular political position is, quite obviously, to increase spending and to cut taxes. Prior to the presidency of Ronald Reagan, most Republicans advocated reducing both taxes and spending, while many Democrats favored increasing both. Whether consciously or otherwise, Reagan adopted the most popular approach. Like previous Republicans, he castigated the "tax and tax, spend and spend" policy of the Democrats. But instead of replacing it with the traditional Republican alternative, Reagan merely cut taxes without any reduction in overall spending. His method can accurately be described as "spend and spend, borrow and borrow." This approach works well with the electorate—at least for a while—because it allows current voters to enjoy the benefits of government spending without the sacrifices needed to pay for them. "Fly Now—Pay Later" would be a fitting slogan for the Reagan program. Although Reagan poses as a conservative, he is only a *social* conservative. In *fiscal* terms, he is in fact an extreme, reckless liberal.

The relative prosperity in New York during his administration has made it possible for Mario Cuomo to adopt a different and much more responsible—but equally popular—approach. Walter Olson of the Manhattan Institute has called Cuomo's program "pay-as-you-go liberalism" (fiscal conservatism and social liberalism). Cuomo himself has called his approach "the New York idea," by which he means being compassionate and fiscally responsible. It is a tough combination to challenge. As long as an economy is growing at a rate sufficient to pay for increased spending without raising tax rates (and, perhaps, even with *reducing* them), pay-as-you-go liberalism is the way to go, in terms of both morality and politics.

Should Cuomo become president, though, he would inherit a vastly different fiscal situation in Washington from what he found in Albany. The enormous Reagan deficits place severe constraints on what presidents in the near future will be able to accomplish in the way of social programs. Reagan's fiscal irresponsibility makes it most difficult for his successors to be socially responsible. That, many observers believe, was a major goal of the Reagan policies from the start.

Cuomo's fiscal policies have sought to address the complexity of the issues involved in budget-making. He said from the outset of his administration in 1983 that his method would be "to tax selectively and to cut selectively, without the blanket actions that substitute speed and simplicity for parity and equity." This was prior to the advent of Gramm-Rudmanism and its meat-cleaver approach. Cuomo believes that chief executives and legislators ought to make decisions and set priorities—that they should do the job they were elected to do, not save themselves from making choices by instituting mindless mechanisms.

Opponents insist that for all his talk about fiscal responsibility Cuomo is just another big-spending Democrat. "We're dealing with a guy who's a spender," says State Senate Majority Leader Warren M. Anderson, a Binghamton Republican.

He is right, up to a point. Part of the rapid increase in New York spending under Cuomo was caused by problems that he inherited, including the $1.8 billion deficit and lavish labor contracts providing state workers with a 30 percent pay hike over three years. But much of the spending has been the result of decisions over which the governor had some control. They reflect the priorities he set for the state. The operating budget (exclusive of capital expenditures) of the Department of Correctional Services rose by 88.4 percent during Cuomo's first term. Cuomo and the legislature decided to provide substantially more aid for localities and schools, in part to offset cuts in federal aid. The state began picking up a larger share of Medicaid costs, which have soared.

The governor wanted to make a stronger effort in education. "Providing a quality education for all, unimpeded by economic and social barriers, is a basic responsibility of government," Cuomo proclaimed while campaigning in 1982. Few would question his sincerity in making such statements, but many educators and students were disappointed in Cuomo's early record on education, particularly when it came to providing financial support. Everette D. Joseph, president of the State University of New York Student Association, said of Cuomo in 1986: "His first budget was like a hurricane, wiping us all out, so all of the budgets since then, even if they've seemed good, are really just less of a storm than the first one."

The fact is that on spending for education at all levels, Cuomo has usually recommended less than has the legislature, and the increases to which the governor points have sometimes been less reflective of his desires than those of leading legislators in both parties. (If this somewhat diminishes Cuomo's reputation as a champion of education, it also blunts Senator Anderson's criticism of Cuomo as a spender.) In 1986, for instance, the governor proposed a $300 million increase in aid to local schools, but wound up agreeing, at the legislature's insistence, to boost aid by twice that figure.

None of this is to say that Cuomo has not been supportive of education. He launched Centers for Advanced Technology at seven universities and provided each with annual funding of $1 million. He advocated more than $100 million in increases in the state's Tuition Assistance Program and pushed a new merit scholarship program to keep New York's best students in the state. Overall, education spending in New York increased by $3 billion in Cuomo's first four years. By the end of that term, the state was paying 44 percent of school costs, up from 39 percent when Cuomo took office. He made available $95 million to raise teachers' salaries above negotiated increases. And he started programs aimed at decreasing dropout rates and maintaining small class sizes.

But Cuomo approaches spending on education in the same way he does everything else. His pay-as-you-go liberalism is a liberalism designed for an age of limits. Whenever anyone tells him of a need for the government to do something, Cuomo responds, "That's great. What can I cut from somewhere else?" People are not accustomed to such a response from a politician, especially if that politician is supposed to be a liberal. Someone will come up to the governor at a forum and say: "Oh, my daughter—it's too bad—she's in a state institution and it's awful. They only change the sheets twice a day. Can't you do something—can't you have them change the sheets at least three times a day?"

"Great," Cuomo responds. "I'll have them changed three times a day. Now what are you going to give me so that I can pay for it? Do you want to wait longer in line at the Motor Vehicles office to get your license renewed? Do we stop paving the road in front of your house? Do you mind if we plow the snow less often?"

"Well, no, I don't want you to cut any of those things."

MARIO CUOMO

"Well, then, I don't understand," Cuomo says to such seekers of increased assistance. "Where do I get what I need to do what you want?"

Cuomo's idea is simply that, given limited resources, choices must be made. We cannot afford to do everything we would like to do. You must "give to get," he says.

Press Secretary Gary Fryer says that Cuomo's insistence on pointing out the need for trade-offs "really pisses people off, because they can't figure out a way around it. I mean, the way it's supposed to be with a politician is you say 'Give,' and he says, 'Okay.' But if you say 'Give' and he says, 'Fine, now you give me something,' that doesn't compute. You know, 'You're not supposed to do that. You're the government. You're supposed to figure it out.' But that's the way he is."

The realization that Cuomo will not simply agree to anything that seems worthwhile in the way of government spending comes as a shock to some liberals. According to Fryer, they will suddenly say, "Jesus Christ, this guy isn't a liberal!" And they're right if they are talking about a "knee-jerk" liberal. It is plain that political taxonomists should not number Mario Cuomo among that endangered species. The genus is correct, though. His strong social conscience justifies placing Cuomo among the liberals. But he is a pragmatic liberal, in the tradition of Franklin D. Roosevelt. Certainly he believes in doing what we *ought* to do, but only within the reasonable limits of what we *can* do.

Cuomo's basic philosophy of government is evident in a rule he gives to his cabinet members: "It's not what your constituency *wants*, or what you as a commissioner or director want; it's what your constituency *needs* that must determine what we try to do."[9]

Mario Cuomo's commonsense liberalism is based upon his belief in the necessity of cooperation. "What I wanted to do mostly," he told me, "was to get the people thinking of themselves as a family—get them to see that synergism was the necessary characteristic of a government that would succeed, given all the diversity and disparate elements that we have in this society—the idea of swapping and sharing, of mutuality, that's the one idea I pushed hard."

Family. Synergism. Swapping. Sharing. Mutuality. These are the terms of a true liberalism, but they imply a willingness to give

as well as to get. Compromise and conciliation are the essence of
Cuomo's approach to government. From the beginning of his administration, he emphasized the idea of maximizing cooperation.
When he was asked at his first postelection press conference how
he would deal with Mayor Koch, Cuomo recited a poem that sums
up his belief in the way government should operate, Edwin Mark-
ham's "Outwitted":

> He drew a circle that shut me out,
> Heretic, rebel, a thing to flout.
> But love and I had the wit to win:
> We drew a circle that took him in.

Cuomo tried to make the philosophy expressed in this poem the
basis of his dealings with the legislature. In 1984 he restored a
practice started by Governor Alfred E. Smith but then abandoned:
holding informal cocktail parties at the Executive Mansion for
legislators of both parties. The legislators appreciated this gesture,
for Cuomo seemed to be treating them with respect, which most
of them felt had not been the case with Hugh Carey.

"I've never been invited here except for a ceremonial occasion,"
five-term Democratic Assemblyman William Hoyt said. Cuomo
made no speeches at these affairs, concentrating instead on listening to what legislators had to say. "It builds a reservoir of good-
will," Speaker Fink told Ken Auletta. "Look, the governor is a
very simpatico guy. Very earthy."

"This is my fourteenth term," Republican State Senator John
Marchi of Staten Island noted in 1983, "but this was the first time
I'd ever received a call from the governor saying he was available
and would be in touch with me."

Through his first term, Cuomo had an unusually good relationship with the legislature. He went out of his way to give credit to
the legislators for important accomplishments, even those that he
had initiated himself. The idea of the "family of New York" carried with it a sharing not only of benefits and burdens, but also of
the credit for what was achieved. In keeping with his personal
history as a conciliator, Cuomo generally prefers to govern by
mediation rather than confrontation. Dealing throughout his governorship with a Republican majority in the Senate and a Democratic majority in the Assembly, Cuomo "puts himself in a position
where he's trying to get two parties to agree," notes Union College
political scientist James Underwood, a student of Cuomo's prac-

tices as governor. "He has a knack for finding a common ground between disagreeing parties."

"More often than not," Cuomo said to me, "you have to work out compromises. You have to be able to work together with your own party, certainly, and with the other party as well. I work very hard at that, and I will continue to." But there are exceptions to his conciliatory method. "He believes that reasonable compromise is the way to get things done," Fabian Palomino says of his friend. "But there are times when you don't compromise. You just don't always do it to get something done and look good. If it's not the right thing to do, you don't do it." "There are times when you have to draw the line, and I obviously have," Cuomo says. A clear example is his annual veto of the capital-punishment bill. The number of times the governor threw the gauntlet down before the legislature increased early in his second term, as we shall see in the next chapter.

There was, however, one other important issue on which Cuomo fought hard against a majority in the legislature in his first term. The governor found himself at odds with the legislature over his proposal to raise the legal drinking age to twenty-one. He felt very strongly about the issue. It seemed reasonable, rational, and lifesaving. He showed a willingness to take on a special interest for the public good. The legislators, though, saw it as a chance to show their power. Here was something on which they could show their independence from the governor. When he lost on the issue in 1984, Cuomo did not denounce the legislature. They came for a fight when he addressed them, but the governor caught both legislators and media off guard by saying he knew when he was beaten. He said the defeat meant that he had not worked hard enough. If he had, Cuomo said, he might have won the first time, but he would go back and work harder to convince both the legislature and the public. It was just the right tack to take. In 1985 a strong campaign with the public raised consciousness on the issue and put sufficient pressure on the legislature to get the bill passed.

The governor also pushed through the first mandatory seat-belt law in the United States. The combination of this measure with the twenty-one-year-old purchase age and raising the number of state police to the highest in the state's history produced the lowest highway mortality rate in New York in four decades.[10]

* * *

During Mario Cuomo's first few years as governor, his confidence in his ability to do the job and do it very well grew week by week. It was not so much any particular accomplishment, although the successful handling of the Ossining crisis before he had been in office two weeks was obviously a great confidence builder. Rather, his administration unfolded in a way that fit with his incrementalist view of government. "This is a process I think you do by accretion," he said after the 1985 legislative session, "pick up a little piece here, a little piece there, and you have to keep working at it. . . . It took five years to get a Medicaid pickup. It took nine years to get them to vote on life imprisonment without parole. . . . It took me two years to get the 21 year old purchase age. Look at the time it took to get this tax cut, the best tax cut in the history of the state. It took me a long time. So, you don't get everything the first shot."

Cuomo's accomplishments as he began to move beyond New York to the national stage were both tangible and intangible. In the latter area there is simply the fact that, despite a flood of very serious new problems that have arisen during his time in office—AIDS, crack, and the rapid growth of the homeless population, to name a few—he has presided over a very good era in the state's history. He has made New Yorkers proud. They feel good about their governor and what he has accomplished. All the national attention he gets gives them vicarious pleasure. It's very much like New Yorkers identifying with the Mets or Giants in their championship years: "That's *my* team" is similar to "He's *my* guy; he's *my* governor!"

Cuomo also restored stability to a state that had come to expect volatility in its government. Hugh Carey had been, well, a bit strange. He had a good record as governor, but he did things like miscoloring his hair so that it came out orange and allegedly having the state seize land because buildings on it were blocking his view of the ocean. No matter how good Carey was in a technical sense as governor, New York residents had the understandable feeling that things were somehow amiss.[11]

Mario Cuomo was refreshing in many ways. He was serious, friendly, competent, honest, inspiring, and able to get things done. He cut taxes, increased services, and balanced the budget at the same time. And in 1984 he rose in the estimation of many to the stature of a national leader second only to the president of the United States.

11

LEADER

ALTHOUGH Mario Cuomo's
first inaugural address in 1983 and his early accomplishments as
governor had brought his considerable talents to the attention of
a substantial number of political insiders around the country prior
to the summer of 1984, the public at large had its first introduction
to him on the evening of July 16, 1984, when New York's governor
delivered the keynote address at the Democratic National Convention in San Francisco. Many observers ranked the speech with
such landmarks of modern American political oratory as Franklin
D. Roosevelt's second inaugural and John F. Kennedy's inaugural.
Cuomo's speech instantly transformed him into a major national
leader and likely presidential candidate. No address had done so
much to advance the career of an American politician since William Jennings Bryan's "Cross of Gold" speech at the 1896 Democratic convention.

Although "the Speech" did so much to propel Cuomo into the
national limelight, he repeatedly resisted requests that he deliver
it. There was a long tradition of keynote addresses having an effect
on the careers of their deliverers opposite that which the 1984
address wound up having on Cuomo's. Several people had destroyed their political futures by giving less than stirring keynote
speeches. In 1976 John Glenn had lost the vice presidential nomination by delivering what was basically a good speech, but doing
so poorly.

On June 14, Charles Manatt, chairman of the Democratic National Party, called Cuomo to say that Fritz Mondale's campaign
committee had decided that the New York governor should be the
keynoter. Cuomo said he thought Ted Kennedy should be asked
to give the speech. The next day—Cuomo's fifty-second birthday—

Mondale called three times. Cuomo spoke with him about 6 P.M. and Mondale said that he did not want Kennedy to be the key-noter, he wanted Cuomo.

"It's very important to me," Mondale told Cuomo. "I want you to do it."

"I couldn't stand having him ask so insistently—not for this," Cuomo said, "not for me to give a lousy speech. I don't know why it is so important to him, but it appears to be."

Cuomo tried to persuade Mondale that he could get Kennedy's endorsement in exchange for the keynote spot, and that would be worth much more than having Cuomo give the speech while Kennedy remained neutral or perhaps even "quietly hostile." "Mondale," Cuomo says, "showed a surprising disregard, almost contempt [for the political considerations of getting Kennedy's support before the convention]. I kind of liked it in a man who had been accused of being too conciliatory."

Michael Del Giudice urged Cuomo to consider accepting the offer. There would be a television audience, he anticipated, of 30 million people. He thought it was a marvelous opportunity for Cuomo to tell this huge audience what he thought was right. If it worked, it might make a big difference in the Democratic cam-paign. If the speech did not go over well, little would be lost, because people don't vote against a presidential candidate on the basis of a poor keynote address.

Del Giudice was right. *Mondale* stood to lose little if Cuomo gave the keynote speech and it turned out to be a dud. *Cuomo,* on the other hand, would be risking a great deal. Risk, though, is usually the traveling companion of opportunity. It was a chance that Cuomo remained willing to pass up.

Tim Russert agreed with Del Giudice that it was too great an opportunity to be missed, but Cuomo remained reluctant. His reluctance should have grown when Russert put together a video-tape of several previous keynote addresses. They all contained shots of the crowd, with people yawning and scratching. It was enough to give almost anyone pause. Not Russert. "I had every confidence that that would not be the case this time. I don't know why, but I just felt it very deeply," Russert told me. "To tell the truth, I don't know why—how I knew what he could do in terms of that platform, how he would compensate and get the attention of that crowd. I knew he'd work out something."

If the past record of disaster in keynote speeches failed to discourage Russert, it seems actually to have *en*couraged Cuomo. Many people told him not to do it. David Burke of ABC was one of those who told the governor it would be a big mistake. Anyone who understood Cuomo's psyche would expect that telling him how much the odds were against success would be the surest way to convince him to do it. It was a challenge; a new chance to be the underdog; a situation that would demand great effort—hard work. How could Mario Cuomo resist?

Ted Kennedy still wanted to be the keynoter and, Cuomo said, was "unhappy over Mondale's refusal to give it to him." Kennedy and his staff argued that the keynoter should be someone who was neutral in the contest among Mondale, Hart, and Jackson, and that Cuomo would be seen as a Mondale man. "I agree with them," Cuomo wrote in his diary, "although the Kennedy people don't believe me and Manatt doesn't believe anybody."

Cuomo indicated to the Mondale people that if they wanted him to do it, they must make it clear to Kennedy that it was Mondale who did not want Kennedy and that Cuomo had in fact pushed for Kennedy to be given the task.

Senator Kennedy called Cuomo on the evening of June 20. "The senator was circumspect and a bit disjointed," Cuomo says. "He started a bit tentatively, so I took the conversation away from him." Cuomo told Kennedy that he had declined Mondale's invitation to give the keynote address and tried to talk the candidate into asking Kennedy to do it.

Kennedy said his people had spoken to Mondale's "surrogates," but Mondale himself had not gotten back to the senator. The surrogates told Kennedy's staff that Mondale wanted Cuomo. "I am calling, Mario, to say I think you should say yes," the Massachusetts senator said. "I can't think of anyone better. You would be great. I think there's a role for me. All I want to do is unify the party. Lord knows, God knows, all I want is to be helpful. . . . I know you have been good to me. I have gotten the word that you have been loyal and kind, and if they get back to you, you ought to say yes. I will do whatever they want me to do. I'm afraid that they just don't think I'm for them."

By the end of his conversation with Kennedy, Cuomo was convinced that he should do the keynote. "If I walk away from them," he said, "it looks like I'm reading the polls."

An hour after his conversation with Kennedy, Cuomo received a call from both Mondale and Manatt. Cuomo then realized that

Kennedy's call had been part of a plan. "It was all constructed," he wrote in his diary. "It doesn't happen spontaneously. They were both on the line and were formal. They tried very hard to sound warm, sincere, and endearing, and none of it worked." (Cuomo burst out laughing when he read this to me from his unedited diary.) Mondale again offered the keynoter position to Cuomo, and he accepted, although he told Mondale that he still thought he was making a mistake in choosing him for the job.

Cuomo drafted the speech on Saturday, July 7. In some respects it was a typical Saturday in the summer for him. Maria and Christopher and some friends were enjoying the splendid facilities at the Executive Mansion. From the time he had entered the place, the ascetic Cuomo had been taken aback by the splendor of the house and grounds. "The Mansion is an extraordinary place," he wrote in his diary on the second day of his gubernatorial tenure. "It will take me some time to get used to it: 40 rooms, 6½ acres, 100 years of history. The Governor's suite is lavish. It opens onto an enormous bedroom area with a huge double bed looming up directly in view of the door as though it were designed to boast of the role that rest plays in the Governor's life. This bedroom area has a large fireplace, sofas facing each other in front of it, a breakfast nook and enough room by itself to serve as a barracks."

Even while Cuomo was sternly disapproving of the luxury and the decadence to which it seemed to testify, one can detect a small note of pride in the fact that this son of an immigrant grocer had risen to such surroundings.

"The *pièce de résistance*," Cuomo continued in his initial survey of his new manor house, "is the bathroom. It has to be seen to be believed. It is immense. One side of it—some 20 feet long—contains a full-length dressing table with mirrored walls, two sinks and special 'make-up' mirrors circumscribed by rows of light bulbs like in an old-fashioned actor's dressing room. . . .

"There's a tub like few I have ever seen. It was built into a platform about three feet high. There are three wooden steps that are ascended in order to reach the tub. The faucet is simulated gold, like the shower handles. It is located on the far side of the tub, away from the steps." He goes on to explain that there is no way to turn on the water without sliding into the tub first "and thereby risking scalding or freezing." Two entire walls adjacent to the tub are covered with mirrors. "That's so that you can see yourself either freezing or burning to death."

The dressing area, Cuomo relates, has a room in which to store clothing that has enough space for the gear of an entire basketball team. "In order that I should not be humiliated, I have had to separate my jackets and pants so as to occupy as much space as possible. There's a series of cubicles for storing accessories, underwear, shirts, etc.

"Here, to get decent coverage, I have placed one shirt—and in some cases a pair of socks—in each cubicle."

Cuomo's amazement that anyone actually lives like this—or would *want* to—is apparent. He saw the Executive Mansion as a treasure belonging to the people of New York. For the first time in its history, the mansion has been opened by Matilda Cuomo for public tours on one day each week.

In his nineteenth month in office, Mario Cuomo was more accustomed to the surroundings at his official residence, but as he sat down to work on what, at least up until that time, would be the most important speech of his life, he once again mused about the facilities. "It really is like a resort here in the summer," he wrote. "I don't know what else one could ask for—putting green, tennis courts, pool, recreation room, basketball court, gardens for strolling."

It was nice to know that it was there, and that the family got some use out of it. But to the Dedicated Worker, the magnificent facilities were of little consequence. His pleasures were far more spartan: "For myself, none of it counts for much. I spent the day indoors, in my shorts, without a shave. That by itself is half a vacation." Perhaps Cuomo takes more vacations than people give him credit for. They just don't define vacations in quite the same way he does.

As Cuomo sat in his shorts with his whiskers growing that Saturday, he spent seven or eight hours working on the draft of the keynote speech. But that was not the reason he spent so much of Saturday working. "If I hadn't the keynote to do," he said truthfully, "I would have spent the day on some other kind of work." He knows himself.

The governor read his draft to speechwriter Peter Quinn, who thought it was "even better than good." But the author was not satisfied. "I think it is too long, not punchy enough, doesn't focus enough on the future," he wrote that evening. Cuomo continued to tinker with the speech over the next several days. He had intended to get plenty of rest before the day of the address, but he wound up making major revisions in the speech on Friday night, July 13, just three days before he was to deliver it. Several members of his inner circle gave him a flat response to a reading of the speech, and the governor decided to rework it once more.

"I worked so much on the speech in the last week that now the whole thing is predictable and dull to me," he wrote on the thirteenth. "I can no longer judge its potential effectiveness. It's almost certain, however, that I won't be able to reach the expectations that have been created. Over and over, I hear and read about what a dynamite speech is expected. I'm afraid I'm going to pay a big price for the inaugural success. Nevertheless the uncertainty about how it will go, the curiosity and the challenge, create a special kind of excitement that's not altogether unappealing."

There is, in fact, no greater excitement for Mario Cuomo than to face a stiff challenge, the outcome of which is in much doubt. Such a situation is infinitely preferable to one in which he is expected to succeed, as he was in his 1986 reelection campaign and as he would have been had he entered the 1988 presidential contest at the beginning of 1987.

Those who expected Cuomo's keynote address to the Democratic delegates in San Francisco and a national television audience to be dynamite were mistaken. The explosive force of the speech was more akin to that of nuclear fisson than dynamite.

In order to rivet the attention of the audience in the convention hall and to avoid television shots of people yawning, the Cuomo forces decided that instead of having someone introduce the governor they would use a six-minute movie about his growing up in New York. The houselights were off as the film ended and a spotlight focused on Cuomo as he walked out. Nary a nodding head could be seen. From this point Cuomo had about two minutes in which to captivate the crowd. If he did not, he was likely to go the way of John Glenn.

Cuomo began by noting that ten days earlier President Reagan had said that he didn't understand why some Americans were fearful or unhappy. The president had said: "Why, this country is a shining city on a hill." Cuomo used this assertion as a springboard to attack the Reaganites for not seeing the parts of the nation beneath that hilltop, and to state the differences between Democratic and Republican policies in the most moving terms.

"There is despair, Mr. President, in faces you never see, in the places you never visit in your shining city," the governor of New York declared.

"In fact, Mr. President, this nation is more a 'Tale of Two Cities' than it is a 'Shining City on a Hill.' "

Cuomo castigated Reagan for his apparent belief in social Darwinism. As the keynoter began to outline the differences between Republicans and Democrats, he was hitting his stride and won the rapt attention of the crowd both inside the Moscone Center and those sitting before their television screens across the nation:

The Republicans believe the wagon train will not make it to the frontier unless some of our old, some of our young, and some of our weak are left behind by the side of the trail.

The strong will inherit the land!

We Democrats believe that we can make it all the way with the whole family intact.

We have. More than once.

Ever since Franklin Roosevelt lifted himself from his wheelchair to lift this nation from its knees. Wagon train after wagon train. To new frontiers of education, housing, peace. The whole family aboard. Constantly reaching out to enlarge that family. Lifting them up into the wagon on the way. . . .

Some of us are in this room today only because this nation had that confidence.

It would be wrong to forget that.

. . .

We must get the American public to look past the glitter, beyond the showmanship—to reality, to the hard substance of things. And we will do that not so much with speeches that sound good as with speeches that are good and sound.

Not so much with speeches that bring people to their feet as with speeches that bring people to their senses.

. . .

To succeed we will have to surrender small parts of our individual interests, to build a platform we can *all* stand on, at once, comfortably—proudly singing out the truth for the nation to hear, in chorus, its logic so clear and commanding that no slick commercial, no amount of geniality, no martial music will be able to muffle it.

. . .

We would rather have laws written by the patron saint of this great city, the man called the "world's most sincere democrat"—St. Francis of Assisi—than laws written by Darwin.

We believe, as Democrats, that a society as blessed as ours, the most affluent democracy in the world's history, that can spend trillions on instruments of destruction, ought to be able to help the middle class in its struggle, ought to be able to find work for all who can do it, room at the table, shelter for the homeless, care for the elderly and infirm, hope for the destitute.

Cuomo closed with a stirring call to recognize the fact that we are all part of a "Family of America" and lines about his immigrant parents that were taken straight from his inaugural speech. There was, in fact, little that was new in Cuomo's keynote speech. He had been saying similar things for years. It was not even his best speech. But it was far better than anything most of those in attendance or watching on television had heard from a politician in so many years that it absolutely stunned them. As had happened in Albany a year and a half before, hardened politicians choked back tears. A thunderous ovation, far beyond what is to be expected on such an occasion, arose, calling Cuomo back to the podium. The crowd continued to go wild.

As Cuomo came down the stairs from the platform after the speech, he appeared dazed by the response to his message. "What happened?" he said to staffers and others who surrounded him to congratulate him. Many people who were on the floor of the Moscone Center that night say that there was a real possibility that the convention might have stampeded to Cuomo, as the 1896 convention had rushed to nominate Bryan following his speech. This was an eventuality that Cuomo had no desire to see occur. He was not yet ready to run for the presidency. And, in any case, the nomination to oppose Ronald Reagan in 1984 hardly seemed worth having. Cuomo quickly returned to New York, although CUOMO IN '88 buttons suddenly appeared at the convention site and sold out almost immediately.

The reason that the speech moved people to the extent that it did is well summed up by Matilda Cuomo: "He spilled his guts out in that speech," Mrs. Cuomo said to me. "He was saying to people, 'For God's sake, this is the Democratic party. If you're Democrats, this is what you must believe in.' And he spoke the language of all people. Even the Republicans have to believe those basics, because that's what we're here on earth for—not to make work for our fellowman, but to help. There are certain basics we all want and feel deeply and a lot of them don't know how to say it—and he *did!* He verbalized it for everybody."

That's just it. Cuomo spoke for the better side of the natures of all of us. He put the distinction between traditional Democratic principles and the Reagan Republican doctrine of "every man for himself (and every woman for a man)" into sharp definition. He reminded people who had begun to forget in Ronald Reagan's America whence they came. Those who have been successful should not be ashamed of their success, Cuomo was saying, but some of them ought to be ashamed of the way they have used—or abused—that success. The speech was a wakeup call urging Americans to arise from the slumber of self-centeredness that had dominated the preceding decade. "You can't forget a person who says those things and believes them with all his heart and soul," Matilda Cuomo maintains.

Plainly *what* Mario Cuomo said in San Francisco deeply moved millions of people. But of nearly equal importance was *how* he said it. The speech reads very well, but lacks the extraordinary power it has when one sees and hears Cuomo deliver it. "What I've always thought about the keynote," Peter Quinn told me, "is if Mondale had given that speech, no one would have ever remembered it." Surely that is an accurate assessment. The same words delivered by Fritz Mondale—or one of the early contenders for the Democratic nomination in 1988, most of whom took up Cuomo's themes—would not elicit the same response. "He's the only person I ever met in politics who has a real feel for words—not just for putting arguments together, but for the sound and power of words," Quinn says of his former boss.

What makes Cuomo's talent all the more remarkable is that he is able simultaneously to captivate both of the very distinct audiences for a speech such as the keynote address: that in the building and that watching via television. The sort of animated delivery that often works well in a large auditorium is much too "hot" for TV. Ted Kennedy's powerful address to the 1980 Democratic convention is a case in point. It was a great speech to read or to hear in the arena, but it was considerably less effective on television. Cuomo, though, manages in his oratory to achieve just the optimum temperature for both convention hall and living room.

The impact of Cuomo's keynote address was much greater than either he or even the most sanguine of his advisers could have hoped for. The television ratings were extraordinary. An estimated 79 million people saw the speech. It instantly turned Mario Cuomo into a truly national figure. As far as the politically active and intellectual segments of the nation are concerned, the speech completely reinforced what most of them had been reading about the governor of New York. *It's all true,* they concluded after hearing him.

"I knew what that speech did that night," Tim Russert said to me. Its impact was so great that it made Mario Cuomo something very close to the front-runner for the 1988 Democratic presidential nomination before the 1984 campaign was fully underway. For most politicians, that would be wonderful. It made Cuomo uneasy. If he decided to run in 1988, he would have to find some way to shed the front-runner status and turn himself once more into an underdog. *That* would be a task of sufficient difficulty to provide Cuomo with the sort of challenge he loves.

In the meantime, the speech served briefly to lift the spirits of Democrats, but it had no particular effect on the 1984 election. Mario Cuomo, after all, was not the candidate. Mondale and many other leading Democrats had wanted him to accept the vice presidential nomination, but Cuomo had pledged during the 1982 gubernatorial campaign that he would serve his full term. Besides, there was little point in becoming first mate on the *Lusitania.* And such a ticket would have seemed upside down. Once Cuomo had said no to the vice presidential nomination, he showed no regrets. The more the Democrats saw of Fritz Mondale's well-intentioned but uninspiring campaigning, the more they pined for the unavailable Demosthenes they had heard in San Francisco. "Wait Till '88" became the desperate cry of Democrats as they gazed longingly in the direction of Albany.[1]

For his part, Cuomo did what he could to assist the hopeless cause of the Mondale-Ferraro ticket in the summer and fall of 1984. But he had another major concern during those months. A few weeks before the Democratic convention, Archbishop O'Connor had launched his attack on Cuomo. (See Chapter 3.) In August the governor took the offensive with his extended interview in the *Times.*

The main event toward which Cuomo directed much of his energy after the keynote speech was his address on "Religious Belief and Public Morality" at Notre Dame in September 1984. When the governor told Peter Quinn that he was going to make a speech on this question, the speechwriter told him he was mak-

ing a big mistake. It would intensify his argument with the archbishop, Quinn warned, and even those Catholics who disagreed
with O'Connor "don't like to hear you argue with him in public
and they are not going to hear the words—they are just going to
hear the music."

Cuomo's response to this argument, Quinn told me, was "the
damnedest thing I've ever heard any politician say: 'I don't care;
I want to get it straight—on the record.'"

So they went ahead with work on the speech. If he was going
to insist on proceeding with this foolhardy venture, Quinn told
Cuomo, he must at least be sure that he kept it brief. Quinn noted
that speaking is no longer a form of public entertainment. Television, he pointed out, has "molded the mind—ten minutes before
they want a commercial." Quinn said the draft of the speech was
more than three times too long. "He's talking to eight hundred
kids; it's gonna be on TV, and if one of them yawns, that's all the
camera has to pick up and you're dead." But Cuomo was adamant.

"I don't care if it takes an hour and forty-five minutes," he
declared. "I want to say what I have to say."

Quinn says that when someone tells Cuomo that he is going
against all the odds, "that is when he digs his heels in." So they
worked on the speech off and on for five weeks. It went through
at least seventeen drafts. Yet when he delivered it, Cuomo did so
as if he had never said the words before.

Knowing how important the speech was to Cuomo and to his
career, members of the governor's staff tried to get him to South
Bend early, so he could walk around the campus, chat with students, and relax before the speech. But Cuomo does not like to
arrive very early. He considers it a waste of time that he could
better spend working in the office. So he delayed the departure.
Then the notorious state plane that Cuomo refuses to replace, even
though he places himself and others in mortal danger every time
they climb aboard, ran into bad weather on the way to Indiana.
The old turboprop plane cannot get above storms. "It was a terrible flight," then Press Secretary Martin Steadman told me. (He
had gone out earlier, but heard all about it from those on board.)
"Everybody thought they might die."

As a result of the "horrendous" flight, the Cuomo party arrived
only about an hour before the program was to begin. In the little
room his hosts had provided for him, Cuomo immediately sat
down to make last-minute alterations in the speech. Somebody

asked if the governor wanted anything. All he wanted, he said, was a glass of orange juice. He promptly spilled the sticky juice on the only copy of the speech that had his markings and written notations on it. "It was a riot," Steadman told me. "Fabian was holding the pages up to the air-conditioner blower to get the goddamn things to dry. Meanwhile they're sticking together. It was just awful—and it's all because he *won't* go early. He's stubborn."

Despite the behind-the-scenes problems, the Notre Dame speech was another masterly performance. Cuomo fully understands the theatrics of public speaking. But that does not alter the content of the speech. The fact that he held the audience in rapt attention for about fifty minutes—way beyond what professionals think is the normal attention span of a modern American—was as much the result of what Cuomo was saying as it was his accomplished delivery. The music may have gotten the listeners' attention, but the speaker got them to hear his words as well.

The Notre Dame speech was extremely important to Cuomo. A man who takes his Catholicism seriously, he thought deeply about his subject and fashioned a generally persuasive case. (The speech is discussed in detail in Chapter 3.) The keynote address had shown a man who believed passionately in the values for which Democrats had stood for more than a half century—and a man who could blend powerful emotion into a speech of some substance. Notre Dame proved that Cuomo was a man of deep thought as well as great compassion. It showed a national audience of influential people that he did more than give good speeches—he also gave hard thought to complex issues. And a Cuomo appearance on ABC's "Nightline" after the speech brought its significance and its author's ideas to a much wider audience.

In "picking a fight with a bishop" and making the Notre Dame speech, Cuomo defied a host of standard political rules: arguing with his own church, talking too long, and addressing a serious subject in intellectual terms. Political opponents thought Cuomo's struggle with the Church might amount to political suicide. After Cuomo's initial shots against O'Connor, President Reagan told a prayer breakfast that there was a time in America when "a politician who spoke to or of [religious leaders] with a lack of respect would not long survive in the political arena." It was a fate the president clearly hoped would befall New York's governor. But Cuomo not only survived his confrontation with O'Connor and his disagreement with his Church, he thrived. His popularity among all religious groups—Catholics, as well as Protestants and Jews—soared from mid-1984 through the first half of 1985. There is some evidence, though, that the controversy hurt Cuomo among Catholics for a brief time. His favorable rating among Catholics in New York in a June 1984 Marist poll stood at 58.1 percent, almost the same as his 59.0 percent approval from the state's electorate as a whole. By September—following his Democratic convention speech and his run-in with Archbishop O'Connor, and at the time of his Notre Dame speech—Cuomo's approval rating with the state's voters had jumped seven points to 66.1 percent. But among New York Catholics the governor's favorable rating remained virtually unchanged, at 58.7 percent. The controversy with the Church had not diminished his support among New York Catholics, but it seems to have prevented him from gaining among them as a result of his San Francisco speech, as he obviously did among non-Catholic New Yorkers.

In the months following the Notre Dame speech, though, Cuomo's popularity among New York Catholics soared. In June 1985 the Marist poll found that the governor's approval rating had surged to 69.6 percent among Catholics, identical to his rating with the electorate as a whole.[2]

In the summer of 1985, with his popularity at new highs and with a substantial reputation as a national leader, Mario Cuomo once again took up a cause that most political experts said was one that would surely be both unpopular and unsuccessful. In fact, Cuomo dares to go against prevailing opinion whenever he believes prevailing opinion to be wrong. He thinks that a politician who merely goes along with popular opinion is "not a shepherd but simply part of the flock."

President Reagan and leading figures in both parties were backing "tax reform." The notion of "reforming" a tax system that Jimmy Carter had in the mid-seventies called "a disgrace to the human race" was an idea whose time had come a decade later, with opinion polls indicating that a vast majority of the American people favored it. Those who opposed were castigated as "special interests." The issue of tax reform in 1985 had come to be something like that of opposing "the trusts" in 1890, when many members of Congress simply wanted to vote for a bill with the term "antitrust" in its name.

Cuomo had nothing against the concept of tax reform in the abstract. Who could? It was a classic motherhood-and-apple-pie issue. Everyone loved the idea of simplifying taxes, making them fairer, and reducing them. " 'Tax reform, tax reform'—it was like a choir singing, Democrat and Republican," Cuomo political aide Andrew (Drew) Zambelli said to me, recalling the situation in 1985. But Cuomo's singing voice had always been too singular for choir participation. New York's governor refused to join the rush to remodel the nation's tax code. In fact, his opposition dated from the unveiling of the Reagan plan shortly after the 1984 election. The very morning the plan first appeared in the papers, Cuomo was doing a radio program in New York. He said that the Reagan "tax reform" was an attack on the middle class and was very likely to be harmful to New Yorkers. Never one to embrace simple answers to complex problems, Cuomo pointed out that any legislation that would reduce the taxes of the rich, remove many of the poor from the tax rolls, and be revenue neutral *must* result in increased taxes for at least part of the middle class.

He particularly focused on the Reagan administration proposal's principal means of offsetting the lowered rates: the elimination of deductibility for state and local taxes. "This is insane. This doesn't make any sense. This isn't tax reform," Cuomo told his staff. Most of them tried to convince him not to take up the fight. "Everybody felt in the beginning that it was a case we shouldn't make. We couldn't win," Cuomo told me. "I said, 'We *have* to win.' "

Well, not quite "everybody." Marty Steadman told me that he could see that it was not going to be an uphill fight at all. "We knew that we were going to win from the beginning." All the logic and solid arguments were on their side.

No other major politician wanted to take up the case against the tax reform proposal. For the governor of "liberal" New York, with one of the highest tax rates in the nation, to lead the fight for what Reagan and others would surely label as a "special interest" appeared to be political madness. But Cuomo believed that his case was right and that it could be won. "You see, I have a great confidence in rationale," the governor said to me. "I think if you're reasonable and you're right, the American people will perceive that—enough of them to make a difference. That comes from my confidence in juries. You give them the most complicated set of facts, and their consensus judgment will be very good, most of the time. I see the American people that way."

So the veteran barrister took his case to the jury. In July 1985 Cuomo testified before the House Ways and Means Committee. The packed house in the ornate hearing room testified to the stature as a national leader that Cuomo had gained in the preceding year. President Reagan had contended that state tax deductibility constituted a subsidy of high-tax states by low-tax states. The former, of which New York was the most notorious, were wasteful, big-spending, liberal states that deserved to have their subsidies cut off, Reagan indicated. States, like individuals, ought to paddle their own canoes, without outside assistance.

Cuomo was not alone in realizing that this argument was nonsense, but he was the only major politician to say so. He pointed out the obvious when he told the Ways and Means Committee that most of the so-called high-tax states, far from being subsidized by the low-tax states, actually paid much more in federal taxes than they received back in federal spending.

Cuomo told the committee that the actual reasons why "high-tax" states had higher taxes was that they had more people in need living within their borders and were more prepared to meet their responsibility to assist them. "This notion that we are manipulating our taxes so that we can attract more homeless, more criminals, more drug addicts, more welfare cases," he declared, "is ridiculous." New York's governor said that taxes could be equalized among the states when "low-tax states" took their share of such people with problems. "How many do you want?" he asked congressmen from those states. No responses were forthcoming.

When someone at the hearing told Cuomo that polls showed that most Americans favored tax reform, the governor said: "I don't like polls." This drew a feigned look of startled outrage from the committee's Polish-American chairman, Dan Rostenkowski of Illinois.

Cuomo kept hammering away on the issue of state tax deductibility at public forums throughout the summer and fall of 1985. "You see, what the president is trying to do is to look good on tax reform by making us pay for it," he said. He noted that deductibility of taxes was simple justice. Without it, people would be required to pay taxes on taxes—on money that was never theirs to spend, because it was already taxed away. It just didn't make sense. In September Cuomo said on NBC's "Meet the Press" that Reagan's tax plan would be "devastating" to the middle class. The president promptly responded, saying that Cuomo's charge was "balderdash" and that he was so angry that he "finished watching that show on the ceiling, looking down."

When he was told of the president's comments, Cuomo said, "It's flattering that he turned to my channel and never turned it off even from the ceiling."

As Cuomo kept the argument going, people began to look a bit more carefully at the molars of the president's gift horse. Many of them realized that Cuomo was right. The elimination of the state and local tax deduction was not reform but regression. In October Cuomo sent a letter to Rostenkowski, contending once more that repeal of deductibility would amount to a double tax. "I'm hopeful under your leadership that the committee will soon report out a bill which retains this deduction and which achieves the fundamental goals of tax reform: simplification, fairness and economic growth. Such a bill would have my enthusiastic support."

The tax reform legislation that was finally enacted contained a compromise on the question of state tax deductibility. All state and local taxes except sales taxes remained deductible. Although eliminating the deductibility of sales taxes constituted a tax on a tax, Cuomo had won most of the battle. It was the sort of compromise he could live with, particularly since he did not want to be seen as standing in the way of genuine tax reform. Sales taxes are, moreover, the most regressive form of taxes and the distinction between them and other types of taxes might encourage states to move toward more progressive forms of taxation. "For this state, we got eighty-six percent of what we wanted," Cuomo told me. "We got all the deductibility preserved except sales tax. Colossal victory—it was one of the biggest victories we've had."

That is a hard proposition to argue with. Mario Cuomo is much more responsible than any other person for the fact that American citizens can still deduct most of their state taxes on their federal tax returns. What started out looking like a foolhardy political act turned out to be very popular. In the end, it looked like a stroke of political genius, but in fact Cuomo's initial opposition to the Reagan position on tax reform was an act of genuine political courage. He did it simply because he believed he was right. His experience has shown him again and again that when one does what is right, people will eventually understand. The fact is, though, that many another politician might not be able to succeed at such an effort. Cuomo's ability to make his case, to communicate with the public, helps him to swing opinion behind his positions.[3]

                    Mario Cuomo had his most successful legislative session in 1986, as both he and the state legislators were preparing to face the voters in November. That double date with the electorate, combined with the governor's extraordinary popularity, made nervous legislators more amenable to Cuomo's entreaties than they had been in previous years. Shortly before the beginning of the 1986 session, Cuomo issued a reminder to those legislators who had been blocking his measures. "How does it help to drive the governor into the position where he has to campaign against you?" he asked. "He's going to come into your district with the toxic tort bill, with the victims who have been exposed to these substances, some of them in wheelchairs."

It was not a vision that comforted Republican state senators. On the one hand, they did not want to hand the incumbent Democratic governor a series of triumphs. On the other, they did not want to give him issues on which to run against them as obstructionists. They opposed him through most of the session, but at its very end in late June and early July, the legislature rushed through a host of significant measures, most of which the governor had been pushing all year. Included were the toxic tort bill, which made it easier for victims to sue polluters; a bill establishing "opportunity zones" with tax and other incentives for businesses to locate in economically depressed neighborhoods and regions; a $1.45 billion environmental bond issue; a plan to refurbish substandard housing in New York City; a bill creating a public authority that could take over the Long Island Lighting Company; a law making it easier to prosecute organized crime; a reorganization of the New York liability-insurance industry; a plan to slash the state's annual short-term borrowing by nearly $1 billion; a requirement that all new school buses have seat belts; and a reorganization of the state's courts.

The 1986 session typified Cuomo's achievements as governor: simultaneous movement on several fronts, with substantial accomplishments, but nothing especially flashy. His legislative successes that year also evidenced Cuomo's growing self-confidence in the role of governor and his increasing mastery of the political and legislative processes. By 1986 Cuomo was a skilled and competent political leader who could get most of what he wanted.

But even Cuomo could not get *everything* he wanted. His "single biggest disappointment" in the session, he said, was the legislature's failure to pass tough ethics and campaign-financing laws. The legislature was prepared to pass a few weak measures, but the major corruption scandals at the time were confined to New York City, and the upstate Republicans who dominated the State Senate were under no significant constituent pressure to enact tougher ethics laws. The issues of ethics and the public financing of campaigns would have to await another year, when Cuomo's popularity had been dramatically demonstrated at the polls and when the scandals had reached Albany. Cuomo was not about to abandon them.[4]

The 1986 gubernatorial contest was not at all the kind of campaign Mario Cuomo likes. His statewide approval rating at the beginning of the election year stood at a stratospheric level above 70 percent. After raising a New York record of $3.4 million at a single dinner in November 1985, Cuomo entered the election year with more than $9 million in his campaign account. No prominent Republican could be persuaded to run against him. The Reagan administration made strenuous efforts to find a strong candidate to oppose Cuomo. Vice President George Bush was among those who tried to find a challenger who might at least make a race of it. At the beginning of 1986, former Secretary of State Henry Kissinger's name was floated as a possibility. Kissinger considered making the race, but decided not to, citing his commitments in national and international affairs. The general assumption was that Kissinger, like other leading Republicans, concluded that there was scant hope of victory over Cuomo.

The Republicans finally had to settle for Andrew P. O'Rourke, the little-known county executive of Westchester County. Although O'Rourke would do his best, it was like pitting the 1985 Columbia University football team against the Chicago Bears of the same year.

Under the circumstances, there was absolutely no way that Cuomo could make himself into an underdog. He was uncomfortable with the situation. As a result, Cuomo did a number of things during the campaign that were not in keeping with his better instincts.

Cuomo's opinion analyst, Bob Sullivan, describes the 1986 re-election campaign as "a nightmare." "That would have tested anybody," Sullivan said to me. "God, what do you do when you don't have an opponent? You've got a whole campaign to run. The national press as well as the New York City press staring at you all the time—'What are you going to do next?' 'What are you going to do now?' That drove him nuts. There was nothing to do but wait."

In fact, Mario Cuomo is incapable of doing nothing but waiting. He has to be active, even when there is no objective need to do so. Some of his actions in 1986 made him the target of sharp criticism for being "arrogant" and "heavy-handed." Part of the problem was simply that an action undertaken by someone with a huge lead will be viewed differently than the same action undertaken by an underdog. Hard, vigorous campaigning by someone trailing in a race may earn him praise as a "scrapper" who is "spirited" and "tenacious." The same sort of campaigning by a heavy favorite is more likely to result in him being castigated as a "bully" who is "combative" and "mean."

Yet this was not the first time Cuomo had been accused of political arrogance. When Walter Mondale asked the governor to run his 1984 primary campaign in New York, Cuomo recalled some of his problems with the Carter-Mondale people in 1980. He said that he would do it, but "we have to run it, and it has to be done our way." Mondale campaign officials Tom Donlan and Jim Johnson resisted Cuomo's desire to have control. Finally Cuomo told Mondale, "You can have the campaign. I'm not going to do it, because I'm not going to let your people do it in my state, and me be responsible for it. I think they'll foul it up; I'm not impressed by them."

Mondale, who was by this time under great pressure from Gary Hart, said, "Okay. You run it."

"Andrew ran it," Cuomo says of the Mondale campaign in the 1984 New York primary. "I worked very hard at it, but Andrew ran it." One prediction the night before the primary had Hart defeating Mondale by six points. In the event, Mondale won by sixteen points. Some of Mondale's people complained that Cuomo was "arrogant." He responds by saying, "Yes. 'Arrogant' means that I said I wouldn't run it unless they let me run it. And we won by sixteen points after having been outspent and ABC having said the night before that we were going to lose by six points."

Obviously Mario Cuomo believes that he knows New York politics. It is a bare-knuckles, rough-and-tumble sort of politics. He has been victimized by it in the past, but now he has mastered it to the point that he believes he is better able than anyone else to run a New York campaign.

The first serious question about Cuomo's hardball politics in the 1986 campaign concerned the governor's actions in forcing Abraham Hirschfeld off the ballot as a candidate for the Democratic nomination for lieutenant governor. Cuomo had chosen Representative Stan Lundine as his running mate and was angered at the attempt by Hirschfeld, a wealthy real estate developer who has often been classified as a political eccentric, to join his ticket.

Cuomo is unapologetic about his role in forcing Hirschfeld off the ballot. "I didn't want him on the ballot," Cuomo bluntly told me. "He had five million dollars. He would have won. He was totally ill equipped to be lieutenant governor. Everybody knew it. He had *no* experience. He was called a 'wacko' by the *New York Daily News,* in a big piece. Why should you allow him to get on the ticket with you—if you can stop it, and you didn't do anything illegal? You simply used the law. Why not?"

The law that Cuomo's operatives used to remove Hirschfeld from the ballot was one detailing how nominating petitions must be filed. A candidate for statewide office in New York was required to have a minimum of twenty thousand valid signatures of voters on nominating petitions. These must be distributed to include at least a hundred signatures in each of seventeen congressional districts. The courts disqualified Hirschfeld because his petitions, which contained more than three times the required total number of signatures, were not properly divided by congressional district and county. This requirement was intended to make it easier for officials to determine if the signatures were valid.

It is clear that Hirschfeld's petitions did not meet the letter of the law. Whether that fact justifies Cuomo's actions is questionable. It was widely believed that Cuomo did not want Hirschfeld to become lieutenant governor because he would not want to leave the state in Hirschfeld's control while he was campaigning for the presidency and would certainly not want Hirschfeld to become governor, should Cuomo be elected president. Those are legitimate reasons for opposing Hirschfeld. But Cuomo's assertion that

Hirschfeld would have won the primary because of all the money he had to spend is dubious. He had spent several million dollars on four previous campaigns for such offices as United States senator and City Council president, and had never won any of those races. Had Cuomo campaigned against Hirschfeld and urged the voters to give him the running mate he wanted, there is little reason to think that he could not have gotten Lundine the nomination.

On this issue it appears that Cuomo's sometime rivals Ed Koch and Andrew O'Rourke were correct. After categorizing Abe Hirschfeld as "a terrible person," Mayor Koch said: "I believe that you don't throw people off the ballot based on technicalities. It's just not right." O'Rourke described Cuomo's successful effort to knock Hirschfeld off the ballot as "brassy politics at its worst, brassy as in knuckles."

The second source of the charge that Cuomo was arrogant in 1986 was his refusal to debate O'Rourke until he fully disclosed his tax returns for the past ten years. No incumbent with a large lead is ever eager to debate his challenger. It simply gives the opponent greater visibility. But it is hard to imagine Mario Cuomo being particularly concerned about debating anyone—certainly not Andy O'Rourke, who is a competent and sometimes humorous fellow, but who is plainly not in the same league with Cuomo.

As the campaign went on, the press began to give Cuomo a beating for not debating. O'Rourke carried a life-size cutout of Cuomo around to appearances and "debated" it. By October the easiest course for Cuomo would have been to have a debate. But he had earlier tied debates to full financial disclosure. Drew Zambelli insists that it had become an issue of principle with Cuomo. "You can't just say, 'Disclosure is important. I'll give ten years of my tax returns; you give ten years of yours,' and then say, 'Never mind. Okay, now that I'm getting beaten up in the press for not debating, even though I'm not wrong, let's change the rules.'"

So Cuomo kept on insisting that he would not debate until O'Rourke made the complete disclosure. About a month before the election, the Republican candidate relented and released his tax returns for the six years prior to the most recent four years, which he had previously released. Cuomo counts this as a significant victory for the public's right to know about candidates seeking high office. "For the rest of history in this state, no gubernatorial candidate will be able to hold back his tax returns. The next election for governor in this state," Cuomo said to me, "you try hiding your tax returns—you can't do it, because the precedent's been set."

But still there was no debate. After O'Rourke released the rest of his tax returns, Cuomo said that the Republican candidate still had not met another demand: that he disclose the names of all his private law clients for the past twelve years. When it was pointed out to him that this would constitute a violation of the state's code of professional ethics for attorneys, Cuomo asked that O'Rourke list only those clients he had represented before county agencies while he was a county legislator.

Cuomo says that the media called him arrogant only because he was not doing what they wanted him to do: have debates. "And when we finally had a debate, nobody put it on television. I pleaded with people to come and televise it; we provided a cassette of it, but nobody would play it, except one station in Albany. When I asked why they wouldn't play it, they said, 'There was nothing controversial; it was just a dry discussion of issues.'" At a press conference after the debate, Cuomo said to the assembled media, "Oh, ye hypocrites."

The only debate of the 1986 New York gubernatorial campaign did not take place until October 30, five days before the election, with Cuomo an astounding fifty points ahead in the polls. It proved to be a marked anticlimax. The long-running debate over whether to debate was much more stimulating than the debate itself. The latter was universally described as dull, subdued, and low-key. The fact was that the election's outcome had long since become a foregone conclusion, and there was no point in engaging in fiery exchanges.

The same condition applied throughout most, if not all, of the campaign. Yet the two men spent months hinting that the other was tainted with corruption. From the moment he entered the race, O'Rourke tried to tar Cuomo with the brush of the New York City corruption scandal, then centered among Queens Democrats. "Mario Cuomo, if you knew about the corruption in New York City, why didn't you do something?" O'Rourke asked in commercials. "If you didn't know anything about what your political buddies were up to, how could you be so dumb?" For his part, Cuomo kept implying that O'Rourke had something to hide in his tax returns or among his legal clients.

"Everyone who has run against Cuomo," O'Rourke said in

August, "—Koch, Lehrman, Hirschfeld—has had their character personally attacked. This is another example of the arrogance of the Cuomo camp."

The worst flare-up of the campaign came in mid-October when O'Rourke created his own debate by calling a radio program on which the governor was answering questions. The Republican angrily attacked Cuomo for insisting that he release his tax returns and client lists. Cuomo kept taunting his opponent, who began to lose his temper. The governor said he would debate as soon as O'Rourke would make a statement saying, "Other than the ones you caught me at, I had no other clients before county offices or agencies or courts."

"Tell me what you caught me doing," an agitated O'Rourke asked. After a few more moments of both Cuomo and the show's moderator talking over O'Rourke, the irate challenger said, "I can't answer that question because you didn't catch me in a god-damn thing."

"Oh, be careful, Andy! Be careful, Andy," Cuomo lectured, as the moderator disconnected O'Rourke.

It was something less than an enlightening intellectual exchange on differing philosophies of government. "Every once in a while his Italian passion comes to the fore," explains a Cuomo friend.[5]

A third charge against Cuomo in the 1986 campaign was that he failed to do enough to help his party's candidates for the legislature. In particular, some critics contended that Cuomo failed to use his huge personal popularity to win control of the state senate for the Democrats.

When I asked the governor about this, his initial response was to suggest that the accusation was baseless. He said that since becoming governor he had done more than ninety fund-raisers, and only six of them were for himself. "All the rest were for others, including legislators. I doubt that you've ever seen any specific, tangible evidence that I didn't support any candidate—or even any [Democratic] candidate saying that I didn't support him or her."

But then Cuomo went on to indicate that the charge that he had not done as much for the senate Democrats as he could have was true. "I did not run around spending a lot of time with the senate minority candidates. The senate minority had *opposed* ethics legislation in the 1986 session. So had the Republican majority, but if I went around campaigning with the senate Democrats, I would have had to say to voters, 'These people opposed ethics legislation.' I don't think they would have wanted me to do that."

It seems, then, that the 1986 legislature's last-minute flurry of activity may have saved Republicans from Cuomo's campaign wrath, but it did nothing to help members of his own party make up for their failure to produce an acceptable ethics bill. Cuomo concentrated on his own campaign while he let Democratic state senators fend for themselves.

For the most part, he allowed the party's candidate for the United States Senate, Mark Green, to do the same. In the Senate primary, Cuomo remained officially neutral, but he was generally believed to favor Green's opponent, John S. Dyson, because the moderate-to-conservative Dyson would have the money necessary to mount an effective challenge against incumbent Republican Senator Alfonse M. D'Amato, while the very liberal Green would not. Green noted before the September primary that there was a certain inconsistency in the position of some state Democrats. Although he did not name the governor, it was clear that Cuomo was one of those to whom Green was referring. "Some Democratic leaders in the state have cognitive dissonance on this point," he said. "They wake up in the morning supporting John Dyson because, although he doesn't excite them, he has the bucks. Then in the evening they go to bed bemoaning an Abe Hirschfeld whose money is giving them all sorts of problems and they just don't understand."

After Green won the Democratic nomination, Cuomo supported him to the extent of transferring campaign funds to him and making some joint appearances with him. The governor also urged Dyson, who had the Liberal party nomination, to quit the race. "Mark Green's a friend of mine," Cuomo told Anthony Lewis of the *Times* after the election. "I gave him $50,000 of my own money. The last three days I campaigned with him every day. I took on D'Amato. There's no way I could have done more for him."

It is probably true that Green had no chance of winning the election. D'Amato is a master of constituent service and the pork barrel. Cuomo's assertion that he could not have done more for Green must be questioned, though. The governor did arrange for the fifty-thousand-dollar contribution to Green's campaign, but the money came from the state Democratic party, not Cuomo's personal campaign funds. And just how and to what extent the governor "took on D'Amato," with whom he has a generally good relationship, is less than clear. "Of course there was a nonaggression pact between Governor Cuomo and Senator D'Amato," Democratic Senator Daniel Patrick Moynihan said after the election. "That's not a theory; it's a fact." Moynihan said that Cuomo, for whom he has often expressed great admiration, had "focused single-mindedly on his own victory margin without offering enough help" to other Democratic candidates.

Although in his concession speech Green himself thanked Cuomo "for doing everything possible to help," many of his backers disagreed. Some of them hissed when the defeated candidate thanked the governor. "The real test of leadership," Green aide Randy Daniels said after the election, "is guiding and building and helping the party, not building up superflous margins. It wasn't a team effort."

The last comment must have cut Cuomo, the team player, deeply. But it was true. The only defense of Cuomo on this issue is that he may have had a more inclusive conception of what his team was. At least as far as the legislature was concerned, Cuomo had been trying to govern as much as possible through a bipartisan approach. His dealings with the legislature did not ignore party as much as did his judicial appointments, but there was plainly a tendency in that direction. Senate Majority Leader Warren Anderson said later that the governor had "made some commitments to [Republican] members that if he went into [their] districts, he would only campaign in favor of the Democratic nominee, not against the Republican." Anderson said that Cuomo had "slipped in a couple of instances," making some Republicans "sore." But his general adherence to the rule—issuing from his bipartisan approach—of not campaigning against Republican incumbents certainly did not endear Cuomo to partisan members of his own party. Yet if he was sincere in wanting bipartisan government, it would be difficult suddenly to start practicing intensely partisan politics.

Cuomo's own campaign *was* intense, despite the lack of serious opposition. "The governor worked no less hard in 1986 than he did in 1982 or in 1977," Drew Zambelli told me, "nor did we run in 1986 any less a competitive campaign than in '82. In fact, we did a lot more. People just never saw it."

Cuomo had nothing against either work or winning big. "We saw what a miserable election he had; it was horrible," former

Cuomo speechwriter Peter Quinn said of the 1986 experience. "I mean he turned it into—he did his best to make it as painful as possible." One of the circumstances that made it so painful was Cuomo's desire to get as close to unanimous approval as possible. He really wants his family to be as inclusive as possible. "The wonderful thing about him, you know," Quinn said to me, "is that he could have had ninety-two percent approval and that eight percent would kill him—why they don't like him."

Zambelli believes that it was a masterful, but nearly invisible, campaign. "When you have a candidate with a hundred percent recognition, you don't have to create scenarios for people to know you better." So Cuomo spent most of the campaign being governor. He made no specifically campaign appearances until the last weekend before the election. Of course he was frequently in the news, carrying out his official duties. Television advertising was used to communicate directly with the voters, circumventing the filter of reporters, editors, and producers. Included were the unique commercials asking voters to return Matilda Cuomo to the Executive Mansion.

The Cuomo operation had learned the importance of direct mail from the way the Lehrman campaign had used it in 1982. Four years later the financial situation was reversed. The Cuomo campaign had a huge advantage in money in 1986. It sent out more than 3 million pieces of direct mail and placed another million pieces under doors. Zambelli estimates that the campaign made 3 or 4 million telephone calls. "Nobody ever saw that," he told me. "People kept saying there was no campaign going on, yet there was a level of campaigning unprecedented in New York."

Obviously it worked. "He embarked on a strategy to win by a huge margin, and he did it," State Senate Minority Leader Manfred Ohrenstein said of Cuomo. "Not everybody liked the strategy. It is a controversial strategy, but it worked enormously well."

The previous record in a gubernatorial election in the Empire State was 58.5 percent, set by Grover Cleveland in 1882. Cuomo obliterated that standard, crushing O'Rourke by a margin of more than two-to-one, 65 to 32 percent. Franklin D. Roosevelt had been reelected in 1930 by a margin of 725,000 votes; Cuomo's relection margin was 1.3 million. In the four normally Republican suburban counties around New York City, where no Democrat had won more than 50.9 percent of the vote in modern history, Cuomo received 62.1 percent in 1986, up from 48.2 percent four years before. And he had brought together the Italians and the Jews, the two ethnic groups in greatest opposition among New York voters.

It was an achievement of which any politician could be justly proud. "It's very, very difficult to accept that you have broken every record there is—I mean, if you think about it, people like Grover Cleveland and Franklin Roosevelt," Cuomo said the day after the 1986 election.

But in some respects it was a costly triumph. Many politicians in his own party, as well as reporters and consultants, were upset by the Cuomo they saw during the reelection campaign. He seemed too political where his own interests were concerned and, perhaps, not political enough with respect to the contests involving other Democrats. A postelection analysis in the *Times* summarized these views by saying that "in a few months of not particularly difficult campaigning, confrontations with political opponents made him appear aggressive, even vindictive, in trying to squeeze every ounce of political advantage from each situation."

If the state and national polls and the clamor in the following year for him to run for president were any indication, the ill effects of Cuomo's disappointing resort to completely unnecessary political hardball in 1986 were not lasting. One does suspect, though, that the realization that he had, as one of his aides put it, "acted irrationally, because he was going against his grain," may have made Cuomo reluctant to enter the 1988 presidential race as the front-runner.[6]

During and immediately after the 1986 campaign, Mario Cuomo and the New York media engaged in a brutal combat that Cuomo's staff dubbed "the press wars."

The genesis of the conflict was a series of stories that appeared in New York papers about the activities of Andrew Cuomo's law firm. No one asserted that the younger Cuomo had broken any laws, but the notion was spread that his firm's representation of clients before state agencies produced the appearance of possible impropriety. William Safire of the *Times* called Andrew Cuomo the new "rainmaker" in New York.

The governor was outraged. "I was angry about the things they were saying about Andrew, which were untrue. I believed that some of them [reporters and columnists] were acting unprofessionally, and I said so."

"When they started attacking Andrew," the governor told me, "I went after them. I let them know exactly what I thought—exactly what I thought about them and their editors. I let them know precisely what was on my mind and in my heart. They responded by killing me—or trying to. They certainly didn't succeed, but they certainly took their best shot."

That sort of thing is just not done in politics. The "normal" thing for a politician to do if someone takes a shot at a member of his family is to say something like, "It's rather unfortunate that you would say something like that. It's certainly not true. Next question, please."

Mario Cuomo is not a "normal politician." That is one of his attractions. He is a real, live person. Just as a nonpolitician would get angry with someone who attacked a member of his family, Cuomo responds the same way when someone fools around with his family. Such responses do not appear to be in his political interests, but he reacts as a person, not a politician. As Press Secretary Gary Fryer puts it, "He's a real, live, honest-to-God human being."

"The press is not accustomed to being dealt with the way they deal with politicians," Cuomo says. "The press finds it very easy to call politicians liars, [but] when you turn around and tell [somebody in] the press, 'I think you're a liar,' they go crazy." He told me that he held the press up to a professional standard and found that some of them were not meeting it. "I was merely measuring them against a professional standard, the way they measure politicians. They can't stand that."

The press "has the last word," Cuomo said to me, "and they have it in print. That's why most politicians don't tell them what most politicians feel. I paid the price for it, and I still do."

At the end of the 1986 campaign, Cuomo's anger at the press overflowed. On the Sunday before Election Day, the governor said to a group of reporters: "Don't flatter yourself that you're the best way to reach the public, because you're not. Rather than your 800 words, I'm probably better off with the 10 seconds on radio because those are my words. When I talk to you, they're your words." Cuomo told reporters that he was thinking about cutting back reporters' access to him.

What happened during the "press wars" was that members of

the New York media, many of whom had been enamored of Cuomo during much of his first term discovered that he is not *always* a charming, wonderful fellow. *Hey, wait a minute,* some reporters suddenly thought. *This guy's morose. He's got a dark side. He gets mad. He can be vindictive.*

All of this is true. Since he *is* a real live human being, Cuomo, like any other mortal, has his shortcomings. That this realization came as a shock to some of the reporters who covered him was probably a result of the fact that they had been so impressed by him that they had come to think of him as something far above other people. To discover that he could at times act like the rest of us was a severe disappointment to some reporters. Cynicism being the established religion of the Fourth Estate, other reporters had taken the opposite position on Cuomo from the start. If he seemed too good to be true, that was simply because he *wasn't* true. Since such reporters assume that *all* politicians are frauds, they thought that Cuomo necessarily must be one, too.

So during the "press wars," few reporters were willing to accept Cuomo for what he is: an extraordinary person in politics, but a person all the same. For some it amounted to disillusionment; for others it was a case of "I told you so."

As 1987 progressed, however, Cuomo's relations with the press improved. Although he did briefly cut back on contacts with reporters right after the 1986 election (including not holding the usual postelection news conference), Cuomo soon returned his high degree of accessibility. Members of the New York media developed a more balanced and accurate view of the governor, and he lowered his hostility toward them. Cuomo says that he likes most of the reporters with whom he deals in Albany. "I don't always like what they write, but I like them as human beings," he told me. Cuomo even allows that over his years as governor he has probably come out a little ahead. He points out that assessments can be inaccurate in two ways: overly generous or overly harsh. Cuomo says that there have probably been at least as many times when the media have been unjustified in their praise of him as there have times when they were unjustified in their negative criticism. "I don't have any complaints overall, I really don't."

But he is completely unrepentant about the press wars. "Would I have done it differently—would I reserve my comments and not share them with the press, knowing how tough they can be in response? *No!* I'm glad I told them the way I told them. I'm glad

I told them exactly what was on my mind. I thought they were unfair when they attacked Andrew—terribly unfair—and I still do."[7]

That's Mario Cuomo. What you see is what you get. He is not the creature of a media consultant or a public relations expert. He flirted with that approach early in his political career, but it didn't work. After his 1977 primary defeat, Cuomo reverted to simply being himself. His image since his 1982 campaign has been that he is *not* an image. He does what he thinks is right, regardless of the political consequences. Sometimes that gets him into temporary trouble with the press, but the "politics be damned" attitude is so unusual among politicians that it usually proves to be the best politics of all.

Coming off both his successes at the end of the 1986 session and his unprecedentedly large reelection victory, Cuomo could look forward to the 1987 legislative session with hope of great accomplishment. Much of that hope was ultimately realized, but not before what Cuomo describes as an "all-out war" was waged between himself and most of the state legislature.

The *casus belli* were four: Cuomo's insistence on a tough ethics bill, resentment on the part of Democrats in the legislature (and especially the Senate) at Cuomo's failure to share his popularity with them in the recent election, the desire of Republicans—especially until February 19, and to a lesser extent thereafter—to cause Cuomo as much trouble as possible to hurt his expected presidential campaign, and the replacement of Stanley Fink as assembly speaker by Mel Miller of Brooklyn. The new speaker wanted to demonstrate his independence from the governor, and got along with him considerably less well than had Fink. "Mel Miller decided to go back to the idea of the legislature as an institution, independent of the governor," Marty Steadman says. "It didn't work."

The first major conflict got underway even before 1987 did. The issue was taxes. New York, like thirty-two other states, would gain revenue as a result of the federal tax reform unless it took action to lower its state rates. Governor Cuomo called the legislature into special session in December 1986 to consider his plan to lower state levies. His economic advisers estimated that the state would collect an additional $1.7 billion as a result of the federal changes. Republicans insisted that much larger cuts—at least $2.8 billion—should be made, in order to make New York tax rates more competitive with those of other states. Cuomo argued that the state could not afford bigger cuts. Republicans and some independent analysts suggested that Cuomo wanted to be particularly cautious in cutting, lest slashes that went too deep might necessitate a tax increase in 1988, when he might be running for the presidency.

Cuomo implied that such analyses were correct when he said in his 1987 budget message, "We must resist being deceived by a dramatic-sounding tax cut now that will next year produce the need for a tax increase or draconian spending cuts." The governor's budget focused on education, where his call to boost state aid to school districts by $405 million would produce a cumulative increase of more than 50 percent since he took office four years before. Overall state spending would be up by almost 50 percent in the same period. This increase in spending was more than twice the rate of inflation. It has produced some criticism of Cuomo as a "big spender," but he points out that he has cut taxes and balanced the budget at the same time he has made needed increases in spending. The "New York idea," Cuomo says, is to be both compassionate and fiscally responsible (neither of which, in his view, applied to the Reagan administration).

The tax question persisted through most of the regular legislative session of 1987. Republican leaders were frank in saying in January that they hoped to oblige Cuomo either to accept deeper cuts or be tagged a "big spender" who opposed tax cuts. "We'll hold his feet to the fire," Assembly Minority Leader Clarence D. Rappleyea promised.

Cuomo proposed the construction in front of the State Capitol of a thermometer on which revenue surpluses could be measured. He said that it would be reckless to cut taxes before the size of the surpluses had been determined.

Given the Republicans' open intention of using the tax issue to hinder a Cuomo presidential bid, it seemed odd that on the day after his announcement that he would not seek the presidency Cuomo proposed an additional tax cut of $1.7 billion. He explained his reversal by noting that it had just been determined that state revenues for the previous December were more than $200 million above projection. Republicans cheered, but most Democrats were more restrained. "This is a total surprise from a very unusual man," one Democratic legislator told a *Times* reporter. "I don't know if he's good unusual or bad unusual, but he's certainly unusual."

In April Cuomo signed into law the largest tax cut in New York's history, totalling $5.5 billion. The bill removed eight hundred thousand low-income New Yorkers from the state's tax rolls and scheduled the gradual reduction of the highest bracket from 9 to 7 percent by 1991. Five days after signing the tax cut bill, Cuomo proposed a $1-billion-per-year increase in a host of nuisance taxes and fees. The money was needed, the governor said, for road and bridge repairs. His concern with the issue was not new. As we have previously seen, in the late 1970s Cuomo had been one of the first public figures to point to the growing need for what came to be known as "infrastructure" spending. But the need had recently come much more to the public's attention with the collapse of a bridge on the Thruway that resulted in ten deaths. In his January State of the State address (before the Thruway tragedy), Cuomo had warned the legislature not to cut taxes too much, because they would need an additional $1 billion for roads and bridges. The legislators had not listened to him, Cuomo now contended, and had made an excessive cut in revenues. Why, then, had he signed the tax cut bill? He said he had "no alternative. They were so overwhelmingly for it that it was clear they would have gotten it anyway."

Probably so, but if the governor actually believed that the cut was too deep, but signed it in order to avoid having his veto overridden and the appearance of opposing tax cuts, it seems that he slipped into a politics of expedience rather than principle.

Only two weeks after his call for a $1-billion-a-year increase in taxes and fees, Cuomo reversed himself again. On May 15, 1987, the governor announced that the increase could be deferred because of a "dramatic" and unanticipated rise in 1986 state income tax revenues of $850 million. He said that this windfall could be used as a "down payment" on the repair program. Cuomo apparently realized that, whatever his intentions, the discovery of the excess revenue eliminated any possibility that the legislature would pass a bill to raise taxes and fees. The governor and the legislators finally agreed to divide the revenue surplus among the road and bridge repairs sought by Cuomo, the prison construction desired by Senate Republicans, and the rehabilitation of middle-income housing wanted by Assembly Democrats.

Another notable event in the 1987 legislative session was passage of a law ending archaic milk regulations, left over from the Great Depression, that kept up prices to the point that they cost New York consumers an estimated $100 million a year. Cuomo also gained the agreement of upstate legislators to a desperately needed $8.7 billion project to rebuild the New York City transit system. And the governor and the legislature agreed to reduce corporate taxes to offset the windfall from federal tax reform. Cuomo refused to go along with Republican attempts to make cuts in corporate taxes beyond what was necessary to eliminate the windfall, as had been done with personal income taxes.[8]

The major confrontation of 1987 between Cuomo and legislators was over government ethics. Cuomo had been pushing for stricter ethics laws since he entered government as secretary of state. The burgeoning New York City corruption scandal, the emergence of new scandals in Albany involving legislators providing no-show state jobs for campaign workers, and Cuomo's monumental endorsement by the voters combined to give the governor a new opportunity in 1987 to obtain passage of a meaningful ethics bill.

Cuomo began the process in January, when he announced the appointment of a new state commission to investigate corruption. The panel, called the Commission on Government Integrity, was to be a successor to the earlier State-City Commission on Integrity in Government, which had made recommendations for legislation and had called for a new panel with subpeona power. The Republican-controlled state senate had so far refused to act on the recommendations of the earlier commission, which was headed by Michael Sovern, the president of Columbia University. The new commission Cuomo announced in January was to be headed by Joseph Califano, who had been Secretary of Health, Education, and Welfare under President Carter.

The Califano Commission was quickly aborted by the state legislature, members of which wanted to confine any investigation of corruption within the city limits of New York. They refused to provide funds for the commission until Califano agreed to step down as its chairman. Cuomo had considered financing the commission through private donations, but Califano thought that would be unwise.

When the legislature passed—by a combined vote of 199 to 1—a milquetoast ethics bill in April, Cuomo asked that it be recalled and strengthened. The legislature failed to take the action he requested, and Cuomo promptly vetoed the bill, risking the first override of his governorship. The guerrilla engagements of the first three months of the session now gave way to the all-out war to which Cuomo later referred.

Cuomo said that the bill "simply does not do enough, and goes backward in certain critical areas." If this meant confrontation with the legislature, he said, "so be it, we'll have a confrontation." Senator Anderson called the veto an "arbitrary and capricious act" that showed "deliberate hostility towards the Legislature."

The bill was in fact a shabby affair. As two examples of its many shortcomings, it would have banned only formal appearances by legislators for clients before state agencies. The far more effective behind-the-scenes contacts would be permitted. And the bill included a provision that if the courts invalidated any provision in the huge bill, the entire law would be considered overturned. This was precisely the opposite of the usual procedure, and seemed to indicate that lawmakers did not in fact even want to be subject to the diluted provisions in their own bill. Most of them would have preferred no ethics bill at all, and the strange invalidation provision provided them with an opportunity to say they voted for ethics legislation at the same time it held out for them the hope that the whole bill might quickly become a dead letter.

In retrospect, Cuomo is more generous in his appraisal of the motives of legislators than he was at the time. He told me that they simply did not like the idea of changing the way they had been doing things for many years and resented the implication that they had been involved in wrongdoing.

Cuomo's fight on the ethics issue can be seen in at least two ways. His opponents point out that the fight enhanced his image as an opponent of corruption at just the time when the various New York political scandals might have tarnished him—albeit unjustly—through geographical proximity. The governor's supporters counter this argument by noting that, although hindsight makes it clear that the ethics fight helped his image, that was by no means certain when he vetoed the bill. The veto might have been overridden, which would not have been good for Cuomo's image. Or his opposition might have produced such a stalemate that no bill was passed. In either of those cases, Cuomo would not have emerged from the struggle with a better public image.

Cuomo's confrontation with a nearly unanimous legislature carried high risks. Inevitably, it aroused bitter resentment among many legislators. They saw him as building his image as "St. Mario" at their expense, by fostering the impression that they were corrupt. The strong possibility existed that members of the legislature would seek revenge by blocking the governor's programs wherever they could.

The governor's backers insist that, as usual, he was shunning the easy path, which would have been to sign the weak bill, and instead was seeking to do what was right. With the bar association and the editorial writers of the major papers behind him, Cuomo took his case to the people. He is very skillful at making a case with the public. If he does it on an issue on which most of the legislature is opposed to him, the cry arises that he is "going around the legislature." But there is nothing wrong with that. One of the most important functions of a governor—or a president—is to raise public consciousness and rally public support in order to pass legislation that is worthwhile but is facing strong opposition in the legislative branch.

By 1987 Cuomo was very skilled at using the levers of political power. One tactic he successfully employed in the ethics struggle was to hold up agreement on a pay raise for legislators until they approved an ethics bill the governor found acceptable. His forcing of a confrontation with the legislature, his translation of his personal popularity into meaningful legislation, and his unwavering stand for a tough ethics bill combined to produce the most important victory of Cuomo's years as governor.

The ethics bill that was finally passed at the beginning of July 1987 did not contain everything Cuomo had sought. By almost all accounts, though, it was one of the strictest in the United States. Almost unnoticed at the the time was a companion internal control measure added by Cuomo that provides for regular internal audits and periodic external audits of all agencies of the state government. The ethics bill addressed the way public officials run their private lives, which is of great importance when public funds are involved. But the internal control bill deals with how public officials spend the public's money, which may be even more important to the efficient functioning of state government. Both of these measures were pathbreaking efforts in which New York took the lead. And it is beyond question that Mario Cuomo deserves the overwhelming share of the credit for these achievements.

When the governor signed the two bills into law in August, he was generous in his praise of legislators for their ultimate cooperation. This was partly fence-mending, in anticipation of future dealings with the legislature. But Cuomo is usually willing to share credit for accomplishments with others.

Although the ethics and internal audit laws were major achievements, much remained to be done. For example, efforts to enact legislation providing for public financing of political campaigns in New York State and New York City died in the 1987 legislature. After the legislative session closed, Cuomo vetoed two other bills that had passed unanimously in both houses of the legislature. One dealt with the way hospitals are reimbursed by insurance companies and the government. Cuomo maintained that it would have cost the people of New York $400 million each year. In addition, in basing the level of reimbursement on the rates previously charged by each hospital, the bill would reward hospitals that had been overcharging patients.

The second Cuomo veto of a unanimously passed bill in the summer of 1987 was on the issue of supplementing the pensions of previously retired city and state employees. Cuomo contended that the bill as passed was "legally flawed" because it created new supplements without repealing old ones and so would allow certain pensioners to collect twice. He also agreed with Mayor Koch that the costs of the bill would be too high and that the benefits should be directed toward those retirees who were actually being shortchanged, because they had retired before 1968, rather than at all state and city retirees.

Legislators, still simmering over the ethics fight, threatened to reconvene and override the governor's vetoes of these two bills. Cuomo headed off this threat by making it clear that he would push for additional, stiffer ethics legislation if the lawmakers returned to Albany. By September negotiators from the executive and legislative branches had worked out a compromise on the hospital bill. It was generally agreed that the new version would save a minimum of $100 million—and possibly as much as $300 million—a year from what the original bill would have cost. Chalk up another victory for the governor—and the people of New York.

As this is written, a compromise on the pension bill appears to be close. If so, it means that by standing up to a unanimous legislature on three important issues in 1987, Mario Cuomo will have achieved one of the most stringent ethics laws in the United States and prevented the unnecessary expenditure of hundreds of millions of dollars of the taxpayers' money.

While the 1987 legislative session was one of considerable triumph for Mario Cuomo, he did not succeed on all fronts. One important example of legislation pushed by the governor but not enacted by the legislature was Cuomo's call for tougher penalties for crimes motivated by racism or other prejudice. Another was the inability of the governor to obtain Republican agreement on a plan to restructure New York's confusing hodgepodge of courts into a single, unified system. On the whole, though, 1987 was a banner year for Cuomo on the legislative front. The price he paid for his victories was to sow a large crop of resentment among the legislators. How costly the victories might ultimately prove to be could not be known until that crop was harvested in 1988. If the reasonably amicable negotiations over the health care and pension compromises in the fall of 1987 can be taken as indicative of future relations, the final price for the governor's victories may turn out to be very small.

One other Cuomo initiative in 1987 should be mentioned. As he had done on such earlier issues as infrastructure rebuilding, Cuomo took a leading position in dealing with the Acquired Immune Deficiency Syndrome epidemic. In August 1987 New York's governor instituted a large-scale, anonymous test of blood samples to determine if the deadly AIDS virus had begun in any significant degree to spread beyond promiscuous homosexuals and intravenous drug users. At the same time, Cuomo denounced the hysteria-fed demand of some politicians for mandatory testing of such groups as foreigners entering the United States, all people entering hospitals, and people applying for marriage licenses. He similarly denounced attempts to institute discriminatory practices against groups or individuals deemed likely to be carriers of the disease.

In warning of the potentially massive impact of AIDS on our society, attempting to collect accurate information on its spread, and resisting hysterical reactions, Cuomo was demonstrating responsible leadership on what could prove to be an explosive political—as well as health and financial—crisis.[9]

Those who have seen Mario
Cuomo as a budding national leader of extraordinary potential
have often pointed to his lack of foreign-policy experience and
knowledge as his major weakness in a national campaign. He was
well aware of the deficiency, and has devoted a substantial amount
of time, beginning in 1985, to remedying it. He has read widely in
the field, had long discussions with foreign- and defense-policy
experts, and finally started to travel abroad.

Although somewhat sensitive about his lack of background in
diplomacy and national defense, Cuomo has believed that the same
fundamental principles and values that have guided his policies at
home can be broadened to form the basis of an approach to international affairs. These include "family" and synergism, reasonableness and common sense, mediation and conciliation, and the rule
of law. He has also felt that neutralizing the issue of his lack of
experience in these areas would not prove to be especially difficult.

When I first discussed foreign and military policy with Cuomo
at the beginning of 1986, he stressed these points. "If you're allowed to assume that the people are going to be reasonable, that
they're going to listen to reason when you talk about foreign
policy," Cuomo said to me, "then it's just a matter of making a
commonsense case. And I think the commonsense case starts with
a recognition of the interconnectedness of the world." "If I were
president," he went on, "I'd give a nice simple speech about interconnectedness and [that] there have to be some rules. Can you
imagine any family without some rules? Every society needs some
rules. We have not yet begun to think of the world as a society, and
it is. That's a reality that we haven't dealt with yet. The world *is*
a single society."

Speaking of terrorism as well as the arms race, Cuomo said,
"Somebody has to sit down and make up some rules. You've got
to get the people who are rational in the world to agree on some
rules. . . . You've got to have the predictability of a rule." On the
one hand, this might sound terribly naive; on the other, it's the
only commonsense way to try to deal with a worldwide problem
such as terrorism. "The Germans think they can tell you to go to
hell with your terrorism principle," Cuomo said. "You've got to
have enough leadership to do this." Of course he did not yet know
when this conversation took place in January 1986 the full extent

to which the incumbent president of the United States was then failing to show that leadership. Trading arms to one of the leading backers of terrorism in exchange for hostages while denouncing others for dealing with terrorists would not appear to be the best way to lead the "rational" people of the world to set up and abide by predictable rules.

What of the irrational leaders of the world—or those who may be perfectly rational but refuse to accept international cooperation? Obviously one cannot count on everyone playing by the rules. "You've got to be strong enough to deal with those who will not live by the rules once they are set down," Cuomo answered in 1986. His solution to problems of defense was to apply his basic principles: "Interpolate a little rationality into it. We're just not doing it smart. . . . We're spending too much money on the wrong things. *Everybody* knows it. Goldwater knows it; Aspin knows it; Nunn knows it. What you've got to do is to be strong enough to be apolitical about it. The only reason you pour all that money into defense is that you think it makes you look good and you want to win the next election. We've gotta have somebody who says, 'Screw it. I'm going to do the right thing, and I'm going to take the risk.'"

Which, of course, is exactly the Cuomo approach to controversial issues in New York.

At the beginning of 1986, Cuomo placed the highest priority on achieving an arms control deal with the Soviets. He indicated that he was opposed to President Reagan's Strategic Defensive Initiative, popularly known as Star Wars. "I think eventually the immensity of SDI will become the *enormity* of SDI." (He told me that he had just found out that "enormity" is a negative. He had used it as a synonym for "immensity" in his recent State of the State address and had received several letters from English teachers.) If President Reagan insisted on pursuing SDI, Cuomo said, "it will show what a waste, what a travesty that whole thing is." In order to get a deal that would massively reduce nuclear armaments, Cuomo argued, "you have to give up SDI. I think that's going to be the key. You have to be careful how you do it, though. You can't give it away during the campaign."

The governor seemed to be following that strategy in public statements on the subject. A little more than a year after our conversation (and two nights before his startling announcement that he would not seek the 1988 Democratic presidential nomination), Cuomo answered a question on SDI after a speech he gave at Tulane University. He said that he supported continued research on the proposal, because it was a good "bargaining chip" for use in negotiations with the Soviets, and because such research might produce technological spin-offs that could prove useful in nonmilitary fields. He went on to say he was undecided about whether SDI should be taken beyond research. Unless his views had changed from what he had told me a year earlier, this was intended for public—and, particularly, Russian—consumption.

Although some analysts have criticized Cuomo for being naive about the Soviet threat, the fact is that he began his study of Soviet-American relations from a distinctly Cold War point of view. As he was delving into the subject in 1986 and 1987, Cuomo was talking one morning with press aide Dick Starkey. "He was talking like a cold warrior of the fifties: '[The Communists are seeking] world supremacy'—he didn't say 'evil empire,' but he used everything short of 'evil empire,' " Starkey told me.

"Mario, where did you get all this?" Starkey finally asked him. "That's fifties talk, and it's terribly narrow."

"Well," the governor responded, "you learned that in Catholic school like I did. Why aren't you saying the same thing?"

"He said, in effect," Starkey told me, "that he was influenced—and he is today—by what he learned in Catholic school: 'godless Communism.' So there's a little naiveté, an innocence that shines through . . . with regard to foreign affairs—though maybe not for long."

In order to end that innocence and replace it with well-thought-out positions, Cuomo undertook intensive study and consultation with foreign-policy and defense experts. One strongly suspects that his awareness of his lack of preparation in these fields played an important role in his decision to forgo active campaigning for the presidency in 1987. His time was better spent in reading, talking, and traveling abroad than it would have been in the living rooms and meeting halls of Iowa and New Hampshire.

Few people have ever questioned Mario Cuomo's intellectual capacity; he is a rapid learner. In his studies he delved into a wide variety of books, such journals as *Foreign Affairs,* and the international coverage of the *New York Times* and the *Washington Post,* and he talked whenever he could with people knowledgeable in diplomacy and defense, including experts holding many different viewpoints.

Cuomo began to state his positions on certain foreign-policy issues. Although he questioned whether the Reagan administration had thought out a long-term strategy for dealing with Libya, Cuomo said that he supported the American attack on that country. He criticized the Reagan administration for not doing enough to oppose apartheid in South Africa, and he opposed the Reagan policy of supporting the contras in Nicaragua.

By June of 1987, Cuomo already believed that he had gone a long way toward removing the question mark about his knowledge and ability in international affairs. When I mentioned the perception that he is weak on foreign policy, Cuomo interrupted me to say that he wasn't hearing that anymore. The main reason, he thought, was the commencement address he had given at the Johns Hopkins School of Advanced International Studies a few weeks earlier.

The bases for Cuomo's Johns Hopkins speech were the ones that have informed his developing philosophy of international affairs: a truly *democratic* foreign policy, worldwide interdependence, the need for negotiation and conciliation, and the rule of law. He pointed out that conducting foreign policy on a democratic basis is difficult, but "in this country, policy—including our foreign policy—to be *effective—must ultimately* be a reflection of the public judgment and will."

"Effective policy in this democracy," Cuomo stated, "demands effective communication between the government and the governed. I suggest to you that if we accomplished that, the principal truth we would be making clear to the public today would be our increasing *inter*dependence—within the nation and within the world." Just as it should be evident that all parts of the United States must share in the nation's fate, he said, "today it's just as clear, that with only a small portion of the five billion people who occupy this planet living in the United States, the economic life of every farm and manufacturing community in the nation, of every city and village, is firmly set in a matrix of relationships with the *entire rest* of the world."

"There is no way," Cuomo told the Johns Hopkins audience, "to make ourselves secure from one another's aggressions and mistakes by building a wall around our borders—or an impenetrable shield reaching to the stars. You know that no man is an island. No woman. No village. No town. No state. No nation either."

Cuomo noted that there seemed to be a rare opportunity, "an

unprecedented convergence," that might allow successful negotiations to end the Cold War. "Of course, achieving it [lasting peace] won't be easy and it would be naive—or cynical—to suggest otherwise. Nice words like 'interdependence,' 'mutuality,' 'family' and 'peace,' are easier to utter than to apply. . . . But we should not use the conceded difficulties as excuses for reducing our standards or our aspirations."

On the other hand, Cuomo tried to demonstrate that he understood the danger posed by the Soviets. "All of this we must do without abandoning our wariness of the Soviet Union. Whether they are driven by historical fears or a desire for global supremacy spawned by Marxist-Leninist principles, we should not make the mistake of tempting them with weakness."

In his call for worldwide application of the rule of law, Cuomo took several shots at the Reagan administration (and some of its predecessors):

We need a more reliable set of guidelines than the impulses urging us to do whatever we decide is the very best for *us* at the moment—despite previous understandings or consensual arrangements.

We cannot join in an international court of law and participate only when all the rulings go our way.

We cannot covertly work to assassinate political leaders, no matter how reprehensible, and then expect to lead a moral crusade against terrorism.

We cannot insist that other nations comply with arms control agreements, which we seek to reinterpret to our benefit with casuistic arguments.

And of course, we must insist that *other nations* play by the rules as well. The Soviet Union, for example, has violated treaties, invaded and brutally occupied Afghanistan, and played cynical proxy games in the Middle East and the Third World.

Our negotiations, therefore, should seek to achieve a firmer *mutual* commitment to the rule of law.

Cuomo concluded by telling the foreign-affairs graduates that "while the future may be beyond our vision, it is not beyond our influence. We have you to help us get past the slogans, labels, and the seductive but unreal poetry of politics. To help us form intelligent public policy consensus on our important concerns. To find ways to forge new *mutually*—indeed *universally*—beneficial relationships—North and South, East and West, the Old World, the New World, the Third World."

It was a powerful speech, and Cuomo believed that it had served its purpose well. He told me that he talked with many foreign-policy experts before and after the Johns Hopkins address, and that afterward everyone was accusing him of holding out on them about his extensive knowledge of international affairs. "It was interesting," he said, "really very interesting, how easy it was to persuade them." "It's amazing how Washington—how quickly they will change their attitudes—so I'm not hearing it," he said of the talk about his being weak on foreign policy. "And once I go to the USSR—this is stupid business, [but] you take one trip overseas [and] they see your picture in the paper: 'Hey, he was in the USSR!' "

Before he undertook that trip in September 1987, Governor Cuomo had an opportunity to outline some of his thoughts on dealing with the Soviet Union. He welcomed delegations of American and Soviet citizens to a conference at Chautauqua, New York. He spoke on the same themes he had addressed before, but was sharply criticized by several commentators for failing to stress the evils and abuses of the Soviet system. In emphasizing what we have in common, these critics contended, Cuomo failed to mention what keeps us apart. He said nothing about Afghanistan, nothing about refuseniks, nothing about human rights abuses or treaty violations. "What *you* might regard as a well-ordered society *we* might consider an oppressive one," Cuomo told the visiting Russians. "What we think of as incentive, you may see as inequity." This came too close for comfort to the outrageous idea of "moral equivalence" between the American and Soviet systems. It's all just a matter of different opinions, Cuomo seemed to be saying: different strokes for different folks. He had come a long way in a short time from "godless Communism." Too long. It seemed almost a journey from Barry Goldwater to George McGovern.

Cuomo explained his emphasis on the positive at Chautauqua by pointing out that he was making a welcoming speech. It would hardly have been appropriate, he said, to start lecturing his guests on their sins.

What is inappropriate for a host may be the same for a guest. When Cuomo traveled to the Soviet Union in September 1987, he bent over backward to be polite. A group of dissidents seeking freedom of the press asked Cuomo about human rights violations in Russia, and he told them that he didn't "want to do anything to show disrespect for a government that's been so good to us by inviting us here and allowing me this kind of activity here tonight."

But more than politeness was involved in Cuomo's frequent accentuating of what the two countries had in common. His experience as a mediator had taught him, he said, that agreements are best reached and concessions obtained by focusing on areas both sides agree upon, rather than by stressing differences.

On his first day in Moscow, Cuomo's Soviet hosts tricked him into endorsing a proposal they had made for a joint conference on human rights violations in the two countries. "Moral equivalence" again, but it had the sound of reasonableness, and Cuomo had not been briefed on the subject. When a reporter asked him whether he thought there were extensive human rights abuses in the United States, the governor replied, "That's a provocative kind of question. Why don't you hold a conference and find out?"

Cuomo quickly retreated from his apparent support for the Soviet proposal. Later in the day, after a meeting with dissident physicist Andrei Sakharov, Cuomo said that he had no position on the conference. The next day he held a news conference to clarify his nonposition. He said he certainly did not intend to imply that there might be human rights violations in the United States of anywhere near the magnitude of such abuses in the Soviet Union.

As his weeklong visit to Russia went on, Cuomo became more openly critical of his hosts—and more animated and Cuomo-like as well. After attending Rosh Hashanah services at the Moscow synagogue, Cuomo went to have a holiday meal with twenty-two refuseniks at the apartment of one of them. The immigrant's son seemed genuinely moved by the plight of these Jews who were not allowed to emigrate. Passion replaced the stiff formality of his first few days in Moscow. Cuomo brought smiles to the faces of the Russian Jews as he spoke movingly of freedom. He identified with these victims, as he had so often in the past with suffering Americans.

When Cuomo finished, his host, Alex Lerner, gave *Village Voice* writer Craig Copetas an assessment of the governor that matched what many Americans had said of him. "This man would be a good president," the Jewish scientist said. "I have met most of those who want to be president. Gary Hart was too dry, hard, and unemotional. Mondale was a good man, but lacked strength. Ahhh . . . but this Cuomo is smart and strong and kind. It is a rare combination of features for a leader. Cuomo is a statesman. It is a very great mistake that he is saying no."

The Kremlin shares few views with the refuseniks, but the Soviet leaders who met Cuomo apparently agreed with Lerner that the governor should be president. Georgi Arbatov, director of the Soviet Institute for the USA and Canada, called Cuomo the most effective American leader since Franklin Roosevelt. Copetas was told that when former Soviet ambassador to the United States and current Central Committee Secretary Anatoly Dobrynin met privately with Cuomo, he told him that the Kremlin wanted George Bush to win the presidency. "Bush would be the easiest one for us to deal with," Dobrynin reportedly told Cuomo. "We don't want you to be president because you're too tough." As Cuomo kept insisting that he was not running, Dobrynin interjected, "But you're the best possible candidate." Sources told Copetas that Cuomo smiled at this comment.

Despite a few rough spots, Cuomo's trip to the Soviet Union was a notable success. He grew much more at ease as the week progressed, and he showed obvious joy at being able to discuss world affairs with high Soviet leaders. Although he insisted that he never expected to meet with General Secretary Mikhail Gorbachev, Cuomo must have been disappointed that the Soviet leader did not return to Moscow from an extended vacation to see him. But the governor told reporters that he had found exhilaration in talking with Soviet officials about questions affecting the future of the world.

Cuomo got very good reviews from both Soviets and Americans who observed him on the trip. *Pravda*, the official Soviet newspaper, printed a long and favorable article on Cuomo's visit. Several weeks later NBC newsman Tom Brokaw interviewed Mikhail Gorbachev, showed him a page with photos of the twelve active presidential candidates, and asked him to circle the one he thought would be elected in 1988. Gorbachev circled the entire group, but two of his top aides said that the face of the next American president was not on the page.

Officials at the American embassy said that on the trip Cuomo had shown himself—a few faux pas notwithstanding—to be well versed in Soviet affairs.

Cuomo told me that he thought the trip was "great." "We didn't sleep at all, just about. Jet lag was horrible. I've still got it," he said three weeks after his return. "I think I'll always have it—I'll be tired for the rest of my life. But we saw so much, talked to so many people. I love that sort of thing, being exposed to new situations, confronted with new problems. That's what I liked so much about practicing law. It was always new and different cases you had to prepare for."

The most important test of what Cuomo had learned and accomplished in Russia came a few weeks after his return, when he delivered a major address on international affairs at the Council on Foreign Relations in Washington. The speech contained the same philosophy that Cuomo had espoused at Johns Hopkins, but the audience was more important—much of the foreign-policy establishment of the United States—and the speech contained a greater emphasis on the need for caution in dealing with the Soviets and on the failings of the Soviet government.

Cuomo reported to the CFR on the findings of his trip. The Russian economy, he said, "is weak and growing weaker." More significant, he indicated, was his perception that many people in the Soviet Union were beginning to become restive. "There is a stirring—a reaching—a curiosity about other, better possibilities." Cuomo contended that the Soviet leaders "are faced with a dangerous dilemma and they know it: they need to give their people more freedom in order to make progress, but if they give too much freedom they risk losing power." Their precarious position makes the Soviets eager to achieve arms reductions so they can meet the demands of their people for more consumer goods. While making it very clear that we must insist upon changes in Soviet behavior before agreements are finalized, Cuomo argued that an unusual opportunity exists to make the world safer and save a fortune at the same time.

After his twenty-five-minute speech, Cuomo answered questions in a two-and-a-half-hour, off-the-record session that amounted to a kind of oral comprehensive exam in foreign affairs. Cuomo's 250 interrogators gave him high marks, most of them saying they were impressed with the governor's knowledge in this area. "What he said was unexceptional," said conservative Democrat and former Reagan Defense department official Richard Perle. "But the manner in which he said it was exceptional. He was unusually candid. He's forceful and lively."

"I have never had such a reaction to a speech," Cuomo told me a few days later. "The reaction to the convention speech was great, but this was even better. That was all emotion. This was much more intellectual."

In the Council on Foreign Relations speech, Cuomo several times referred to the need for strong presidential leadership. "Historians and philosophers have always quarreled about how much influence individuals have on events," he said. "But for the leaders of nations there can be only one working principle: events will be what they make them."[10]

His denials continued, but by late October 1987 there could be little doubt that Mario Cuomo was thinking very seriously about becoming a leader of nations who could influence the future of the world.

12

CUOMO

At THE OUTSET of this book, I said that many people find Mario Cuomo to be an enigma. The extensive analysis of his life in the pages since should have made him less of a puzzle. It remains, however, to try to take the measure of the man.

Cuomo does not fit readily into political categories. Although he is most often pigeonholed as a "liberal," his aides go to great pains to try to persuade people that he is not a liberal. And several articles in liberal publications have expressed shock at the discovery that Cuomo may not be so liberal after all. In an unrelentingly hostile early 1987 piece in *Mother Jones*, *Newsday* Albany bureau chief Miriam Pawel said, "If Cuomo is their best bet, liberals may be in big trouble." In New York, she contended, many liberals "don't believe [in Cuomo] anymore. They've applauded the stirring speeches and been moved by the rhetoric, but they've despaired of the results."

The governor himself insists that such labels as liberal and conservative are meaningless. He prefers to call himself a "progressive pragmatist." The public that knows him best—the people of New York State—tend to see Cuomo as they see themselves. In a 1985 Marist poll, a plurality of self-identified liberals (41.6 percent) called Cuomo a liberal. A substantial majority of self-styled moderates (69 percent) saw Cuomo as a moderate. And far more self-proclaimed conservatives (26.4 percent) labeled Cuomo a conservative than did members of either of the other groups. (A wide plurality—46.1 percent—of those calling themselves conservative Democrats identified their governor as a conservative.) It reminds one of the Alfred S. Burt–Wihla Hutson Christmas song, "Some Children See Him":

Some children see Him lily white
The baby Jesus born this night
. . .
Some children see Him bronzed and brown
. . .
Some children see Him dark as they.

Cuomo's remarkable ability to relate his experiences to those of people anywhere is part of the explanation of why people with divirgent backgrounds and philosophies identify with him. It was, perhaps, not especially surprising that Cuomo was able to convince an audience in San Antonio at the beginning of 1986 that his experience growing up as an Italian-American in Queens was similar to that of Mexican-Americans on the West Side of the Texas city. But it *was* remarkable when he managed to persuade most of the audience at the 1987 state Democratic party dinner in Indianapolis that "in a very real sense we [in South Jamaica] were a lot like 'Hoosiers.' " In fact, Cuomo has little difficulty in making his urban-ethnic-immigrant-Catholic background sufficiently universal that it seems familiar to a rural, "native" WASP from the heartland. He tells them that the folks in his neighborhood were "people whose values were rooted in family, faith, and community. People who believed passionately in the dignity of hard work—the chance to earn one's bread. People who knew, by instinct, the necessity of sharing. . . . Maybe the immigrant languages of South Jamaica, Queens, were different from what you'd hear in Terre Haute or Bloomington. The complexions were probably darker, a shade more olive, a little more black and brown. But the struggle was the same. And the strivings. And the dreams."

After he did an article for *Life* on growing up in an ethnic neighborhood in Queens, Cuomo got letters from people all over the country, saying how similar their experiences in Montana, or wherever, had been to his in South Jamaica.

Those who think that Cuomo could not win much support in some regions of the country, such as the South, the Rocky Mountain West, or the rural Midwest, do not understand the special aspects of the man and his abilities. There is no question that a degree of prejudice persists in some areas against Catholics, Italian-Americans, New Yorkers, and those suspected of being "liberals." Those biases would not vanish because Cuomo sought the presidency. But in order for someone to maintain a prejudice, it is necessary for him to make exceptions. Any member of a target group who does not fit a bigot's stereotype must be classified as an exception. If it were otherwise, the prejudice would have to be abandoned. Even Hitler was said to know a dozen or so people he considered to be "good Jews." People who do not fit one's preconceived notions about a category are quickly and conveniently removed from that category. Early in 1980 more than one-fourth of the Americans surveyed in a national opinion poll said that they could never vote for a divorced man for the presidency. As far as I know, there was no follow-up poll after the election, but it would be very surprising if most of those people did not vote for Ronald Reagan. One suspects that many of the people who were most adamantly opposed to divorce would have liked Reagan so much for his positions on issues that he would, in their minds, cease to be a divorced man. Something similar would very likely happen when people in other regions of the country heard Cuomo talk about his universal values. Many of those who remained biased against the *categories* to which Cuomo belongs would exempt him from those categories. In their minds Catholics, Italians, New Yorkers, and liberals might continue to be anathema, but they would cease to consider Cuomo to be any of them.

As I have said, Mario Cuomo is a complex man who defies simple categorization. But the associate who told political journalist Fred Barnes that Cuomo's "heart is on the left, but his wallet's on the right" spoke the essential truth. The influences that shaped Cuomo's beliefs molded him into a compassionate but frugal man. His religion and his family orientation gave him a social conscience and made him sensitive to the needs of others, but he is also the son of a shopkeeper. He approaches finances—both his own and the public's—with the thinking of a small merchant who counts his pennies. Although money has never held any great attraction for him, Cuomo is always mindful of the need to make ends meet. Occasionally a member of the governor's staff will make the mistake during a discussion of a budget item of saying something like, "It doesn't really make much difference; it's only fifty thousand dollars." Cuomo's response will be something to the effect of: "Oh, just fifty thousand dollars, huh? *Whose* fifty thousand dollars is it? Is that *your* fifty thousand dollars or is that *my* fifty thousand dollars?" He makes clear to all present that while such transactions may seem minimal to others, they are important to him. He knows that money is finite. Resources are limited and choices must be made. This blend of social liberalism and fiscal conservatism is one that a majority of New York voters find extremely appealing. It seems certain that people across the nation would agree.

Those who are most critical of Cuomo may see him as too liberal or too conservative, but a better label for what some of them dislike about him might be "mugwump." The name was applied to Republican reformers who bolted their party in 1884 because they could not support the party's tainted presidential nominee, former Senator James G. Blaine. "Mugwump" was derived from a word in the Natick dialect of the Massachuset tribe, and was used to mean "holier than thou." What some politicians find most troublesome about Mario Cuomo is that he sometimes acts as if he is the only person in politics with pure motives. Like the 1884 mugwumps, Cuomo often shuns partisanship and acts independently.

The term "mugwump" points up one of the greatest dangers Cuomo faces: giving the appearance of believing that he is better than other people—what *Time* magazine has called "a kind of conspicuous moral vanity." "It ought to be possible," George F. Will has noted, "for a man of Cuomo's intelligence to call attention to problems without, in the process, seeming to disparage the public's moral sensibilities and to celebrate his own." Cuomo has to avoid giving the appearance of being someone who thinks, "I'm fundamentally a damn fine person." Will quotes *American Scholar* editor Joseph Epstein as describing this type of person (Epstein coined the term "Virtucrat" to classify the breed) as "a modern Diogenes who, in search of one good man, knocked off after turning his lantern on himself."

Cuomo does not in fact believe—at least not consistently—that he is much better than others. His diaries make it clear that he harbors large self-doubts. But he must be careful not to give the *impression* that he thinks he is moral and others are not. It is essential that Cuomo make it plain that when he calls upon people to help others, he is not lecturing them on how they should be good *like him*. He should emphasize—and often does—that we are *all* imperfect and need substantial improvement that can be achieved through working together. Seen in this light, Cuomo's self-doubts can be an advantage. They can enable him to show that he shares in the problems and imperfections against which he preaches. A good motto for him might be "Do as I Say, Not as I Sometimes Do."

The Democratic candidate to whom the Republican mug-wumps threw their support in 1884 was Grover Cleveland. Cleveland was elected to the governorship of New York in 1882, exactly a century before Cuomo. Some interesting similarities between the two men can be identified. Cleveland was noted for his remarkable degree of honesty. When he was nominated for the presidency, he was called "the unowned candidate." As governor of New York, he stood as a man of principle. One example of this was Cleveland's veto of a bill that would have lowered the fares on the elevated railroads of New York City. Signing the bill clearly would have been the popular course to take, but Cleveland insisted that the measure was wrong and irresponsible and so vetoed it. As president, Cleveland pushed for lower tariffs, an effort that may have cost him the 1888 election. When he was told that his stance on tariffs might result in his defeat, Cleveland said, "What is the use of being elected or reelected unless you stand for something?" "Perhaps I made a mistake from the party standpoint," he later declared, "but damn it, I was right."

Grover Cleveland's integrity, his stand on principle regardless of popular opinion, and his "politics be damned" attitude all sound like Mario Cuomo. But it would be a mistake to carry very far the notion of similarities between these New York governors. Cleveland was a man of principle, but his principles were steadfastly conservative. As historian Richard Hofstadter put it, Cleveland was "the ideal bourgeois statesman for his time: out of heartfelt conviction he gave to the interests what many a lesser politician might have sold them for a price."

Certainly Mario Cuomo is a pragmatist, but one with a large social conscience. His philosophy is eclectic, but it is grounded on certain firm values and principles. They, in turn, originate in Cuomo's religion.

Cuomo's belief in the principles of affirmative government for which the Democratic party generally has stood since the New Deal has remained unshaken. The fact that such beliefs became unpopular in the early eighties, Cuomo said in a 1985 speech at Yale, was no reason to abandon them. Recounting Galileo's whisper after being forced by the Church to deny that the earth orbits the sun, *"E pur si muove"* (But still it moves), Cuomo said that despite the outcome of the 1984 election, he would continue to say of the Democratic principles, *"E pur si muove."*

"Our Constitution isn't simply an invitation to selfishness,"

Cuomo said in what may have been his most inspiring speech, the sermon he gave at New York City's Cathedral of St. John the Divine in November 1983, "for in it is also embodied a central truth of the Judeo-Christian tradition—that is, a sense of the common good. It says, as the Gospel says, that freedom isn't license; that liberty creates responsibility; that if we have been given freedom, it is to encourage us to pursue the common good." He went on to say that we must affirm "as our moral and political foundation the idea that we *are* our brother's keeper, all of us, as a people, as a *government;* that our responsibility to our brothers and sisters is greater than any one of us and that it doesn't end when they are out of the individual reach of our hand or our charity or our love."

Cuomo extends his philosophy of mutual responsibility to the entire planet. "I'd like to write a Declaration of Interdependence, about the relationships between all the parts of a disparate world," he says, echoing John XXIII.

"Let's not forget," Cuomo often says. Others helped us to get where we are. There is nothing wrong with success, as he sees it. "Get rich—but don't forget those you leave behind who are in the same boat you were in. Pay your dues to the society that has made your success possible." He worries, Matilda Cuomo says, that "we may be developing a whole society of soft people, people who don't realize their obligations." This attitude filters down through the society. "You bring children into the world," Mrs. Cuomo said her husband tells young people. "It's your responsibility, not the next guy's. Don't think they're society's or anybody else's."

Helping others is good for the giver as well as the recipient, as Cuomo sees it. "Lord knows they need the help," Cuomo said of Italian earthquake victims in 1980, "and we need to give it." "I feel almost guilty about our good fortune," Cuomo wrote in his diary in 1981. "I've always had the feeling that I've been given much more than I deserve and much more than most others and that most of my life should be spent trying to give something back. It's important to be even. Although I've never been able to figure out exactly why."[1]

Mario Cuomo's abilities are extraordinary. In the assessment of his former speechwriter Peter Quinn, Cuomo is "the single most amazing man in American politics." Perhaps his most evident ability is in the realm of public speaking. Cuomo can communicate with anyone. When he talks to kids in Harlem about drugs, he doesn't patronize them. He doesn't lecture them; he just says, "Hey, that's stupid." When he gave one such talk, the kids, twelve to fifteen years old, stood and applauded. A teacher who was in attendance said later that those were not children who are easily fooled—or easily impressed. But Cuomo had impressed them. They would not forget him, or what he told them, she said.

Cuomo was already a brilliant speaker before he entered politics. He was able to go before an appellate court and make an argument that was emotional and eloquent, forceful but controlled. He had a good sense of theater, knowing when to turn on his heels at the end of a speech and walk away. He could leave those in the courtroom gasping. It took some time for him to shift from the rather aggressive approach that served him well in the courtroom to the more measured tones that could persuade the general public. Once he had learned the lesson, he became as much of a virtuoso at political speaking as he had been at legal presentation.

In one-on-one discussions or in small groups, Cuomo still uses his skills as an attorney. He is usually able rapidly to shoot holes into the arguments of others. Those who go into the governor's office intending to argue with him, former chief of staff Michael Del Giudice told me, often wind up "walking out of the room sheepishly—carrying their heads in their hands, because he blew 'em apart."

He can also walk into a room without notes and handle almost any question that someone throws at him. When he starts to speak, Cuomo can convert or disarm any but the most obdurate opponent. He knows how to be charming (although of course he is not always so) and is astute at judging an audience. He can manage and work a crowd as well as a stand-up comic can. Del Giudice says that Cuomo is like Johnny Carson. "Carson never bombs, because if he's bombing, he makes a joke out of bombing. Mario used to call it 'jujitsu thinking.' 'We'll do it jujitsu-wise. If there's a problem, you turn it inside out and make it your asset.' " Cuomo seldom lets anything fester. Whatever he says publicly is either a success to begin with or he "turns it inside out" to his advantage. As Del Giudice says, "it's very tough to defeat somebody like that."

Yet Cuomo can have an off day as a speaker. When he is nervous, he tends to speak too quickly. But his off days have been very rare in recent years, and when he is on a roll there seems to be nothing that Cuomo cannot do with words. "His active vocabulary is larger than most people's passive vocabulary," Fabian Palomino says of his friend. Yet in employing that vocabulary, Cuomo does not talk above his audience, or in a condescending manner. He makes connections with any audience, if not in his prepared remarks, then in question-and-answer sessions, in which he is almost invariably more impressive than he is in formal speeches. As a rule, he can teach without seeming to preach. (There are always exceptions to rules, and it is most often when he starts to sound preachy that Cuomo runs into trouble.)

He can talk to an audience of hundreds—or millions—and make each of them feel as if he were his or her next-door neighbor. Yet if he sounds like a neighbor, he also sounds like the most impressive and inspirational orator that one has ever heard. "When he's hot," Nicholas D'Arienzo says of Cuomo, "he touches the nerve—he *burns* it." Cuomo can bring moisture to the eyes of people whose tear ducts had previously seemed to be vestigial organs. Marie Vecchio put her finger on the most important aspect of her brother's oratorical ability when she said she's heard again and again from people that his words are deeply inspirational. "People have told me, 'After listening to him, you want to go out right away and *do* something.' "[2]

While Cuomo is certainly a "Great Communicator," it is hardly accurate to classify him, as some in Albany have, as "the ethnic Ronald Reagan." The reason such a characterization is off target is that Cuomo has the substance with which to back his rhetorical ability. Not only can he communicate brilliantly; he also has something worthwhile to communicate. Reagan's skill was that of an actor, and, as became increasingly evident, his words suffer from lacking substance, lack of concrete specifics or value.

Being his own scriptwriter distinguishes Cuomo from almost all other modern American politicians. Even his harshest critics would acknowledge that no one is pulling Cuomo's strings or putting words in his mouth. His words are actually *his* words. It is dismaying to face this reality, but the fact is this is extremely rare in modern politics. Jefferson and Lincoln were presumably the actual authors of the words carved in stone on their monuments in Washington. But in recent decades most of the memorable phrases uttered by political leaders have been the work of professional ghostwriters. Senator Joseph Biden got into trouble in 1987 for plagiarizing the speeches of other politicians. But where did most of the words he expropriated originate? More than likely not in the minds of the men who publicly pronouced them.

Mario Cuomo is different. This is not to say that he never uses a phrase he picked up elsewhere or that he does not employ speechwriters. That is a necessity for anyone who must give as many speeches as he does. But Cuomo's major speeches—and the memorable lines from them—*are* his own work.

Cuomo's intelligence is on a level that is uncommon among politicians. "His intellect is enormous," Michael Del Giudice says. "He's a giant brain—raw IQ is enormous." There are few subjects on which he cannot converse knowledgeably.

Drew Zambelli, a former college professor who joined Cuomo's political staff after working with leading academicians, maintains that the governor is "one of the smartest people I've ever met—and I've worked in a world of smart people. . . . And he combines his vast intellect with tight reasoning ability." Zambelli told me that he had never before admitted to himself that another person was clearly more intelligent than he, but after working with Cuomo he finally had to do so.[3]

Part of the secret of leadership is a deeply felt belief in oneself. Cuomo certainly has this belief, although it is tempered by persistent self-doubt. He has often been accused of playing Hamlet on major decisions, but for the most part Cuomo does not show hesitation or give any hint that he is unsure of himself. As his brother Frank puts it, "Nothing fazes him."

"He has such a personal magnetism and presence," Cuomo's former law associate Sal Curiale said to me. "There is something about him." "Something" in this case refers to the same undefinable quality that we often call "charisma." Matilda Cuomo puts it differently. "He's got that kind of softness that people can feel easy with." Women, she told me, especially older women, "want to hug him and kiss him, and a lot of them do. It's like they knew him forever. That, I think, is fascinating." Curiale told me that the attraction Cuomo holds for women is shared by more junior members of the sex. "You could see it in their eyes. But he would pretend not to notice," Curiale says. "There was not a woman in New York [who knew Cuomo] who was not enthralled—in love with him." Cuomo says that such assertions are without foundation.

Just about everyone who has ever worked with Cuomo says it is exciting but extremely demanding. There is, to begin with, the sheer volume of labor. "He's the only guy I've ever worked for that I could not outwork," Michael Del Giudice told me. "He always outworked *everybody*. You just *can't* outwork him; he's just tireless."

Gary Fryer describes working with Cuomo as "more like a roller coaster than it is like a plane. There are ups and downs all over the place. He will dip down to the most minute of details on an issue and then, two seconds later, he's up above everybody else talking about philosophical implications. To people who work for him, that is mind-boggling, because trying to stay up with him requires a hell of a lot of intellectual tenacity. But for the people who work for him, it is the source of the fascination."

As he is always testing himself, Cuomo frequently tests staff members. Zambelli finds the constant intellectual demands the most stimulating aspect of working for Cuomo. Del Giudice agrees. "He's very demanding," he told me. "In an intellectual argument, he will give precision analysis to your position. That makes it very exciting to work for him. You can't ever lower your guard, because he'll get you right between the eyes." Fryer uses another sports cliché—one more fitting to the former baseball star—to describe the same Cuomo proclivity: "Don't take your eye off the ball."

Although Del Giudice says Cuomo is "a generally gracious guy," he does "get pissed off periodically." "If you do something dumb," the former chief of staff says, "you're going to know about it. And if you have a lot of weak arguments in your case, you're going to know about it." Sal Curiale told me that Cuomo was "basically a real good guy" to work for, "a tremendous sense of humor, great to be around, funny, [but] on the other hand, he could freeze you with a look. He could be very short at times—not the yelling and screaming times, but the look that would turn you into jelly, and you would proceed out of the office with your tail between your legs."

Curiale was talking about working with Cuomo in the early

1970s, before he entered politics. Certainly, as Del Giudice put it, he still gets "pissed off" on occasion. But there is general agreement among those who are frequently around him that Cuomo has mellowed over the last several years. His fuse has gotten longer. Curiale says Cuomo rarely loses his temper these days, "unless you can get his goat, which is what his opponents try to do most of the time." Cuomo "has a range of emotions," Del Giudice says. "I think he used to be a lot more impatient than he is now with people."

While it appears that Cuomo has gotten better mastery over his temper, the degree of control depends upon the situation. He almost always keeps his cool when he is involved in mediation or dealing with an issue in which he has no large personal involvement. But he is still susceptible to losses of temper if someone strikes him in a personal manner. This was apparent in the governor's reaction to attacks on his son during his 1986 reelection campaign. And if Cuomo turns on someone, he can be as ferocious as a pit bull. "I wouldn't want to be one of Cuomo's enemies," Peter Quinn told me, "because I think he'd be relentless in chasing you down."

Although he can be tough on staff members, Cuomo is very loyal to those who work for him—too much so, in the view of many critics. It may be that it is the best of his people who suffer the most abuse from Cuomo. He has always had great compassion for people of lesser ability. It just may be that this attitude extends all the way into the government he runs: those who prove themselves to be extremely capable are subjected to greater demands, because Cuomo knows they can handle such demands; those who are not up to their assignments are treated gently and eventually moved elsewhere. "He's good that way," Fabian Palomino told me. "Employees, people he should really fire—incompetence, disloyalty, and everything else—he'll call them in and he'll talk to them and he'll say, 'I got a job for you.' Instead of firing them, he gets them another job where they fit in better." Shortly after the 1986 election, Cuomo himself said, "I don't ever fire anybody, but I don't ever have to fire anybody. They go. They leave."[4]

Mario Cuomo is a man given to few diversions. He has no hobbies. He never had any interest in golf, and has only taken up tennis in a most casual way in recent years. His sports have always been team sports, in which his individual striving could be part of a larger effort. Taken by itself, this would mean little. Many people participate only in team sports and never develop Cuomo's social attitudes. But placed in the context of the rest of Cuomo's life, his love of team sports seems to be of considerable significance in understanding the man.

Cuomo will occasionally watch a baseball game, and he participates in a rotisserie baseball league. In this game, players from major-league teams are organized into fantasy teams. Participants draft various players to create ersatz teams. Standings are calculated on the basis of the statistics compiled by the real players during the season. Near the end of the 1987 season, the team Cuomo owned with Marty Steadman was mired in eighth place in a ten-team league. The governor said it was all Steadman's fault, since he had been in charge of drafting team members.

Almost all of Cuomo's time is occupied by work, family, or such solitary pursuits as reading and thinking. Each morning he does about a quarter hour of yoga to help with his chronic back pain. His back problem is serious. He always carries a board with him to sit on in the car, and has a sort of whoopee cushion that massages his back when he leans against it. He likes to give the latter to unsuspecting guests and tell them to sit on it.

Most early mornings Cuomo also spends a substantial period of time writing on the loose-leaf pages of his diary. Mary Tragale, his long-time executive assistant who types the diary, says that when Cuomo writes anything—including all but the most important speeches, as well as diary entries—he "never rewrites, rearranges, or crosses out. Once he starts writing—he will think it out first—it just flows continuously onto the paper. He never changes anything."

The only habit that might lead even a strict Mormon to disapprove of Cuomo is his insatiable desire for black coffee. He partakes of a glass of wine now and then, but in recent years has usually refrained from stronger beverages. For many years Cuomo was a heavy smoker—two or more packs of Kools a day. Then on Good Friday 1976, Matilda sent Christopher, then six years old, in to see his father.

"Daddy, Mommy says you don't love me," the boy said.

"Your mother's said a lot of rotten things about me," Cuomo responded, "but never that. *Why* did she say that?"

"Because you smoke, and because you could *die* from smoking. And you wouldn't want to die if you really loved us."

It was, Cuomo told me, "one of the true cheap shots—and also one of the most effective—she's ever delivered."

"Your mother has a point," Cuomo said, putting out his cigarette. His intention was to stop for the weekend and see what Monday brought. It brought headaches and a swollen tongue and lips. "I was absolutely *sick* for a cigarette," he recalls. "Christopher came in and said, 'Mommy says now that the weekend's over, you're going back to smoking. You *lied* to us!' I was beside myself. I was *very* angry. I said, 'Okay, I won't smoke.' "

A few days later Cuomo got hives all over his body. Frantic, he called a doctor, who told him that he was experiencing withdrawal. That frightened him. After a few smokeless weeks, he came to the unhappy realization that he would never lose the desire to smoke. "I knew I'd have to beat it every day, the way an alcoholic does," he told me. "And that's what I've done—despite campaigns, crises, calamities—and despite the continuing desire to smoke."

Cigarettes had become an opponent, and Cuomo the competitor resolved to beat them. He is proud to count this contest among his victories.[5]

As he did as a child in his own world in the room behind his father's store, Cuomo still cherishes his time alone. "I've never been totally satisfied with having to deal publicly," he wrote in his diary in 1982. ". . . I've always preferred privacy." A few months later he wrote of his tendency "to yearn for privacy, quiet, the time to think and be left alone. It continues to be the greatest tension I feel—wanting to be remote and having to be immersed." He gives a great deal of personal attention to answering letters he receives—an activity that both satisfies his affection for the written word and can be done in private. Cuomo seems to derive no particular pleasure from the adulation of crowds on the street. Glad-handing and backslapping have never held any appeal for him.

"He's one of those guys who can stand in the middle of a mob scene and compose a poem," says Norman Adler, political director of District Council 37 of the American Federation of State,

County, and Municipal Employees. "He just pulls a curtain around himself."

Even on his increasingly frequent trips around the country, Cuomo usually remains secluded. He contends that there is no way he could gain any insight into a place or its people if he's surrounded by the media, staff, and security people. He can learn much more about a locale and its inhabitants through reading, the governor maintains. His general *modus operandi* on a trip is to fly into town shortly before the scheduled time of his speech, be driven from the airport to the site of the talk, deliver the address, answer questions, and return directly to the airport and thence home as quickly as possible. The major reason for this procedure is that he hates to waste time. He wants to get back to work as rapidly as possible. Surely the prospect of spending countless evenings making small talk in the living rooms and civic-association meeting halls of Iowa and New Hampshire was one of the factors that led Cuomo to pass up the early campaigning for 1988. He believed he had better things to do. He was probably right. It's a hell of a way to choose a president.

Although he cannot stand failure, Cuomo is uncomfortable with success. The pre–Vatican II Church in which he was raised taught people to be suspicious of success. It was seen as something tainted. It might be better to fail. God loved those who failed. To pursue success was an unchristian endeavor. So the more success Cuomo achieves, the more nervous it makes him.

"My mind tells me that 'success' is little more than good luck attached to efforts you make that aren't much different from the efforts of many others who don't get touched by the good luck," Cuomo wrote in 1982.

The pursuit of success is, in Cuomo's value system, evil. But what if success (that is, the presidency) pursues you? That may be a different matter. Then it might seem more like duty than egotism.

If his Catholic background left Cuomo distrustful of success, his Italian peasant ancestry may account for his frequent reluctance to admit that he is in as good a position as he in fact is. The peasant never has a good year. There isn't enough rain. Or there's too much rain. The crop is never as good as it should be. Cuomo is given to similar sentiments. After a tremendously successful speech, he is likely to say, "But the lighting was terrible," or "I saw someone in the third row who didn't look interested."

Like Abraham Lincoln, with whom he identifies, Cuomo experiences periods of melancholy. He lapses into what some of his friends call "dark moods" in which he suddenly becomes silent and thoughtful. Judge Sol Wachtler told me that one can "be sitting, having a very light, very fun exchange, and all of a sudden—almost like a cloud coming over him—suddenly, some other thought is crossing his mind." Wachtler says that it is "not a negative kind of darkness. It's almost an intellectual retreat. You can almost see him thinking. It's more visible with him than with many people." Wachtler thinks that it is Cuomo's penchant for sinking deep into thought that led to his reputation for being indecisive. As Wachtler sees it, rather than being a Hamlet, Cuomo is like a Talmudist: "On the other hand—what if?"

Cuomo's slides into darkness are more than offset by his wit and sense of humor, which are frequent behind the scenes and are regularly put on public display. He is blessed with natural wit, a quality of inestimable value to a public figure. People will forgive a great many mistakes by someone who can make them laugh.

With friends, Cuomo uses storytelling and jokes as a means of relaxation. He is especially good at relating anecdotes, but likes straight jokes, too. On such occasions, he is a real pleasure to be with. Cuomo is, as Norman Adler told Ken Auletta, "the kind of person you'd like to invite to the house."

The governor often employs humor as an ally. He likes to kid people during negotiating situations, in order to lighten things up and make the process go more smoothly. In meetings with the press, Cuomo is likely to interrupt a questioner who is just beginning to speak with a loud "I deny it!" and a smile. He understands that self-deprecating humor is the most effective sort, and often pokes fun at himself. As in his partiality for self-criticism, Cuomo much prefers making fun of himself to others doing it.

For the most part, Cuomo does not aim his humor at others. "The one thing I admire most about his sense of humor," Wachtler says, "is that he turns it on himself. He does not hurt other people, and that's a great gift. Too many people who pride themselves on having a good sense of humor exercise it at the expense of others. He does not." He does like hard teasing, but he usually directs it at those he knows can take it. This practice is at least in part the product of Cuomo's youthful training in verbal sparring with friends in front of Tiedemann's ice cream parlor. It is the give-and-take that is so emblematic of New York.

Cuomo can be very sarcastic at times, but much of his sarcasm passes over the heads of those at whom it is directed. They do not catch his inflection and so miss the point. "I've been to so many places when he said something to someone and they thought it was a compliment," Nicholas D'Arienzo told me. "He doesn't mean it as a compliment." On the rare occasions when Cuomo gets very tired, his friends say, he can get angry and his usually gentle wit can become cutting.

The vast majority of the time, though, Cuomo's humor serves him well. "The most effective thing I am able to do on a stage is make people laugh," he wrote in his diary during his first gubernatorial campaign. Planned jokes in speeches can be effective, but it is the quickness of Cuomo's wit that is its most striking characteristic. When he told reporters after the revelation of Gary Hart's cruise with a young woman that Matilda would "split her sides laughing" if she was told *he* had done something like that, Cuomo added, "but she's Sicilian, and if she believed it, she'd probably have me killed."

Once when the governor was listening to a woman from Queens, Press Secretary Marty Steadman, who was standing nearby, sneezed. "That's a Yiddish sign that the person talking is telling the truth," the woman said.

"Next time, see if you can sneeze while *I'm* talking," Cuomo immediately said to Steadman.

It is because he can come up with such quick responses that Cuomo always insists on speaking last at any function. He can pick up on whatever the other speakers say, make witty remarks about their comments, and leave the crowd happy.[6]

A good deal can be learned about someone by finding out whom he or she most admires—and does *not* admire. I asked Cuomo who his heroes in American history are. His response: "Jefferson, for the Declaration. Madison. Not Washington. Washington was a great father figure, but . . . I would say Lincoln. I would say [Franklin] Roosevelt. That's it."

He said what he admires about Lincoln is "his language—the magnificent way he communicated profound truths with simple images, simple words. The way he was able to communicate a morality for the people. I find it less easy to justify him as the man who kept the country together, because then you get into the argument of whether he should have kept the country together without war." He went on to say that "there are many ways in which you could judge Lincoln and he would fail. He was no good at managing, apparently. And he had his defects personally."

I asked him what he thought about some other American political figures who are sometimes classified as great leaders.

Andrew Jackson? "What were his legacies? I'm not impressed by tall generals. He doesn't ring any bells for me."

Theodore Roosevelt? "He was a New Yorker, so I have to include him, and he was a progressive, which is fine. But I don't think of him as a hero. You've gotta give him points for 'bully pulpit,' though, even if it weren't an excellent forum for delivering ideas to the people, 'bully pulpit' would have made it so—just the words would have made it so."

Woodrow Wilson? "He had the one unrealized idea that we need to come to eventually, and that is that the *only* way to keep peace and have progress in an interconnected universe like this one is to have some formal way to resolve disputes, some rules of law. You'll have sovereignties of all sorts, and they can't surrender to a supersovereignty. But you need a world court, a world forum, with certain rules. It's no good just to say we'll negotiate on everything on an ad hoc basis. It just doesn't work."

Franklin D. Roosevelt? "Great politician. First of all, he's a New Yorker. Second, he's a governor. Third, I use his table as my desk. He helped lead the country onto safer ground. He helped tie us together, mostly I think by the force of his personality. He was a man without a philosophy. He is now regarded as the godfather of progressive, positive government. Well, that was the product of his very, very insistent kind of pragmatism—stringing together a series of solutions to a series of problems, and doing it through government. At another time he might have believed in remote government. He was a pragmatist. He liked the challenge. Presumably liked people—had an extraordinary power to communicate with the vulnerable. Like Lincoln, he was there at a time of crisis, and managed to get through."

Adlai Stevenson? "No—no. He used words well. But so does Bill Buckley."

John Kennedy? "Charismatic." A long pause followed. And you'll leave it at that? "Well, he was charismatic, he was personally very appealing. You can't say he was a great communicator; Sorenson wrote the speeches. Kennedy was a great *spokesperson*. Mostly it was the force of his looks and his persona—bold, refreshing, a function of his youth, and he made a major achievement in acknowledging himself to be a Catholic and winning anyway. That was important."

Lyndon Johnson? "Great senator. And the part of his presidency that worked best was working with Congress. He was a substantial contibutor to the advancement of civil rights. You needed a southerner to do it. You need a strong man to make peace."

Richard Nixon? "Two or three presidents. The Watergate president, the Cambodia president, and all the rest of the presidency. On all the rest of the presidency, good-to-excellent, including his social programs. Watergate—terrible, terrible. Cambodia, in retrospect, a mistake. He was very logical, strong in foreign policy, but you can't separate him."

Hubert Humphrey? "33⅓ Adlai Stevenson being played at 45rpm."

Jimmy Carter? "Very smart. Very unlucky. Especially on Iran. And oil. The OPEC price increase gave us inflation, or a lot of it."

Ronald Reagan? "If he makes the INF [intermediate nuclear forces] deal and, maybe, even another one on strategic weapons, he will have made a great contribution. I will be grateful to him for an excellent contribution to our welfare. He's done a lot of bad things, from my point of view. He helped make the denial of compassion respectable. And that I found very bothersome."[7]

One of Mario Cuomo's many attractions is his unquestioned personal integrity. People are accustomed to being disappointed by politicians. The fact that Cuomo seems to "tell it like it is," whether that's pleasant or not, is impressive. His own nearly lifelong lack of interest in money is similarly reassuring. There are, however, two distinct but related areas that have the potential to cause a national Cuomo campaign some difficulty. One is the proven corruption of several people with whom Cuomo has been politically associated in the past. The other is the whispering campaign that some member of his family might have been involved with another sort of "family," the Mafia.

On the first point, Cuomo could not help but associate with the late Queens borough president, Donald Manes, who committed suicide in 1986 after being indicted in the New York City corruption scandal. Manes was the Democratic leader of Cuomo's home county, and the rising politician often sought his support. The same is true of several other New York City Democratic leaders who were involved in the scandals. It is important to remember, though, that Cuomo arose outside the Democratic club system that proved to be an incubator for corruption. He dealt with Manes and his ilk out of necessity, not choice. Cuomo certainly had nice things to say about the borough president from time to time. And when the stories of Manes's misdeeds first became public, Cuomo said that he thought he should withhold his opinion at least until formal charges were made. This was a reflection of Cuomo's sense of fairness and his reluctance to rush to judgment, even when that is the politically wise course to take.

When I asked Cuomo about the possible effects of the city scandals on a national campaign, he answered: "I would guess that there would be a certain percentage of people who would vote against you at the slightest provocation. But I think there would be just as many people who, seeing what happened in Queens, and New York, and seeing how none of it ever happened to *me*, could arrive at a different conclusion, and that is that the same forces and environment that produced corruption didn't do it to *him*. So I think it would work both ways."

Cuomo had nothing to do with selecting the city political bosses. The same cannot be said of some of his own staffers who have been implicated in illegal or questionable practices. Besides William Cabin's 1981 phony-payroll scheme (described in chapter 9), there occurred another incident in 1987, when Cuomo's long-time close aide and associate Alexander A. Levine, at that time executive director of the New York State Thruway Authority, was accused of having steered state business to a computer software company that he had helped to establish. Levine, who had been with the secretary of state's office when Cuomo took over that department, had replaced Cabin as the lieutenant governor's chief of staff in 1981, and later directed purchasing and personnel for the governor. Cuomo's executively created Inspector General's Office sent a report on the Levine matter to prosecutors in October 1987. At this writing the case remains under investigation.

The discovery of corruption and possible wrongdoing among his top aides is the source of serious embarrassment for Cuomo. No one even suggests that he has personally been involved in such activities, but the revelations fuel the charges that he is not a good administrator and does not make the best choices in his appointments.

Obviously such incidents are not helpful to Cuomo, but they do not seem serious enough to cause significant damage to the reputation of a man who has so many positive qualities. The potenial for real damage seemed to many people to lie in another area, one that was not spoken of openly until the fall of 1987, but which had been passed around the nation in hushed tones: Cuomo—or some relative of his—was involved with organized crime.

The Mob rumors have taken many forms. Among the stories that have been bandied about are the following: 1) while a young attorney Cuomo represented members of organized crime; 2) Cuomo met with a Mafia figure in the mid 1970s; 3) Cuomo's former law firm made secret payments to someone involved in organized crime who was later charged with killing an undercover cop; 4) a mobster made a large contribution to Cuomo's 1982 gubernatorial campaign; 5) Cuomo's father-in-law, Charles Raffa, was an arsonist and the brutal 1984 attack on him was perpetrated by the Mafia; 6) Cuomo blocked the police inquiry into the Raffa mugging; 7) the record of an arson arrest of Raffa was deleted from the state crime computer.

Cuomo suspected that the rumors were the result of an organized campaign by some political opponents of his. This suspicion was at least partially confirmed late in 1987 when it was revealed that a Republican staff member on a state senate committee, Jeremiah B. McKenna, was a major source of the rumors and that some of the stories had been passed along to McKenna by two lawyers, Michael Nicholson and Diana Long Nicholson, who had taken over Cuomo's law firm and have been engaged in a bitter dispute with him over fees. But while some people who have opposed him have participated in spreading stories and shown no apparent concern for their accuracy, it seems that there are two more important reasons for the crime rumors: Cuomo is an Italian-American and, despite the fact that he seemed almost perfectly to fit what the country was looking for in a president, he decided in 1987 that he would not run.

The twin beliefs that all organized criminals are Italians and that most successful Italian-Americans are organized criminals have become ingrained in American popular thought. This is, of course, absurd. But television and movies consistently reinforce the notions. No other ethnic group in America is as regularly portrayed in a negative way as are Italians. When Cuomo was first considering a run for statewide office in 1974, he commissioned a poll to be taken in the state, but outside New York City. It found, as he had expected, that his name recognition upstate approached zero. But 6 percent of those polled said that the possibility of Cuomo's Mafia connections would be held against him. They had never heard of the individual, but just seeing the name "Mario Cuomo" led some people to assume an automatic association with organized crime.

When a politician with Mario Cuomo's gifts declines to seek the presidency, people naturally wonder why. Since most Americans assume that everyone wants, as the television commercials tell us, to "be all that you can be," and "have it all," there simply *must* be some dark, hidden reason why a person with such an apparently good chance of success would not go after the office. The ready assumption is that there must be a "skeleton in his closet." If the noncandidate in question happens to be of Italian extraction, many people will jump instantly to the conclusion that the unseen skeleton wears cement shoes. A public that is receptive to any rumors of Mob connections, no matter how farfetched, is thus created.

The notion that Cuomo decided to opt out of the presidential race because of fear that participation in it would expose him to intense scrutiny that would uncover criminal connections ignores the fact that many news organizations have been investigating the Cuomo-crime stories for years. Several supplemented their own investigative teams with former New York City policemen and private detectives. They found *nothing*. The microscopes that come into use in a presidential campaign are no more powerful than those that both the New York and national media have already used on Cuomo. He has, moreover, run against opponents in New York who were well financed and not above using anything they could to discredit him. "I've been running since 1974 in this jungle called New York," Cuomo said to me, "and I've had people like David Garth trying to kill me, for Ed Koch, and doing every kind of investigation, all through the '77 campaign."

If there was anything there, it seems almost certain that it would have come out long ago.

Still, confronting rumors can be a dangerous business. Even showing them to be wholly without foundation gives the stories greater exposure. And many people operate on the "where there's smoke, there must be fire" assumption. In fact, in the case of the crime rumors around Mario Cuomo, all the available evidence indicates that where there's smoke, there's a chunk of ice.

The story that Cuomo represented mobsters when he was a young lawyer apparently arose out of the fact that Joseph "Joey Narrows" Laratro, a Luchese family capo, was a part owner of one of the fifteen junkyards that Cuomo represented in his fight against Robert Moses and the World's Fair. He never represented Laratro as an individual, and actually took pains to make sure that he never took anyone involved in organized crime as a client. "I never represented wiseguys," Cuomo told crime reporter Nicholas Pileggi. "I was asked thousands of times to do appeals for this guy and that guy, but I never did one. I had friends who were prosecutors, detectives, and FBI men, and if I wasn't sure, I could go to them and they'd warn me about who anyone was."

The story that Cuomo had met a mobster in the mid-seventies is true. Both Cuomo and Colombo family capo John "Sonny" Franzese were among the guests at a large wedding. The two of them, along with most other people in attendance, shook hands. There is no indication that Cuomo even knew who Franzese was.

As for the charge that Cuomo's firm made payments to a mobster, two checks dated July 25, 1977, from someone named Gualtieri, went into the firm's account. Whether the man whose name was on the check was mob figure Carmine Gualtieri is unknown. In any case, the payment was *from* someone of that name, not *to* him. And it all happened three years after Cuomo left the firm.

Five dummy corporations set up to avoid payment of gasoline taxes paid $1,000 each for tickets to a Cuomo fund-raising dinner in 1984. The dinner took in $1.2 million, and Andrew Cuomo says that there was no way to check out every corporate check that came in. "As soon as we found out what happened," the younger Cuomo told Pileggi, "we tried to send the money back, but it turned out the companies were already out of business. We sent the money to charity."

All of the rumors about Mario Cuomo himself having any connection with organized crime appear to be absolute nonsense. "They're not talking about me personally [anymore]," he told me in the fall of 1987. "They gave up on me personally a long time ago. They're talking about my in-laws, frankly. It's sick, terrible."

The rumors concerning Cuomo's father-in-law are more complicated, but similarly without foundation. Charlie Raffa's major crime seems to have been to be an uneducated Italian-American who succeeded. In the books of many people, that automatically makes him suspect. As Cuomo put it in a conversation with me, it "allows stupid people and cruel people to suggest all the worst possibilities."

Cuomo has had a warm relationship with his father-in-law. From the time Mario started seeing Matilda regularly, Raffa began talking about "my future son-in-law, the lawyer." Cuomo always treated Raffa like a second father. When Andrea Cuomo died before his son was elected governor, Mario seems to have had his wife's father fill in, to help him enjoy the glory that Andrea had missed. Even so, the relevance to Cuomo of any questionable associations of Raffa—if any were ever found—would be slight.

When Raffa was beaten and nearly killed in the basement of a vacant building he owned in Brooklyn in 1984, stories began to circulate that the eighty-year-old man was an arsonist and his assailants were mobsters. No witnesses to the attack have been found, and Raffa himself has given sharply differing descriptions of his attackers. The latter problem is readily explained by the severe head injuries that the man suffered. The idea that Raffa planned to burn the building does not stand up to any scrutiny. He had arranged to meet possible tenants there, and there was no fire insurance on the property.

Stories that Cuomo rushed to the scene to cover up what had happened are patently untrue. It has been verified that he was never near the scene of the attack. One of the governor's bodyguards, New York City police detective Sebastian Pipitone, was dispatched to the 75th Precinct station house to make inquiries about the case so that the governor's office could keep abreast of developments. Raffa's car was given to Detective Pipitone to return to the family, and he took it to a car wash to remove Raffa's blood from the exterior before Mrs. Cuomo saw it. Pipitone has been criticized for this, but the car did not at that time figure in the investigation.

The rumor that the governor had Raffa's name erased from the state police computer is also without foundation. In fact, Raffa's name *is* in the computer, but only for having offered a gift to a government employee in 1973. Any serious crime, such as arson, would have been placed in the FBI computer as well as the New York system, and the FBI has no record of any kind on Raffa. Unless one thinks that Mario Cuomo can also get the FBI to delete files, the whole business must be seen as malicious, baseless gossip.

The trouble with rumors and fabrications, of course, is that, as Adolf Hitler said in describing his Big Lie technique, they leave behind a residue even after their falsity has been demonstrated. Many people will say, "Well, there must have been *something* there." Nicholas Pileggi, who frequently writes on organized crime, tracked down all the rumors of Cuomo-crime links for a late 1987 article in *New York* magazine. He could find no substance to any of them. It is impossible to prove a negative, but Pileggi came as close to giving Cuomo a clean bill of health on the subject as any journalist is ever likely to give any politician. Several newspapers followed Pileggi's article with editorials decrying the spreading of false stories about Cuomo and his family.

The crime charges aside, the question of voter prejudice against an Italian-American presidential candidate still looms over any national Cuomo campaign. It is beyond question that bias of all types has been greatly reduced in the last three decades. As Judge Wachtler said in making a presentation to Cuomo in 1986, "We have come so far in this country that even wearing a yarmulke and a prayer shawl would not bar someone from the White House—provided, of course, that he isn't Jewish."

Cuomo's ethnicity might actually be turned to his advantage. I have already noted the likelihood that many people would exempt him from their biases when they heard him talk about his universal values. Some might also be susceptible to the argument John Kennedy so skillfully used in overwhelmingly Protestant West Virginia in 1960: I know that you're not prejudiced, and that you wouldn't vote against me just because I'm a Catholic. The only way people could show that they were not prejudiced was to vote *for* him.

There is also the possible positive effect that Cuomo's ethnicity would have in galvanizing Italian-American voters (most of whom are concentrated in such large electoral-vote states as New York, California, Florida, Massachusetts, and New Jersey, and many of whom have voted Republican in recent national elections). Their pride in a man who shares their heritage and can give them a different image than the criminal stereotype might lead even those who disagreed with Cuomo on some issues to support him. His origins as a member of an ostracized out-group would also be useful to Cuomo in gaining the backing of many other ethnic and racial groups. At the end of the 1982 campaign, Cuomo visited the Italian neighborhood of Arthur Avenue in the Bronx. Everyone was with him. Then he said, "Look, we're Italian, we're very proud of it. . . . Wouldn't it be great if those of us who remember being called guineas and wops and dagos will now stop talking about people as spics and niggers? Wouldn't it be terrible if we did to the people that came after us what we think some people did to us?" Cuomo says the talk was "very well received, *very* well received."[8]

It was Cuomo as a teacher and moral leader. He might be able to do a lot more such instructing in a national campaign, and reduce bias in the process.

Then why has Cuomo been so reluctant to get into a national campaign? If it was not a skeleton in the closet, and it was not the likelihood of defeat, what was his problem?

Although he had been saying for more than two years that he probably would not run, particularly if he sought a second term as governor, Cuomo's February 19, 1987, announcement of noncandidacy came as a shock to most political observers. I heard people say in the following days that they would remember where they were when they heard the news in much the same way that they remember where they were on November 22, 1963, April 4, 1968, or June 6, 1968. That reaction might be a bit extreme, but for a small but politically significant group of people around the country, Cuomo had come to represent something that had nearly vanished from American public life since the late sixties: hope. All they could do was mutter something akin to the young boy's lament upon learning of the "Black Sox" baseball scandal of 1919: "Say it ain't so, Mario."

In fact, the very next day, Cuomo did indicate that there was a slim possibility that it might not be so. In his withdrawal statement he had said the Democratic party "offers a number of presidential candidates who can prove themselves capable of leading the nation toward a more sane, a more progressive and a more humane future." When a reporter at his news conference the day after the announcement misquoted him as having said "a number of presidential candidates who have proven themselves capable," Cuomo interrupted with a significant correction: "No, no. I said, 'who *can* prove themselves.' " The door was left ever so slightly ajar—just enough for a draft to enter should none of the other candidates catch on.

Cuomo's withdrawal made him the forbidden fruit of the Democratic party. His reluctance to run, apparently based upon his sense of duty, made him seem all the more desirable. The reasons he stated for not seeking the nomination did not seem sufficient, and growing numbers of Democrats hoped that he might yet be brought into the race.

The need for someone like Cuomo seemed to grow steadily as 1987 unfolded. The American public was sinking ever more deeply into a crisis of confidence. Cynicism, on the rise since such early sixties events as the U-2 incident and the Bay of Pigs, and in the saddle since Vietnam and Watergate, had reached truly dangerous proportions. A litany of the distressing events in the twelve months beginning in the fall of 1986 provides some sense of the crisis: the Iran-contra scandal, the insider-trading scandal on Wall Street, Wedtech, Michael Deaver, the Marine sex scandal in Moscow, the unholy wars among television evangelists, the problems of Democratic presidential hopefuls Gary Hart, Joe Biden, and—to a considerably lesser extent—Michael Dukakis, and of President Reagan's various nominees for the Supreme Court, and the Wall Street crash that occurred eight months after Cuomo's withdrawal.

A substantial majority of the American people seemed eager to be inspired to believe in something beyond the self. But fighting off cynicism was very difficult in the midst of all the evidence of greed, egoism, and corruption in high places. The decline in confidence in all American public and private institutions, after being briefly stemmed by the apparent success of the Reagan administration, continued apace. If nothing was done to reverse this decline, the consequences for American democracy could be devastating. The frightening rise in the summer of 1987 of a national mania centered on Lieutenant Colonel Oliver North offered a chilling glimpse of where the public's need to believe in something and somebody might lead. If that need to believe was not satiated by something noble and worthwhile (and some*one* of integrity, with respect for our legal system and values of compassion and responsibility), the void might be filled by a movement or demagogue who could conceivably become a real threat to the American system.

When I spoke with Cuomo's friend Nicholas D'Arienzo in April 1987, prior to Gary Hart's fall, he said something that later became most interesting. "I think if, say, the leading contender in the Democratic party—something [were to happen] like the Tammy Faye/Jim Bakker thing, then he would think it was necessary, his duty, to run. It would have to be a duty imposed upon him."

Within short order, precisely that had happened. The forced withdrawals first of front-runner Gary Hart and then of Joseph Biden, combined with embarrassing revelations about some of the other Democrats seeking their party's 1988 presidential nomination and a general failure by all of them to excite the electorate made a growing number of people turn wistful eyes toward Albany. *Someone* had to be found who was capable of reversing the national slide into cynicism and despair. Mario Cuomo looked more and more like that person.

Cuomo's statement that there were a number of people in the party who could prove themselves capable leaders simply did not seem to be finding any takers. One who was given to such explanations might detect the hand of destiny in the thinning of the Democratic ranks and the polls indicating that the nation yearned ever more passionately for a president with precisely the qualities Cuomo possesses. Gary Hart's startling reentry into the race at the end of 1987 added to the confusion and made a Cuomo candidacy more likely.

The reasons for Cuomo's reluctance to run were complex. Several factors can be identified, some of which I have mentioned before. One, certainly, was just what he said in his statement of noncandidacy: his feeling of obligation to the the state of New York. This was admirable—but only up to a point. Responsibility is in all too short supply among politicians these days. But a larger responsibility to the nation and the world, one that superseded his responsibility as governor was becoming clearer. The chances that Cuomo would heed this call to a higher duty seemed to be increasing in the closing weeks of 1987.

Another reason for his reluctance to run was also stated at the time of his declaration: concern for his family. This concern was genuine, but it was misinterpreted by the media. It was not so much that he was worried about new press attacks on Andrew. Those, as he said, would continue as long as he was governor. But Cuomo realized that the days of having two of his children at home—one of them studying his beloved law—were distinctly numbered. It was entirely understandable that he would want to savor those days.

A third factor was one Cuomo did not discuss at any length with the press: his constant wrestling with his own motivations. He wants to do things for the right reasons—to serve others—but he is troubled by the knowledge that, like all humans, his motivations are not always pure and selfless. If he actively sought the presidency, he might never be sure that he was not doing it for the wrong reasons.

If, on the other hand, the presidency actually sought him, he would be much more comfortable. In that case, he could be confident that he was doing it out of a sense of responsibility. It would be clear in his own mind that he was doing it for the public good, not his own ego. If the party and the nation clearly *needed* him to be president, it would be a duty to answer that call. By late 1987 it appeared that such a call existed. A sophisticated opinion survey done by the Gallup organization for the Times-Mirror Company indicated that two-thirds of the American people wanted a leader with a profile that if fed into a computer dating service would print out Cuomo's name as the one perfect fit.

But Cuomo kept resisting the conclusion that the presidency was seeking him. As his friend Jack Newfield puts it, "Mario doesn't have a messianic complex. He can't believe he's indispensable." "It's very hard for me to say, 'I should be president; I'm better than all those people,' " Cuomo told me. "I don't *feel* it, and I don't believe it. Some people *do* believe it. They come to me and say, 'I think you're better than this guy.' I say, 'Okay, but I don't.' I don't know whether it's a psychic barrier of some kind. I don't know, maybe it's the first definition of sin I ever read—sin not being sex, but *pride*. Sin in the Garden wasn't really sex; it was pride. That's what eating the apple was."

That explanation is quintessential Mario Cuomo. Many people would take it with a large dose of salt, but he seems to be serious.

A fourth factor behind Cuomo's reluctance to run surely was that he is uncomfortable with the status of being the favorite in any contest. As I have pointed out earlier, he has always loved to be the underdog. This problem occurred to me as early as 1985. I wondered how Cuomo would react to being the front-runner in 1988. After he said he would not run, I postulated a scenario in which he would make himself the underdog by waiting until everyone said it was too late and then jumping in.

On his flight to Indianapolis in July 1987, to address the state Democratic party dinner, Cuomo talked with reporters about death. "I would like to die sliding into third base," he said. "*No!* Into home! Sliding into home would be better." He continued the conversation, trying to determine the exactly perfect circumstances of his fatal slide. Stealing home might be an acceptable way to go, he allowed. After Cuomo dismissed the idea of coming in on a squeeze bunt, someone suggested an inside-the-park home run. "That's it!" Cuomo exclaimed. "That would be the way to go."

Journalist Joe Klein, in recounting this episode, pointed out that "an inside-the-park home run is a small bolt of lightning, a small miracle. It demands a certain amount of chutzpah and a great deal of luck (and, often, a series of mistakes by the opposition)— sort of like running for the presidency without entering any of the primaries."

Such a scenario clearly holds an appeal for Cuomo. It sure beats being the favorite.

Cuomo told me shortly after his announcement that he would not run that a large part of the reason was simply his instinct. I got the impression that his instinct was not telling him that he should not become president, possibly even in 1988, but that it was not *then* the time to be running. Events in subsequent months proved his instinct correct. Not running in 1987 was the best position for him to be in.

The possibility must be considered that the whole thing was a ploy—part of a grand and daring strategy. As early as the spring of 1985, some Cuomo advisers told Fred Barnes that Cuomo might pursue a "reverse Mondale strategy." Whereas Mondale spent four years doing nothing but running for president, Cuomo might try the opposite approach: do everything but run. "Cuomo's strategy would be this," Barnes wrote in 1985, "win a smashing reelection victory next year, sit out presidential politics in 1987 as a Cuomo ground swell mounts, noisily defy a few traditional Democratic pressure groups, and then jump into the race around the time of the early primaries."

It was a forecast that seemed disturbingly accurate two and a half years later.

Other hints that there might be a method to Cuomo's apparent madness could be found. "I believe it's too early to be as prominent a potential candidate as I now am, but I have little choice," he wrote in his diary in 1981. Six years later he may have felt that he had more of a choice. He has also indicated that success in politics requires "exquisite timing." Perhaps that is

what his 1987 noncandidacy was all about. No one can say with
any degree of certainty. My feeling is that it was not a conscious
strategy, but that Cuomo felt all along that he would have no
objection if lightning struck. He is, after all, a rather fatalistic
person. When the propeller on the decrepit state airplane that
he refuses to replace conked out on a July 1987 flight, threatening panic among reporters, Cuomo calmly told them not to
worry. "You've never done anything really terrible in your
life," he said. "You're in a state of grace." He then resumed an
interview as the plane returned to Albany for an emergency
landing. *Che sarà sarà.*

But sometimes what will be may need a little help to come into
being. Cuomo was willing to stoke the fires beneath his noncandidacy whenever necessary in 1987. Pressed on what he would do
in the unlikely event that he was drafted for the 1988 Democratic
presidential nomination, Cuomo responded with "I would do the
right thing." Then he smiled.

Assuming that Cuomo's reluctance to run was genuine, there
were a couple of other possible reasons for it. One was the question
of whether 1989 would be a good time to become president. Cuomo
told me early in 1986 that he thought there was a fairly good
chance that the next president might wind up playing Hoover to
Reagan's Coolidge. It seemed a role better suited to George Bush
than Cuomo. The pragmatic progressive governor of New York
would rather be cast as FDR. But the stock market crash of October 1987 seemed to alter the script by cutting out one act. As the
first professional actor to occupy the White House, Ronald Reagan
may have won for himself the difficult dual role of playing Hoover
as well as Coolidge. The possibility of worsening economic problems made Cuomo look all the more attractive.

Perhaps the most important reason Cuomo hesitated was that
he has always wanted to be completely prepared for any undertaking in which he became involved, whether a legal case, the position
of mayor, or that of governor. "Cuomo will never, *ever* do something unless he feels he is as prepared as he can be," Marty Steadman says. "He prepares and prepares and prepares. . . . He just
simply will not embarrass himself or his family. He has to be as
perfect as he can be, or he *won't* do it."

Clearly Cuomo did not in 1987 feel fully prepared for the presidency of the United States. Equally clearly, he was right. No one
is *ever* completely prepared for the presidency. Surely Jimmy

Carter and Ronald Reagan were not. Neither was Abraham Lincoln or Franklin Roosevelt.

The question of readiness is in fact a relative one. It is not one of whether one is fully prepared, but of whether one is as well prepared as other potential candidates—or better prepared. Cuomo himself has said, "The test should be: Is there anyone who can do it better, or at least as well, who has the same chance or a better chance to win?" That is a test that most observers late in 1987 would find Cuomo passing easily. "Cuomo would obliterate the [Democratic] field if he entered," former Reagan political director Haley Barbour said to me in the fall of 1987. Cuomo's values, vision, communications ability, and executive experience appeared to many people to outweigh the Washington experience of a few other candidates.[9]

The readiness question can be viewed in the light of the two worst crises in American history: the Civil War and the Great Depression. What made Lincoln ready in 1860? He had served only one term in Congress and had lost six elections before winning the presidency. But what if he had declined to run because he wasn't ready? The nation would have had to face its worst crisis without his leadership. The Union might very well not have been preserved. Lincoln may not have been ready, but the early 1860s was the time when the country needed him.

And what of Franklin D. Roosevelt? He did have more national and international experience at the beginning of the 1930s than Cuomo did at the end of the 1980s, but not that much. His stint as assistant secretary of the navy gave him important Washington experience, and his losing vice presidential campaign in 1920 exposed him to much of the country. But FDR was only in his fourth year of statewide office in 1932. Cuomo is in his fourteenth year in statewide office in 1988—and his sixth year as governor.

Ever since 1912 FDR and his adviser Louis Howe had pointed toward 1936 as *the* year for Roosevelt to seek the presidency. He may not have been fully ready in 1932, but that was when the country needed him. What might have happened had FDR, with his pragmatism and his remarkable ability to ease people's fears, not become president in 1933? Of course no one can say with any certainty, but it is plain that democracy and the free-enterprise system were in peril. They might not have survived without Roosevelt's leadership in that time of crisis.

There are two sides to the readiness question. The potential candidate may not feel entirely ready, but what if the nation is "ready" for him or her? That is to say that at certain points in history a country *needs* a certain type of leader. Such was the case with Lincoln in 1860 and Roosevelt in 1932. It may also be the case with Mario Cuomo in 1988.

There are three reasons why the nation may need Cuomo now as it needed Lincoln and Roosevelt in past crises. We all hope that no crisis even approaching the magnitude of the Civil War or the Great Depression awaits us in the next few years. Yet the economic prospects are alarming. If a collapse is to be averted, some very tough actions will be necessary. Persuading the American people to take those actions—to make those sacrifices—will be an extremely difficult task. There are many who can see the need for such actions, but very few who are capable of inspiring the people to do what is necessary. Figuring out what needs to be done will not be easy. Cuomo proposed a bipartisan commission to provide some of the answers. The real difficulty may be in implementing the solutions that are proposed. It is not the sort of thing that Walter Mondale could do. Nor could Jimmy Carter, George Bush, Robert Dole, Jack Kemp, Gary Hart, Michael Dukakis, Paul Simon, Jesse Jackson, Richard Gephardt, Bruce Babbitt, or Albert Gore. Not even the Great Communicator himself could do it. He never even *tried.* President Reagan was great at preaching guiltless egoism and painless panaceas, but he never even tried to ask for sacrifice. There is no certainty that Mario Cuomo could succeed in convincing the American people that they must be willing to make some sacrifices for the common good. But he would seem to have a better chance to do so than anyone else who might win the presidency in 1988.

What is needed is someone who can make us see that we are in this mess together and that the only way we are ever going to get out of it is to cooperate—like a family, sharing benefits and burdens. Sacrifice will only be accepted if it is clear that it is being fairly shared. This is a vision that many politicians can and do talk about, but it is doubtful that anyone else can get it across to the public as well as Cuomo can.

The second reason that it may be something approaching a historical necessity that Cuomo become president of the United States is closely related to the first. However the economic crisis of the coming years may unfold, there can be no doubt that we are already deep into a crisis of confidence that poses a long-term threat to our democracy. For two decades now, we have reeled from one scandal to another, from one untrustworthy or incompetent leader to another. During these five failed presidencies (and countless lesser examples of political corruption and ineptitude), the confidence of the American people in their government and political leadership has declined to the point where it endangers our very commitment to democracy.

There is, then, a desperate need for someone who has the integrity, vision, values, character, and communications ability to restore public faith in our political institutions. Many of the candidates who have actively sought the presidency have one or two of the needed qualities. None seems to possess them all. I have become convinced, after researching and writing this book and reflecting on what I have learned, that Cuomo does.

FDR had to restore confidence in the government to save the economy—and, indirectly, our democratic system. What we need now is someone who can restore confidence in the government in order to save our democratic system—and, perhaps indirectly, the economy.

Cuomo first entered the public arena out of a sense of obligation—to try to rehabilitate politics and show that government could work for people rather than against them. Today there is a plain need for a similar undertaking on the national level.

The third factor that may make Cuomo's assumption of national leadership in the near future almost essential is international in scope. As Mikhail Gorbachev becomes a more and more effective spokesman for the Soviet bloc, the need grows for a leader in the West who can effectively present a vision rooted in freedom, democracy, *and* social responsibility. Cuomo seems much more likely to fit this role than anyone else on the political horizon. And his concept of family may well offer the basic vision that is needed internationally as well as nationally.

If Mario Cuomo in fact possesses the qualities that the nation and the world so much need today, it might be argued that the selfish course for him to follow would be *not* to run.

No one on this side of the Jordan is perfect—or even very close to it. I greatly admired Mario Cuomo when I started this project. At its conclusion I still admire him. But my admiration is not blind. I have found and in the preceding pages detailed many examples of his imperfections. I was not expecting to find someone ready for canonization, and I did not. What I did find was a human being who has a very large ego that he must struggle to keep in check, who enjoys winning a bit too much, who is not as selfless as he knows he should be, who can be vindictive, plays hardball politics more than there is any reason to, sometimes constructs an image of himself that is not entirely in keeping with reality, works obsessively, and spends less time with his family than he knows he ought to. I also found a man who is more aware of his faults than most of us are of ours, who has great compassion rooted in deep religious belief, possesses extraordinary talent and intellect, and whose abilities seem almost perfectly to match what America needs at this point in its history.

Notes

Preface

1. Author's telephone interview with Mario M. Cuomo [hereafter, MMC], from Albany, N.Y., October 17, 1987; John Gunther, *Roosevelt in Retrospect: A Profile in History* (New York: Harper & Brothers, 1950), pp. 5, 50.

Introduction

1. James A. Farley, as quoted in James MacGregor Burns, *Roosevelt: The Lion and the Fox* (New York: Harcourt, Brace, 1956), p. 123; MMC, *Diaries of Mario M. Cuomo: The Campaign for Governor* (New York: Random House, 1984), p. 269; Mary McGrory, "Democrats' Last Liberal Hope," *Washington Post,* November 11, 1984; author's interview with Sal Curiale, New York City [hereafter, NYC], April 7, 1987; author's interview with Fabian Palomino, NYC, May 21, 1987; author's interview with Matilda Cuomo, Albany, May 19, 1987.

2. Author's interview with Arthur M. Schlesinger, Jr., NYC, July 15, 1985; author's interview with Mayor Edward Koch, NYC, May 22, 1987; author's interview with Beth Smith, Sen. Gary Hart's communications director, Washington, D.C., January 27, 1986; author's interview with Patricia Derian, Washington, D.C., June 18, 1985.

3. Seymour Martin Lipset and William Schneider, "The Confidence Gap During the Reagan Years," *Political Science Quarterly* Vol. 102 (Spring 1987), pp. 1–23; Robert S. McElvaine, "Why the Debacle Shouldn't Hearten Liberals," *New York Times* [hereafter, *NYT*], December 9, 1986; Jonathan Yardley, "The Thrill is Gone," *Washington Post National Weekly Edition,* May 18, 1987; MMC, Sunday service, St. John the Divine, NYC, November 27, 1983; MMC, *Diaries,* pp. 464, 107, 182, 95, 394, 253, 396, 68, 215, 254; author's interview with MMC, NYC, January 21, 1986.

4. MMC, *Diaries,* pp. 287, 171, 197, 165, 196, 310, 428, 448, 458–60, 412, 11; MMC interview, January 21, 1986; MMC, speech to Black Ministers' Association, Rochester, N.Y., August 16, 1982; MMC, first inaugural address, Albany, January 1, 1983; MMC, "A Case for the Democrats, 1984: A Tale of Two Cities," keynote address, Democratic National Convention, San Francisco, Calif., July 16, 1984; Robert S. McElvaine, "Liberals Go Back to the Flag," *NYT,* September 2, 1984; author's interview with Gov. Bill Clinton, Little Rock, Ark., April 17, 1986.

5. Arthur Schlesinger, Jr., interview; MMC interview, January 21, 1986; MMC, *Diaries,* pp. 245, 236, 141, 243, 246, 36, 113, 121, 215, 120, 191, 240, 320; "What Makes Mario Run?" *Newsweek,* March 24, 1986, pp. 22–30; Matilda Cuomo interview; Palomino interview, May 19, 1987.

6. Author's telephone interview with MMC, from Albany, December 6, 1987; author's interview with MMC, Albany, March 12, 1987; *NYT*, May 9, 1987; author's interview with Fabian Palomino, NYC, April 9, 1987.

7. Colleen O'Connor, Howard Fineman, and Martin Kasindorf, "Wherefore Art Thou, Mario?" *Newsweek*, February 3, 1986.

8. Hearing of the House Committee on Ways and Means on President Reagan's proposal for comprehensive tax reform, Washington, D.C., July 17, 1985; *NYT*, July 19, 1985, December 18, 1985, January 21, 1986, January 23, 1986, January 24, 1986, January 27, 1986; MMC, *Diaries*, pp. 269, 78, 187, 329, 41; author's interview with Rep. Morris Udall, Washington, D.C., July 16, 1985; *Washington Post*, January 20, 1986, January 24, 1986; Rowland Evans and Robert Novak, "Cuomo's High Wire Act," *Washington Post*, January 24, 1986; James Reston, "Cuomo Sets a Standard," *NYT*, January 22, 1986; editorial, "Could an Italian-American Win?" *NYT*, January 22, 1986; Michael Kramer, "After the Fall, Here Comes Cuomo," *New York*, November 19, 1984; author's interview with Frank Cuomo, Copiague, Long Island, N.Y., May 20, 1987; author's interview with Sen. Christopher Dodd, Washington, D.C., January 28, 1986; *Newsday*, May 13, 1985; Ellen McCormick, *Cuomo vs. O'Connor: Did a Catholic Politician Make an Anti-Catholic Appeal?* (Commack, N.Y.: Dolores Press, 1985), p. 20.

9. Author's interview with Janie Eisenberg, NYC, April 9, 1987; author's interview with Richard Starkey, NYC, April 7, 1987; author's interview with William A. Carrick, Jr., political director for Sen. Edward M. Kennedy, Washington, D.C., July 17, 1985; author's interview with Richard Goodwin, Bourne, Mass., July 8, 1985; MMC, *Diaries*, pp. 373, 221, 367.

10. Paul West, "Cuomo's Complaint," *New Republic*, February 17, 1986, pp. 10–12.

11. Author's interview with former Gov. Charles Robb, Fairfax, Va., January 29, 1986; MMC, *Diaries*, pp. 179, 332, 7, 362; author's interview with MMC, January 21, 1986; *NYT*, February 16, 1985.

12. MMC, *Diaries*, p. 69; Lee M. Miringoff and Barbara L. Carvalho, *The Cuomo Factor* (Poughkeepsie, N.Y.: Marist Institute for Public Opinion, 1986), p. 18.

13. Author's interview with Jack Newfield, NYC, April 9, 1987; author's interview with Immaculata Cuomo, Copiague, May 20, 1987; author's interview with Frank Cuomo, Copiague, April 8, 1987.

14. *NYT*, May 17, 1987, May 19, 1987; MMC, speech at Tulane University, New Orleans, La., February 16, 1987; author's interview with Gov. Michael Dukakis, Boston, Mass., May 10, 1986; George F. Will, "Does It Have to Be Mondale?" *Washington Post*, May 24, 1984; "What Makes Mario Run," *Newsweek*, March 24, 1986.

Chapter 1

1. WPA, Federal Writers' Project, *The Italians of New York* (New York: Random House, 1938; reprint ed., New York: Arno Press and the *New York Times*, 1969), pp. 3–4, 36, 49; Nathan Glazer and Daniel P. Moynihan, *Beyond the Melting Pot: The Negroes, Puerto Ricans, Jews, Italians, and Irish of New York City* (Cambridge, Mass.: MIT Press, 1963; 2nd ed., 1970), pp. 184–85, 195, 197, 339, 186; MMC, *Diaries of Mario M. Cuomo: The Campaign for Governor* (New York: Random House, 1984), pp. 412, 406; Leonard Covello, *The Social Background of the Italo-American School Child* (Ph.D. dissertation, New York University, 1944), p. 276; MMC, Sunday Service, St. John the Divine, NYC, November 27, 1983, in MMC, *Diaries*, p. 463.

2. WPA, FWP, *Italians of New York*, pp. ix, 51, 59–62, 15–16, 18; Herbert Gans, *The Urban Villagers* (Glencoe, Ill.: Free Press, 1962); Glazer and Moynihan, *Beyond the Melting Pot*, pp. 186–207; author's interviews with Rosario Cuomo, Maria Cuomo, and Jenny Brand, Holliswood, Queens, N.Y., April 6, 1987.

3. Rosario Cuomo, Maria Cuomo, and Jenny Brand interviews; author's interview with Immaculata Cuomo, Copiague, Long Island, N.Y., May 20, 1987; MMC, address at New York State Fair Dinner, Syracuse, N.Y., September 1, 1981, in MMC, *Diaries*, p. 406.

4. Rosario Cuomo and Jenny Brand interviews; Immaculata Cuomo interview; author's interview with Marie Cuomo Vecchio, Mineola, Long Island, N.Y., June 19, 1987; Marie Vecchio, letter to Robert McElvaine, June 24, 1987, in possession of the author; Ken Auletta, "Governor—I," *New Yorker*, April 9, 1984, pp. 50–57; MMC, *Diaries*, pp. 8–10; author's interview with MMC, NYC, June 18, 1987; author's interviews with Frank Cuomo and Joan Cuomo, Copiague, April 8, 1987, and May 20, 1987; MMC, Sabbath service at Temple Sholom, Glen Oaks, Queens, N.Y., February 20, 1981, in MMC, *Diaries*, pp. 401–2.

5. Oscar Handlin, *Al Smith and His America* (Boston: Atlantic Monthly Press/Little, Brown, 1958), p. x; Wickersham Report, as quoted in WPA, FWP, *Italians of New York*, p. 55; MMC, "A Case for the Democrats, 1984: A Tale of Two Cities," keynote address, Democratic National Convention, San Francisco, Calif., July 16, 1984.

Chapter 2

1. Author's interview with Marie Cuomo Vecchio, Mineola, Long Island, N.Y., June 19, 1987; author's interview with Matilda Cuomo, Albany, N.Y., May 19, 1987; author's interview with Frank Cuomo, Copiague, Long Island, N.Y., April 8, 1987; author's interview with Joe Austin, Jamaica, Queens, N.Y., May 22, 1987; MMC, Sabbath service at Temple Sholom, Glen Oaks, Queens, N.Y., February 20, 1981, in MMC, *Diaries of Mario M. Cuomo: The Campaign for Governor* (New York: Random House, 1984), pp. 399–400; "What to Make of Mario," *Time*, June 2, 1986; author's interviews with Immaculata Cuomo, Frank Cuomo, and Joan Cuomo, Copiague, May 20, 1987; MMC, speech to Police Conference of the State of New York, Albany, March 24, 1982, in MMC, *Diaries*, p. 414.

2. Author's interviews with MMC, Albany, March 12, 1987, and NYC, June 18, 1987; Marie Vecchio interview; author's telephone interview with Peter DeNunzio, June 11, 1987; Nathan Glazer and Daniel P. Moynihan, *Beyond the Melting Pot: The Negroes, Puerto Ricans, Jews, Italians, and Irish of New York City* (Cambridge, Mass.: MIT Press, 1963, 2nd ed., 1970), p. 197; Immaculata Cuomo, Frank Cuomo, Joan Cuomo interviews, May 20, 1987; Frank Cuomo interview, April 8, 1987.

3. Immaculata Cuomo, Frank Cuomo interview, May 20, 1987; MMC interview, June 18, 1987; Marie Cuomo Vecchio, letter to Robert McElvaine, June 24, 1987, in author's possession; MMC, *Diaries*, pp. 9, 191; MMC interview, March 12, 1987; MMC, Sabbath service at Temple Sholom, in MMC, *Diaries*, p. 400.

4. Glazer and Moynihan, *Beyond the Melting Pot*, pp. 199, 202; author's interview with Anthony Sarno, Hicksville, Long Island, N.Y., April 8, 1987; MMC, *Diaries*, p. 344n; MMC interview, June 18, 1987; Frank Cuomo interviews, April 8, 1987, May 20, 1987; Immaculata Cuomo interview, May 20, 1987; MMC, speech at Henry Gonzalez Dinner, San Antonio, Texas, January 18, 1986; Marie Vecchio interview; James Reston, "Cuomo Sets a Standard," *NYT*, January 22, 1986; MMC, *Diaries*, p. 13; Ken Auletta, "Governor—I," *New Yorker*, April 9, 1984, p. 51.

5. Joan Cuomo interview, May 20, 1987; Frank Cuomo interviews, May 20, 1987, April 8, 1987; Immaculata Cuomo interview, May 20, 1987; MMC interview, June 18, 1987; author's interview with Arthur Foster, NYC, June 22, 1987.

6. Immaculata Cuomo interview, May 20, 1987; Frank Cuomo interviews, April 8, 1987, May 20, 1987; Foster interview; Marie Vecchio interview; Glazer and Moynihan, *Beyond the Melting Pot*, p. 207.

7. Frank Cuomo interview, April 8, 1987; MMC interview, March 12, 1987; Austin interview.

8. "What Makes Mario Run," *Newsweek*, March 24, 1986, p. 24; William Foote White, *Street Corner Society: The Social Structure of an Italian Slum* (Chicago: University of Chicago Press, 1943; 2nd ed., 1955); Herbert Gans, *The Urban Villagers* (Glencoe, Ill.: Free Press, 1962); Glazer and Moynihan, *Beyond the Melting Pot*, pp. 189, 197; Lawrence W. Levine, *Black Culture and Black Consciousness* (New York: Oxford University Press, 1977), pp. 344–58;

author's telephone interview with MMC, from Albany, July 14, 1987; Robert Ajemian, "Inside the Diaries—and the Mind," *Time,* June 2, 1986, p. 36; Immaculata Cuomo interview, May 20, 1987; Auletta, "Governor—I," p. 51.

9. Glazer and Moynihan, *Beyond the Melting Pot,* p. 197; author's interview with Fabian Palomino, NYC, April 9, 1987; author's interview with Peter Johnson, NYC, May 20, 1987; WPA Federal Writers' Project, *The Italians of New York* (New York: Random House, 1938; reprint ed., New York: Arno Press and the *New York Times,* 1969), p. 52; Ajemian, "Inside the Diaries—and the Mind," p. 37; MMC, speech to the Order of the Sons of Italy Convention, Kiamesha Lake, N.Y., June 5, 1982, in MMC, *Diaries,* p. 435; Frank Cuomo interview, April 8, 1987.

Chapter 3

1. Charles Krauthammer, "The Church-State Debate," *New Republic,* September 17 & 24, 1984, p. 16; MMC, Sunday service, St. John the Divine, New York City, November 27, 1983, in MMC, *Diaries of Mario M. Cuomo: The Campaign for Governor* (New York: Random House, 1984), p. 464; Pete Hamill, "Cuomo, in Church, Preaches the Politics of Love," *New York Daily News,* September 12, 1977; author's interview with Richard Starkey, NYC, April 7, 1987; author's telephone interview with Richard Starkey, from NYC, December 7, 1987; author's interview with Nicholas Sallese, Colonie, N.Y., May 18, 1987; author's interview with Matilda Cuomo, Albany, N.Y., May 19, 1987; *Current Biography, 1983,* p. 78; author's telephone interview with MMC, from Albany, July 14, 1987.

2. Henry J. Browne, "The 'Italian Problem' in the Catholic Church of the United States," Catholic Historical Society, *Historical Studies and Records,* Vol. 35 (1946), pp. 46–72; Nathan Glazer and Daniel P. Moynihan, *Beyond the Melting Pot: The Negroes, Puerto Ricans, Jews, Italians, and Irish of New York City* (Cambridge, Mass.: MIT Press, 1963; 2nd ed., 1970), pp. 202–5; MMC, *Diaries,* pp. 39, 11–13; WPA Federal Writers Project, *The Italians of New York* (New York: Random House, 1938; reprint ed., New York: Arno Press and the *New York Times,* 1969), p. 75; MMC, St. John the Divine service, p. 463; author's interview with MMC, NYC, June 18, 1987.

3. MMC interview, June 18, 1987.

4. Author's interview with Frank Cuomo, Copiague, Long Island, N.Y., April 8, 1987; author's interview with Immaculata Cuomo, Copiague, May 20, 1987; author's interview with Bernard Babb, NYC, April 7, 1987; author's interview with Dr. Nicholas D'Arienzo, Forest Hills, Queens, N.Y., April 6, 1987; author's interview with Anthony Sarno, Hicksville, Long Island, N.Y., April 8, 1987; author's interview with Joseph Mattone, Flushing, Queens, N.Y., June 19, 1987; author's interview with MMC, Albany, March 12, 1987; author's interview with Fabian Palomino, NYC, April 9, 1987; author's interview with Sal Curiale, NYC, April 7, 1987; Matilda Cuomo interview; MMC telephone interview, July 14, 1987.

5. MMC interview, June 18, 1987; Mattone interview; Nat Hentoff, "Cuomo Rising: Will New York's Great Smart Hope Run for Mayor?" *Village Voice,* April 18, 1977, p. 32; *Prep Shadows,* 1949 (St. John's Prep yearbook).

6. MMC telephone interview, July 14, 1987; Nicholas D'Arienzo interview, April 6, 1987; Richard Starkey interview, April 7, 1987; Ken Auletta, "Governor—I," *New Yorker,* April 9, 1984, pp. 51–52; author's interview with Philip Astuto, Jamaica, Queens, N.Y., June 22, 1987; Sarno interview; Mattone interview; author's interview with Judge James Starkey, Brooklyn, N.Y., May 23, 1987; *Vincentian,* 1953 (St. John's College yearbook); Sallese interview; MMC interview, June 18, 1987; Babb interview; author's interview with John Gerity, NYC, April 9, 1987; author's interview with Marie Cuomo Vecchio, Mineola, Long Island, N.Y., June 19, 1987.

7. Sarno interview; Astuto interview; Mattone interview; Babb interview; Sallese interview; author's interview with Ted Vecchio, Mineola, June 19, 1987.

8. Mattone interview; Joseph Vann, ed., *Lives of the Saints* (New York: John J. Crawley, 1953), pp. 309–23; Alistair Fox, *Thomas More: History and Providence* (New Haven: Yale University Press, 1982), pp. 13, 51, 55; Anthony Kenny, *Thomas More* (New York: Oxford University Press, 1983), p. 11 and *passim;* MMC telephone interview, July 14, 1987; Hentoff, "Cuomo Rising," p. 32.

9. Pierre Teilhard de Chardin, *The Divine Milieu,* introduction by Pierre LeRoy (New York: Harper & Row, 1960, 1965), pp. 21–22, 16, 32, 15, 13, 14, 41–42, 56, 60–62, 45, 63, 51, 35–36; MMC, Sunday service at St. John the Divine, p. 464.

10. MMC, "Religious Belief and Public Morality," address at the University of Notre Dame, September 13, 1984, reprinted in *New York Review of Books,* October 25, 1984, p. 36.

11. "Man of the Year," *Time,* January 4, 1963, pp. 50–54; Norman Cousins, "A Declaration of Interdependence," *Saturday Review,* May 4, 1963, pp. 18–20; Roger Williams, as quoted in John A. Garraty, *The American Nation* (New York: Harper & Row, 1966; 2nd ed., 1971), p. 33; Elisabeth Mann Borgese, "The Church Embraces the Future," *Nation,* January 12, 1963, pp. 23–27; "Vatican Revolutionary," *Time,* June 7, 1963, pp. 41–43; Michael Novak, "Act One of the Vatican Council," *New Republic,* January 12, 1963, pp. 15–17; author's interview with Rev. Elvin Sunds, Clinton, Miss., June 29, 1987; Ari L. Goldman, "Cuomo and the Church: Some Vexing Questions," *NYT,* September 12, 1986; R. W. Apple, Jr., "The Question of Mario Cuomo," *New York Times Magazine,* September 14, 1986, p. 49; MMC telephone interview, July 14, 1987.

12. MMC, Sunday service at St. John the Divine, p. 464; author's interview with Jack Newfield, NYC, April 9, 1987; Hamill, "Cuomo, in Church"; Marie Vecchio interview; author's interview with Fabian Palomino, NYC, May 21, 1987; *Time,* January 4, 1963, p. 53; Krauthammer, "Church-State Debate," p. 16; MMC interview, June 18, 1987; MMC, "Religious Belief and Public Morality," p. 36; Richard Reeves, "Jerry Brown Offers 'New Perspectives' Worth Reading," *Atlanta Constitution,* July 29, 1986.

13. *NYT,* August 24, 1974, as quoted in Ellen McCormick, *Cuomo vs. O'Connor: Did a Catholic Politician Make an Anti-Catholic Appeal?* (Commack, N.Y.: Dolores Press, 1985), p. 42; author's interview with Janie Eisenberg, NYC, April 9, 1987; Kenneth Briggs, "Cuomo vs. Bishops," *NYT,* September 14, 1984; *NYT,* August 3, 1984, September 9, 1986; Goldman, "Cuomo and the Church"; "What to Make of Mario," *Time,* June 2, 1986, pp. 33–34; "Cosmo Talks to: Mario Cuomo," *Cosmopolitan,* October 1985, p. 129; Edward I. Koch, *Politics* (New York: Simon & Schuster, 1985), p. 228; Matilda Cuomo interview.

14. Matilda Cuomo interview; *NYT,* August 3, 1984; McCormick, *Cuomo vs. O'Connor,* pp. 31, 43, 79, 65–66; Mary McGrory, "Cuomo Makes a Difference by Being a Different Sort of Pol," *Washington Post,* August 7, 1984; Frank Cuomo interview, April 8, 1987; author's interview with Peter Johnson, NYC, May 20, 1987; editorial, "The Prelate and the Politician," *NYT,* August 8, 1984; MMC, "Religious Belief and Public Morality," pp. 32–37; Gerity interview; *New York Daily News,* October 7, 1984; author's telephone interview with MMC, from Albany, December 9, 1987; Krauthammer, "Church-State Debate," p. 17; "Cosmo Talks to Cuomo," p. 129.

15. *NYT,* September 6, 1986, September 8, 1986, September 9, 1986, October 3, 1986; Goldman, "Cuomo and the Church"; Johnson interview.

16. Mattone interview; MMC, *Diaries,* pp. 239–40, 36, 37, 320; Anthony Lewis, "Cuomo's Turn," *NYT,* November 10, 1986.

Chapter 4

1. Author's interview with Nicholas Sallese, Colonie, N.Y., May 18, 1987; author's interview with Judge James Starkey, Brooklyn, N.Y., May 20, 1987; Paul Taylor, "Cuomo's Not So Tough, As Long as He Gets What He Wants," *Washington Post National Weekly Edition,* December 1, 1986.

2. David Shribman, "Mario Cuomo Emerges as a Major New Voice in Democratic Circles," *Wall Street Journal,* September 4, 1986; author's interview with Bernard Babb, NYC, April 7, 1987; author's interview with Frank Cuomo, Copiague, Long Island, N.Y., May 20, 1987; author's interview with MMC, NYC, June 18, 1987; author's interview with Lou Carnesecca, Jamaica, Queens, N.Y., June 18, 1987; author's interview with Arthur Foster, NYC, June 22, 1987; MMC, *Diaries of Mario M. Cuomo: The Campaign for Governor* (New York: Random House, 1984), pp. 13–14.

3. Mike Lee, "Reports," *Long Island Press,* June 23, 1949, January 21, 1950, and April 26, 1964, clippings in MMC scrapbooks, Executive Chamber, State Capitol, Albany, N.Y.; Frank Cuomo interview, April 8, 1987; author's interview with Joe Austin, Jamaica, May 22, 1987; author's interview with Fabian Palomino, NYC, April 9, 1987; author's telephone interview with MMC, from Albany, July 14, 1987; author's interview with MMC, NYC, May 21, 1987.

4. Author's interview with Joseph Mattone, Flushing, Queens, N.Y., June 19, 1987; author's interview with Richard Starkey, NYC, April 7, 1987; James Starkey interview; Babb interview; unidentified clippings in MMC scrapbooks, Albany; Sallese interview; author's interview with Nicholas D'Arienzo, Forest Hills, Queens, N.Y., April 6, 1987; author's interview with Anthony Sarno, Hicksville, Long Island, N.Y., April 8, 1987; Carnesecca interview; *Vincentian,* 1953.

5. Babb interview; Frank Cuomo interview, May 20, 1987; Carnesecca interview; author's interview with Fabian Palomino, NYC, May 21, 1987; MMC telephone interview, July 14, 1987; Ken Auletta, "Governor—I," *New Yorker,* April 9, 1984, p. 52; undated clipping from *The Torch* (St. John's college paper), 1951, MMC scrapbooks, Albany; author's interview with Matilda Cuomo, Albany, May 19, 1987; Nat Hentoff, "Cuomo Rising: Will New York's Smart Hope Run for Mayor?" *Village Voice,* April 18, 1977, p. 32; unidentified clippings in MMC scrapbooks.

6. Ed McCarrick, Inter-Club Communication to Mickey O'Neil, Subject: Outfielder Mario Cuomo, May 31, 1952, in MMC scrapbooks, Albany; Auletta, "Governor—I," pp. 50, 52; Babb interview; Matilda Cuomo interview; Sarno interview; Carnesecca interview; Murray Kempton, "A Hard Case" (review of MMC, *Diaries of Mario M. Cuomo: The Campaign for Governor*), *New York Review of Books,* July 19, 1984, p. 5.

7. MMC, *Diaries,* p. 14; *Brunswick* (Ga.) *News,* June 6, 1952, June 7, 1952, August 26, 1952, *Albany* (Ga.) *Herald,* June 23, 1952, clippings in MMC scrapbooks, Albany; D'Arienzo interview; "What to Make of Mario," *Time,* June 2, 1986, p. 32; Auletta, "Governor—I," p. 52.

8. Matilda Cuomo interview; unidentified clipping in MMC scrapbooks, Albany; *The Torch,* September 19, 1952; Austin interview; Sallese interview; MMC telephone interview, July 14, 1987; Mario Matthew Cuomo, player record card, in MMC scrapbooks, Albany; MMC, *Diaries,* p. 14.

9. Sarno interview; author's interview with Peter Johnson, NYC, May 20, 1987; Frank Cuomo interview, April 8, 1987; Richard Starkey interview.

10. Babb interview; Hentoff, "Cuomo Rising," p. 31; Palomino interview, April 9, 1987; author's interview with Alexander Levine, Albany, May 18, 1987; Frank Cuomo interview, April 8, 1987; R. W. Apple, Jr., "The Question of Mario Cuomo," *New York Times Magazine,* September 14, 1986, p. 50; MMC telephone interview, July 14, 1987; Palomino interview, May 21, 1987; Johnson interview.

11. Author's interview with Sal Curiale, NYC, April 7, 1987; Frank Cuomo interview, April 8, 1987; Paul West, "Cuomo's Complaint," *New Republic,* February 17, 1986, p. 12; Mary McGrory, "If Only the Primaries Were Over," *Washington Post,* January 28, 1986; George F. Will, "Cuomo's Skin Not Too Thin," *Clarion-Ledger* (Jackson, Miss.), December 8, 1986; "What Makes Mario Run?" *Newsweek,* March 24, 1986, pp. 23, 28; Robert Ajemian, "Inside the Diaries, and the Mind," *Time,* June 2, 1986, pp. 36–37; Apple, "The Question of Mario Cuomo," p. 86; Taylor, "Cuomo's Not So Tough."

12. Hentoff, "Cuomo Rising," pp. 32–34; Frank Cuomo interview, April 8, 1987; Auletta, "Governor—I," p. 58; Palomino interview, April 9, 1987; Anthony Lewis, "Cuomo's Turn," *NYT*, November 11, 1986.

13. MMC, *Diaries*, pp. 182, 78, 81–82, 187, 342, 273, 182; Taylor, "Cuomo's Not So Tough"; editorial, "Mario Cuomo, Then and Now," *NYT*, November 2, 1986; Will, "Cuomo's Skin Not Too Thin."

14. "You and Me Against the World," lyrics and music by Paul Williams and Ken Asher, © 1974 Almo Music Corp./ASCAP; MMC, *Diaries*, pp. 314, 182.

Chapter 5

1. MMC, *Diaries of Mario M. Cuomo: The Campaign for Governor* (New York: Random House, 1984), pp. 7, 406–12, 459–60, 396; author's telephone interview with MMC, from Albany, N.Y., July 14, 1987.

2. Author's interview with MMC, NYC, June 18, 1987; Nat Hentoff, "Cuomo Rising: Will New York's Great Smart Hope Run for Mayor?" *Village Voice*, April 18, 1977, p. 31; author's interview with Ted Vecchio, Mineola, Long Island, N.Y., June 19, 1987; author's interview with Joseph Mattone, Flushing, Queens, N.Y., June 19, 1987; author's interview with Frank Cuomo, Copiague, Long Island, N.Y., April 8, 1987; MMC, *Diaries*, pp. 333–34, 114, 92; author's interview with MMC, August 13, 1987; author's interview with Peter Johnson, NYC, May 20, 1987; author's interview with Immaculata Cuomo, Copiague, May 20, 1987; author's interview with Nicholas Sallese, Colonie, N.Y., May 18, 1987; Nathan Glazer and Daniel P. Moynihan, *Beyond the Melting Pot: The Negroes, Puerto Ricans, Jews, Italians, and Irish of New York City* (Cambridge, Mass.: MIT Press, 1963; 2nd ed., 1970), p. 195; R. W. Apple, Jr., "The Question of Mario Cuomo," *New York Times Magazine*, September 14, 1986, p. 48; "What to Make of Mario," *Time*, June 2, 1986, p. 32.

3. Author's interview with Matilda Cuomo, Albany, May 19, 1987; Sallese interview; author's interview with Nicholas D'Arienzo, Forest Hills, Queens, N.Y., April 6, 1987; author's interview with Anthony Sarno, Hicksville, Long Island, N.Y., April 8, 1987; Mattone interview; author's interview with Fabian Palomino, NYC, May 21, 1987; Ken Auletta, "Governor—I," *New Yorker*, April 9, 1984, p. 57; "What to Make of Mario," p. 32; Frank Cuomo interview, April 8, 1987.

4. MMC, *Diaries*, pp. 14–15; Hentoff, "Cuomo Rising," p. 32; "What to Make of Mario," p. 32; author's interview with Fabian Palomino, NYC, April 9, 1987.

5. Auletta, "Governor—I," pp. 57–58; MMC telephone interview, July 14, 1987; Palomino interview, May 21, 1987; Matilda Cuomo interview; St. John's Law School Yearbook, *Res Gestae*, 1956, pp. 65, 112.

6. MMC telephone interview, July 14, 1987; "What to Make of Mario," p. 32; Frank Cuomo interview, April 8, 1987; Mattone interview; Apple, "Question of Mario Cuomo," p. 48; "What Makes Mario Run?" *Newsweek*, March 24, 1986, p. 23; Hentoff, "Cuomo Rising," p. 32; MMC, *Diaries*, p. 216; Palomino interview, May 21, 1987; author's interview with Marie Cuomo Vecchio, Mineola, June 19, 1987.

7. Author's interview with John Gerity, NYC, April 9, 1987; William Reel, "Our Man Goes Looking and Finds an Honest Lawyer," *New York Daily News*, October 17, 1975; Auletta, "Governor—I," pp. 57–61; author's interview with Sal Curiale, NYC, April 7, 1987; Palomino interviews, April 9 and May 21, 1987; Mattone interview.

8. Gerity interview; Curiale interview; Hentoff, "Cuomo Rising," p. 31; Matilda Cuomo interview; Robert S. McElvaine, *The Great Depression: America, 1929–1941* (New York: Times Books, 1984), p. 61; author's interview with Richard Starkey, NYC, April 7, 1987; Palomino interview, May 21, 1987; Marie Vecchio interview; "What to Make of Mario," p. 31; author's interview with MMC, Albany, March 12, 1987; Frank Cuomo interview, April 8, 1987; author's interview with Alexander Levine, Albany, May 18, 1987; MMC, *Diaries*, p. 373.

9. D'Arienzo interview; Mattone interview; Palomino interviews, April 9 and May 21, 1987; Matilda Cuomo interview; author's interview with Rosario Cuomo, Holliswood, Queens, N.Y., April 6, 1987; Auletta, "Governor—I," p. 57; Curiale interview; Sallese interview; MMC, *Diaries*, pp. 341, 31, 70; MMC telephone interview, July 14, 1987.

10. Matilda Cuomo interview; Mattone interview; author's interview with Judge James Starkey, Brooklyn, N.Y., May 20, 1987; author's telephone interview with Jacques Tuchler, from Brooklyn, N.Y., December 17, 1987; Palomino interviews, April 9 and May 21, 1987; author's telephone interview with Fabian Palomino, from Albany, December 9, 1987; author's telephone interviews with MMC, from Albany, December 6 and 9, 1987.

11. Matilda Cuomo interview; Curiale interview; Palomino interview, May 21, 1987; D'Arienzo interview; Johnson interview.

12. Matilda Cuomo interview; Sallese interview; Robert Ajemian, "Inside the Diaries—and the Mind," *Time*, June 2, 1986, p. 37; Michele Willens, "Cosmo Talks to: Mario Cuomo," *Cosmopolitan*, October 1985, p. 126; *NYT*, October 20, 1986; MMC, *Diaries*, pp. 94, 46, 106, 11, 194; Frank Cuomo interview, April 8, 1987.

Chapter 6

1. MMC, *Diaries of Mario M. Cuomo: The Campaign for Governor* (New York: Random House, 1984), p. 411; author's interview with Margaret Swezey, Jamaica, Queens, N.Y., June 16, 1987; author's interview with Sal Curiale, NYC, April 7, 1987; Pete Hamill, "Northside Blues," unidentified clipping in MMC scrapbooks, Albany, N.Y.; author's interview with John Gerity, NYC, April 9, 1987; MMC, *Forest Hills Diary: The Crisis of Low-Income Housing* (New York: Random House, 1974), pp. 38, 80, xiv, 109, 43; author's interview with Nicholas D'Arienzo, Forest Hills, Queens, N.Y., April 6, 1987.

2. R. W. Apple, Jr., "The Question of Mario Cuomo," *New York Times Magazine*, September 14, 1986, p. 49; *The Tablet* (Brooklyn, N.Y.), May 30, 1963; *Long Island Press*, April 26, 1964; James J. Sexton, Jr., Brooklyn, N.Y., letter to Harold F. McNiece, February 19, 1963, copy in MMC scrapbooks, Albany; author's interview with Fabian Palomino, NYC, May 21, 1987; Ken Auletta, "Governor—I," *New Yorker*, April 9, 1984, p. 61; *NYT*, March 7, 1965, April 16, 1965, April 21, 1965, July 20, 1965, December 16, 1965, December 17, 1965, December 18, 1965, December 23, 1965, December 27, 1965, December 29, 1965, January 2, 1966, January 3, 1966, January 5, 1966, January 7, 1966, January 9, 1966, January 18, 1966, January 30, 1966, February 5, 1966, March 13, 1966, April 30, 1966, May 1, 1966, March 8, 1967, June 20, 1967, July 25, 1967, August 22, 1967, November 5, 1967; author's interview with Richard Starkey, NYC, April 7, 1987; author's interview with Anthony Sarno, Hicksville, Long Island, N.Y., April 8, 1987; author's telephone interview with MMC, from Albany, July 31, 1987.

3. Robert Caro, *Power Broker: Robert Moses and the Fall of New York* (New York: Alfred A. Knopf, 1974), pp. 6–8, 1082–90, 1098; MMC telephone interview, July 31, 1987.

4. MMC, *Forest Hills Diary*, pp. 3–23, 28, 36, 42; Ross Gelbspan, "Corona: Cause for a Day," *Village Voice*, July 8, 1971; MMC telephone interview, July 31, 1987; author's interview with Matilda Cuomo, Albany, May 19, 1987; Nicholas D'Arienzo interview; Jimmy Breslin, preface to MMC, *Forest Hills Diary*, pp. vii, xi; *New York Daily News*, October 5, 1969, December 3, 1970, June 11, 1971, July 10, 1971; *NYT*, December 3, 1970, May 23, 1971, May 25, 1971; author's interview with former Mayor John V. Lindsay, NYC, August 6, 1987; *Long Island Press*, April 10, 1969, January 22, 1971, March 2, 1971, June 10, 1971, June 15, 1971; unidentified clippings in MMC scrapbooks, Albany; anonymous broadside in MMC scrapbooks, Albany; Curiale interview.

5. Andy Logan, "Not You, Not You," *New Yorker*, November 11, 1972, pp. 169–82; MMC *Forest Hills Diary*, pp. 12–13, 15–16, 24–26, 39, 31, 42, 30, 101, 97–98, 36, 92, 110, 81, 108, 49, 62, 100, 114–16, 123, 134, 117–20, 141–46, 55, 118, 106; Lindsay interview; *Time*, November 29, 1971; *Newsweek*, November 29, 1971; Breslin, preface to MMC, *Forest Hills Diary*, pp.

vii–viii; author's interview with Joan Cuomo, Copiague, Long Island, N.Y., April 8, 1987; *NYT,* October 31, 1985, April 27, 1987.

6. MMC, *Forest Hills Diary,* pp. 56, 122, 99, 131, 133.

7. Author's interview with MMC, NYC, June 18, 1987; MMC, *Forest Hills Diary,* pp. 127, 145, 151.

Chapter 7

1. *Observer-Dispatch* (Utica, N.Y.), October 24, 1978; author's interview with Frank Cuomo, Copiague, Long Island, N.Y., May 20, 1987; MMC, *Forest Hills Diary: The Crisis of Low-Income Housing* (New York: Random House, 1974), pp. 111, 106, 71, 143, 138; author's telephone interview with MMC, from Albany, N.Y., July 14, 1987; *New York Daily News,* October 17, 1975; author's interview with Fabian Palomino, NYC, April 9, 1987; Nat Hentoff, "Cuomo Rising: Will New York's Smart Hope Run for Mayor?" *Village Voice,* April 18, 1977, p. 32; Woodie Fitchette, "Cuomo Seen as Albany's 'Conscience,'" *Ithaca Journal,* December 2, 1975; author's interview with Matilda Cuomo, Albany, May 19, 1987; author's interview with Joseph Mattone, Flushing, Queens, N.Y., June 19, 1987.

2. Palomino interview, April 9, 1987; author's interview with Peter Quinn, NYC, August 7, 1987; author's interview with Fabian Palomino, NYC, May 21, 1987; Jimmy Breslin, preface to MMC, *Forest Hills Diary,* p. xii; author's interview with MMC, Albany, N.Y., August 14, 1987; Mattone interview; author's interview with Nicholas Sallese, Colonie, N.Y., May 18, 1987; MMC, *Forest Hills Diary,* p. 120; MMC, "Ethics—Impossible in Public Office?" *Newsday,* April 6, 1975; author's interview with Nicholas D'Arienzo, Forest Hills, Queens, N.Y., April 6, 1987.

3. Edward O'Neill, "City Hall," *Newsday,* December 12, 1972; Robert Mindlin, "JVL Man to Beat in Mayoral Stakes," *Long Island Press,* February 4, 1973; author's interview with John V. Lindsay, NYC, August 6, 1987; author's interview with Frank Cuomo, Copiague, Long Island, N.Y., April 8, 1987; author's interview with Bernard Babb, NYC, April 7, 1987; MMC, *Forest Hills Diary,* pp. 116, 136; MMC interview, August 14, 1987; unidentified clipping, MMC scrapbooks, Albany; D'Arienzo interview; Mattone interview; author's interview with Judge Sol Wachtler, Mineola, Long Island, N.Y., May 20, 1987; Hentoff, "Cuomo Rising," pp. 31–32; *Long Island Press,* March 14, 1973, March 23, 1973; author's interview with Richard Starkey, NYC, April 7, 1987.

4. *New York Daily News,* October 9, 1973, June 2, 1975; MMC interview, August 14, 1987; Edward I. Koch, *Mayor* (New York: Simon & Schuster, 1984), pp. 339–40; Hentoff, "Cuomo Rising," p. 34; *NYT,* March 8, 1974, May 1, 1974, May 10, 1974, June 15, 1974, August 5, 1974, August 24, 1974; author's interview with Mary Anne Krupsak, NYC, August 11, 1987; author's interview with Joan Cuomo, Copiague, April 8, 1987; Auletta, "Governor—I," pp. 64–65; author's interview with Marie Cuomo Vecchio, Mineola, June 19, 1987; Woodie Fitchette, "Cuomo Expected to be Influential," *Tarrytown* (N.Y.) *News,* January 7, 1975; *Knickerbocker News* (Albany, N.Y.), February 5, 1975; Gene Spagnoli, "Socking Catcher's Mask Taught Him Tact," *New York Daily News,* March 30, 1975; Richard Starkey interview.

5. Judith Bender, "The Governor's Favorite Mr. Fixit," *Newsday,* April 21, 1975; David Shaffer, "Cuomo's Appointment Looms as Significant," *Buffalo Courier Express,* December 23, 1974; *NYT,* December 20, 1974, January 17, 1975, March 11, 1975, March 14, 1975; Fitchette, "Cuomo Expected to Be Influential"; Richard Ryan, "Mario Cuomo: New State Secretary of State Should Be Better," *The Tablet* (Brooklyn), January 2, 1975; Spagnoli, "Socking Catcher's Mask"; *New York Daily News,* January 6, 1975, January 17, 1975, February 5, 1975, March 9, 1975, February 12, 1976; *Albany Times-Union,* January 17, 1975, February 20, 1975; *Long Island Press,* February 17, 1975; MMC, "Ethics—Impossible in Public Office?"; *Binghamton* (N.Y.) *Sun-Bulletin,* April 4, 1975; *Niagara Falls Gazette,* March 4, 1975; Vic Ostrowidski, "Cuomo Seeks Lobby Reform," *Albany Times-Union,* March 5, 1975; Woodie Fitchette, "Disputes on Lobby Bill," *Binghamton Evening Press,* June 20, 1975; *Utica Daily*

Press, February 16, 1977; *Niagara Falls Gazette,* March 5, 1977; *Brooklyn Bulletin,* May 20, 1975; Peter Harrigan, "Cuomo: The Job's Not 'Ceremonial,' " *Staten Island Advance,* May 12, 1975.

6. *Brooklyn Bulletin,* June 13, 1975, July 21, 1976; Hentoff, "Cuomo Rising," pp. 34–35; *New York Post,* December 18, 1975, May 13, 1976, June 26, 1976, June 30, 1976; *Long Island Press,* May 19, 1976, July 20, 1976, July 28, 1976; *Amsterdam News* (NYC), January 4, 1975; editorial, "Bravo Mario!" *Amsterdam News* (undated clipping in MMC scrapbooks, NYC); Fitchette, "Cuomo Seen as Albany's 'Conscience' "; *New York Daily News,* May 12, 1976, June 29, 1976, July 1, 1976; Auletta, "Governor—I," pp. 66–68; MMC, "The Bitter Alternatives for Co-op City," *New York Daily News,* November 30, 1976; *Albany Times-Union,* July 27, 1976; *Utica Observer-Dispatch,* August 12, 1976; *Newsday,* December 2, 1976; *Watertown* (N.Y.) *Daily Times,* March 22, 1977; *Niagara Falls Gazette,* March 30, 1977; Judith Bender, "Cuomo: The Modest Mediator," *Newsday,* March 20, 1977; MMC interview, August 14, 1987; Harrigan, "The Job's Not 'Ceremonial.' "

Chapter 8

1. Author's interview with MMC, Albany, N.Y., August 14, 1987; *New York Post,* December 3, 1976; Woodie Fitchette, "Will 'Good Soldier' Cuomo Take Over?" *Utica Observer-Dispatch,* November 22, 1976; *Schenectady Gazette,* November 29, 1976; *Newsday,* November 19, 1976, December 4, 1976; *Buffalo Evening News,* November 27, 1976; *NYT,* November 28, 1976; *New York Daily News,* December 5, 1976.

2. Author's interview with Felix Rohatyn, NYC, August 17, 1987; author's interview with Herman Badillo, NYC, August 8, 1987; author's telephone interview with MMC, from Albany, August 15, 1987; *NYT,* December 26, 1976, February 23, 1977, February 28, 1977, March 2, 1977, March 3, 1977, March 4, 1977, March 24, 1977, April 7, 1977; Arthur Browne, Dan Collins, and Michael Goodwin, *I, Koch* (New York: Dodd, Mead, 1985), p. 125; Ken Auletta, "Meat-Eating Gorillas, Mayoral Fever, and Other Seasonal Woes," *New York,* August 16, 1976, p. 6; *Utica Daily Press,* March 23, 1977; Nat Hentoff, "Cuomo Rising: Will New York's Great Smart Hope Run for Mayor?" *Village Voice,* April 16, 1977, pp. 31, 35–36; *New York Post,* March 1, 1977, March 3, 1977, March 21, 1977; *New York Daily News,* April 7, 1977; *White Plains* (N.Y.) *Reporter Dispatch,* March 18, 1977; *Canandaigua* (N.Y.) *Messenger,* March 23, 1977.

3. MMC telephone interview, August 15, 1987; *New York Post,* March 21, 1977; Pete Hamill, "Cuomo's Plan: Fed Help, Self-Help, and Hope," *New York Daily News,* April 15, 1977; Hentoff, "Cuomo Rising," p. 36.

4. Edward I. Koch, *Mayor* (New York: Simon & Schuster, 1984), p. 41; author's interview with Robert Sullivan, NYC, August 15, 1987; *NYT,* April 14, 1977, April 15, 1977, April 18, 1977, April 19, 1977, May 2, 1977, May 7, 1977, May 8, 1977, May 9, 1977, May 10, 1977; Browne, Collins, and Goodwin, *I, Koch,* p. 126; author's interview with Jack Newfield, NYC, April 9, 1987; author's interview with Richard C. Wade, NYC, August 17, 1987; MMC telephone interview, August 15, 1987; author's interview with Judge Sol Wachtler, Mineola, Long Island, N.Y., May 20, 1987.

5. *NYT,* June 20, 1977, June 30, 1977, July 21, 1977, August 8, 1977, August 20, 1977, August 24, 1977, August 25, 1977, September 1, 1977, September 3, 1977, September 10, 1977; Hentoff, "Cuomo Rising," p. 31; Wachtler interview; Sullivan interview; *Staten Island Advance,* August 15, 1977; MMC telephone interview, August 15, 1987; *New York Daily News,* August 24, 1977, September 2, 1977; Browne, Collins, and Goodwin, *I, Koch,* pp. 149–54; *New York Post,* August 19, 1977.

6. MMC, *Diaries of Mario M. Cuomo: The Campaign for Governor* (New York: Random House, 1984), pp. 158–59; Sullivan interview; Wade interview; Koch, *Mayor,* pp. 36–37; Badillo interview; MMC telephone interview, August 15, 1987; Margot Hornblower, "East Side, West Side, Corruption Is All Around the Town," *Washington Post National Weekly Edition,* September 7, 1987; author's interview with Eugene Callender, Albany, August 12,

1987; Pete Hamill, "Cuomo, in Church, Preaches the Politics of Love," *New York Daily News*, September 12, 1977; *NYT*, September 10, 1977, September 11, 1977, September 12, 1977, September 13, 1977, September 15, 1977, September 16, 1977, September 17, 1977; Murray Kempton, "A Hard Case," *New York Review of Books*, July 19, 1984, p. 3; author's interview with Nicholas D'Arienzo, Forest Hills, Queens, N.Y., April 6, 1987; author's interview with Mayor Edward Koch, NYC, May 22, 1987; Wachtler interview.

7. Browne, Collins, and Goodwin, *I, Koch*, pp. 127–29; Jane Perlez, "Koch: The Media Whispers," *Soho Weekly News*, November 10, 1977; Koch, *Mayor*, pp. 33–36; Geoffrey Stokes, "Smear News Is No News," *Village Voice*, November 7, 1977, p. 27; MMC telephone interview, August 15, 1987; Koch interview; *Knickerbocker News* (Albany), April 28, 1976; *Newsday*, January 3, 1978, January 5, 1978; Hamill, "Cuomo, in Church"; *NYT*, August 31, 1977, November 6, 1977, November 10, 1977, November 18, 1977, November 22, 1977; author's interview with MMC, aboard helicopter en route from Albany to NYC, August 13, 1987.

8. Sullivan interview; MMC telephone interview, August 15, 1987; Wade interview; *NYT*, August 31, 1977, September 20, 1977, September 21, 1977, September 27, 1977, October 14, 1977, October 17, 1977, October 27, 1977, November 9, 1977, November 11, 1977; author's interview with Marie Cuomo Vecchio, Mineola, June 19, 1987; Ken Auletta, "Governor—I," *New Yorker*, April 9, 1984, p. 73.

Chapter 9

1. Author's interview with Judge Sol Wachtler, Mineola, Long Island, N.Y., May 20, 1987; author's interview with Nicholas Sallese, Colonie, N.Y., May 18, 1987; author's interview with Peter Johnson, NYC, May 20, 1987; author's interview with Bernard Babb, NYC, April 7, 1987; Ken Auletta, "Governor—I," *New Yorker*, April 9, 1984, p. 82. The Harding quote comes from a highly reliable source who does not wish to be identified.

2. *New York Post*, February 22, 1978, April 24, 1978, June 13, 1978; author's telephone interview with MMC, from Albany, N.Y., August 15, 1987; *Newsday*, February 9, 1978, May 12, 1978; Wachtler interview; Doug Ireland, "Polls and Pols," *Soho Weekly News*, May 11, 1978; Frank Lombardi, "Just Wait Till This Year," *New York Daily News*, May 11, 1978; *Utica Observer-Dispatch*, October 24, 1978; Jane Perlez, "Cuomo Forgives Murdoch," *Soho Weekly News*, May 11, 1978; MMC, *Diaries of Mario M. Cuomo: The Campaign for Governor* (New York: Random House, 1984), p. 25; author's interview with Robert Sullivan, NYC, August 15, 1987; author's interview with Richard C. Wade, NYC, August 17, 1987; author's interview with Mary Anne Krupsak, NYC, August 11, 1987; author's interview with Carol Bellamy, NYC, August 11, 1987; *NYT*, June 13, 1978, June 14, 1978; author's interview with Richard Starkey, NYC, April 7, 1987; author's interview with MMC, Albany, August 14, 1987.

3. Author's interview with Frank Cuomo, Copiague, Long Island, N.Y., May 20, 1987; MMC, *Diaries*, p. 25; Richard Starkey interview; Edward I. Koch, *Mayor* (New York: Simon & Schuster, 1984), p. 329; Auletta, "Governor—I," pp. 73–74; MMC interview, August 14, 1987.

4. MMC telephone interview, August 15, 1987; author's telephone interviews MMC from Albany, January 12, 1988, and February 8, 1988; author's interview with Jack Newfield, NYC, April 9, 1987; author's interview with Sen. Edward M. Kennedy, Washington, D.C., February 27, 1986; *NYT*, July 30, 1987; MMC, *Diaries*, pp. 26-27; MMC interview, August 14, 1987.

5. Author's interview with Michael Del Giudice, NYC, June 19, 1987; MMC, *Diaries*, pp. 64, 102–5, 241; Richard Starkey interview; Auletta, "Governor—I," p. 74.

6. MMC telephone interview, August 15, 1987; Newfield interview; MMC interview, August 14, 1987; Arthur Browne, Dan Collins, and Michael Goodwin, *I, Koch* (New York: Dodd, Mead, 1985), pp. 235, 241–42; Koch, *Mayor*, pp. 330–31; MMC, *Diaries*, pp. 28, 67, 43,

48–49, 68–70, 71, 76–77, 82–83, 89, 92, 99, 102, 109–12, 114; Wachtler interview; *NYT,* June 13, 1981, August 1, 1981, August 9, 1981, November 8, 1981, December 31, 1981.

7. *NYT,* January 16, 1982, February 23, 1982, February 24, 1982, March 12, 1982, March 17, 1982, March 25, 1982, April 5, 1982, May 17, 1982, June 19, 1982, June 22, 1982, August 24, 1982, September 17, 1982, September 19, 1982; MMC, *Diaries,* pp. 118–20, 140, 154, 175, 211, 228n, 270–71, 441–45; MMC interview, August 14, 1987; Koch interview; Browne, Collins, and Goodwin, *I, Koch,* pp. 246, 247, 250, 253–58; Auletta, "Governor—I," p. 74; Koch, *Mayor,* pp. 331–32; MMC telephone interview, August 15, 1987; Wachtler interview.

8. MMC, *Diaries,* pp. 165, 197, 204, 215, 216, 237–41, 243, 245–46, 298, 301–2, 303, 314, 320; Auletta, "Governor—I," pp. 74–81; author's interview with MMC, NYC, January 21, 1986; Koch interview; MMC telephone interview, August 15, 1987; Browne, Collins, and Goodwin, *I, Koch,* pp. 258–59; *NYT,* July 8, 1982, September 24, 1982, September 25, 1982; Sullivan interview; Wade interview; Lee M. Miringoff and Barbara L. Carvalho, *The Cuomo Factor* (Poughkeepsie, N.Y.: Marist Institute for Public Opinion, 1986), p. 3.

9. MMC telephone interview, August 15, 1987; MMC, *Diaries,* 317–19, 321–25, 329, 330–31, 348; *NYT,* October 1, 1982, October 6, 1982, October 9, 1982, October 12, 1982, October 20, 1982, October 26, 1982, October 28, 1982, October 29, 1982, October 31, 1982, November 3, 1982, November 4, 1982; Miringoff and Carvalho, *Cuomo Factor,* pp. 8–9, 10; Auletta, "Governor—I," p. 81; author's interview with Drew Zambelli, Albany, August 12, 1987; Sullivan interview; author's interview with Gary Fryer, Albany, August 12, 1987; author's interview with Martin Steadman, NYC, August 17, 1987; author's interview with Frank Cuomo, Copiague, April 8, 1987.

10. Miringoff and Carvalho, *Cuomo Factor,* pp. 10–13; Auletta, "Governor—I," p. 81.

Chapter 10

1. Author's interview with Michael Del Giudice, NYC, June 19, 1987; Ken Auletta, "Governor—I," *New Yorker,* April 9, 1984; author's telephone interview with MMC, from Albany, N.Y., August 15, 1987; author's interview with Mary Tragale, NYC, May 21, 1987; MMC, First Inaugural Address, Albany, January 1, 1983, in MMC, *Diaries of Mario Cuomo: The Campaign for Governor* (New York: Random House, 1984), pp. 455–61.

2. Auletta, "Governor—I"; MMC, "State of the State," January 5, 1983; Del Giudice interview; author's interview with Timothy Russert, NYC, August 11, 1987; MMC telephone interview, August 15, 1987.

3. MMC telephone interview, August 15, 1987; Auletta, "Governor—I," pp. 94–113; author's interview with MMC, NYC, January 21, 1986; author's interview with Gary Fryer, Albany, August 12, 1987; Ken Auletta, "Governor—II," *New Yorker,* April 16, 1984, pp. 65–66, 68, 74, 78.

4. Auletta, "Governor—I," p. 110; author's interview with Peter Quinn, NYC, August 7, 1987; author's interview with MMC, aboard helicopter en route from Albany to NYC, August 13, 1987; author's interview with Drew Zambelli, Albany, August 12, 1987.

5. Auletta, "Governor—II," p. 56; Del Giudice interview; Quinn interview; author's interview with Robert Sullivan, NYC, August 15, 1987; Russert interview; author's interview with Martin Steadman, NYC, August 17, 1987; author's interview with Peter Johnson, NYC, May 20, 1987; author's interview with John Gerity, NYC, April 19, 1987; author's telephone interview with William Stern, from NYC, August 4, 1987; author's telephone interview with Fabian Palomino, from Albany, October 26, 1987; *NYT,* June 26, 1984; MMC telephone interview, August 15, 1987; author's telephone interview with MMC, from Albany, October 17, 1987; "What to Make of Mario," *Time,* June 2, 1986, p. 33; "What Makes Mario Run?" *Newsweek,* March 24, 1986, p. 26.

6. Author's interview with Judge Sol Wachtler, Mineola, Long Island, N.Y., May 20, 1987; author's interview with Fabian Palomino, NYC, April 9, 1987; *NYT,* August 12, 1986, January 18, 1987, June 21, 1987; *Wall Street Journal,* September 4, 1986.

7. Del Giudice interview; *NYT,* September 7, 1987; Fryer interview; Lee M. Miringoff and Barbara L. Carvalho, *The Cuomo Factor* (Poughkeepsie, N.Y.: Marist Institute for Public Opinion, 1986), pp. 18, 79; Auletta, "Governor—II," p. 53; author's interview with Fabian Palomino, NYC, May 21, 1987; Wachtler interview; Paul Taylor, "Cuomo's Not So Tough, As Long as He Gets What He Wants," *Washington Post National Weekly Edition,* December 1, 1986; Marist Institute for Public Opinion, New York State Poll, January 1988, p. 18.

8. Author's interview with Margaret Swezey, Jamaica, Queens, N.Y., June 16, 1987; MMC telephone interview, August 15, 1987; Del Giudice interview; Zambelli interview; *NYT,* May 23, 1984, October 3, 1984, October 10, 1985, October 16, 1986, January 14, 1987, January 20, 1987, January 25, 1987, April 29, 1987; author's interview with Matilda Cuomo, Albany, May 19, 1987; MMC interview, January 21, 1986; Fryer interview; "What to Make of Mario," p. 32; Palomino interview, April 9, 1987; author's interview with Nicholas Sallese, Colonie, N.Y., May 18, 1987.

9. MMC telephone interview, August 15, 1987; Walter Olson, "Cuomo's Pay-as-You-Go Liberalism," *Wall Street Journal,* October 6, 1986; *NYT,* January 31, 1983, March 30, 1986, January 21, 1987; *Chronicle of Higher Education,* September 17, 1986, pp. 21–23; *Wall Street Journal,* September 4, 1986; Fryer interview; Sallese interview.

10. MMC telephone interview, August 15, 1987; MMC, *Diaries,* p. 356; Auletta, "Governor—II," pp. 65, 72; Zambelli interview; author's interview with MMC, Albany, August 14, 1987; *Wall Street Journal,* September 4, 1986; Palomino interview, April 9, 1987; Russert interview.

11. Del Giudice interview; Miringoff and Carvalho, *The Cuomo Factor,* p. 5; Matilda Cuomo interview; Fryer interview.

Chapter 11

1. Author's interview with Peter Quinn, NYC, August 7, 1987; author's telephone interview with MMC, from Albany, N.Y., August 15, 1987; excerpts from unpublished MMC diaries, June-July 1984, Executive Mansion, Albany; author's interview with Timothy Russert, NYC, August 11, 1987; MMC, *Diaries of Mario M. Cuomo: The Campaign for Governor* (New York: Random House, 1984), pp. 389–91; MMC, "A Case for the Democrats, 1984: A Tale of Two Cities," keynote address, Democratic National Convention, San Francisco, Calif., July 16, 1984; author's interview with Matilda Cuomo, Albany, May 19, 1987; author's interview with Mary Tragale, NYC, May 21, 1987.

2. Quinn interview; author's interview with Martin Steadman, NYC, August 17, 1987; MMC, "Religious Belief and Public Morality," address at the University of Notre Dame, September 13, 1984, reprinted in *New York Review of Books,* October 25, 1984; Charles Krauthammer, "The Church-State Debate," *New Republic,* September 17 & 24, 1984, p. 16; Lee M. Miringoff and Barbara L. Carvalho, *The Cuomo Factor* (Poughkeepsie, N.Y.: Marist Institute for Public Opinion, 1986), p. 86.

3. Author's interview with Drew Zambelli, Albany, August 12, 1987; Steadman interview; MMC telephone interview, August 15, 1987; Erwin M. Yoder, Jr., "Demagoguery Over a Deduction," *Washington Post,* June 18, 1985; Robert S. McElvaine, *The End of the Conservative Era: Liberalism After Reagan* (New York: Arbor House, 1987), pp. 91–92; MMC, testimony before the House of Representatives, Committee on Ways and Means, July 17, 1985; MMC, "Meet the Press," NBC News, September 8, 1985; *Washington Post,* September 13, 1985; *NYT,* November 12, 1985; Miringoff and Carvalho, *Cuomo Factor,* p. 81; author's interview with Michael Del Giudice, NYC, June 19, 1987.

4. Paul Taylor, "Cuomo's Not So Tough, As Long as He Gets What He Wants," *Washington Post National Weekly Edition,* December 1, 1986; *NYT,* July 6, 1986; Steadman interview.

5. *NYT,* November 20, 1985, February 4, 1986, April 17, 1986, August 5, 1986, August 28, 1986, August 29, 1986, September 15, 1986, October 3, 1986, October 17, 1986, October

31, 1986; Anthony Lewis, "Cuomo's Turn," *NYT*, November 10, 1986; author's telephone interview with MMC, from Albany, October 17, 1987; Zambelli interview; editorial, "Drop the Smokescreen; Start the Debates," *NYT*, October 16, 1986; author's interview with Nicholas Sallese, Colonie, N.Y., May 18, 1987.

6. MMC telephone interview, October 17, 1987; *NYT*, August 28, 1986, September 9, 1986, September 29, 1986, October 20, 1986, October 22, 1986, November 5, 1986, November 6, 1986, December 7, 1986; Lewis, "Cuomo's Turn"; Zambelli interview; Quinn interview; Miringoff and Carvalho, *Cuomo Factor*, p. 54; author's interview with Richard Starkey, NYC, April 7, 1987.

7. *NYT*, November 5, 1986, November 6, 1986; MMC telephone interview, October 17, 1987; MMC telephone interview, August 15, 1987; author's interview with Gary Fryer, Albany, August 12, 1987.

8. Steadman interview; *NYT*, December 11, 1986, December 14, 1986, January 18, 1987, January 20, 1987, January 21, 1987, February 21, 1987, February 23, 1987, April 30, 1987, May 2, 1987, May 5, 1987, May 16, 1987, July 4, 1987, July 10, 1987, August 14, 1987; editorial, "The Governor's Thermometer," *NYT*, January 23, 1987; editorial, "Tax Turnaround in Albany," *NYT*, February 25, 1987; editorial, "The Albany Scorecard," *NYT*, July 16, 1987.

9. *NYT*, January 16, 1987, April 7, 1987, April 10, 1987, April 15, 1987, April 16, 1987, April 17, 1987, April 18, 1987, June 10, 1987, June 27, 1987, July 1, 1987, July 2, 1987, July 10, 1987, July 12, 1987, August 12, 1987, September 19, 1987, October 10, 1987; editorial, "A New Look at New York Ethics," *NYT*, January 16, 1987; editorial, "A Tatter of Loopholes in Albany," *NYT*, April 16, 1987; MMC telephone interview, October 17, 1987; editorial, "The Albany Scorecard," *NYT*, July 16, 1987.

10. Author's interview with MMC, NYC, January 21, 1986; MMC, speech and question-and-answer session, Tulane University, New Orleans, La., February 17, 1987; *NYT*, May 1, 1986, February 18, 1987, September 21, 1987, September 22, 1987, September 23, 1987, September 24, 1987, September 26, 1987, September 28, 1987, October 15, 1987; Richard Starkey interview; author's interview with MMC, NYC, June 18, 1987; MMC, commencement address, School of Advanced International Studies, The Johns Hopkins University, Washington, D.C., May 28, 1987; MMC, remarks at Chautauqua Institute Conference, Chautauqua, N.Y., August 23, 1987; A. Craig Copetas, "Mario's Mission to Moscow," *Village Voice*, October 13, 1987, pp. 31–36; author's telephone interview with Fabian Palomino, from Albany, October 26, 1987; Michael Kramer, "The Man Gorbachev Didn't Circle," *U.S. News & World Report*, December 14, 1987, p. 20; MMC address to the Council on Foreign Relations, Washington, D.C., October 13, 1987; MMC telephone interview, October 17, 1987.

Chapter 12

1. Miriam Pawel, "Nine Great Myths About Mario Cuomo," *Mother Jones*, February-March 1987, pp. 27–49; Fred Barnes, "Meet Mario the Moderate," *New Republic*, April 8, 1985, p. 17; Lee M. Miringoff and Barbara L. Carvalho, *The Cuomo Factor* (Poughkeepsie, N.Y.: Marist Institute for Public Opinion, 1986), p. 85; MMC, speech at Henry Gonzalez Dinner, San Antonio, Texas, January 18, 1986,; MMC, speech at Indiana Democratic State Committee Dinner, Indianapolis, Indiana, July 28, 1987; author's interview with Peter Quinn, NYC, August 7, 1987; author's interview with Judge Sol Wachtler, Mineola, Long Island, N.Y., May 20, 1987; author's interview with Richard Starkey, NYC, April 7, 1987; "What to Make of Mario," *Time*, June 2, 1986, p. 30; George F. Will, "Cuomo and a Self-Righteous Minority," *Boston Globe*, May 8, 1986; author's interview with Gary Fryer, Albany, N.Y., August 12, 1987; Richard Hofstadter, *The American Political Tradition* (New York: Alfred A. Knopf, 1948; 2nd ed., Vintage, 1973), pp. 231–39; MMC, Chubb Fellowship Lecture, Yale University, New Haven, Conn., February 15, 1985; *NYT*, February 16, 1985; MMC, Sunday service at St. John the Divine, NYC, November 27, 1983, in MMC, *Diaries*

of Mario M. Cuomo: The Campaign for Governor (New York: Random House, 1984), pp. 462–68; R. W. Apple, Jr., "The Question of Mario Cuomo," *New York Times Magazine,* September 14, 1986, p. 47; author's interview with Fabian Palomino, NYC, May 21, 1987; author's interview with Matilda Cuomo, Albany, May 19, 1987; MMC, *Diaries,* pp. 59, 107.

2. Quinn interview; author's interview with Peter Johnson, NYC, May 20, 1987; author's interview with Lou Carnesecca, Jamaica, Queens, N.Y., June 18, 1987; author's interview with Drew Zambelli, Albany, August 12, 1987; author's interview with Nicholas D'Arienzo, Forest Hills, Queens, N.Y., April 6, 1987; author's interview with Sal Curiale, NYC, April 7, 1987; author's interview with Michael Del Giudice, NYC, June 19, 1987; author's interview with Fabian Palomino, NYC, April 9, 1987; author's interview with Marie Cuomo Vecchio, Mineola, June 19, 1987.

3. Michael Oreskes, "Cuomo's Personal Touch," *New York Times Magazine,* January 29, 1984, p. 33; Marie Vecchio interview; Del Giudice interview; Zambelli interview; Curiale interview; Palomino interview, May 21, 1987; Matilda Cuomo interview; author's interview with Robert Sullivan, NYC, August 15, 1987.

4. Fryer interview; author's interview with Frank Cuomo, Copiague, Long Island, N.Y., April 8, 1987; Curiale interview; Del Giudice interview; Zambelli interview; Quinn interview; Pawel, "Nine Great Myths," p. 30.

5. Author's interview with Martin Steadman, NYC, August 17, 1987; *Albany Times-Union,* September 22, 1987; Palomino interview, May 21, 1987; "What to Make of Mario," p. 31; author's interview with Mary Tragale, NYC, May 21, 1987; author's telephone interview with MMC, from Albany, July 14, 1987.

6. MMC, *Diaries,* pp. 120–21, 228, 232; *NYT,* September 7, 1987; Ken Auletta, "Governor—I," *New Yorker,* April 9, 1984, p. 76; Quinn interview; author's interview with Jack Newfield, NYC, April 9, 1987; Wachtler interview; Richard Starkey interview; Palomino interview, May 21, 1987; Marie Vecchio interview; Ken Auletta, "Governor—II," *New Yorker,* April 16, 1984, p. 65; Nicholas D'Arienzo interview; *Washington Post,* June 20, 1985; "What to Make of Mario," p. 30.

7. Author's telephone interview with MMC, from Albany, October 17, 1987.

8. Palomino interview, May 21, 1987; MMC telephone interview, October 17, 1987; author's interview with Alexander Levine, Albany, May 18, 1987; Nicholas Pileggi, "Cuomo and Those Rumors," *New York,* November 2, 1987, pp. 44–51; author's interview with MMC, January 21, 1986; Frank Cuomo interview, April 8, 1987; author's telephone interview with MMC, from Albany, October 31, 1987; NYT, October 28, 1987, December 1, 1987, December 6, 1987; Wachtler interview; Marie Vecchio interview; "What Makes Mario Run?" *Newsweek,* March 24, 1986, p. 23.

9. *NYT,* February 20, 1987, February 21, 1987; Seymour Martin Lipset and William Schneider, "The Confidence Gap in the Reagan Years," *Political Science Quarterly,* Vol. 102, Spring 1987, pp. 1-23; Nicholas D'Arienzo interview; Zambelli interview; Anthony Lewis, "Cuomo's Turn," *NYT,* November 10, 1986; David S. Broder, "The American Voters' New Stripes," *Washington Post National Weekly Edition,* October 19, 1987; Newfield interview; author's interview with MMC, Albany, August 14, 1987; Fryer interview; Joe Klein, "The Kibitzer," *New York,* August 10, 1987, pp. 9–13; Quinn interview; Barnes, "Meet Mario the Moderate," p. 20; MMC, *Diaries,* p. 91; Steadman interview; author's interview with Haley Barbour, Jackson, Miss., September 25, 1987.

Index